IMMIGRATION AND SOCIAL CHANGE

ASSOCIATES:

Mrs. Z. Ben-Zimra—co-author of Chapter 9.
Mrs. F. Bernstein—co-author of Chapter 6.
Mrs. T. Horowitz—who contributed part of the material in Chapter 5.
Mrs. T. Parness—co-author of Chapter 8.
Mrs. M. Shapira—co-author of Chapter 7.
Miss H. Weihl—co-author of Chapter 10.

DOV WEINTRAUB

AND ASSOCIATES

IMMIGRATION AND SOCIAL CHANGE

Agricultural Settlement of New Immigrants in Israel

ISRAEL UNIVERSITIES PRESS

MANCHESTER UNIVERSITIES PRESS
HUMANITIES PRESS, INC.

Published in the United Kingdom, 1971
by
MANCHESTER UNIVERSITY PRESS
316–324 Oxford Road
Manchester M13 9NR
ISBN O 7190 03830

Distributed in the USA
by
HUMANITIES PRESS, INC.
303 Park Avenue South
New York, N.Y. 10010
U.S.A. SBN 391 00125 6

Published in Israel, 1971
by

ISRAEL UNIVERSITIES PRESS
a publishing division of
KETER PUBLISHING HOUSE, LTD.,
a wholly owned subsidiary of
ISRAEL PROGRAM FOR SCIENTIFIC TRANSLATIONS, LTD.
P.O. Box 7145, Jerusalem, Israel
IUP cat. no. 2646

This book has been composed, printed and bound at Keter Publishing House, Ltd., Jerusalem, Israel.

Acknowledgements

It gives me great pleasure to acknowledge my indebtness to the following people and institutions who have helped in the research contained in this book, and in the preparation of the book itself, and with my gratitude I gladly absolve them from any responsibility whatsoever for the shortcomings of our work.

Professor S. N. Eisenstadt, who supervised and encouraged the research programme throughout.

Dr. M. Lissak, who shared with me the early planning of the research; Mrs. T. Horowitz, who helped in the preparation and the supervision of field work in the first stage of the project; and Mrs. Ben-Zimra, Mrs. P. Morag, Mrs. T. Parness and Miss H. Weihl, who did this in the second stage.

Professors J. Ben-David, E. Katz, M. Gluckman and the late Y. Talmon, who at various times gave me the benefit of their advice.

The Land Settlement Department of the Jewish Agency for supporting the first stage of the research, and the United States Department of Agriculture for supporting the second phase (under Grant No. FG.Is.139—Social Factors which Promote or Impede Changes in Agricultural Organization and Production).

The Department of Geography of the Hebrew University, Jerusalem, for the maps prepared for the book.

Last, but not least, Mrs. Rinna Samuel, for turning my english into English.

I am also most grateful to those publications which first published some of the present data, and then permitted their inclusion here in modified form:

Sociologia Ruralis, for material included in the Appendix, giving the conceptual framework of the study, and first published in *A Study of New Farmers,* No. 1, 1964; and for the General Remarks, which owe much to The Concepts Traditional and Modern in Comparative Social Research—an Empirical Evaluation, No. 1, 1965;

Arid Zone Studies of UNESCO, for material included in Chapters 1, 2, and 3, and drawing upon *Agricultural Planning and Village Community in Israel.* J. Ben David, (ed), Paris, 1964.

The American Journal of Sociology, for Chapter 6, based upon Social Structure and Modernization—A Comparative Study of Two Villages, No. 1 1966.

The British Journal of Sociology, for Chapter 7, based upon The Traditional Family in Israel—Crisis and Continuity, No. 3, 1968.

Rural Sociology, for Chapter 8, based upon Rural Life, Orientation to Change and Modernization, Vol. 33, No. 3, 1968.

CONTENTS

LIST OF MAPS, FIGURES AND CHARTS

MAPS

FIGURES

CHARTS

LIST OF TABLES

INTRODUCTION

The purpose of this book is to analyze some of the salient social problems of rural colonization and development in Israel. The scope of our study, however, is narrower than this opening sentence might imply. We are concerned, specifically, with new immigrants and new farmers, and their settlement in newly established smallholders' cooperative villages—known in Hebrew as *moshavim* (singular *moshav*).

Even so, the presumption is great, for the subject matter of this book is an experiment which is perhaps unique both in nature and in scope: namely, the creation, within the period of only a few years, of hundreds of new agricultural villages, populated by people of diverse social and cultural backgrounds, who were frequently devoid of any farming background or experience. We do not aim here, therefore, at a definitive examination; nor shall we presume to make any final evaluation. All we shall try to do is to raise certain questions and discuss certain issues—bearing in mind that the empirical data on which the book is based are, as will be seen, of essentially modest proportions. As a result, our findings are sometimes preliminary and quite tentative, and since we are focusing on the present situation (or on the very recent past), we have dealt somewhat ungenerously with the remarkable historical setting of these contemporary problems. Similarly, we have made no effort to relate the scheme under discussion to the general situation in the country. In other words, we have treated the new immigrant village in Israel as a slice of life, valid and interesting in itself.[1]

Furthermore, our treatment is frankly sociologically biased, certainly insofar as specific economic conditions and processes are introduced as background and limiting factors.

A word now about the *moshav* type of village: it was originally created by Jewish immigrants to what was then Palestine, people who profoundly believed in the values of national service, agricultural pioneering, equality, and cooperation. Originally, settlers like these were a tightly knit group, with common ideals and a strong and well-articulated desire to evolve a new way of life both for Jews and for mankind in general. The basis of their settlement (the first of these was established in 1921) was undoubtedly the common goal of all of the pioneering movements in Palestine—namely the three-fold ideal of productivization (or inversion of the

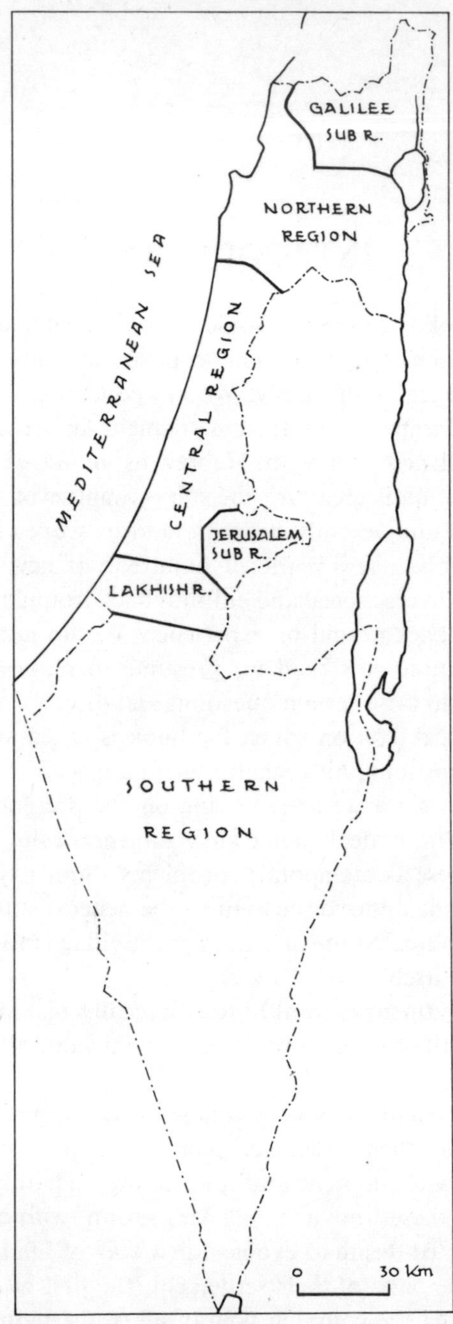

MAP 1. Settlement Regions of Israel

"traditional" Jewish occupational pyramid),[2] of non-exploitation of others, and of service for the common good. In concrete terms, this ideal was embodied in (a) national ownership and non-alienation of land, which was considered a value in itself and seen as the basis of a new way of life rather than as a marketable commodity; (b) mobilization for special national tasks: (c) public financing, planning and guidance of the settlement, which were considered a condition for accelerated development and growth, and which both symbolized and safeguarded mutual bonds and responsibility; (d) emphasis on manual labour, without the use of hired labour; (e) non-acceptance of gainful employment outside the *moshav*; and (f) mixed farming, signifying both farm autarky and the all-round farmer's attachment to his homestead via a wide range of ties rather than agricultural specialization which was regarded as the creation of yet another type of commercial enterprise.[3]

This general pioneering image was embodied in the *moshav* in a way (both in terms of an agrarian and a social system) which was quite different from that of the more veteran (and better known) *kibbutz*: instead of the collective itself, i.e, the *kibbutz* or group, being the unit of production, consumption and socialization, in the *moshav* the emphasis was on a cooperative community made up of individual households, each working a family small-holding.

In each *moshav*, there was an equitable division of the means of production (chiefly in respect to the size, quality and distribution of plots, water resources, and capitalization),[4] but this equality was not mechanical, but rather of life chances: the village itself constituted an intensive market-oriented economy; and within the limitations of overall planning, the utmost development and utilization of means of production was a national duty as well as a realization of individual potential. Maximization of production, however, while giving scope to the more enterprising and the more skilled farmers, was not to be made the cause of either clear social differentiation within the village, or, more importantly, of a consumer-oriented way of life. The first was kept in check by assuring a minimal standard of living for everyone, and making the community responsible for this as well, and by using corporate incentives and providing help for farms in trouble; the second was limited by constraints (social rather than legal) against conspicuous consumption, against investing in outside property, etc.

The various families which constituted the *moshav* formed a small compact community made up of about a hundred units, which formed a tightly-knit *gemeinschaft*: this *gemeinschaft* involved very close social interaction, and much mutual help and responsibility. It was sustained by an elaborate network of agricultural, credit, supply, and marketing services, and by a corporate local authority.

This basic pattern, only sketched here,[5] was adopted in 1949 as the major instrument for the settlement of new immigrants on the land. By then, of course, the structure had been somewhat modified, several sub-types had developed, and some of its rules and regulations had been relaxed.[6] But, the fundamental image and the ultimate aim of the *moshav* remained essentially unchanged since its beginnings in 1921; and the new population was sometimes even viewed as a means of regaining ground previously lost.

At the 18th Agricultural Convention in 1949, Mr. Levi Eshkol, who was later Israel's Prime Minister, and then Head of the Land Settlement Department, said: "I know that the great stream of popular immigration has brought with it a man who is very different from the one to whom we have become accustomed over the decades during the breakthrough years of the pioneering movement; he is a man who, due to circumstances, perhaps lacks the old social qualities, but he may have other qualities which will enable him to adjust to our reality. One way or the other, he is a fact. And over the next five or six years, these men will come to this country, and will have to carry on, and it is on them that we must count. We must, therefore, struggle and strive to turn this new immigrant into a farmer, into a creator of agricultural villages which embody the new way of life."

Or to quote A. Assaf, then secretary of the *Moshav* Movement, in his book on *moshavim* in 1948:[7] "Now especially with the establishment of the State and the mass immigrant settlement—settlement of people who work the land for their livelihood without having been ideologically prepared for it and without the benefit of village experience in Israel, people whose ideas of work and of property, and of satisfaction, are taken from other lands and other systems—now especially, it is necessary, it is even imperative for us to consolidate our way of life and to protect it, so that deviation can be avoided and we can continue on our chosen path—the vitality and the importance of which are more crucial now than ever before."

Although this self-image was later shown to have been over-idealized and over-optimistic, it is not presented here in any spirit of debunking—in which the smug sociologist shows up the naive visionary or the harassed policy maker. On the contrary, the situation was an extreme one; it required extreme measures, and the idea of the immigrant *moshav* was most relevant to it. In this respect, two factors in particular must be borne in mind:

A. The enormous pressure under which the new State of Israel laboured in matters of security, development and immigrant absorption. This pressure was felt very acutely in rural settlement: the extended and hostile borders had to be settled fast; thinly inhabited areas waited to be filled, so that the new State's claim to them should not be disputed, and to achieve population dispersion; numerous new jobs and openings had to be created, and this was considered easier and cheaper in agriculture than in other branches, as was social absorption; food and other staples had to be provided for the increasing population, and to replace the lost production of the former Arab sector, while the recent War of Independence (like the First World War in Holland) was thought to point to the necessity of autarky in this sphere; and over all these factors there hovered the pioneering ethos—as well as the concrete interests of its upholders—striving to project into statehood as much as possible of the historical ideals, traditions, and achievements of the Jewish community in Palestine.[8]

B. In this situation, the *moshav* pattern offered a convincing solution, especially as the constant and unrelieved pressure of time and circumstance, during the period of preliminary planning and initial absorption, obviously prevented the working-out of a systematically differential approach. Because of the security situation, and because most of the people concerned had had no previous agricultural experience, completely individual, independent and scattered farming was not considered practical for their settlement. To facilitate their introduction to agriculture, it was necessary to release the new settlers—at least at first—from ultimate responsibility for the productive process, and to give them special and intensive training. All these considerations led to the conclusion that a closely-knit and well-supervised economic and community organization, within which the absorption agencies might operate, would provide the best possible solution. This decision was influenced also by the fact that several types of corporate villages had already been successfully developed in what was now Israel and these could provide fundamental settlement models, organizational know-how, and even experienced personnel. And of the various such possibilities (namely the *kibbutz*—or collective village, the *moshav shitufi*—or cooperative village,[9] and the *moshav*—or smallholders' cooperative village), the last was decided upon as the most suitable for the new immigrants, since it seemed to be a much more flexible and adaptive system, and more likely to absorb the newcomers quickly.

Also, while the absorption agencies did not, of course, ignore the possibility that difficulties might arise as a result of the unique size and tempo of the immigration, the characteristics of the immigrants themselves, and the fact that the various goals of settlement were not always compatible (for example, such border areas as the Judean mountains, colonized primarily for security reasons, were not most suitable for farming), there were some grounds even for guarded optimism. Most of the objective hardships which had confronted the earlier settlers could now be eliminated. Until the creation of the State, prospective farmers in Palestine had to wait up to eight years before land was allocated to them; similar difficulties also attended the provision of capital; and the Jewish community institutions were limited in their ability either to plan for or to modify the market situation. The full development of the farm, therefore, had to be deferred for a long time, and settlers often had to resort to outside work. Agriculture, as a whole, had faced severe competition with the more primitive, but cheaper Arab production and labour.[10] Now, however, the greater resources of the State were considered capable of smoothing the settler's path and compensating him for the difference in the human material and the size of the absorption problem. This was so, particularly, on two counts: on the one hand, the settlement authority could provide each new village of about 70 families with a local team of extension workers.[11] And on the other, it was able to work out an intensive development and capitalization schedule, leading up to potential farm consolidation within seven years.[12] Additionally, the colonizing plan also envisaged far greater flexibility—and a longer time span—in the actual realization of a full-fledged community pattern by the new settlers.

It can thus be said that while new rural colonization was largely a matter of necessity, the specific immigrant *moshav* scheme relied on the prevailing opinion that although the process of absorption and of socio-economic consolidation could be a long one, the achievements would ultimately equal those of the veteran settlers.

The translation of this vision into reality—the actual experience gained during the first decade and a half of the programme, the successes achieved, and the difficulties and obstacles encountered—is thus the subject of this book. An idea of the growth and the scope of the *moshav* settlement scheme described, in comparison with other forms and earlier periods, is given in the following maps and tables. Maps 2 and 3 show the development of the veteran *moshavim* between the years 1922 and 1948, while Map 4 shows the *Moshav* Movement in 1956, after the establishment of 241 new immigrant villages. Tables 1–2 reflect 10 years of the new settlement programme—1949–1958, in terms of the number of villages established and of households actually settled on the land, in respect also to distribution by farm-type[13] and geographical area (for orientation, see Map 1). Table 3, on the other hand, shows the social complexity of the programme, reflected in the extreme heterogeneity of the villages. (The data relate to the year 1958–1959 when our research began. However, since settlement had been reduced to a trickle by then, the figures also provide a fairly good idea of the situation as it is today.)

The nature of the varied backgrounds of the new immigrants constitutes a focal point of our study, and we will analyze it in a number of sociological ways later on. But even the formal presentation of the diversity of areas of origin seems sufficient to show the magnitude and challenge, in purely human terms, of the task which was undertaken. No wonder, therefore, that the settlement programme soon ran into trouble. The problems it encountered were reflected in two ways.

To begin with, there was a large number of "drop-outs", so that over ten years, 8,587 households (or 34.7 percent) of all those settled in *moshavim* left them altogether (this excludes transfers from one village to another). Table 4 summarizes this movement of population. For the sake of comparison, those who left are combined here together with the total of those who were settled (as in Table 1).

Secondly, in only a very few of the new *moshavim* development followed the prescribed schedule and achieved the effect planned. Crises characterized settlement

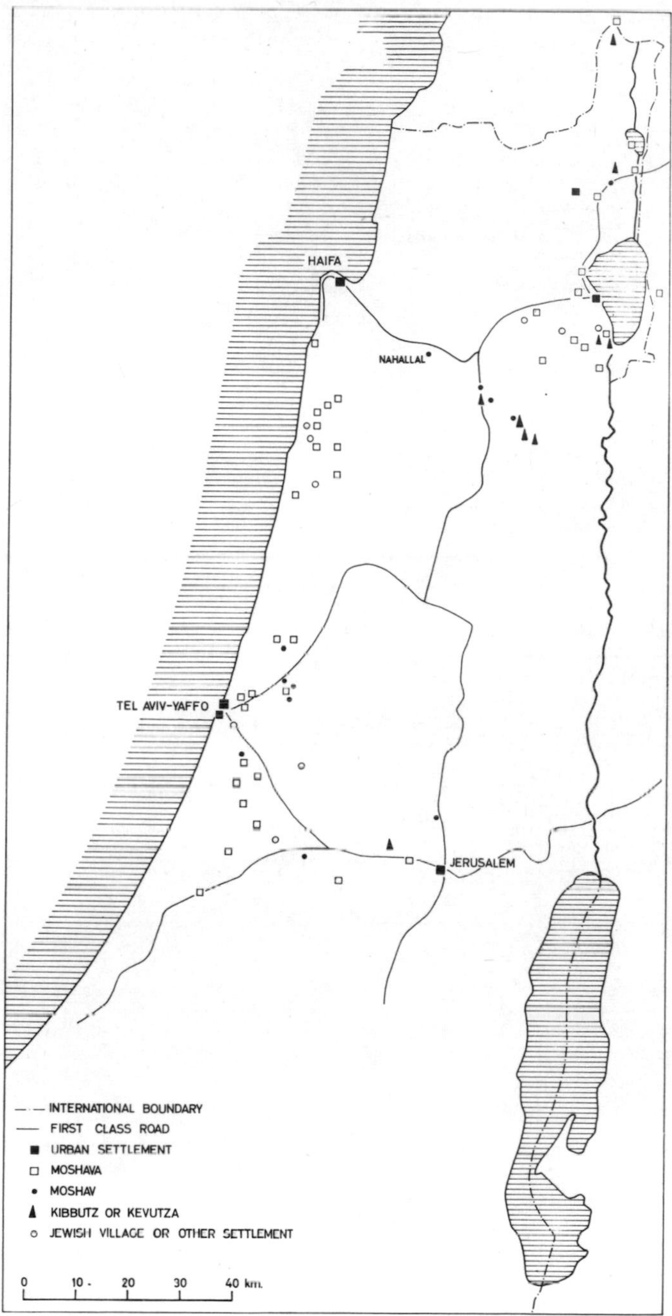

MAP 2. Jewish Settlements 1922

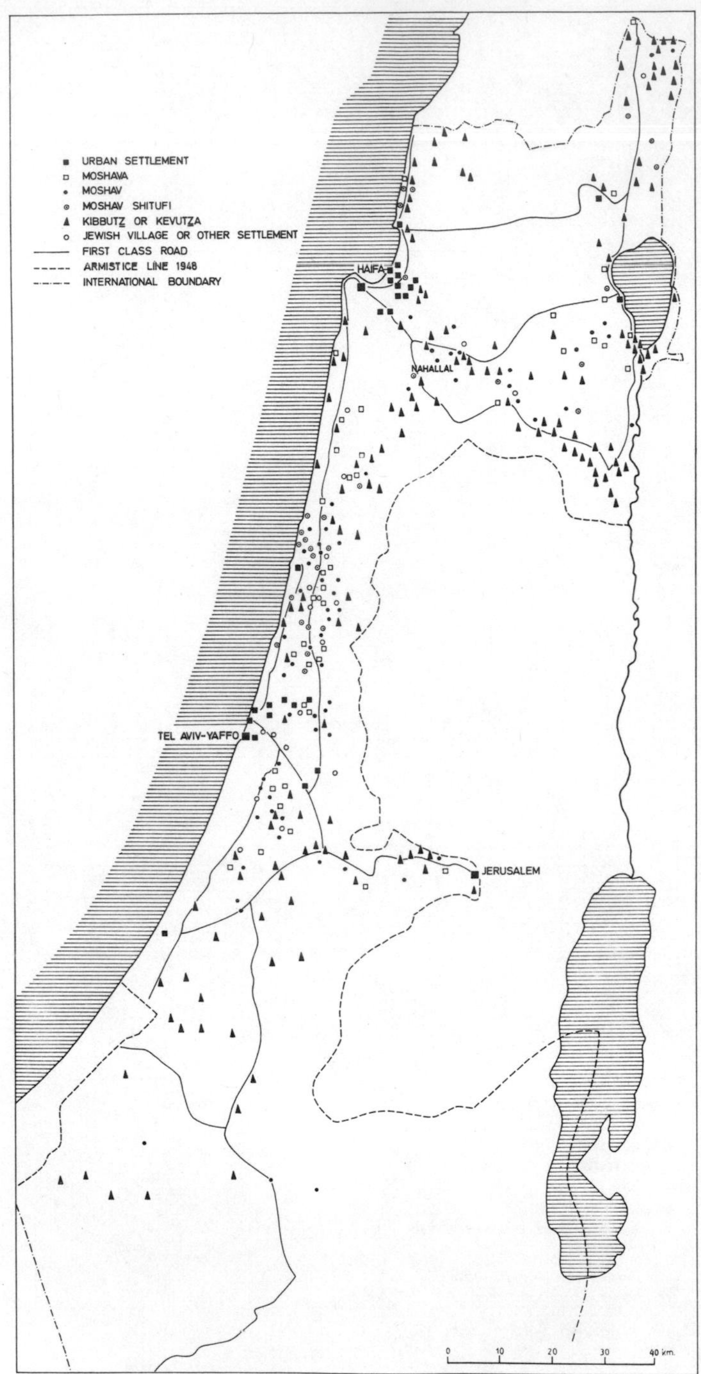

MAP 3. Jewish Settlements 1948

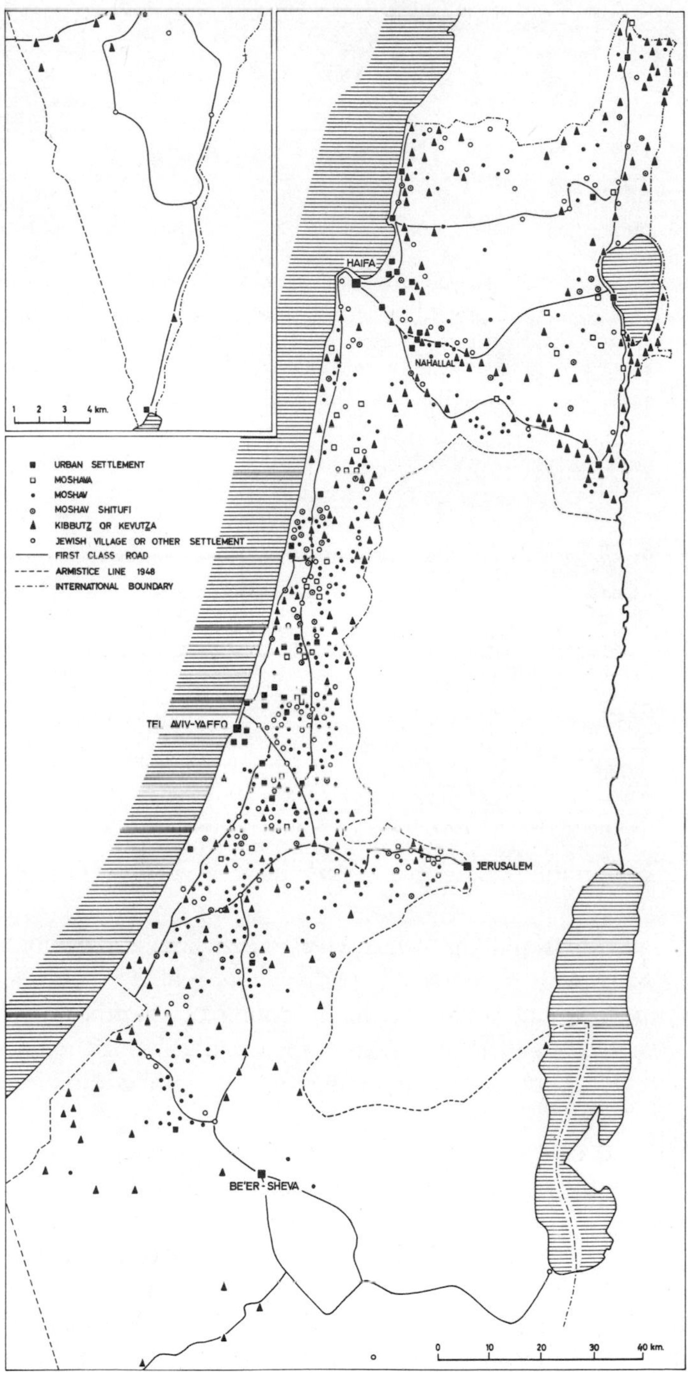

MAP 4. Jewish Settlements 1956

TABLE 1—New Moshavim Between 1949 and 1958

	1949	1950	1951	1952	1953	1954	1955	1956	1957	1958	Total
Villages established	73	84	14	19	27	4	12	8	5	5	251
Households settled	4086	7265	1609	1942	1457	2487	2340	1818	1118	645	24,767

Note: Households settled also include those distributed among previously established immigrant villages.

Source: compiled from statistics of Land Settlement Department of the Jewish Agency.

TABLE 2—Distribution of New Villages (1958–1959)

By area	No. of villages	By farm-type	
Northern	53	Field	57
Central	72	Mountain (mixed)	38
Mountain Jerusalem sub-district	33	Hills (mixed)	23
Galilee sub-district	29	Dairy (mixed)	121
Lakhish	30	Citrus	12
Southern	34		
Total	251	Total	251

Source: compiled from statistics of Land Settlement Department of the Jewish Agency.

on both the individual and the village level. There was a growing trend toward part-time farming, with a consequent waste of allocated resources. There were gross deviations from, and inequalities in, the planned farm production and income. And—last but not least—there were cases of the social disintegration of communities which proved incapable of functioning within cooperative and municipal frameworks.

There were (and still are) no comparative data on the incidence and impact of the various difficulties which were encountered. The "sum-total", as it were, of underdevelopment expressed itself, however, in the fact that of 171 villages established between 1948 and 1951 (those which by 1958 should have absorbed and activated the basic seven year capitalization and production timetable) only 24—or 14 percent—actually did so, and thereby achieved formal consolidation status.[14]

The significance of this lag can be—and in fact was—evaluated in various ways.

TABLE 3—Structure of Actual Settler Population in New Immigrant Moshavim (1958)

Area of origin	By households			By villages
	Country of origin	No. of households	Percentage	No. of villages
Eastern and Central Europe	Poland	867	5.3	
	Hungary	1363	8.4	
	Rumania	2183	13.5	
	Czechoslovakia	418	2.6	
Total		4831	29.8	76
America	U.S.A.	48	0.3	
	Argentina	88	0.5	
Total		136	0.8	2
The Balkans	Yugoslavia	250	1.5	
	Bulgaria	350	2.2	
	Greece	130	0.8	
Total		730	4.5	10
North Africa	Morocco	2455	15.3	
	Algeria	31	0.2	
	Tunisia	1026	6.3	
	Libya	1113	6.9	
Total		4625	28.7	85
Middle and Far East	Kurdistan (incl. Persia and Turkey)	1500	9.3	
	Persia (rest)	786	4.8	
	Turkey (rest)	158	1.0	
	Syria and Lebanon	75	0.5	
	Egypt	312	1.9	
	Yemen	2168	13.5	
	Cochin	246	1.5	
	China	38	0.2	
Total		5283	32.7	71
Others		575	3.5	7
Total		16180	100.0	251

Source: compiled from statistics of Land Settlement Department of the Jewish Agency.

TABLE 4—Out Movement from the Moshav in 1949–58

	Left		Remained		Settled	
	No	%	No	%	No	%
1949–50	5215	45.9	6136	54.1	11351	100.0
1951–52	884	25.3	2667	74.7	3551	100.0
1953–54	738	18.7	3206	81.3	3944	100.0
1955	707	30.2	1633	69.8	2340	100.0
1956	327	10.0	1491	82.0	1818	100.0
1957	328	29.0	790	71.0	1118	100.0
1958	388	60.0	257	40.0	645	100.0
Total	8587	34.7	16180	65.3	24767	100.0

Source: compiled from statistics of Land Settlement Department of the Jewish Agency

The situation is reminiscent of the celebrated definition which claims to distinguish between an optimist and a pessimist on the grounds that the former, looking at a partly filled concert hall, comments on the fact that it is half-full, while the latter emphasizes that the hall is half-empty. Be that as it may (the author, for one, is impressed with how *much* was achieved under the circumstances, and how relatively *little* social waste was involved), the time was ripe for some serious stocktaking.

Without question, some of the phenomena observed could be traced immediately to obvious economic factors. For example, many of the villages (particularly those in mountain regions), which had been established primarily for other than purely economic reasons, were lacking in sufficient land and water to begin with. Also, in many cases, villages were founded without any detailed planning or any preliminary survey of the soil, sometimes resulting in the establishment of settlements which had no sound economic basis. More generally speaking, the supply of capital to the settlements (a supply which depended largely on Jewish donations from abroad) fluctuated and often fell short of over-optimistic estimates. Similarly, it was realized that agricultural planning had been largely on the micro- or farm level: not based on the food-basket or on market requirements. Consequently, there were inevitable surpluses and equally inevitable price crises.[15]

Attention was also drawn to administrative confusions and snarls which, of course, hampered various activities on the village level, and even higher. Lack of proper administrative routines, organs and personnel caused snags in marketing, in credit arrangements, in supplies, and in various other areas.[16]

All these problems, however—many of which were soon, at least to some extent, solved[17]*—only explained part of the situation. It became clear that various villages*

somehow produced different results although their hardships and overall conditions were much the same. It was this conclusion which finally gave the impetus to the social research with which this book deals.

Our study falls into two analytically (and chronologically) distinct but interrelated parts:

A. Examination of the *initial* confrontation of the new settler with the *moshav*: this focuses on the primary impact, and attempts to isolate and compare the elementary and fundamental (even crude) dimensions and forms of the settlers' reaction and adjustment to the new reality. The dominant theme of this part of the study is, consequently, the analysis of the various strains which were created by the absorptive situation on the one hand, and the salient *predispositions* of the newcomers in various relevant spheres on the other.

This phase, which lasted from 1959 to 1962, was based on a sample of eleven villages studied systematically by the author and a team of researchers in the Department of Sociology within one comparative analytical framework. Some reference was also made, however, to two case-studies done by a sociologist of the Land Settlement Department.[18]

Table 5 specifies the villages included in the first phase of the study (with the two settlements external to our basic sample last on the list):

B. An inquiry into some of the processes of mutual *social change*—between the absorbing and the absorbed—which took place under these various stress situations.

TABLE 5—Population of First Phase of Research

Code name of village	Origin	District	Year of establishment	Type of farm
Azor	Yemen	Jerusalem	1951	Hills
Biyoun	Tunisia	Central	1950	Citrus
Levanon	Yemen	Jerusalem	1949	Mountain-mixed
Resissim	Mixed*	Jerusalem	1948	Milk
Savel	Yemen	Lakhish	1950	Field crops
Shalekhet	Hadramaut**	Central	1952	Hills
Ta'amon	Central Europe	Central	1949	Milk
Te'ena	Persia	Lakhish	1950	Milk-mixed
Zimriya	Morocco	Central	1949	Milk-mixed
Torem	Atlas Mountains	Lakhish	1955	Field crops
Zeviya	Central Europe	Northern	1949	Milk
Koresh	Iraq and Persia***	Jerusalem	1950	Mountain-mixed
Oranim	Yemen	Jerusalem	1950	Mountain-mixed

* The two largest groups being immigrants from Rumania and Persia respectively

** Yemeni cultural area

*** From the area populated by Kurdish tribes

Map No. 5 shows the location of these villages in the country

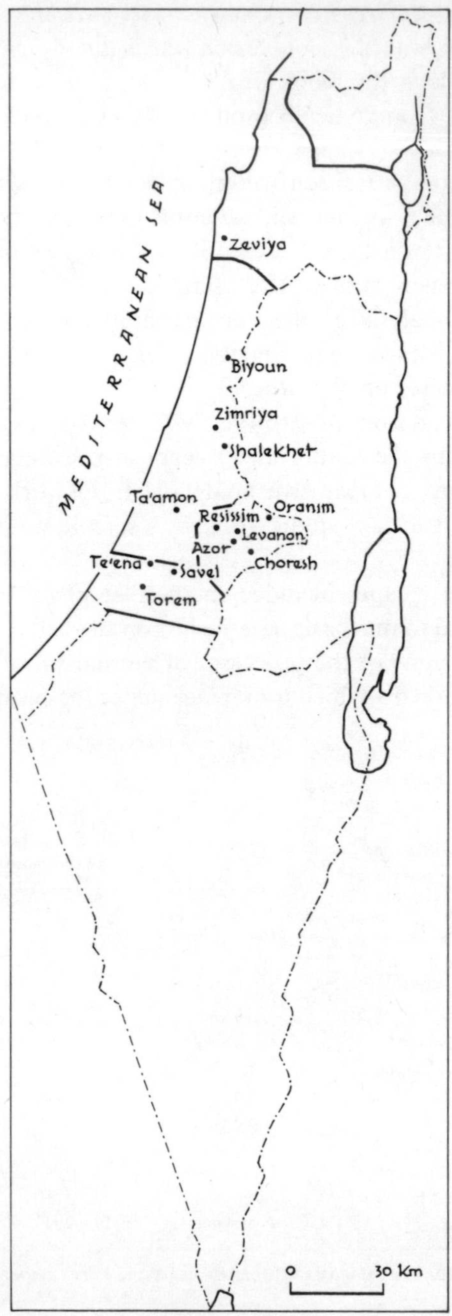

MAP 5. Location of Sample Villages

Here, the emphasis is on *development* patterns within the new villages, and on their future trends.

The second stage took place from 1963 to 1965 and consisted of studies of selected situations of change, and of the young generation. This phase was more limited in its scope but—we hope—more clearly focused and perhaps more sophisticated—since it was possible to build upon already existing foundations.

These themes form, as it were naturally, the two main parts of this book. Our material is presented largely in a descriptive vein; and the various topics, though related, are not organized within an explicit theoretical scheme or model. At least, this is so on the overt level: for while the study—and in particular its first part—was carried out on the basis of an elaborate conceptual framework (which the curious can find in the Appendix), we believe that the reader should not be burdened accordingly; and that the conclusions and generalizations—if any—should flow naturally from the material itself. In other words, a model should be somewhat like basting, i.e. withdrawn as soon as the various pieces are securely put together.

One final note: in broad terms of agrarian patterns, the scheme described embodies development which is (a) "expansionist" rather than "intrinsic" (that is, based on colonizing new areas, not on the intensification or reform of existing units)[19]; (b) based on public planning, guidance and financing; (c) embodying induced social change, implying the adjustment of many social groups to one prearranged blueprint. However, while the data are indeed relevant to these general aspects, and will be related to them analytically, this book is definitely *not* a sociology of rural development, even in the limited sense mentioned; nor is it even a sociology of the new immigrant *moshav* in Israel. It is simply a series of papers on one topic or social reality; and we can only express the pious hope that it forms an integrated whole rather than a random collection.

NOTES

1 The reader is, of course, referred to relevant literature. At the risk of offending the historian, however, we have generally included only the most accessible (that is, the English language) publications—however inadequate—rather than quote a host of impressive but essentially foreign sources.

2 The Jews in the Diaspora had been characterized by the predominance of tertiary and secondary occupations, and by a relative paucity of farmers and industrial workers.

3 Of course, the ideal of the mixed (dairy) farm was also reinforced by the then existing agricultural economic theory, brought into being largely as a result of the failure of the monocultures of some of the private farm colonies, occasioned by separation from export markets during World War I. See chiefly: I. Eleazari Volcani: *The Dairy Industry as a Basis For Colonization of Palestine* (Tel Aviv, Palestine Economic Society, 1928).

4 Concretely, each of these units was designed to average 50 dunams (12.5 acres), 30 of which were to be intensively irrigated and cultivated, while the remaining area was to serve for dry farming, to give scope for intensification, and to constitute a reserve for one unit of the second generation. The new immigrant *moshav*, by the way, was slightly different in this respect: it was planned without this reserve.

[5] For brief examination of the *moshav*, the *Moshav* Movement and the movement's place in relation to other colonization forms established in Palestine since the end of the 19th century, see: D. Weintraub, M. Lissak, and Y. Azmon, *Moshava, Kibbutz, Moshav: Jewish Settlement and Colonization in Palestine* (Ithaca, New York, Cornell University Press, 1969).

[6] For example, the growing export orientation dictates a partial transition to industrial crops and greater specialization, as did price crises in some of the overcrowded branches of the mixed farm; and this, together with the development of the veteran farms, paved the way for the systematic use of hired labour. This use was even initially validated by the all-important function of absorbing, and employing new immigrant workers; but, in time, what had originally been regarded as a matter of duty came to be considered as a prize or a special privilege. This ideological relaxation was reinforced also by the second generation members, who were more economically rather than ideologically minded.

[7] A. Assaf, *Moshav Ovdim* (Tel Aviv, Ayanoth, 1948).

[8] Within the present context it is of course impossible to discuss these and other factors, and to evaluate their validity. See, however, the following:
A. Rokach, chapters on land and water: "The Development of Agriculture in Palestine and Israel", and "Agricultural Planning since the Establishment of the State", in: J. Ben-David, (ed.), *Agricultural Planning and Village Community in Israel* (Paris, UNESCO, 1964), pp. 13–44;
S.N. Eisenstadt, *Absorption of Immigrants,* (London, Routledge and Kegan Paul, 1953);
S.N. Eisenstadt, *Israeli Society* (New York, Basic Books, 1969).

[9] The *moshav shitufi* is a "half-way house" between the collective and the small-holding village: in it, the community is the unit of production (all branches being owned and managed by the settlement, and employing the members as workers), but the individual household is still the unit of consumption and socialization. A relative newcomer upon the Israel scene, it is also the smallest and the weakest of the settlement movements.

[10] See chiefly D. Weintraub, M. Lissak and Y. Azmon, *op. cit.*

[11] Each such local team was composed of three resident instructors: a vocational-agricultural instructor, a social instructor (who was also initially the village administrator) and a woman social instructor.

[12] The following was the planned investment programme for each farm unit—70 percent of which was to be by direct public financing—based on 1958–1959 price levels in Israel Pounds:

Type of investment	Total investment (for 80 farms)	Investment per farm
Farm house		
2½ rooms (45 square metres), water installations, shower, shutters, outside water-closet	492,000	6,150
Communal buildings		
2 classrooms, creche and kindergarten	30,000	
Assembly. hall and club	14,000	
Grocery	12,000	
Clinic	8,000	
Armoury	7,000	
Office	6,000	
Kindergarten kitchen	12,000	
Synagogue	11,000	
Ritual bath	7,000	
	107,000	1,338

Type of investment	Total investment (for 80 farms)	Investment per farm
Farm buildings		
Multi-purpose shed (24 square metres) with concrete floor		1,750
Open farm shed (24 square metres) tin roof, 2 walls		850
Chicken run and equipment for 300 chickens (15 square metres)		780
Stable (30 square metres)		750
Poultry batteries for 100 layers		250
	350,040	4,380
Communal farm buildings		
General warehouse-storeroom (210 square metres)	18,000	
Sheep dip (at village centre)	4,000	
Grading station for vegetables (at village centre)	4,600	
Technical supervision of farm buildings and houses (6 per cent of total value)	58,640	
	85,240	1,067
Irrigation equipment		
Central and lateral piping (permanent) for 24 dunams of irrigated land, including orchards, sprinklers, and 13 metres aluminium per dunam		4,320
Water metre		160
Total investment in irrigation equipment	358,400	4,480
Equipment		
Half-share in auxiliary implements for draught animals		460
Poultry equipment		100
	44,800	560
Stock		
100 pullets or cocks and chicks		400
8 head of sheep or 2 beef cows		800
Half-share in traction animal or one work cow		450
	132,000	1,650
Settler's share in heavy equipment (at rural centre)	93,200	1,240
Orchards		
Planting and maintenance of 4-dunam orchard	192,000	2,400
Electrical installations (including cost of linking to main national grid)	30,000	375
Roads		
To storehouse, centre of village, etc.	24,000	300

Type of investment	Total investment (for 80 farms)	Investment per farm
Deep ploughing		
Cost of ploughing 29 dunams of irrigable land	23,000	288
Revolving capital		
For 20 dunams at IL 100 per dunam	160,000	2,000
Water rights, etc.	80,000	1,000
Total investment in equipment and stock	2,178,140	27,228
Planning, instruction and administration costs (15 percent of IL 27,200)	326,721	4,084
Total investment	2,504,861	31,300

Source: Lakhish Region planning section.

Since development was progressive, here, too, the plan called for interim outside employment; the idea, however, was to have a short period of organized public works, designed to fit in with the requirements and growth of the *moshav*.

13 For specification of farm-types (institutionalized between 1953–1956), see note 17.

14 Consolidation status signifies economic and administrative autonomy, reflected in (a) productive investment, (b) the withdrawal of the resident team of instructors.

15 A detailed examination of these problems is beyond the scope of this discussion. The reader is referred to A. Rokach, *op. cit.*

16 For a vivid description of these problems see chiefly: A. Weingrod, "Administered Communities: Some Characteristics of New Immigrant Villages in Israel, *Economic Development and Cultural Change,* Vol. IX, No. 1 (1962).

17 For a detailed discussion of some of the new measures see A. Rokach, *op. cit.* Briefly, however, there were five crucial turning points, introduced between 1953 and 1956:

(a) A more realistic evaluation of the resources at the disposal of agricultural development.

(b) A more realistic evaluation of market potential; and the transition from agricultural autarky to integration in world markets.

(c) The consequent change in farm planning, which now became systematically differentiated in relation to the above mentioned factors, instead of the hitherto predominant mixed-dairy farms. The types of farm envisaged, and actually established, since then are as follows:

The fully-irrigated farm comprising 28 dunams, four or five of which are orchards (citrus and other fruit), the rest being used for field crops, mainly fodder for the milch-cows. The amount of water allotted to each farm varies according to its location: in the coastal regions, it is about 16,000 cubic metres per year; in the Hulah Valley, 17,600 cubic metres, and in the south, about 20,000 cubic metres. The dairy is the mainstay of these farms and should eventually be stocked with five milking cows and with 100 laying hens as a secondary activity.

The semi-irrigated dairy farm: a variation of the above, specially devised for the *Negev* (arid southern region). For an average area of 40–42 dunams, water allocated is about 20,400 cubic metres a year, which is only enough for partial irrigation.

The citrus farm has 28 dunams of irrigated land, of which citrus groves account for ten dunams, while the rest are irrigated field crops, particularly vegetables. The citrus grove supplies about 60 percent of the farm's total income. The annual water allocation is about 15,000 cubic metres per farm. In addition, there is a chicken-run of 100 laying hens. These farms have been developed mainly in Israel's coastal plain where the land is suitable.

The field crops farm consists of 40–50 dunams of irrigated land, intended mainly for industrial crops (cotton, sugar-beet, groundnuts), vegetables for the canning industry (tomatoes and cucumbers), and potatoes. About four to five dunams are used for plantations. Water allotted to each such farm in the central district is about 15,000 to 16,000 cubic metres, and in the *Negev* it is between 19,000 and 20,000 cubic metres annually. Secondary activities are cattle- and sheep-breeding for meat, and poultry-raising (about 200 laying hens). The raising of beef cattle depends upon available pasture.

The hill farm: 35 dunams per unit of which 10 to 15 dunams are irrigated. The irrigated land is intended for fruit-growing—mainly vineyards and deciduous fruit trees. Four dunams of the irrigated area are under field crops. Water allotted to each farm unit is between 3,500 and 6,000 cubic metres per year. The unirrigated area is also cultivated with field crops, mainly tobacco, in rotation with beans, etc. Carob trees are included among the unirrigated plantations. Sheep or cattle are raised for meat, where there is pasture land, and 200–400 laying hens are kept. Most of these hill farms are in the Jerusalem Corridor, in regions which are 200–450 metres above sea level.

The mountain farm: usually 18–25 dunams per unit, of which about ten dunams are intended for irrigated plantations, two to four dunams for irrigated field crops, and the rest for various unirrigated crops, mainly tobacco. Water allotted to each farm unit is 3,000–5,000 cubic metres per year. There are 200–400 laying hens, and, where local conditions are favourable, also cattle. The mountain farms are in the Jerusalem Corridor and in Galilee, at altitudes of 500–800 metres above sea level.

(d) A radical change in the *pattern* of farm-development. True, the main measures adopted in more recent stages of planning are not in themselves very different from the *ad hoc* measures instituted earlier; but now they have been consciously incorporated in the *moshav* plan, the basic assumption of which was that development should be phased over a prolonged period and that the problems involved in each stage should be anticipated. A new term—the "managed farm"—was introduced to describe early stages of the immigrants' settlement. Obviously, these stages of planned development differ in different types of farm, but basic problems are the same everywhere. Our description is derived mainly from the experience of "managed" villages in the Lakhish area, where farms are based on the cultivation of industrial crops.

Introductory stage. Upon his arrival in the *moshav,* the settler is given a standard house, including basic furniture and kitchen equipment. He is also allocated some four dunams of land (of the 40-odd which he will ultimately get) on which to grow vegetables. He is then employed as an agricultural labourer, either by a public or by a private organization, which acts as a contractor for the village's arable land. The contractor is only allowed to employ settlers from this particular village; not to bring workers in from outside. He must develop and work the land in accordance with the crop rotation scheme and water schedule planned by the settlement authority. The wages paid to the settlers for this work are based on the rates of unskilled labourers (approximately IL7 a day), and include about twenty working days per month per family. These earnings, however, are supplemented by the vegetables grown for home consumption as well as for marketing.

After about a year, the settler is given another 13 or 14 dunams of irrigated land, and the area cultivated by the contractor is reduced accordingly. The settler now derives half of his income from his work as a labourer and the other half from working his own land.

By the third year, additional land is allocated to each household, and the contractor gradually withdraws until, by the fourth year, the settler is farming his own 20 irrigated dunams independently (though he is still, of course, under the control and supervision of the settlement authority). By this time, his entire income should be derived from working his land. This is still a period of development and consolidation, and his income is, as yet, far from that ultimately envisaged, approximating about IL1,800–2,200 per annum (1958 prices). Families which fall behind in developing their farms at this stage can still be given outside work to supplement their income, while needy cases can apply to a special fund.

Intermediate stage. By this time (the fourth year) the settler is supposed to have been allocated his 20 dunams of irrigated land, as well as about half of the other resources he is eventually scheduled to receive. Vegetables are an important source of income, otherwise the small irrigated plot would not provide sufficient livelihood. The crop rotation scheme envisaged for this stage is, accordingly, of an intensive nature, as is the water schedule. The greater part of the budget in the intermediate stage goes to irrigation equipment to bring the total area under intensive cultivation up to 35 to 37 dunams. As has already been stated, this period continues until both the settlement authority and the settler himself have invested the entire basic development and revolving capital, and the farm is brought into full production. The income from the farm, which by now should be exclusively agricultural, is expected to reach roughly two-thirds of the final output. The planned rate of investment and development, and the resources from which this investment originally derives, are shown in the following table. As may be seen, the basic seven-year schedule is maintained, but is made more flexible and is conditional upon previous development.

Period	Object of investment and concurrent activities	Source of capital	Percentage of total investment
Before actual settlement	Surveying, planning, water development, area development, roads, buildings (houses), school, armoury, office and other communal buildings.	Settling authority exclusively	30%
First and second year	Costs of transportation, central irrigation pipes, agricultural equipment, initial provision of revolving capital	Settling authority exclusively	20%
Third year	Construction of other communal buildings and farm sheds, acquisition of stock, planting of orchards and vineyards	Largely settling authority	15%
Fourth to ninth year	The remaining investment, in irrigation, revolving capital, electricity, etc.	Largely settler himself	35% (7% per year)

Source: Joint Planning Centre.

The village's financial responsibilities, and the payments due from individual settlers, are also subject to a process of gradual increase. Without now going into the question of the social conditions necessary for the *moshav* to assume these obligations, we should note that a village administration ought to be established early on—at the latest towards the end of the introductory period. Whether this is, in fact, the case, or whether the "team" actually carries out the requisite functions, all these economic and municipal tasks must be undertaken and paid for. They are, usually, as follows:

1. Payment of salaries for staff engaged in various services, for which the village is itself responsible, including a part-time secretary, a part-time treasurer or bookkeeper, a clerk for the cooperative store,

and a school janitor. (In the new villages, all school expenses are paid by the Ministry of Education and Culture. As the *moshav* develops, however, it shoulders a progressively larger share: initially, the janitor's salary, and the cost of repairs, replacement and acquisition of new equipment, later also a part of the other expenses.)

2. Maintenance and services of public buildings and the village office; sanitation.

3. Other expenses, such as cultural activities, welfare cases, etc.

These expenditures are met by direct taxation of each household. In the early stages of settlement, village dues are generally collected at a flat rate of five percent of the settler's income, later a progressive scheme can be worked out (although this is not common). In addition, each household pays income tax (in the early years, of course, the settler's income is below the taxable minimum); district council rates which are a poll tax and a land tax, but are very low; national insurance and social security (compulsory), sick fund (this is not compulsory, but no private medical services are available in the villages and insurance with this fund is practically universal), water and electricity rates.

(e) Regional settlement planning, in which production and services are integrated on the regional level.

[18] O. Shapiro, *Koresh—A Kurdish Village in the Jerusalem Mountains* (Jerusalem, Land Settlement Department, 1958 [Hebrew]).
O. Shapiro, *Oranim—A Yemenite Village in the Jerusalem Mountains* (Jerusalem, Land Settlement Department, 1960 [Hebrew]).

[19] For discussion of development systems, and in particular, as regards "expansionist" versus "intrinsic", and "free" versus "guided", see Bert F. Hoselitz, "Patterns of Economic Growth", in *Sociological Aspects of Economic Growth* (Glencoe, Illinois, The Free Press, 1960).

PART ONE

As mentioned in the Introduction, this part of the book reports on the first phase of research in new *moshavim*. The purpose of this phase was to obtain a general overview of the settlement scheme, and to identify and trace the basic emergent patterns of farm and community among the diverse social groups. Towards this end, a sample of villages, as representative as possible within the limitations imposed on the study, was selected; and the following pages include their comparative analysis along five major dimensions:

1. Demographic patterns in the rural households, and their economic and other implications;
2. Problems of know-how of the new farmer;
3. Social structure and integration in the new communities;
4. Types and characteristics of village organization—cooperative and municipal;
5. Motivation for settlement among different groups.

All data in this part refer to the year 1959/1960.

CHAPTER 1

WORKING HANDS AND MOUTHS—THE MOSHAV AND THE DEMOGRAPHIC STRUCTURE OF NEW IMMIGRANT HOUSEHOLDS

Introduction

The importance of demographic factors in development has, of course, long been recognized everywhere. One might even say that it was the first area to be explored systematically within this context, and a very fruitful one. However, most of these studies have, not unnaturally, been devoted primarily to the macro or the societal level, and have examined such questions as population types, movements, and secular cycles, and their implications for general employment policy, patterns of industrialization and mechanization, levels of investment and rate of growth, etc.[1]

Our study of the demographic factor in the *moshav* settlement scheme was much more modest, dealing with the level of the individual farm and household, and the single rural community; and the particular problem which we set out to examine in this context was the significance for the new *moshav* of *patterns of manpower and consumption*. As seen earlier, the settlement plan of the *moshav* clearly implies definite demographic criteria and expectations and therefore requires specific characteristics of the villagers. The immigrant groups, however, were not selected by age, health, or the size and structure of their family units, and they present a great variety of demographic patterns, most of which depart from what the original planners conceived as the "norm" We shall try to examine the results of the confrontation with these patterns and see how different demographic types have affected development.

The Demographic Implications or Requirements of the Moshav

As we have already said, the *moshav* economy, once it has attained the stage of full investment and production, is intended (a) to provide uniformly for all the needs of an agricultural family on a level deemed adequate by society, and (b) to do so without recourse either to additional employment or to hired help.[2] The crucial factor here is that not only was this general intention adopted as the guiding image of the new *moshav,* but that this image was also spelled out in the same agricultural norms, although these specifications had initially been worked out by and designed for a particular type of European settler who bore little resemblance to the kind of immigrant now expected to settle on the land. In other words, the newcomer was confronted with one basic, relatively undifferentiated kind of smallholding, characterized (despite the variety in farm types) by a firm set of work requirements on the one hand, and a given income potential on the other. Thus the new settler had to adjust to a pattern which had very specific demographic implications as regards both production (or manpower) and consumption.

Let us examine the two specifications in some detail. For simplicity's sake we shall refer to only one type of farm[3]—the field-crops farm. Table 6 gives us the manpower requirements for this kind of farm.[4]

Close analysis of these specifications shows that: the farm as a whole, including as it does 367 Standard Work Days per year, requires roughly 1⅓ standard units (on the basis of 280 working days per person per year). This total, however, is spread unevenly over the various seasons and months. The household then must invest between 36½ and 48½ days per month during the peak months; between 24 and 28 days during spring and autumn (April, November, and December); between 6½ and 11½ days only during the rest of the time. That is to say, the farm requires—depending upon the season—from *less* than one standard worker per day up to *two standard workers per day*. This higher limit, needed over 5 months, can be taken as the requirement, although calculations show that since extra effort of a limited kind is possible by fewer people—this norm is really more flexible and stands at between 1½ up to 2 standard workers per farm per year. But the overall total must be evaluated in terms of the quality or structure of this labour force. If we examine each crop as to the physical strength and vocational qualifications needed to raise it,[5] we see that about 270 Standard Work Days must be done by one adult male who is a qualified worker, i.e., the farmer himself. The rest, on the other hand, can be split among marginal cultivators, such as the farmer's wife and his adolescent children, whose summer holidays fall during the peak season.

In other words, the productive or labour force implication of the schedule calls for one fully employed farmer, and for seasonal additions which can easily be supplied by two or three other members of the household, working part-time. Although it is nowhere stated so explicitly, the image is clearly that of a European middle class household of the sort common between the two world wars.

No less definite are the implications concerning the *moshav* household as a consumption unit.

As was mentioned earlier, the *moshav* farm aims at providing a generally uniform level of living which should approximate the national average (actually characterizing the skilled urban artisan).

In Table 7 we see that the field-crops farm was designed to produce a net income (before taxes) of IL4,782 (at 1958–1959 prices). If we take off taxes and payments

TABLE 6—Manpower Requirements in a Field-Crops Farm

Crop	Area in dunams	Work days per dunam	Total work days	Distribution according to months											
				Jan.	Feb.	March	April	May	June	July	Aug.	Sept.	Oct.	Nov.	Dec.
Cotton	4	15	60	—	—	—	2	6	6	4	4	12	18	8	—
Sugar beet	4	12	48	2	2	—	2	16	4	—	2	6	8	6	—
Groundnuts	3	11	33	—	—	—	7½	4½	4½	3	1½	3	6	3	—
Spring tomatoes	1	35	35	—	—	—	1	3	6	5	9	6	4	1	—
Spring cucumbers	1	27	27	—	—	—	3	3	15	6	—	—	—	—	—
Autumn cucumbers	1	24	24	—	—	—	—	—	—	5	7	11	1	—	—
Spring potatoes	1	15	15	—	2½	2	2	1½	7	—	—	—	—	—	—
Autumn potatoes	1	13	13	—	—	—	—	—	—	—	2½	2	1½	1	6
Various summer vegetables	1	20	20	—	—	—	—	3	1½	8½	7	—	—	—	—
Various winter vegetables	1	16	18	1	—	—	—	—	—	1½	2	3	2½	3	3
Onion	1	20	20	1½	2	3½	3½	—	—	—	—	—	—	1	8½
Cauliflower	1	10	10	2	—	—	—	—	—	—	1	2	1½	½	3
Hay	3	0.66	2	—	—	—	—	1	—	—	—	—	—	1	—
Green manure	4	0.5	2	—	1	—	—	—	—	—	—	—	1	—	—
Farm-yard branches			18	1½	1½	1½	1½	1½	1½	1½	1½	1½	1½	1½	1½
Vocational training			24	2	2	2	2	2	2	2	2	2	2	2	2
			369	10	11	9	24½	41½	47½	36½	39½	48½	47	28	24

Notes: 1. 1 dunam = 1/4 acre.
2. The table excludes common orchard or vineyard, cultivated by the cooperative as a whole.

on long-term agricultural loans (estimated at IL 1,030 a year), we set a theoretical income of about IL 3,800 per annum.

On the other hand, as Table 8 makes clear, the average standard of living when this study was made was based on an annual consumption of some IL 1,000 per person. And although again it is not explicitly stated anywhere in these words, it is quite easy to calculate that, since food and lodgings are cheaper in the village, the above-mentioned income can assure this standard to a household of five (or less).

The crucial point is, obviously, not that different farms deviate from this norm, but that *within the uniform production and income plan, households with different demographic structures are bound to find themselves in an* a priori *differential situation.*

TABLE 7—Planned Yearly Income for Established Family Farms of the Field-Crops Type (1958–59)

	IL
Gross income from field-crops	6,819
Gross income from yard branches	280
Gross income from orchard or vineyard	1,344
Total gross farm income	8,443
Inputs	3,901
Net farm income	4,542
Value of use of house	280
Total net income	4,782

TABLE 8—Average National Consumption in 1956–58

Type of consumption	Expenditure per person	Percentage per person
	(IL)	
Food, drink, tobacco	453	43.2
Clothing, shoes, etc.	159	15.2
Other items	437	41.6
Total	1049	100.0

Different Demographic Patterns and Their Significance

Taking the above-mentioned norms of manpower and consumption as points of departure, the demographic nature of any given household can be expressed in terms of the relationship between the (a) *actual manpower of the family* (with the age curve of the unit and the number of its members determining the *size* of the labour force, and the physical constitution and the state of health of each individual on this force defining its *quality*)[6] and (b) *consumption needs* (measured by the number of the consumers). Formulating each dimension as a trychotomy (>, =, and < than the norm) nine composite demographic types are obtained:

A Manpower in relation to requirements		B No. of consumers in relation to earning potential	
(a) Less	(0 to 1)*	(a) Fewer	(1 to 3)
(b) Equal	(1.5 to 2)	(b) Matched	(4 to 5)
(c) More	(2.5 and more)	(c) Greater	(6 and more)

	A	B
1	Less	Fewer
2	Less	Matched
3	Less	Greater
4	Equal	Fewer
5	Equal	Matched
6	Equal	Greater
7	More	Fewer
8	More	Matched
9	More	Greater

* As is obvious from what was said earlier, here we also take into consideration the *structure* of the manpower. A household which has no one "complete" standard worker is classified as (a), even if other members combine to more.

In our actual research population, three of the theoretically possible profiles were either indistinct (2 from 1), or else unreal (7 and 8). Our attention in this paper is thus focused on six basic types, presented in "sociological", rather than numerical order—the frame of reference being their social background, on the one hand, and their significance in the *moshav*, on the other.

Type 1 (or No. 4 in the above) can be called the "pioneering" type, the fully productive, but childless family. In this structure manpower equals requirements, but there are fewer consumers; and the relationship of A > B is established. This structure is obviously ideal for the duration of intensive capital formation and development: and it has indeed been characteristic of many of the young collective settlements. In the population we studied, it has—whenever maintained consistently over a critical period of time—been associated with a take-off "spurt". But this phenomenon existed only among the few family-planning conscious Western immigrants who settled in the village as soon as they were married, or who married "into" a farm. In the traditional family, on the other hand (from backgrounds we will discuss later), this was usually both an unintentional and a transitional situation. On the whole, this is a marginal structure in smallholding farming; and something of a side-issue in the present study.

Type 2 (or No. 5 in the above) is the "balanced" Western demographic structure, in which A = B, both aspects corresponding to the implications of the farm plan. Concretely, this type appears in Israel primarily in the old established *moshav*, and is that structure basically implied by the blueprint of the smallholders' cooperative. The prototypical agricultural household was indeed founded by relatively young people, its children did not, on the average, exceed three, and their age distribution was moreover favourable to the smooth functioning of the farm. As a matter of fact, most of the people who colonized the original *moshavim* were in their early thirties and had children already of school age. Unlike the founders of the *kibbutz* or some of the more recent *moshav* settlers, they had not gone through a period of intensive development before their children were born, but neither did they now have to care for infants. These characteristics promoted full utilization of the factors of production, on the one hand, and achievement of an adequate income per head on the other, without creating overwork or underemployment, and without affecting other basic activities. This type, in fact, is the fairly standard pattern of the Western farmer; and, though as such it frequently appears also in some of the new settlements, it is far too well known to require further elaboration by us.

Type 3 (No. 1 or 2 above) may be termed the "war survivors", or the "unbalanced" Western Jewish family, whose manpower is so small that it often cannot support itself through agriculture even though the number of consumers in the family is also restricted and often falls short of what is envisaged in the norm. As, however, the productive capacity[7] is less than the requirements of profitable commercial farming, the relationship of $A < B$ is established in the household, either transitionally or for an entire generation. The destruction of families in the holocaust of World War II, the frequent second marriages of survivors and the children of these late marriages resulted in a skewed pyramid, characterized by a rather large number of small children with more or less elderly people, and very few age groups in between. Among settlers of this kind, many farms are owned by couples in their fifties who are either childless or who have children at kindergarten and elementary school. In a typical (European) *moshav*, for instance, namely Ta'amon, this demographic datum constitutes the most important single factor in the shaping of the economic activity of its population—immigrants from Yugoslavia and Rumania.[8]

The *actual* specific impact of the demographic imbalance depends on the availability of an alternative occupation and source of income. This "availability" in turn is usually determined by the settler's own skills and by the market situation

TABLE 9—"War Families" in Ta'amon, by Country of Origin and Number of Children [8]

No. of children	Yugoslavs		Rumanians		Total	
	No.	%	No.	%	No.	%
No children	10	50	8	53	18	51
1 child	4	20	3	20	7	20
2 children	5	25	4	27	9	26
3 children	1	5	–	–	1	3
Total	20	100	15	100	35	100

TABLE 10—"War Families" in Ta'amon by Country of Origin and Age of Children

Age of children	Yugoslavs		Rumanians		Total	
	No.	%	No.	%	No.	%
Up to 13 years	8	40	6	40	14	40
14–18	2	10	1	7	3	9
No children	10	50	8	53	18	51
Total	20	100	15	100	35	100

TABLE 11—Relationship Between "Imbalanced" Demographic Structure and Withdrawal from Agriculture (Auxiliary Farming Only)

Demographic structure \ Farming	Full farm	Auxiliary farm	Total
Balanced (Type 2)	127	4	131
Imbalanced (Type 3)	2	33	35
Total	129	37	166

$x^2 = 132.72$
df: 1
$p < 0.01$

in the area, and by the extent of the settler's commitment to agriculture. Since the villagers of Ta'amon on the whole are well educated and since their village is close to urban centres with good employment opportunities, there has been a turn towards a severe limitation of cultivation. Many Ta'amon households only have auxiliary farms and for these people, the *moshav* is primarily a place of residence.

By contrast, in *Moshav* Zeviya the situation is quite different. Although here, too, the families (of war survivors) are not particularly committed to agriculture, they are significantly less educated and are situated some distance from employment centres. Consequently, it is hard for them to find an equally lucrative alternative. As a result, the demographic imbalance is reflected not in limited production, but in a change of method; or, more precisely, in compensating through hired labour on the one hand, and intensive mechanization (which is seldom economically justified), on the other.

TABLE 12. Alternative Production Factors in *Moshav* Zeviya

(a) *Agricultural Machinery*	
1. Farms with milking machines	21
2. Farms with mechanized reapers	1
3. Farms with both	23
	—
Total of mechanized farms	45

correlation coefficient between demographic structure (imbalanced versus balanced) and extent of mechanization—$r = 0.62$.

(b) *Hired Labour*	
1. Farms with hired labour	25
2. Total of hired workers	29

correlation coefficient between demographic structure (imbalanced versus balanced) and hired labour—$r = 0.32$.

It is worth noting, however, that even with the above-mentioned compensation, the imbalanced demographic structure affects the range of development: when we examine the relationship between standard workers at the disposal of the farm (ranked from $\frac{1}{2}$ to 3), and the intensity of farming activity itself (measured by the size of the farm in Standard Work Days), we see a correlation coefficient $r=0.52$.

This situation is probably fluid—and some of the non-agricultural families with children may become productive when their children grow up; or, conversely, agricultural families without children, as they grow older, may stop their production altogether (especially since lack of direct heirs, understandably enough, weakens the motivation for developing the farm fully). At any juncture, however, at which the structure described appears, it plays a significant role in the *moshav* reality.

The following three types of household are all based on the "traditional" Jewish family pattern, characterized by a high fertility (the result of early marriage and no family planning);[9] and the extended family (vestiges of which persist in the *moshav*). But, of course, cultural and other variations have produced definite demographic distinctions in this pattern.

Type 4 (or No. 9 in the above) is the opposite number of the second demographic structure described, namely a "balanced" Oriental or traditional family. Households of this kind, like those that follow, include many children and extended family connections; but owing to good health and strong constitutions (especially among the elder people), its productive manpower is much larger.[10] Potentially, therefore, that is, under different production possibilities, it could meet consumption requirements, thus establishing an $A = B$, or even $A > B$ relationship. Given the existing requirements, however, this excess and *non-utilizable* productive capacity also results, paradoxically, in the $A < B$ imbalance. The crucial factor is thus the ability of the nearby employment market to draw off excess manpower.

To illustrate, let us briefly analyze eight families in a North African *moshav*—Zimriya.

TABLE 13—The "Balanced" Oriental Family

Families \ Members of the family by age	55 and over	55–46	45–35	34–25	24–14	Up to 14	Total
1	1–	1–	2*	1°	4′	2′	11
2		1*	1*		3′	2′	7
3		1–	2*		2′	5′	10
4	3–	1–			1* 2°	1′	8
5	1–	1–		2*		3′	7
6		2*			5′	3′	10
7	1–		1*	1*	3°	2′	8
8		1*	1*	1*	4′	1′	8

* = owner of farm
° = brothers and sisters of owner
– = parents of owner
′ = children of owner

(We have, of course, a complete tabulation of the demographic structure of the other agricultural families in Zimriya—58 in all: but such a large table would have been unwieldy here. Of those other families, eight are "assorted" near-social cases (see later), 25 belong to demographic type 5 (see below), seven may be classified as "balanced" Western families of type 2, and 18 are also of type 4.) All eight families adduced have fully cultivated farms, and all of them—having at least two full workers—send members of the family to work outside the farm. Four of these are permanent, full-time jobs (teaching, baking, orange-grove management, cultivation of additional farm), while the other four constitute full-time seasonal employment.

We see the same picture at *Moshav* Biyoun—a village characterized by a particularly good labour market situation, since "internal" work can be found easily in the extensive fruit orchards cultivated by the local cooperative.

Table 14 shows the advantage of this type in good market conditions.

So, despite the fact that the level of income in this village is, on the whole, lower than the national average (mainly due to inefficient farming), the situation of the "balanced" traditional household is only a little worse than that of the "balanced" Western one.

These, though, are cases in which advantageous market conditions have permitted settlers to exercise their own initiative and modify the purely farming

TABLE 14—Demographic Structure and Income in Two *Moshavim*

Demographic Type / Net monthly income (in IL in 1958/59 prices)	*Moshav* Zimriya			*Moshav* Biyoun		
	"Balanced" traditional	Other	Total	"Balanced" traditional	Other	Total
0 – 149	—	11	11	1	24	25
150 – 249	—	23	23	12	19	31
250 – 349	13	26	39	11	6	17
350 +	13	—	13	—	—	—
Total	26	60	86	24	49	73
x^2	49.93			17.65		
df	3			2		
p <	0.01			0.01		
Average Monthly Income Per Person by Type of Household						
"Balanced" traditional (type 4)	IL. 47.60			IL. 41.00[11]		
"Pioneering" (type 1)				IL. 90.30		
"Balanced" Western (type 2)	IL. 50.60			IL. 51.00		
"Unbalanced" Western (type 3)				IL. 26.30		
"Unbalanced" traditional (type 5)	IL. 20.95			IL. 18.60		

Notes: 1. The table does not include income from the communal orchards, which is rent, unrelated to the factor under discussion; we have also omitted social cases, two farms whose owners were abroad, and non-agricultural village functionaries.

2. Other demographic structure includes: 3 "pioneering" households (type 1); 16 "balanced" Western households (type 2); 12 "unbalanced" Western households (type 3); and 18 "unbalanced" traditional households (type 5).

opportunities. A striking contrast is presented by *Moshav* Koresh, a Kurdish village located in an isolated part of the Jerusalem Mountain District.

Here, the same demographic structure actually means an unemployed manpower surplus on the one hand, and a relatively low income per capita, on the other. The first of these is felt most sharply, of course, during the dead agricultural season; but all in all, the contrast between the family needs and income, and between the manpower potential and realization, not only creates dissatisfaction with agriculture as such, but also leads to feelings of forced inactivity and the undermining of work habits.

Type 5 (or No. 6 in the above) conveniently falls in the category of the "unbalanced" Oriental or traditional family. Here, by contrast to the structure we have just described, the consumption needs are inordinately large, but manpower barely equals the agricultural requirements. Formally—though obviously for different structural reasons—here, too, $A < B$; and here, too, the basic suitability to smallholding agriculture as such may be questioned—especially since capitalization for mechanization and hired labour is impractical if not impossible in this case (see Chapters 2 and 5).

In our analysis, we shall employ a concrete example which, though perhaps extreme, vividly illustrates the case in point and at the same time is far from being marginal. Shalekhet is a Yemenite *moshav* (based chiefly on vegetables and industrial crops) characterized by the fact that, though the majority of the families have enough manpower to cultivate their farms, this cultivation—which is dependent on a large number of workers whose physical capacity is limited—does not suffice for the families' considerable consumption needs, and at the same time also limits other activities.

TABLE 15—Age Structure of *Moshav* Shalekhet

	No. of persons
Adults	
Males in the formal work age groups (up to 55)	80
Females in the formal work age groups	83
Old people (over 55)	30
Total	193
Children and Youths	
Below age 13	255
Youths aged 13–17	33
Total	288

(In the age groups of young people, we have not distinguished between boys and girls, since this is not particularly significant as regards the partial help expected from them on the farm.)

The mean number of children per family in this population is five (although the proportion of young people is small), and at first glance it seems similar enough to the "balanced" type we discussed earlier. But there is a significant departure here in respect to the qualitative aspect of the manpower component.

True, the settlers energetically entered the production cycle. The crops planted and sown in the spring of 1957 were very successful—in size and quality. But this initial impetus (1957 was the first fully productive year in the village's history) was by no means based on a balanced and reasonable working effort. The settlers, including women, children from 7 to 13, and the old people, worked long, hard hours in the fields, over and above the input usually required by this type of farm even in peak production periods—the special effort being inevitable for people of weak physical constitution and generally poor health.

Among these settlers there were many cases of sickness[12] and physical debility; in the summer the children suffered from diarrhoea and boils; while the women, constitutionally frail, were additionally exhausted by frequent childbirth. In spite of this they worked side by side with men, creating a vicious circle, and increasing sharply the necessity for cesarean sections performed as a result of weakness, which made normal delivery difficult. On top of this, malnutrition—further intensifying unsuitability to hard manual labour—has often led, without the people concerned being aware of it, to further debility and weakness.[13]

The situation is somewhat different in respect to the children, because the School Nutrition Scheme provides them with better food; but the school lunch (which often represents half of the children's total food intake) is not given during the summer vacations, which extend over the peak work seasons; and the youngsters' meals then are exactly the same as those of the adults. Thus, though the settlers work willingly, even the young ones tend to return home at noon exhausted; and filling the production norm is only made possible by a large number of workers, each of whom produces only a small part of the standard output. This lessens both the relative adequacy of the economic rewards of the farm, and harms the future work potential of the individuals concerned.

The utmost use of *all* the available manpower, attendant upon farming in this demographic type, also has an adverse affect on the possibility of establishing new units of production via the natural process of fission within each family. In a village, similar to the one we are describing now, both as to origin of the settlers and demographic structure, several farms became vacant when their owners left the settlement, and allocation of these units to the young people of the *moshav* seemed an obvious solution. But, in most cases this was impossible because then the parent farm would be too severely undermined by the withdrawal of a working son; and the establishment of a new household endangered the very existence of the old one.

The extreme form into which this demographic structure is liable to shade is exemplified by some of the village's *agricultural* families. These were not considered significantly different from the average household in the *moshav*, and accordingly were given regular plots for cultivation and subsistence. Actually, in terms of our demographic variable (and, in fact, in terms of reality), they are almost welfare cases, quite incapable of making farming pay.

TABLE 16—Agricultural Families in Shalekhet with a Border-line Structure

	Age of head of family	Structure of the unit	Remarks
1	52	Wife + 9 small children + old mother	
2	42	2 wives + 8 small children[14]	
3	40	2 wives + 8 small children	sickly

All in all, Shalekhet has 43 households of type 5 of a total of 77 (not counting the welfare cases proper, of whom more later). This demographic structure inevitably influences other spheres of activity; the first being education and child-rearing, since neither parents nor elder siblings are able to carry out this function properly. The Yemenite population in general has a positive and intelligent attitude towards education and towards the activities of local educational institutions. The Shalekhet settlers understand the need for regular school attendance, they are interested in the children's studies, and grown-up brothers and sisters recognize their obligation to help younger children with homework. In practice, however, only school attendance is really observed; the burden of farming not only often prevents the adults from participating in the children's education, but the child himself is often unable to do his part since work on the farm awaits him as soon as he returns from school. Even worse, mothers work in the fields all day, and the small children, including babies who are not breastfed, are left to roam the village, without food, without care, without shade, and without attention to hygiene and cleanliness. Sometimes babies are even shut up at home all day, with only a bottle of tea and a piece of dry bread by their side.

The demographic factor, in fact, influences the very allocation and performance of family roles: *moshav* reality forces women to undertake a substantial share of farm work, which the man, or men, of the household cannot accomplish alone. This leads not only to reorganization of the woman's spheres of work and neglect of some of her household duties, but also, necessarily, confers upon her a more authoritative status than heretofore. It is interesting to note that when—as has happened in several cases—the settlers recognize this connection between the requirements of the farm and the process of the woman's encroachment upon "masculine preserves" of saving, investment, consumption, etc., they begin to object to the full development of the farm, to crops grown at a distance from the homestead, and so forth.

Similar impact of the demographic imbalance is felt also in adult cultural and educational activities. This is due, of course, to the fact that the demographic structure, directly or indirectly, determines two data which are basic to the fulfillment of social roles: economic means, and time. And although the nature and relative importance of various aims will not be primarily related to questions of manpower and leisure, the demographic type does, nevertheless, act as a limiting factor, and establishes the means and level on which these aims can be implemented.

Relative limitations on social, cultural, recreational and civic activities are, in any case, inherent in the household which runs a family farm; unlike modern American farmers who are aided by large investments and automation, the Israeli settler (like most smallholders all over the world) is subject to the constant pressure of very long working hours. Even if his income permits him, for example, to pay for modern, city-centred, commercial recreation, in many cases he simply has no time for it. Such recreation is, of course, an optional activity, and, in any case, not very significant in the *moshav,* which usually provides its own cultural facilities, emphasizing reading and interaction as the chief forms of relaxation. By the same token, however, where the new immigrant adult is concerned, much more basic functions are inevitably affected, such as resocialization and absorption.

One of the most difficult problems encountered by organizers of cultural activity in new immigrant *moshavim* is, without doubt, the lack of communicative readiness and receptivity, caused largely by the lack of free time and by fatigue. The greater these factors are, the lesser the immigrant's ability—all other things being equal—to participate in those routine and special activities which are designed to promote his identification with the values and symbols of the State, and also the less his chance of assimilating the norms of behaviour in Israel's social and political framework.

Active farmers of demographic type 3—the "war-survivors family" are also affected in this respect. But the communicative distance to be covered by the Yemenite immigrant is much greater than that of the European newcomer. And the correlation of traditional background with an imbalanced demographic structure is thus particularly significant. The following report by an active observer in Shalekhet is of interest in this respect:

"The *moshav's* cultural life presents a contradiction between the supply of material and activity, and the possibility of utilizing it. The Federation of *Moshavim* for some years now has conducted various regular groups in the *moshav* club, including dancing, singing, story-telling and topical talks. Each Saturday morning, special youth activities have been held, including a review of the week's events, singing and games. It has also been the custom for a Rabbi to come once a week to give religious lessons for the men, while a special instructor for the women has come even more often. Sometimes, students and army units have come to contribute to the programme. All these activities were very popular; recently, however, (1957) there has been a sharp, continuous drop in attendance. This does not seem to be due to lack of interest on the part of the settlers (there is no feeling of surfeit or boredom)—but rather to the development of the farm. It would appear that—at least from the viewpoint of cultural absorption—this development has come at too early a stage; there is a clear connection between adding of fields to the original small plots near the houses, and the relegation of cultural activity to a very low second place. At present, agricultural work takes up practically all the settlers' time and the only 'attractions' which still command large participation are the religious lessons for the grown-ups, and the games for young people."

The step from this type to the welfare case proper is unfortunately short.

Type 6 (No. 3 above) is just such a household, characterized by a total (or almost total) lack of productive manpower, as against a wealth of consumers. Table 17, from the above-mentioned *moshav,* illustrates this type.

TABLE 17—Recognized Social Cases in *Moshav* Shalekhet

	Kind of case	Age of head of family	Structure of the family	Monthly allowance	Remarks
1	blind	35	wife + 4 children	50	Sometimes sells kerosene at home
2	blind	20	+ old mother	32	
3	blind	40	single woman	15	Also receives alms from settlers
4	crippled	30	single woman	5	Husband divorced her for another woman and does not pay alimony (he has 6 children)
5	widows	40	+ 3 small children	35	
6	old men	65	+ 2 wives + 6 children		

The prevalence of demographic structures of types 3 and 5 and, of course, 6[15] has serious implications for the total *moshav* economy. First of all, it is clear that withdrawal of families from the common economic organization (either because of non-membership of the auxiliary farm in the cooperative or because of inability to further stretch the minimal income) affects the financial situation of the collective and reduces its ability to provide public services. As regards type 3 (or at least in respect of the specific example given), this withdrawal may only diminish the profitability of the agricultural cooperative (since the non-members make a good living from other sources and are usually willing at least to pay municipal rates). Even in these cases, however, the *moshav* must depend largely on the willingness of the settler to pay his taxes. *Moshavim* do not have elaborate mechanisms for the collection of taxes, since they can collect arrears from the farmer's shares in the profits of the cooperative (see Chapter 4). This sanction, of course, can not be used against people whose main income does *not* derive from agriculture. In the village settled by types 5 and 6, though, both agricultural and other services are severely affected by the large number of families who are unable to share the financial burden of any assessment. Since most of these services are contracted by the *moshav* as a whole, default of payment by some families may deprive the entire *moshav* of an essential service.

In Shalekhet, for example, the medical services provided by the Sick Fund were suspended for four months because some families did not pay their dues. The dues, therefore, had to be redistributed, increasing the burden of most of the settlers who, in any case, could hardly make ends meet. In 1958, the inclusive dues per household (all families included) were set at nearly IL 17 per month; the share of the nine non-paying units should have amounted to some IL 150. Non-payment of this sum increased the assessment of each of the 77 families by two Israeli pounds per month (i.e., by 12%). Additionally, the village commitments and individual taxes had to be increased in order to establish a local welfare fund. Although welfare cases in new immigrant villages are formally the responsibility of State and regional authorities, the allocation received from these is so small that the *moshav* feels constrained, morally and socially, if not legally, to contribute its share.

Conclusion

To sum up, it is evident that standardization of the agricultural unit and disregard for differences in household structure have given rise to critical problems both in agricultural production and farm subsistence. Some of these discrepancies will probably resolve themselves sooner or later. Thus the special case of the "war survivors" is not likely to repeat itself; cultural changes raising the age of marriage and reducing fertility will affect the "Oriental" structure and bring it closer to the "Western" one; while different standards of nutrition and better medical care should eliminate the particularly problematic Oriental pattern (type 5). At the same time, the need seems to have been established for differential planning, taking into account the diverse predispositions of the settlers. In this way, greater mechanization and incorporation of hired labour might solve the problem of type 3. On the other hand, more land or assured additional employment might significantly regularize the situation of type 4[16]. But there seems to be no solution, within the *moshav,* for the type 6 families. Although these families would have difficulty in any community, the varied educational, employment and welfare services of a city may be more helpful than the small tightly knit *moshav* in helping them.

NOTES

1 See for example:
W.S. Waytinski and E.S. Waytinski, *World Population and Production* (New York, Twentieth Century Fund, 1953);
Joseph J. Spingler and Otis Dudley Duncan, *Population Theory and Policy* (Glencoe, Illinois, The Free Press, 1956);
Kingsley Davis, "Social and Demographic Aspects of Economic Development in India", in S.S. Kuznetz, ed., *Economic Growth; Brazil, India, Japan* (Durham, North Carolina, Duke University Press, 1955);
Kingsley Davis, "The Demographic Transition," in Amitai and Eva Etzioni, *Social Change* (New York, Basic Books, 1964).

2 Except in cases of special family need (sickness, military reserve service, etc.) when the village cooperative is expected to step in itself.

3 As mentioned above, the demographic implications of all farm types are, by and large, similar, and the example referred to throughout the analysis is representative:

Farm type	Yearly work requirements
Milk	395
Field crops	367
Citrus	380
Mountain	375
Hills	350

All these types have an unequal work-curve; and all are equally able to employ auxiliary family labour (see below). Their earning potential is also much the same, a factor discussed later. For example: compare the yearly net income of the field crops farm (specified in Table 1) of IL4,782 with those of the milk and the citrus farms, which are IL5,110 and IL5,200 respectively.

4 Table 6 is based on the standards of Central Agricultural Planning Commission, but we have adjusted it on the basis of our own observations as to the real situation. Two corrections in particular have been made:
(a) we have added time spent on vocational training and courses, which is omitted by the Planning Commission, but which does constitute work expenditure and which stands roughly at 24 days a year;
(b) we have taken the *real* average level of the immigrant farmers as our basis rather than the "norm", and since this former falls below the latter, the expenditure of time and of effort on each crop is inevitably greater.
For example:

Crop	Theoretical work requirements per dunam per year	Actual average per dunam
Cotton	10.0	15
Sugar beet	8.3	12
Groundnuts	6.6	11
Spring potatoes	11.0	15
Cucumbers	23.5	26
Onions	15.5	20

Table 6 refers actually to the anticipated family farm situation at the end of the seven to ten years of orderly development, when the unit reaches consolidation status. The development is thus not the maximum envisaged, since further intensification of production is possible. This, however, does not change the work-requirements situation, since the intensification—if any—will come *pari passu* with the lessening of instruction and with greater work-efficiency.

[5] These two requirements are, of course, distinct: pruning of fruit trees, for instance, can be done by children from the point of view of the effort required, but not from the point of view of vocational skill.

[6] In the actual identification of households we used, in addition to indices of disability, etc., also indices of actual time, institutionally or structurally available to agriculture: e.g., women in advanced stages of pregnancy, or mothers with infants, were considered to be fully preempted by other roles, etc.

[7] In "standard" man-hours; some families, of course, overcome this handicap by longer working hours, but this does not change the basic imbalance.

[8] Tables 9 and 10, which distinguish between this specific structure and other families in the village, should properly comprise both groups. We have, however, tried to avoid large and unwieldy statistical presentations; and as the omitted households are entirely of the stable type 2 mentioned above, we feel this procedure to be justified.

[9] This is, of course, a good example of a "skewed" or unbalanced demographic modernization, in the course of which mortality sharply declines, ahead of fertility. Here, the steep change in the former is the result of immigration to a modern institutional framework, which has, however, not affected the latter as yet.

[10] Insofar as it is possible to generalize about ethnic characteristics (systematic research on the comparative health of groups of origin is of very recent standing in Israel) it would seem that type 4 is more frequent among Jews from Kurdistan and the Atlas Mountains, for instance, than among those from Yemen or Indochina—all communities with similar family structures.

[11] In this village, though, the differences are alleviated by the orchard rent (IL 1500 per year per farm); so that the lowest monthly income (apart of the social cases) is here IL 217.

[12] Tuberculosis, Anaemia, Amoeba, Taenia, Oxyuris, Lamblia.

[13] The usual nutrition pattern: *Breakfast:* (eaten in the field in summer) half a loaf of bread, one egg or yoghurt, hot peppers, two tomatoes, and tea. *Lunch:* (during the summer season it is eaten only by 10 percent of the population which does not work in the fields) half a loaf of bread, hot peppers, olives, yoghurt and coffee. *Dinner* (main meal): bean or potato soup, half a loaf of bread, tea.

[14] In *Moshav* Shalekhet there are 9 welfare case households out of 86, and in *Moshav* Levanon, 10 out of 50.

[15] Polygamy is illegal in Israel, but immigrants from Oriental countries who came to the country with more than one wife have been allowed to keep them.

[16] One possibility now being studied is, in fact, the so-called "combined farm" which includes agriculture and outside employment in regional or cottage industries, specially established for this purpose. This form has been proposed chiefly for the mountain area, to meet special problems of scarcity of land on the one hand, and lack of employment openings on the other.

CHAPTER 2

LAND, THE TASK-MASTER

Introduction

To enlarge upon problems of agricultural skill and proficiency in a population of newly-made farmers—and especially when these are people of traditional backgrounds suddenly placed on modern farms—may seem banal. But in order to present what we have presumed to call "a slice of life", we must state the obvious, primarily because it is there, and also because it is so significant.

It must be borne in mind that the profitability of the small family farm depends mainly on very efficient cultivation. Production factors are rigidly calculated so that a high degree of utilization[1] is necessary, affording only minimum scope for the exchange, or compensation, of one factor by another. Because of its structure, it is impossible in a *moshav* to achieve the same output and income by simply increasing the area under cultivation or the amount of labour expended at a lower level of efficiency. Consequently, there is only a very small margin for any such fluctuations or differentiation, the more so since the anticipated standard of efficiency (i.e., that which is based on the average in well-established farms) serves also as the basis for computing whatever supplementary income must be given to the new farmers in the intermediate stage of production. If the target for this stage is fixed, for example, at IL 3,000 per annum, and the farmer who falls short of this is therefore subsidized by special public works employment, his subsidy is not calculated on the basis of his actual income but rather on the potential income of his unit in terms of the accepted norms. The difficulties involved in acquiring the necessary skills in a comparatively short time become vivid if we bear in mind the complex demands which are placed on the man who runs an intensive family farm today, especially when this is a mixed farm rather than a specialized one.

To begin with, purely *agricultural skills* are necessary. This category includes all of the various skills needed for farming. Efficient field or industrial farming, for instance, requires mastering some 50 different types of activity,[2] each one of which appears in several variations according to the specific crop, to say nothing of the actual planning of the crop rotation programme itself. The difficulty, however, lies not only in the great variety of the *new* skills which must be learned, but also in the high level of abstract thought and understanding which are involved. One basic distinction must be made between two types of knowledge:

1. Manual and mechanical skills, e.g., ploughing, weeding and raking, taking care of livestock, using and maintaining mechanical equipment.
2. Some grasp of the scientific basis of agriculture in such areas as soil mechanics, chemistry, biological development of plants and livestock, and their diseases, knowledge which is essential background for the successful application of the various principles of farming. This theoretical knowledge can be defined as the ability to be intelligently guided by norms of *quantity, quality* and *timing,* which underlie all farm activities,[3] and which are especially important in Israel where research and experimentation result in frequent innovations.

Secondly, the present-day farmer needs a number of *economic and commercial skills,* chiefly the ability to calculate the profitability of a given crop in terms of prevailing market conditions, while still allowing for possible price fluctuations. This is of special importance in the raising of industrial crops, poultry and beef cattle, which not infrequently call for decisions to expand, reduce or even liquidate a certain branch. Obviously, all this also requires considerable knowledge and experience in the marketing of produce, and in the purchase of various production goods such as manure, fertilizers, tools, livestock feed, etc. Although the economy of Israel as a whole and that of its villages themselves are planned, successful manipulation obviously results in more advantageous terms. Most such calculations and activities can be done on the village-unit level, but a considerable share of personal responsibility is inevitable. The individual settler must not only understand and evaluate the steps taken by the corporate body, i.e., the village; he must be able also to apply these to his own specific situation, if only in order to calculate the extent and the variety of his farming activities in keeping with the manpower at his disposal, his personal preferences, and his agricultural and other talents.

Then there are problems which involve *financial and managerial skills,* required mainly to shape the *moshav's* fiscal and financial policy, and allow it to make specific deals and commitments. Applied both to the village as a whole, and to the individual farm, this category embraces all the complexities of capital formation and distribution, in relation to resources, conditions and effective utilization. General as well as individual farm budgets must be prepared, an appropriate taxation scheme decided upon and carried out, and arrangements made for credit, repayment and prolongation of loans. The collective administrative skills of the village must also be applied to the management of various local services, and to execution or supervision of building and development programmes. Although specialized personnel is often partly enlisted from outside, each village must coordinate by itself the deployment of such personnel, and ensure the smooth functioning of services.

As we have already pointed out, most of the settlers under discussion came to the new *moshavim* in Israel without any prior training or experience in agriculture. The significance of this inexperience within different settler groups, and the extent to which it has been made good, form the subject of the discussion which follows.

The Immigrant Farmer—Good, Bad and Indifferent

A clear dividing line can be drawn between agro-technical performance, on both private and public levels, and other types of competence. Acquisition of the various essential manual and mechanical skills needed for farming has almost invariably proved the least difficult; these skills have been learned quite rapidly by people of different occupational and cultural backgrounds, often with little or no farming experience. But this is not true of theoretical comprehension or the application of non-mechanical norms. The ability to analyze new situations, to employ generalized criteria, to calculate and to appraise sensibly are harder to come by. Significant differences deriving from the settlers' previous backgrounds and basic predispositions should be expected here.

The settler with a "modern" general and educational background has the clearest advantage, of course, and is well ahead in this respect. A comparison between the European village of Ta'amon and the "transitional" groups of Zimriya (Morocco) and Teena (Persia) (all in the same region and farm type) shows significant differences, which can be illustrated by their poultry and dairy branches.

TABLE 18—Branch Efficiency in Three Villages[4] (1958/59)

a. *Egg production*

Village	Yearly average of eggs per layer
Ta'amon	199
Zimriya	142

b. *Milk production*

Village	Yearly average, litres per cow	Average input of fodder per litre
Ta'amon	4,560	0.91
Zimriya	2,930	1.1
Teena	1,850	1.4

The difficulty of bridging the initial gap in professional approach emerges just as clearly when we see how some of the farmers of our sample were evaluated by their instructors in relation to the expected norm[5]:

In the European villages of Ta'amon and Zeviya (combined), 63 percent of the functioning farms were classified as good (meaning that they achieved at least the average national standard) and only 3 percent fell into the category of poor performers; in the (combined) villages of Teena and Zimriya on the other hand, 21 percent were rated as good, while 29 percent were classed as problematical. The importance of even the most minimal general education moreover, is demonstrated by the striking differences which appear among settlers whose general background is much the same, but whose educational levels are quite different (Table 19).

TABLE 19—Distribution of Levels of Farming Proficiency according to Levels of (Modern) Schooling

a. *Zimriya*

Level of farming / Level of schooling	Good farming	Mediocre farming	Poor farming	Total
Modern elementary	10	15	1	26
Little or no modern schooling	6	18	12	36
Total	16	33	13	62

$r = 0.38$

$p < 0.01$

b. *Teena*

Level of farming / Level of schooling	Good farming	Mediocre farming	Poor farming	Total
Modern elementary	10	5	1	16
Little or no modern schooling	4	5	4	13
Total	14	10	5	29

$r = 0.36$

$p < 0.05$

The kind of neglect which occurs in "traditional" villages in terms of the abstract norms discussed, is illustrated, in some detail, by a survey of the field crops of seven different farms in the village of Torem. Table 20 thus shows the disregard for both quantitative and qualitative norms in the essential processes of fertilizing and

TABLE 20 Fertilization and Irrigation in a Sample of Seven Farms

Farm Code Number	Type of fertilizer: Nitrates			Phosphates			Irrigation		
	Norm (kg.)	Actual quantity supplied (kg.)	Percentage of norm	Norm (kg.)	Actual quantity supplied (kg.)	Percentage of norm	Norm (m^3)	Actual quantity supplied (m^3)	Percentage of norm
1	1 500	1 200	80	1 700	950	56	17 000	14 000	82
2	950	1 400	147	850	200	24	11 500	14 800	129
3	1 400	700	50	1 555	850	55	15 135	15 000	85
4	1 305	1 400	107	1 385	550	40	13 730	12 250	89
5	1 400	1 400	100	1 300	950	73	14 200	18 767	132
6	1 500	1 400	93	1 440	1 100	76	13 500	12 000	89
7	1 150	1 050	91	1 430	900	63	12 900	11 000	85

irrigation. As we can see, there is perceptible over-fertilization with nitrates, and—even more consistently—insufficient use of phosphates; while the water used falls either well below or well above the norm.

A similar situation exists in regard to timing. In the period under discussion 69 settlers prepared a total of 225 dunams of beet, of which only 143 dunams (65 percent) were sown according to the crop rotation schedule, while the balance followed much later, after the groundnuts crop, and was exposed to a cold and rainy winter. Quantitatively, the yield obtained was uniformly high, and both areas produced an average of 5.75 tons per dunam (comparable to the ideal norm of 6 tons, and to the year's national average of 5.0 tons). But the percentage of sugar content differed significantly. Table 21 shows that while the properly sown plots achieved as much as 17 percent,

TABLE 21—Sugar Content in Beet Root by Areas with Correct and Wrong Timing

Yield by area (in dunams) / Timing	Sugar content by size of area: 13–14%	15%	16–17%	Total area
Correct	—	51	92	143
Incorrect	54	28	—	82
Total	54	79	92	225

$r = 0.80$
$p < 0.01$

the poor areas in no case exceeded 15 percent and in part yielded only 13 percent.

Unsuitable cultivation as regards all three norms in fact affected most crops and branches, and the consequent loss of produce was estimated as follows: autumn potatoes, a loss of 120 tons (at 1.3 per dunam); cotton, a loss of nine tons (at 250 kg. per dunam); groundnuts, a loss of 35 tons (at 300 kg. per dunam); onions, a loss of 80 tons (at 1.5 tons per dunam); dairy, a loss of 130,000 litres (at 3,600 litres per cow). At the prices which the settlers actually got for their products (which were often below par), the loss to the village, because of these poor yields, amounted to some IL 70,000 net—an average of IL 900 per farm.

Additionally and quite apart from the loss of income due to the sugar deficiency in beets, other problems were created by wrong market calculations, bad storage, late reaping, and inefficient marketing. Much of the onion crop, for example, never got to the market at all, in spite of fixed prices (40 percent of the fifty-seven farmers who raised onions sold less than one ton per dunam; 21 percent sold 1.5 tons per dunam; 37 percent sold between 1.5 and 2 tons per dunam; and only two percent sold more than 2 tons per dunam). This was due to poor speculation, as a result of which a large part of the yield was held back until it rotted. The differences in the efficiency of different farmers in marketing are shown in Table 22.

TABLE 22—Onion Production and Marketing in a Sample of Seven Farms

Farm Code Number	Amount (in tons)					Area (in dunams)	Income (in IL)	Average price obtained per ton marketed
	Marketed	Spoilt	Home use	Total production	Yield per dunam			
1	1.30	1.30	0.05	1.65	1.10	1.50	145	111
2	2.00	0.50	0.03	2.53	1.26	2.00	172	86
3	1.90	3.00	—	4.90	2.45	2.00	164	86
4	0.60	—	0.02	0.62	1.24	0.50	51	85
5	3.10	1.00	0.03	4.13	1.38	3.00	285	92
6	14.90	—	0.06	14.96	3.74	4.00	1010	68
7	1.80	—	0.05	1.85	0.41	4.50	168	93

As can be seen in Table 23 this inefficiency was repeated in the handling of autumn potatoes. Regional agreement had assured a fixed price for this item, provided it reached the market not later than February 15th. This price would have grossed an average of IL 200 per ton, or approximately IL 170 net. The actual price realized, however, was only about IL 155 per ton, since 52.5 tons which reached the market long after the stipulated date, were sold at IL 100; 33.5 tons of these potatoes, which had been badly stored and packed, and given a low grade, fetched only an average of

TABLE 23—Potato Production and Marketing in a Sample of Seven Farms

Farm Code Number	Amount (in tons)					Yield per dunam	Area (in dunams)	Income (in IL)	Average price (IL) obtained per ton marketed
	Marketed at price	Marketed below price	Spoilt	Home use	Total production				
1	6.00	1.50	—	0.20	7.70	1.28	6	470	153
2	2.60	0.50	0.50	0.15	4.75	1.28	3	654	159
3	5.00	0.80	—	0.30	6.10	1.35	4.5	409	154
4	—	3.90	1.30	0.20	5.40	1.08	5	230	60
5	5.20	1.00	—	0.30	6.50	1.30	5	538	160
6	7.20	1.00	2.00	0.05	10.25	1.46	7	1329	161
7	4.70	0.90	0.30	0.15	6.05	0.86	7	936	168

IL65 per ton. The *moshav*, as a whole, therefore lost approximately IL8,000 of possible income on 507 tons of potatoes.

It would be interesting to continue this analysis for all the crops and farm branches of the village in question, but even without doing so, we can estimate that the average loss of potential income incurred by each household that year amounts to over IL1,000. These same farms might have easily averaged the scheduled income of IL2,000 for industrial crops. But in point of fact, only 22 out of 69 households achieved this income. Their success was due partly to the size of the plots under cultivation (most of the villagers still did not cultivate the entire plot allocated to them). But the differences in the size of these farms can account for only a part of the difference in income, since only four of eight of the largest farms (30 to 35 dunams) earned IL2,000 or more, while eleven out of the 48 smallest farms had exactly the same income. The main source of the difference was in the quality of the actual farming and of the marketing.

Isolation and analysis of financial and managerial skills is more difficult because management of the *moshav's* economic affairs is closely intertwined with its political functions (see Chapter 4). Economic inefficiency may, therefore, be the result of social and political problems rather than of an inherent lack of financial and managerial ability. In those villages, however, in which a local bureaucracy operated over a period of time, and where we were able to study the situation systematically, we discovered that managerial efficiency was related to much the same factors as efficiency in agriculture and marketing.

So much then for documentation of the obvious: the advantage of a modern background and education in meeting the professional requirements of intensive farming. However, the data also afford a somewhat more subtle insight. The fact is that the Yemenite settler has consistently functioned not according to his "proper traditional" character, out-matching and out-performing his brethren, including the

Kurds and immigrants from the Atlas Mountains. Generally speaking, Yemenite Jewry belongs to the very extreme traditional pole. Its structural purity as a traditional Jewish community was strongly reinforced both by the isolation and the militant conservatism of the surrounding society, as well as by the ecological dispersion of the Jews themselves. Research[6] indicates that the great majority of Yemenite Jews lived in small groups in hundreds of localities which were scattered over all of Yemen[7]. This phenomenon was necessarily reflected in various aspects of their spiritual, social and economic life. The relative isolation of many villages and hamlets in a mountainous desert country which lacks modern roads, transport and communications cut these groups off from any elements of Western culture and education—insofar as these penetrated into the Yemen at all. Isolation also helped to maintain a stagnant and undeveloped economy, with no industry, an extremely primitive technology, a limited money system and markets which were mostly of a local nature and based on barter. In fact, in many places the lineage, or even the isolated extended family, constituted not only the individual's main frame of action and reference, but also his total social horizon. Under such conditions there was little room for a continuous, regular and distinct political structure, and the inevitable internal conflicts and problems of representation before authorities could be and were solved within, and in reference to, the lineage itself, or else they required only sporadic, temporary and ad-hoc measures. These communities thus lacked all experience of "modern" pressure, competition, rational thinking and discipline, and might have been expected to find the transition to the requirements of intensive modern farming in Israel at least as difficult as similar groups. But it was not so. Table 24 shows the place occupied by Yemenite settlers in poultry-farming in the Jerusalem area (measured, as above, by the number of eggs per layer). Since the poultry-farm requires a high-level combination of all the complex skills we have listed, this finding, which confirms our own impressions obtained in a more limited sample, is, we think, of special interest.

One, if not the prime, explanation of this phenomenon seems to lie in the internal discipline and intellectual habits developed almost exclusively by the Yemenites among the traditional Jewish communities in the East. Although their educational curriculum and structure were largely family-oriented and almost entirely religious, education was, nonetheless, of central importance and, without doubt, it promoted the development of individual judgement and understanding[8]. In other words—education was not chiefly concerned with the acquisition of norms and symbols in a primarily ritual, "technical" and heteronomously legitimated way—as has been the case in other societies of this type—but rather with the promotion of a general religious insight characterized by some sophistication and based on personal knowledge. In more generalized terms, this meant that this community developed (or rather maintained) a complex and self-conscious high culture (in the Redfieldian

TABLE 24—Egg Production of Villages in the Jerusalem Area

Villages by origin of settlers \ Production	Number of layers	Eggs per layer	Mean per layer per village
Central European	20 000	100	
Central European	10 000	80	
Central European	8 200	92	95
Central European (Resissim)	6 000	100	
Central European*	2 500	100	
Central European	800	100	
Yemen (Oranim)	5 500	82	
Yemen	4 500	89	
Yemen	4 000	100	
Yemen	4 000	80	
Yemen (Levanon)	4 000	100	88
Yemen	3 300	100	
Yemen (Azor)	2 000	40	
Yemen*	1 500	100	
Yemen*	1 200	100	
Morocco (semi-urban)	1 300	80	
Morocco (semi-urban)	900	50	78
Morocco (semi-urban)	800	80	
Morocco (semi-urban)	500	100	
Morocco (rural)	3 500	68	
Morocco (rural)	500	80	
Kurdish (Koresh)	1 000	80	74
Kurdish	700	71	
Kurdish	500	50	

* In these settlements a minority of settlers originate in Morocco (semi-urban).

sense); and that this high culture was not the esoteric property of a small priestly elite, as in other societies of this kind, but rather that it was generally diffused. In other words, Yemenite Jewry was distinguished by a high cultural (or religious) level, on the one hand, and by little differentiation and specialization in this sphere, on the other[9].

It is reasonable to infer that the above-mentioned distance, small size, and isolation of the Jewish hamlets in Yemen, which prevented the Jews both from having contact with any central institutions and from supporting their own, also contributed significantly to their tendency towards general religious learning. Be that as it may, the results of this learning, as observed in the *moshav*, speak for themselves.

This tradition by no means minimizes the extent of the objective vocational difficulties—the more so since the "learned" Jewish community was, for historical reasons, an exception among traditional Oriental groups. Considering the wide range of skills required in modern mixed family farming, and the enormous gap which had to be bridged by the immigrant, what *was* achieved is far more impressive than what was *not* achieved. This is the more so when one considers the difficulties of the training situation. Although no systematic research into the communicative process has been included in this study, an analysis of conditions and problems of extension work are in themselves illuminating in this respect.

The Instruction Team

As we have mentioned before, a number of instructors were attached to each new *moshav* from the outset, in order to help the settlers gain experience and skill. Their tasks were to teach the newcomers the rudiments of successful farming and responsible membership in the *moshav*, and to assume responsibility for the management of the village itself until the settlers were capable of doing this themselves. The standard team, whose salaries were paid by the Land Settlement Department of the Jewish Agency, consisted of three members: a social instructor, responsible for economic, administrative, social and cultural matters; an agricultural instructor; and a woman home economics and child-care instructor. In addition, teachers, nurses, social workers, doctors and other personnel also work in the *moshavim*; in this particular context, however, their work is not of direct concern to us.

When mass immigration to Israel began in 1948, there were no professional instructors around at all to undertake these responsibilities. The original instructors were therefore "drafted", chiefly from established *moshavim* and they accepted the job as a public service to which they were prepared to devote a few years. Often they were young men and women who had grown up in a village and were competent farmers themselves, as well as being able leaders. Their work had been highly praised by the settlers, and the fact that they had volunteered, out of a genuine desire to help, had not gone unnoticed. Almost always, these volunteers lived right in the *moshav* itself, sharing all of the difficulties and hardships of early settlement. Some of them were regarded by the farmers as model men and expert agriculturalists. But on the other hand, the instructors were recruited from party-oriented movements, which were interested in attaching the new village to their respective networks of *moshavim*. Their loyalty therefore was primarily to the party, and their behaviour was often motivated and determined by their political commitments. The settlers thus often saw their instructor as the direct representative of an outside body, and not unnaturally arrived at ambivalent, and even suspicious, attitudes towards him. Later, when they themselves became more familiar with Israel's political system, they learned, as voters, to use the political factor in order to secure various benefits. (In later years, a different type of instructor emerged, one recruited chiefly from among the new settlers themselves. Many of these social instructors came from the more advanced immigrant *moshavim* and in some cases worked in their own villages.) This situation created a host of problems. First of all there was the lack of any extension framework, in terms of programme, methodology and tools. Vocational training was intended to consist of direct contact with individual farmers, group instruction by way of lectures and experimental plots, and limited special courses and "instruction days".[10] But in the beginning each instructor was forced to rely his own initiative, plus various rough and ready rule-of-thumb methods; and it was only much later that detailed training schedules of any sort were developed.

Moreover, there were no established methods of teaching commercial, administrative or financial skills. The social instructor usually worked through the *moshav* committee, going over all the organizational problems with it and gradually training the membership to take over all outside contacts. Quite early in the development of a *moshav*, the Settlement Department, on the recommendation of the instructors, encouraged appointment of a villager as *moshav* secretary. This secretary, while he was training to become a "manager" was able also to relieve the instructor of some of his multiple tasks. A certain amount of generalized instruction was also given by the woman who served as social instructor (and home economist). Unfortunately she often turned into a kind of technical secretary to the social instructor, which limited the time she could devote to improvement of household and family practices in the village.

Furthermore, qualified candidates to fill vacant positions were very scarce then, and the extent of their duties was seriously underestimated. The instruction teams were too small for their tasks; the settlements were largely isolated and had to run their own services, and the burden fell squarely and solely on the local group. The responsibilities placed upon the social instructor were many and various, including instruction, acculturation and actual management in various spheres of *moshav* life. Proper performance of any one of these duties left very little time for the others. Inefficient organization of the instructor's work schedule, or the settlers' frequent attempts to coerce him into entering into all sorts of peripheral village matters, served further to aggravate the situation. But basically the problems stemmed from the objective scope of the work itself.

The majority of the instructors—in particular those who actually often lived in the villages to which they were assigned—worked long hours often into the night and over the weekend. At the same time, their job also tended to take them away from the village for days on end, thus reducing even more sharply the time available for actual instruction. On top of all this, these commitments grew with time. The instructor's intellectual and physical resources were obviously extended to a breaking point precisely at that critical initial period, when he had to manage village affairs almost entirely on his own, as well as implementing a comprehensive training programme. Little wonder, then, that the results of this situation are still to be felt today in areas of communal or fiscal village activities which lag behind the general development of the *moshav*.

Nor was the picture essentially different in terms of the agricultural instructor. Although his work was more defined and restricted in scope, he also had to carry out an extended and intensive instruction programme, and, at the same time, was charged with supervision of the cultivation of individual and cooperative crops. It is not surprising therefore that he neither could nor did pay adequate attention to each individual farm holding.[11]

Paradoxically enough the situation was sometimes worse in those villages where the instructor was a local settler himself. While it has been generally considered desirable to train a member of the *moshav* to fill the post, any such candidate was, almost by definition, a farm owner, and moreover more successful than his neighbours. The time and attention which he invested in his own holding inevitably had an adverse effect on his public duties.

A third problem was insufficient training—a factor which affected even the experienced farmer-instructor, whose general knowledge and understanding of *moshav* structure, activities and agriculture was not always on the high level demanded by his overall obligations. The agricultural instructor, in particular, was often transferred from a different type of village with a different farm type, and had to undergo a process of reorientation himself. Regional and other specialists were, of course, at his disposal, but their work was frequently restricted to special activities, planning and periodic consultations, and did not extend to the everyday problems and decisions which arose on each individual farm. In consequence, the instructor—no matter how devoted and experienced—sometimes proved professionally inadequate. Fortunately, this did not happen often but the few times it did happen were, of course, magnified. The stories of incompetence and poor judgement went from village to village acquiring new details each time, and had a bad effect which was far in excess of actual severity.

Since they were not qualified agronomists, these instructors occasionally found themselves at a loss in more sophisticated villages, where several farmers had already acquired considerable experience and proficiency, and were certainly beyond the stage of needing basic instruction. These men were almost at the level of the instructor himself, and there was not much he could do to help them.

Very few of the instructors, moreover, had enough teaching experience. Even those who had actually taught were unfamiliar with methods and means which might be suitable for the heterogeneous immigrant population with which they dealt. Language difficulties, in most cases, were overcome, since Israel contains a large number of people proficient in most of the languages of the immigrant groups;

but other skills were conspicuously lacking. How to address someone, and how to make oneself understood; how to prove, or demonstrate, a point; what means to use to maintain discipline among adults—these and many other similar problems could not be anticipated, let alone solved, by the average instructor. In time, these difficulties were mastered, but the setbacks caused by seemingly trivial factors such as failure to use proper visual aids, the inability to understand the need for gradual progress and frequent repetition, or insufficient reliance upon concrete demonstrations, cannot be overestimated. Nor—which is equally important—did the instructors realize the advantage, or perhaps the necessity of initially taking account of and working through the traditional social structure. In some cases, visits to a particular age group or to a specific segment of the population were seen as inimical to the existing order; and an understandable social preference of the young instructor for his peers was regarded as an attempt to rouse the second generation against the first. Demonstration plots and other programmes not carried out in reference to traditional leadership or along the strict lines of kinship status and preference were often doomed to failure. These were probably too heavy a responsibility to be placed upon essentially inexperienced people, who lacked most, if not all, of the specialized vocational, personal, pedagogical and sociological qualifications obviously required by the situation. But again, this was an inevitable result of rapid and continuous settlement.

The fourth problem was related to the timing of the hand-over of the farm by the authorities. Obviously, the appropriate procedure would have been to strike a balance between too protracted a period of preparation, which might undermine the farmer's ability to take full responsibility, and between too swift a transition, which might find him unprepared for it. During the first years of mass settlement, many villages experienced one or the other of the extremes of bad timing. For example, in the village of Teena, the preliminary agricultural training proved insufficient. The settlers, who had been employed chiefly in building and public works, were none-theless plunged into agricultural production and financial responsibility and their lack of psychological preparation, as well as of vocational training was certainly largely responsible for the crisis we shall describe in detail later. Premature switch-over in the supply of know-how and training also occurred in financial and administrative spheres. In almost all the villages where this happened (and there were many), disorder followed. In *Moshav* Biyoun, a settlement with excellent basic conditions (as was proven by its subsequent success), the premature transfer of responsibility during the second year of existence caused a real crisis.

Conversely, too long a process of transition, or too drawn-out a pause between the acquisition of knowledge and its responsible application, obstructed later development no less.

An additional problem, which still exists, stems from the fact that the social instructor's role is oriented towards different institutional frameworks. Actually, he serves three masters, and his success depends on his ability to meet the main demands of all three, though these are not always fully compatible and may even be contradictory. In the first place, the instructor represents the settlement authority, namely the Jewish Agency, which pays his salary and finances the establishment of the village. He is held responsible by the Agency's Settlement Department for the settlement budget, for implementation of instructions and carrying out the development programme, and for various other aspects of the *moshav* organization.

However, he is also the representative of whatever political movement sponsors the village. In this capacity, he is required to secure the settlers' political loyalty and instruct them in the relevant ideology. Although these two aims largely overlap, there is still a definite area of potential disagreement between them, which inevitably is reflected in the instructor's role. For instance, the political movement might advocate a rapid acculturation process which would implement its pioneering, co-operative and egalitarian ideology; the settling agency, on the other hand, might prefer, for reasons of expediency and because of its primarily economic-national functions, to allow adjustments in the basic pattern.

Thirdly, the instructor obviously serves the settlers themselves. They expect him to answer those of their needs which seem primary and important to them. During the first years, for example, a settler's main and immediate preoccupation is an adequate standard of living for himself and his family. The Settlement Department, however, thinks in terms of long-range consolidation and over-all development plans. Some settlers want to cultivate their farm only partially, and to supplement their income from outside work. The *moshav* movements oppose this for ideological reasons, while the Settlement Department, acting as the custodian of national planning interests, does so for economic ones. These areas of potential conflict are built into the situation, and the instructor is often pulled in three different directions. Accordingly, he must be selective in the performance of his tasks, yielding as the case may be, to one or another of the pressures to which he is constantly subjected. The net result therefore cannot be effective training and orderly absorption.

The settlers tend to look upon the instruction teams chiefly as outside factors, which do not, properly, belong to the village at all. To a certain extent, this is true even when the instructor has himself actually been a member of the *moshav* in which he works; he still is, primarily, a representative and an employee of the Settlement Department, to which he owes his first loyalty and whose directives he is bound to follow whether or not they run counter to the demands of the village. The *moshav's* attitude toward him is almost always tinged by some suspicion. The settlers are aware enough of their dependence on the instruction team, but also they are aware of their inability to influence, let alone control, its activities.

In other words, the role of the instructor is split and differentiated according to the outside and inside factors he serves simultaneously. More important, this role is not clearly defined, either as regards concrete activities or hierarchy of aims. Even a minimum implementation of these commitments to multiple goals and to distinct tasks requires considerable agility, and the result is almost inevitably a collision.[12]

To sum up—the training of the new settler was characterized by difficult objective conditions; often unstructured, sometimes contradictory, and always meagre in resources. What was achieved therefore—if we may permit ourselves the luxury of a value judgement here—is a tribute to the dedicated amateur.

Conclusion

This discussion has highlighted the vocational difficulties inherent in cultivating an intensive family farm, and has reaffirmed the familiar—namely, the importance of modern education and background in this respect. Significant differences were, however, found also *within* traditional groups, showing some of them to be capable of rapid assimilation and use of abstract norms of a kind which had been completely alien to them. The finding points to the fact that such a basic discipline as a rigorous sense of time is *potentially* easier to learn than we have supposed. This is not to deny the validity of the customary antithetical image of a traditional and a modern concept of time: the one is religious/agricultural, the other wholly mechanical; the one is present-bound, the other has a long perspective. But the transition from one to the other—at least, on the level of understanding and observance—does not necessarily involve (or may even be divorced from) time as a basic component of reality; it may indeed "merely" imply learning a new skill. (This difference between the intellectual-vocational, and the motivational-symbolic levels of farming—in relation to a traditional culture—will become more sharply delineated in a later chapter.)

NOTES

1 The standards set follow, and change with, the average results achieved in established and consolidated farms, usually cultivated under optimal conditions, and regularly utilizing improvements provided by the agricultural research service. The following figures give some idea of these norms (in selected crops of the field-crops farm), in comparison with the *best* results achieved throughout the country:

Crop	Norm (average for consolidated farms)	Maximum results achieved
Cotton	0.3 tons per dunam	0.4
Sugar beet	5 tons per dunam at 17% sugar	7 tons per dunam at 16% sugar
Groundnuts	0.35 tons per dunam	0.43 tons per dunam
Potatoes	2.25 tons per dunam	3 tons per dunam
Onions	1.8 tons per dunam	3 tons per dunam
Eggs	200 eggs per layer a year	230 eggs per layer

When we consider that average egg production in the new villages in 1958-59 was only 130 eggs per layer, we see the distance that must be covered before the norm is actually achieved.

[2] For the main farming activities on industrial farms, see Note 3.

[3] Granted that intensive cultivation of the type discussed here requires, above all, rational acceptance and frequent modification of precise norms of *timing, quantity* and *quality,* the *moshav* farm is very highly loaded in this respect. This is because, on the one hand, each unit has many "sophisticated" activities (for instance: irrigation, pest control, fertilization, complex mechanization, classification, disease prevention and care); and on the other hand certain major crops—on which the household income largely depends—are outstanding in this respect. The requirements, and the distribution of skill and specialization in the field crops farm for example is as follows:

(a) Cotton: a very complex crop, requiring high agro-technical skills (especially pest control). Main types of agricultural work needed: ploughing, mechanical weeding, fertilizing, deep raking, mechanical sowing, thinning, hand weeding, sprinkle irrigation, spraying and dusting, picking, weighing and loading, cutting the stalks.

(b) Groundnuts: a complex crop, requiring high agro-technical skills (especially computing the relationship between spraying and irrigation). Main types of agricultural work needed: ploughing, harrowing, hand weeding, deep raking, furrowing, hand sowing, sprinkler irrigation, spraying, mechanical digging, heaping, mechanical threshing, transporting hay.

(c) Sugar beet: a relatively simple crop, no spraying, and an uncomplicated irrigation scheme. Main types of agricultural work needed: ploughing, fertilizing, smoothing the earth, hydraulic weeding, mechanical sowing, hand weeding, thinning, sprinkler irrigation, hand cropping, mouse control, mechanical digging, loading, packing and transport, leaf raking.

(d) Potatoes (spring and autumn): a crop requiring high specialization, especially in terms of spraying. Main types of agricultural work needed: ploughing, manuring, fertilizing, harrowing, seed preparation, sprinkler irrigation, hand sowing, deep raking, hand weeding, mounding, spraying, mechanical digging, loading, packing and transport.

(e) Onions: a relatively simple crop. Main types of agricultural work needed: ploughing, manuring, fertilizing, harrowing, deep raking, furrowing, sowing, sprinkler irrigation, hand seeding, gathering, packing and transport.

(f) Tomatoes: a relatively simple crop. Main types of agricultural knowledge needed: ploughing, manuring, fertilizing, hand weeding, semi-hot housing, planting, sprinkler irrigation, tieing, mounding, spraying, picking, packing and transport.

(g) Miscellaneous vegetables (chiefly winter and summer carrots): a relatively simple crop. Main types of agricultural knowledge needed: ploughing, manuring, fertilizing, harrowing, deep raking, mechanical sowing, thinning, chemical weeding, sprinkler irrigation, hand weeding, gathering, washing, packing and transport.

(h) Hay: a highly complicated and mechanical crop. Main types of agricultural knowledge needed: ploughing, fertilizing, harrowing, hand sowing, mouse control, mechanical reaping, mechanical stacking, mechanical packaging, transport.

(i) Green manure: a relatively simple crop. Main types of agricultural knowledge needed: ploughing, fertilizing, hand sowing, deep raking, driving greens into the ground.

(j) Vines: a very complex crop requiring a specialized knowledge of spraying and dusting. Main types of agricultural knowledge needed: ploughing, harrowing, hand weeding, fertilizing, spraying and dusting, wire training, pruning, picking, packing and transport.

(k) Farmyard animals: (i) Poultry: a specialized branch, both technically and commercially. Main types of agricultural knowledge needed: care of chicks in the incubator, heating, mixing and measuring food, disease prevention and care, classification; feeding and care of layers, lighting, disease prevention and care of layers, laying control. (ii) Sheep: a very simple branch. Types of knowledge needed: milking, shepherding (communal).

4 The indices used here—the number of eggs per layer and litre of milk per cow, and input of fodder per unit of production—neutralize other factors (e.g. size of farm, prices, etc.) and are therefore sound indicators of the skill required for each operation.

5 At this early stage of our research, we had not yet developed the more sophisticated measurement of skill we used later on (see Part II, Chapter 6), in which the grading of farmers was done by a panel of experts on the basis of a questionnaire plus observed performance. Data there included a sample of activities in a sample of crops (and livestock) within each production branch. The skill expended on each operation was actually defined and measured specifically against established norms relating to timing, quantity and quality. The degree of skill was then weighted according to the importance of the crop within the farm type (so that proficiency in a marginal crop would not be given an undue place) and according to how badly needed the activity was for the success of the crop. Here, unfortunately, we base ourselves only on general evaluation.

6 Chiefly by Prof. S.D. Goitein, then in the Institute of Oriental Studies of the Hebrew University of Jerusalem.

7 Only about one fifth of the total Jewish population of about 50,000 lived in the bigger towns, such as the capital San'a, Damar, Rada, Al Bayda, and a few others.

8 This was not so in respect to the development of individual personality—an aim which no traditional community acknowledged.

9 This does not mean of course, that there were no specialized centres of religious learning and law. On the contrary, these existed in the capital (San'a) and several other towns. But the average Yemenite Jew almost always received religious education which, in our system, would be equivalent to the secondary level of schooling. (For details, see, for instance:

E. Brauer, *Ethnologie der Yemenitischen Juden.* (Heildelberg, C. Winter, 1934) and

S.D. Goitein, "Jewish Education in the Yemen as an Archetype of Traditional Jewish Education", in *Between Past and Future,* K. Frankenstein, ed., (Jerusalem, The Henrietta Szold Foundation for Child and Youth Welfare, 1954).

10 Later on—a point taken up in Chapter 9—village youths were also sent to agricultural schools, mainly the following:

1. The agricultural secondary schools, which primarily serve the established agricultural population of Israel. The number of new immigrant children in them is negligible.
2. The more recently established regional agricultural schools. A few years ago, a number of regional rural councils set up two-year post-primary schools. Their curriculum consists of basic agricultural theory and practical training, as well as some general education. The students (contrary to the ordinary agricultural schools) do not live in but commute daily in organized transport, and are thus able to help on their parents' farms. Also they do not grow up in an environment which is entirely different from that of the group of origin.

   These seem to be very important factors, because otherwise many parents would not send their children to these schools at all, even if scholarships and other grants were available. Thus, supplementary vocational schooling is, as has been said, of comparatively recent standing and no analysis of its functioning can be made as yet.
3. The pre-secondary vocational boarding classes. In 1950, the Department for Youth Immigration of the Jewish Agency decided to give young boys and girls of the new settlements systematic agricultural training, especially designed to meet their needs and level of formal education. Special classes were established, and vocational training was focused on preparing these youngsters to take an active part in the farming and the management of their villages. Of all the formal educa-

tional settings mentioned, this scheme has, in fact, drawn the largest number of children from new immigrant *moshavim.*

11 The following was, in fact, the schedule of the agricultural instructor in *Moshav* Zimriya in 1958:

a. The Instructor's Tasks

Branch	Task	Action taken
Dairy	feeding cows	2, 3, 1
	cleaning padding	3
	general hygiene of cow-shed, routine care of cows	4,6
	milking	3
	care of births, and sucklings	1, 5
	veterinary care	5, 7, 6
	purchases, sales, insurance development	2, 5, 8
	general management of village, dairy branch	8,5
Fodder	cultivation (preparation of ground, fertilization, etc.)	6, 7, 5, 3
	water and irrigation	1, 2
	pest control	1, 3, 6, 5
	manual cultivation (e.g. weeding)	1, 6, 4
	cutting and gathering	3, 6, 7, 2
	general management	7, 8, 5
Chicken coop	feeding	6, 2, 5, 4, 7
	general hygiene and veterinary care	1, 6, 5, 7
	care of equipment and stocking egg laying and profitability calculation	1, 6, 7, 8, 5
	general management	8, 7, 6, 5
Vegetables	cultivation (preparation of ground) fertilization	6, 3, 2, 1
	water and irrigation	6, 1
	pest control	6, 3, 7, 1, 5
	manual cultivation	6, 5, 4, 1
	picking	6, 3, 7, 8, 4, 5
General	home gardens—horticulture (pruning, fertilization, etc.)	6, 1
	care of village book	5, 6
	current reporting to regional office and instructors	5
	economic analysis of farms	5, 1, 7, 6
	work conflicts	5, 6
	village and farm planning	5, 1, 8
	outside contacts—Jewish Agency	5
	agricultural institutions	5
	economic institutions	5
	social and cultural institutions	5

Legend:

1 = Intensive personal instruction, for clarification of fundamental concepts and activities
2 = personal instruction for backward farmers
3 = periodical instruction in specific areas
4 = general instruction (advice, general education, etc.)
5 = action by the instructor himself
6 = handing of instructions to settlers
7 = supervision and follow-up of settlers' work
8 = planning

b. Division of Instructor's Time (yearly average in 1958)

Instructor's Contacts	Days per month
District Director (or his deputy) of Land Settlement Department	3
Assistant Director in charge of extension	4
District irrigated crops instructor	4
Orchard instructor	0.5
Dairy instructor	1.5
Poultry instructor	0.5
Draught animals instructor	0.5
Home economics instructor	0.5
Veterinary surgeon	3
Land Settlement Department	0.5
Farm planning unit	0.5
Chicken hatchery	1.0
Cow insemination service	1.5
Tnuva (marketing organization)	0.5
Village institution	3
Individual farmers	5.5
Total	30.0

Note :

The table is based on reconstruction and on selected observations, utilizing our own data and those of a survey carried out by the Israel Institute of Productivity. Contacts expressed in the table do not include those that are few and far between, or those that overlap with other contacts.

As is seen in the table, the agricultural instructor devotes only 5.5 days, on the average, to direct contact with his farmers (66 farms). This despite the fact that his working load is much in excess of the formal 25 days.

We can, of course, imagine eyebrows being raised at this evaluation, when in comparable development areas (such as the island of Crete, or parts of Ireland, or the Mezzogiorno, etc.) the ratio is one agricultural extension worker per every 30 villages. But the comparison is not really relevant, due to the greater variety and intensification of the *moshav* farm and the kind of population which must be trained.

12 However, some of the difficulties referred to were principally characteristic of the early settlement period. No panacea has been discovered to cure these or other ills, and most solutions attempted have been partial or have not yet been sufficiently tested. It still seems worthwhile drawing attention to some of the improvements introduced:

1. The "managed farm" system, designed to cope with the settler's difficulties in learning his new occupation. Under this system, it will be remembered, the farm, in its initial stage, is worked and administered under the direct control and responsibility of an outside factor. This is particularly advantageous when the settler has had no previous experience of farming.
2. A thorough reorganization in the structure and methods of instruction, as well as in recruitment and preparation of the absorption teams. In this way it is now required of all instructors, as far as

possible, that they receive some basic sociological and educational grounding. This grounding is given first in regular preliminary courses, and then in lectures and in refresher courses.

The same applies to the level of vocational qualifications of the various instructors. The selection processes for employment have now become more severe and are more rigorously applied, within the budgetary and manpower limitations.

Teaching techniques have also been streamlined and improved, and are intended to utilize the settlers as a group and to secure their active co-operation and participation. Mention must be made of the "observation plot" which is, in fact, a form of instruction involving the use of model units chosen in conjunction with the settlers themselves, on which the village's agricultural problems are carefully worked out, production norms exactly followed and noted, and results clearly demonstrated. These observation plots usually serve a number of neighbouring villages and have, by now, become a regular part of the teaching process. In fact, all training is now differentiated and tailored to fit the agricultural (and other conditions) of specific areas, or even individual villages.

3. The setting-up of rural centres to improve instruction:

(a) special facilities for meetings and for demonstration of heavy agricultural equipment available in a rural centre make for lower costs and higher standards;

(b) the rural centre ensures better living conditions for the professional and absorption teams, as well as some provision for their cultural and social needs (the previous arrangement—living in the village—drew few qualified personnel because of the lack of basic material comforts and recreation; the centre thus contributes toward the provision of better service for the villages).

CHAPTER 3

THE GROUP: SOLIDARITY AND DISINTEGRATION IN THE NEW MOSHAV

Introduction

In this chapter we will discuss the different types of social structure which were found in the new villages of Israel, examine the way in which they evolved, and analyze the extent to which they reflect a sense of belonging to the community and a willingness to support village institutions.

Originally, as we said earlier, the *moshav* was created by people who believed in the values of agricultural pioneering, of equality, and of cooperation. These early settlers constituted rigorously selected and very tightly knit groups, bound by common and pervasive ideals, and they strove to build a *Gemeinschaft* society—a family of families.

Among subsequent waves of immigration there were few groups as well organized or prepared. For most immigrants, the *moshav* was an alien form of village community to which they tried to adjust as well as they could, while still preserving as much as possible of the social structure which they brought with them from abroad. The variety of new social forms brought into being via this confrontation can be classified along two dimensions:

A. The nature of the social relations introduced to the *moshav*, which varied between the traditional-familistic (or ascribed) principle on the one hand, and the modern-associational or contractual one, on the other.

B. The actual social composition of the population—whether the *moshav* was culturally and socially homogeneous or heterogeneous. (The concept of homogeneity is, of course, not absolute but relative to the first variable; and the more permissive and voluntary the interaction is, the more tolerant it is of heterogeneity).

These two dimensions in practice combined into a variety of types, including "mixed" and "intermediate" structures. These latter form a broad, diversified category, since they include villages whose populations are on various levels of the familistic-associational "scale", and have various compositions and arrangements.

Within the present context, however, we shall concentrate on the "modern" and the "traditional" poles, whether homogeneous or heterogeneous. Our four main types therefore are as follows:

the modern-homogeneous, or "subdivided" community (Type 1);
the modern-heterogeneous, or "sectoral" community (Type 2);
the traditional-homogeneous, or "familistic" community (Type 3);
and
the traditional-heterogeneous, or "split" community (Type 4).
By way of illustration we shall offer two intermediate examples.

The New Moshav Society

1. THE MODERN-HOMOGENEOUS OR "SUBDIVIDED" COMMUNITY

The villages of Ta'amon and Zeviya, in our sample, belong to the homogeneous modern type; here we shall describe the former.

Ta'amon is situated in the southern part of Israel, on fertile land, relatively far from the frontier. It is connected to a central water pipeline, a main electricity line, and a good road. In addition, the adjacent area is dotted with established villages and towns, and the regional authority is both active and very experienced. The settlement thus enjoys the most favourable conditions as regards agriculture, security and services.

This *moshav* was founded by some 40 Yugoslav families who settled on the land in 1949, after they had spent some time waiting in temporary quarters in an abandoned Arab village. Shortly after they settled, they were joined by additional groups, also from Yugoslavia. In 1950, with the consent both of the *moshav* itself and the Settlement Department, new farm units were added and a Rumanian group settled on an area near the original centre of the village. In the course of time other families settled, partly to occupy farmsteads that had been abandoned by some of the original settlers, and partly to cultivate new ones. The newcomers were also mainly Yugoslavs and Rumanians, with an admixture of other Central European, Oriental and local families. Today, the Yugoslav group represents some 48 percent of the population of Ta'amon, the Rumanians 22 percent, the rest being individuals from other, mainly European, countries.[1]

The Yugoslavs themselves are divided into two distinct sub-groups—the Ashkenazi group which is the larger of the two and the Sephardi group.[2] The difference between the two communities is not great, and though the former seem to be somewhat more "westernized" than the latter, the characteristics attributed to the Yugoslav immigrants as a whole apply, in the main, to both groups. All these settlers are of middle-class urban or semi-urban backgrounds, and have a predominantly secular outlook on life. They consist mainly of former businessmen, civil servants and members of the free professions; among the original founders of Ta'amon were a lawyer, an agronomist, a banker, a diplomat, a musicologist and a few senior civil servants. This elite constituted some 20 percent of all the heads of families in the original nucleus; the rest were also predominantly composed of men and women who had had high school education and good social standing. Most members of the group had some experience as active participants in the public life of the communities to which they had once belonged. Religious tradition and practice had already become somewhat alien to them; before World War II there had, in fact, been little Jewish consciousness among them at all, and their activity in Jewish religious and community organizations was largely marginal to the roles they performed in society in general.

This, then, was the foundation from which the *moshav* was to develop. Although part of this elite left Ta'amon as soon as opportunities to resume an urban way of life arose, and the Yugoslavs no longer command an absolute majority in the *moshav*, its specific character is, nevertheless, still very much the product of the work and character of the original founders.

The second largest group in the village, namely the Rumanians, is made up of somewhat different elements. Some of these families came from relatively developed parts of Transylvania and from urban middle class backgrounds and their education was more or less similar to that of the Yugoslav settlers. Most of the Rumanians, however, came from small towns and villages, and were of a lower socio-economic status—small merchants, artisans and a few farmers. Almost none of them had had a secondary education; and the majority had attended traditional Jewish religious schools. They had larger families than did the Yugoslav settlers, and they had previously belonged to traditional religious communities.

These two patterns, though both are "European", represent an urban type and a village type, and their confrontation in one small unit makes the social fabric of Ta'amon especially interesting.

The single most conspicuous social characteristic of this village is the multiplicity and variety of its social groups. There are eight main lines of association over and above the family nucleus: friendships begun abroad; friendships formed during the period of common training; friendships based on a mutual mother tongue; blood and family relationships; ethnic origin; age; religious observance; similar schooling. These lines intersect and act in conjunction; yet it seems that the factors of education and language are the most decisive at present. The ethnic factor, by itself, scarcely acts as a barrier between the Ashkenazi and the Sephardi Yugoslavs, while Hungarian-speaking Yugoslavs and Rumanians associate closely, and this circle also includes the few Hungarian immigrants in the village. Similarly, people with academic and secondary education tend to draw together, in clear preference to all other considerations except that previously mentioned. All in all, it can be said that these two criteria are the basic elements of the network of social relationships in the *moshav,* although significant secondary differentiation derives from the other factors.

In effect, then, this is a community formed by plurality of distinct social crystallizations; a plurality which is an explicitly stated principle in the organization of the settlement. When it was founded, the plots were assigned according to the following scheme: (a) the various self-defined social groups were given a number of adjoining plots, equal to the number of their members; and (b) the raffling of the plots was then carried out by each group separately, and only determined the internal distribution within each geographical-social cluster. In this way, friendship and affinity were the cause rather than the effect, of the ecological formation of neighbourhoods. This arrangement was upset when some families left, and new families arrived in their place; but the empty farms were re-distributed, to a considerable degree, by the co-optation of neighbours.

This sub-division, coming as it does between the individual households and the total community, contrasts strongly with the *Gemeinschaft* image of the *moshav*. The "looseness" of social structure was, of course, further emphasized by the physical lay-out of Ta'amon (as seen in Map 6), by its division into two parts, at some distance from each other, and by actual size of the built-up area which measured seven kilometres from one end to the other.[3]

But this social plurality in no way blocked the emergence of solidarity in the *moshav*. As we have already stated, no single predominant factor determines the character of the various associations within the village; these associations are almost entirely social and do not define or reflect cultural separation; nor do they, for this reason, preclude more extensive social activities, celebrations, fetes, or meetings. On the contrary, the attempt of the elite to promote overall frameworks of contact gained support from the "associational" groups. Social standing with these groups themselves is largely derived from, and determined by a given member's overall success in the eyes of the village; and this is measured by his contribution to its economic, political and social life in general. Village society, in fact, is actually the decisive frame of reference, and accordingly can promote common identification and co-operation and prevent social cleavages along any of these lines.

Many settlers are active in Israel's intense political life, working for parties which range from the extreme left to the moderate right and which are traditionally at loggerheads on many issues. But even this activity does not penetrate into or disrupt the fabric of *moshav* society, nor does it bring about ideological divisions (something that happened in a number of established collective settlements) or sharpen already existing tensions (as was the case in several new villages). As a matter of fact, it only happened once, that in the course of elections to the *moshav* council, a list was submitted which consisted wholly of members of a single political party, and even then,

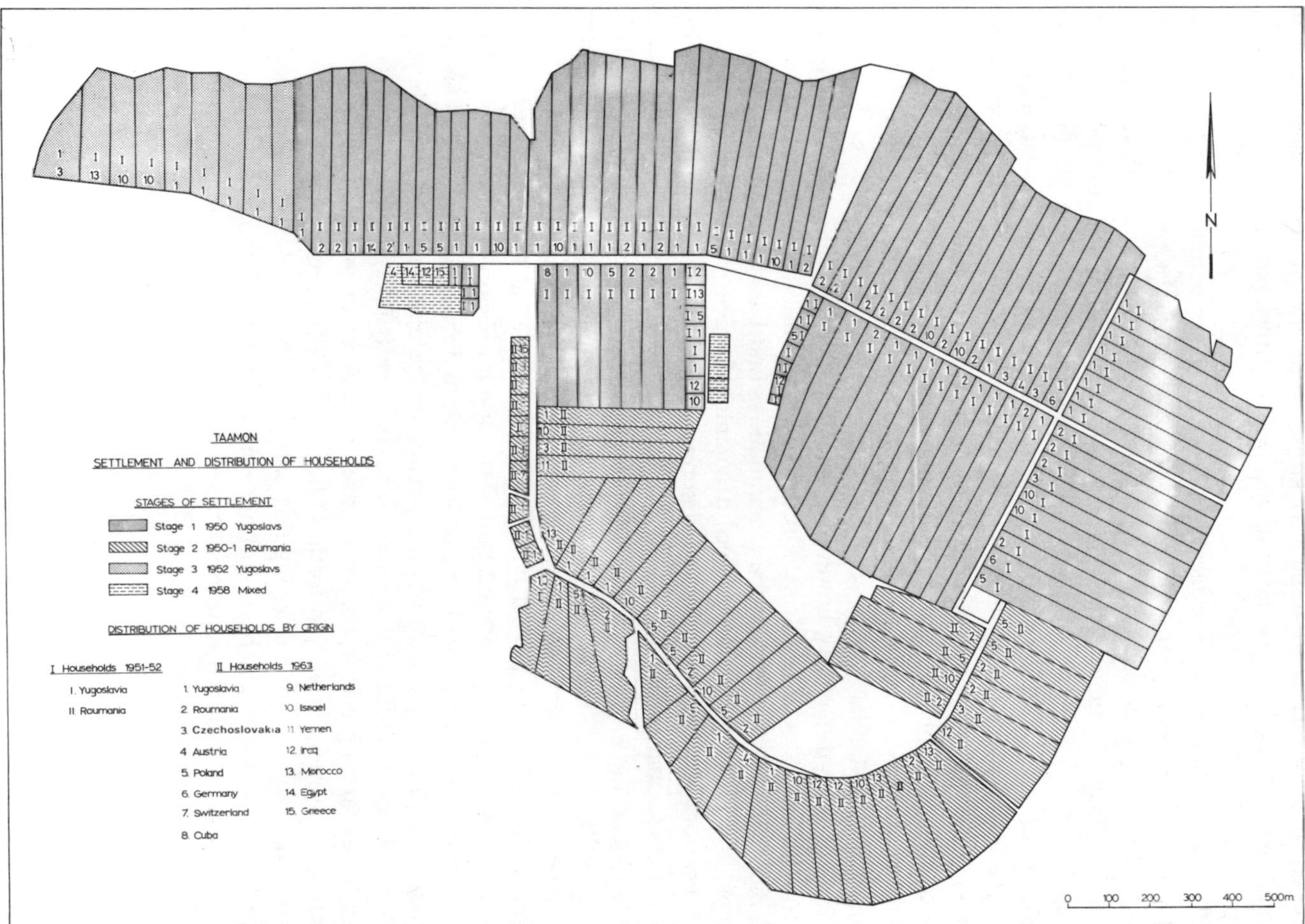

MAP 6. Ta'amon

Note: Due to an omission, ecological data for 1959/60 were not initially collected, and the map refers to 1963, the earliest period for which precise reconstruction was possible

it turned out that this composition was entirely coincidental. In any case, the new council neither discriminated against members of other parties, nor stressed the partisan basis of its own power.

Other social differences have also not led to any major conflicts. We pointed out earlier that there was a clear-cut demographic division in Ta'amon, which resulted in different manpower patterns. These patterns, in conjunction with the settlers' respective socio-economic backgrounds, aspirations, and ability to support themselves outside agriculture, created distinct occupational strata in the *moshav* (agricultural and non-agricultural) as well as different economic interests and ways of life. Some of the Yugoslav immigrants brought furniture and utensils with them and supplemented these subsequently with new purchases. Other groups not only arrived almost completely impoverished, but put their money primarily into developing their farms (see Chapter 5), and the village for a long time contained families whose material standards were very different.

None of these differences, however, crystallized into permanent status divisions or created severe social problems. On the contrary—the pattern of interaction in Ta'amon has incorporated the social inclinations and backgrounds of the various groups, and at the same time evolved a common framework of membership and identification. That this rather loose and permissive structure could support common goals, policies and institutions in other areas of *moshav* life, seems to have been largely due to the way in which the latter were defined by the settlement elite. This definition has been minimal; it has attempted to eliminate from the collective sphere all points of actual and potential tension (explicit and implicit). Economically, emphasis has thus been put on development of individual holdings and on their owners' right to work as they think best. The *moshav* offers expert advice on agricultural matters, but each farmer is free on the whole to decide on crops, area of cultivation etc., and there is considerable variation among the farms in this respect. The same pattern emerges in terms of mutual aid. The community takes care of the individual in so far as farming help is needed in cases of sickness or military reserve service, household emergencies and so forth. Other such needs remain outside the public sphere, there being a general feeling that entrusting them to the community and to its executive organs might be an infringement of individual dignity, and that they are better solved within the more intimate and familiar frameworks of neighbourhood and personal relationships.

This solution of course is not perfect, and some people complained that they were given no help at all, except in the most extreme eventualities. This state of affairs can be understood in the light of Ta'amon's socio-ecological structure: those who were not settled in the "area" occupied by their sub-groups, or who were new to the place, or for some reason or other had few contacts and were not popular, were, in fact, isolated, and as a result suffered some economic hardship. But most of the settlers we interviewed expressed full satisfaction not only with the system itself but also with its success where they themselves were concerned.

Another area of life, in which distinctions exist but are overcome, is religion. We have already mentioned the differences of outlook in this respect. The conspicuous absence of Jewish ritual and folklore in the Yugoslav group was originally a source of friction and conflict in its relations with the Rumanian immigrants. With time, however, both groups underwent a process of mutual adjustment and the orthodox "wing" became more secular, while the secular settlers became more observant.

At the beginning of Ta'amon's history (in 1950) a suggestion that the whole *moshav* celebrate *Seder,* the Passover Eve Feast, together was received quite enthusiastically, both because the elite wanted to strengthen village solidarity and because many of the Yugoslav families had never attended a traditional *Seder*. For various reasons, the plan was not carried out, and the holiday was celebrated separately; and some families which were not familar with the Passover ritual had to do without it altogether. It was, however, the first sign of any religious interest on the part of such a secular group and this interest grew and was strengthened via lectures on the history of Jewish religious festivals, etc. This phenomenon was due partly to the influence of the more orthodox sector of the *moshav,* as well as that of the children who learnt about the holidays and celebrated them in kindergarten and at elementary school; it was also due in part to the blend of national and religious elements which are inherent in the fabric of life in Israel. Mainly, however, it was motivated by the desire of the majority group to meet half-way a large segment of the village and recognize its value system. All in all, the general aspect of the community is still primarily secular, and this with a considerable measure of common approval.

Religious dicta, to the extent that they are observed at all, are confined to private life, and do not affect the freedom of action of the nonobservant settlers. Religious rituals, however, have become part and parcel of the activity and the tradition of the *moshav* as a whole.

To recapitulate: type 1, as represented by Ta'amon, can be considered a loose but stable association of a number of social crystallizations. It is a structure based chiefly on interaction within sub-groups, incorporating various social backgrounds and inclinations; over and above these subgroups, there has also evolved a social identification and participation on the village level, and these frameworks together have been able to support the common goals, policies and institutions of the whole community. One necessary condition for this support has been the *moshav's* collective values, which are so defined as to require a relatively low social consensus and which can accommodate different orientations.

2. THE MODERN-HETEROGENEOUS OR "SECTORAL" COMMUNITY

This type is exemplified, in our sample, by *Moshav* Resissim. Resissim, situated in the center of the country, and blessed by good settlement conditions, is—like Ta'amon—characterized by a diverse population.[4] The socio-economic background of the majority of this population is, moreover, similar to that of the Rumanian group in Ta'amon. The same is true of the pattern of interaction adopted, which is also based on association by friendship, origin, age, kinship, ritual, language and education, with the two last criteria being the most significant. In Resissim, however, there has developed no overall solidarity beyond the emergence of several sub-groups,[5] which constitute almost the entire social universe of the village. These do not promote inter-group activities designed for the community as a whole, and only aim at satisfying the social needs of the individuals who belong to them.

The reason for this relative lack of success in establishing overall community solidarity becomes apparent when we compare the two settlements. First of all, in Resissim the population was much more varied—its main groups, Rumanian, Persian, Moroccan, Turkish and native Israeli, came from different cultural and social *milieux,* and represented very different ways of life. Thus, although the *pattern* of interaction was free and associational, there were few *actual* points of contact—whether in language, religion or tradition. Furthermore, unlike Ta'amon, Resissim had undergone no social selection or preparation, which would make possible less anxiety and a large measure of social flexibility. Finally, Resissim had no elite to set the tone for the *moshav* and provide the necessary leadership. In the type 1 village, this function was fulfilled by the Yugoslav settlers. Here, however, there were two relatively large groups which greatly differed from each other, plus a medley of smaller groups and individual families who had come to Israel from all over the world. Thus, while Resissim, like Ta'amon, was ecologically dispersed (see Map 7), it was much more heterogeneous and this heterogeneity could not be made to merge into a sense of common belonging.

Homogeneity and heterogeneity are of course not necessarily lasting phenomena. Efficient leadership and long experience together gradually overcome the disadvantages of cultural heterogeneity, while homogeneity alone, lacking any effective leadership, does not produce a stable *moshav* structure. It must be pointed out at this stage, however, that homogeneity and leadership are not unrelated. A relatively homogeneous population can provide the proper background for the emergence of leaders, while even very able leaders are not always able to find the social backing they need in a heterogeneous population.

Now, let us turn to types based on the "traditional" pattern of interaction. This pattern is characterized by very strong attachment to kinship and territorial groups, by limitation of social interaction to these groups chiefly, and by lack of confidence in, and the capacity to work together with, people from outside the group. The basic

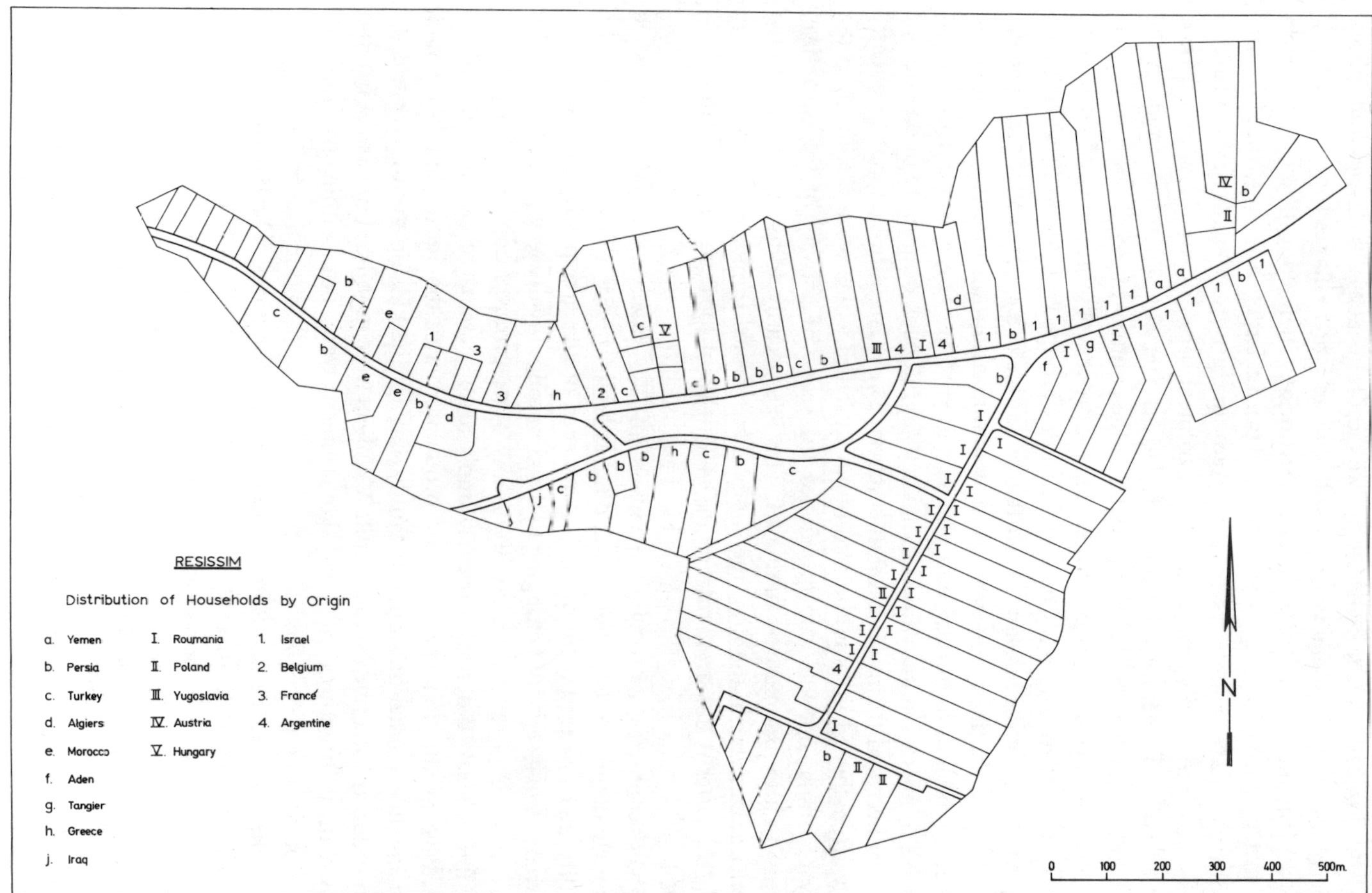

MAP 7. Resissim

framework of this type is the *hamoula* and we meet it in each of the types that follow.

Properly speaking, the origin of what is known in Israel villages today as *hamoula* lies in the Mediterranean patrilineage, territorially defined (although the term itself is in use chiefly in Iraq, Israel and Jordan). In Israel, however, these criteria of membership have sometimes been blurred, and groups which combine several families—not necessarily of common patrilineal descent or common former residence—still call themselves *hamoulas*. This is due not only to changes in the original structure which had already begun in the country of origin, but also to the fact that these groups were often splintered in the process of migration and settlement. In this context, then, the term *hamoula* denotes groups or cliques which actually functioned as such in the *moshav,* rather than in the historical concept of the *hamoula.* In spite of these changes, however, the new organization has often—at least in the initial years—been as important as a unit as it used to be. The reason for this is that the process of migration has caused individuals to fall back even more upon familiar groups and accepted forms of social interaction. The *moshav,* in fact, has frequently not only strengthened links in the traditional structure which were weakened in the country of origin, but has also broadened the scope of activity of this structure, even causing it to assume new functions. This is especially so as regards economic and political activity: in the first, the *hamoula* has gained immensely in importance, while in the latter it has even entered the new fields of local government and party politics.

In their countries of origin, members of the *hamoula* usually formed a neighbourhood group. Membership implied an obligation to afford economic help, hospitality and protection to any other member of the group whenever required. There was a strong sense of belonging to the kin-group, loyalty to which was regarded as being more important than loyalty to any other group. Economic co-operation within the *hamoula* did not, however, imply arrangements of communal or even co-operative production. The unit of production was the individual household, comprising an extended or a nuclear family, but not the kinship group. Nor was the kinship group an effective political unit. Members were mobilized in case of trouble, but permanent functions of local government were not within the *hamoula* jurisdiction or sphere of influence.

But in the *moshav*, the *hamoula* did assume these functions. The *moshav* imposed on the new immigrants co-operative production, and processes of political decision-making through elected representatives and committees. The "Oriental" immigrants, who were not used to acting as individuals, logically enough interpreted the *moshav* institutions in terms of the *hamoula.* Thus the *hamoula* took often upon itself the organization of production and co-operative marketing prescribed by the *moshav* constitution. Even more important, it has become the main political unit in the village, both internally (that is *vis-a-vis* other groups) and externally, as the representative and champion of its members in their relations with the absorbing society. This, in turn, has forced the *hamoula* organization to tighten up, has lent it new strength and endowed it with the power to adopt sanctions. Long "lost" members of the original groups have been sought out all over the country and "drafted" to settle in the villages concerned; and there have even been cases of wholesale exchange of populations between various *moshavim*. This process of social reconstruction and absorption by way of internal selection, and on the basis of kinship or quasi-kinship criteria, has infused the traditional orientations, divisions and strifes with new life.

3. THE TRADITIONAL-HOMOGENEOUS OR "FAMILISTIC" COMMUNITY

Type 3, the homogeneous traditional structure, is based on the *hamoula* pattern. It appears in two fundamental variations, which we shall describe in turn.

The first is the homogenous village proper based on one *hamoula*.

We met with only one case of this kind in our sample at *Moshav* Levanon. This settlement, situated in the Jerusalem Corridor, is on the main road to the capital. The mountainous terrain somewhat limited its agricultural development, but, on the other hand, when the villagers first settled there, terraces and some fruit-bearing trees had already been prepared for them. In this respect, at least, Levanon was more fortunate than many other *moshavim* in the same area which had to start from scratch. The security situation, however, was consistently bad; not only was the *moshav* very near the frontier, but for a long time it was the only settlement in the vicinity. This, and the actual military duties involved, were a constant drain on the physical as well as the moral resources of a far from militant group, particularly since the original nucleus comprised only 25 families.

These first families were actually rather haphazardly chosen and intended as an "advance" party which represented several larger units. Initially, their heterogeneity was not very important. The village and its population were small; there was still no agricultural organization or work (the villages were engaged in ground-breaking and house-building); nor was there any communal or cooperative structure. In fact, the village was a sort of rural workers' camp, and in no way resembled, or was meant to resemble, a *moshav*. This should have made it easier for the new settlers to adjust and should have served as a "breathing spell" before they faced new duties and responsibilities. We shall see, however, that when the situation did change, this preparation proved insufficient.

Within two years, the settlement became a proper *moshav* (insofar as the agricultural resources of the area permitted). Its population was brought up to 130 families, each section of the advance group having in the meantime mobilized members throughout the country. The village now consisted of three almost complete *hamoulas*, each one originating from a different place. These three *hamoulas* crystallized into autonomous, exclusive social groups, which at first segregated themselves, and later entered into a fierce power struggle for political and economic primacy. Since, at this point, the village had more families than had been originally planned, the Settlement Department was not interested in keeping all three units. As a result, the conflict came to a head very soon, and a population upheaval left the *moshav* in the sole possession of the largest group, which numbered 50 households. This change meant a transition from a heterogeneous social structure to a homogeneous one. True, the *hamoula* has continued to constitute the villagers' frame of reference and has even increased its power in the village, but the general cohesiveness and relative freedom from conflict which followed the "Sturm und Drang" brought significantly better social conditions in their wake.

The basic motivation of this one-lineage community seems to be preservation of the group as such and the cohesiveness of its members. The *hamoula* takes good care of its own welfare cases. The village has ten such families, either entirely or partially unable to work. Their continued presence in Levanon is an incessant drain; the farms are in the hands of people incapable of developing them (this is of concern of course also to the Settlement Department); these settlers are exempt from various local taxes and dues, thus impoverishing the communal fund; their meagre competence, provided by various welfare agencies, must be supplemented by the *hamoula*; they are frequent recipients of loans which the *moshav* has to underwrite and invariably repay; and more often than not they are unable to perform any communal roles, not least among these being the heavy guard duties needed. These problems could be solved in various ways, and offers of resettlement have been made by the authorities, but the families themselves are reluctant to leave the *moshav*, and it is reluctant to let them go. This type of solidarity also binds the sceptical, the weak and the vacillating to the village at least for as long as the group as such stays there.

In other respects, however,—economically in particular—the *hamoula* has changed. Economic production in the Yemen almost never transcended the household; the *hamoula* had no duties in this respect, and no experience of any large or combined enterprise. But in Israel the *hamoula* leaders have not only had to accept economic responsibility but also to adopt some form of co-operative production. While auxiliary and livestock farming remains strictly within the control of individual households, the *hamoula* is the unit of production for orchard and field crops. These crops are not communally owned, as often happens in small-holders' villages; the idea is not attractive to the property-conscious group, and the settlers insist on having all the plots legally assigned to heads of families. However, since the greater efficiency of large-scale production is recognized, cultivation is supervised by and entrusted to the group. So is the apportioning of the produce. All in all, then, there is a process in which a traditional structure assumes new roles and functions and redefines its ways of common action, while maintaining its essential system of authority and organization.

The principles which have shaped the social structure and behaviour of the *hamoula* in this new situation are reflected in the status system of the village. There are two distinct scales of social prestige. One expresses the old standards of the traditionally ascribed place of each family within the group. The other represents the level of adjustment to Israel in general, and to the *moshav* in particular. Currently, the traditional scale is the more important: high position on it, due to age, family and religious learning, confers more power and status than do agricultural or administrative achievement. The second scale is complementary rather than conflicting, and subordinate rather than competing.

The second variation of the "familistic" village occurs when, due to common background and place of origin, the population is homogeneous despite a plurality of *hamoulas*. *Moshav* Shalekhet and *Moshav* Torem are in this category. We shall take a close look at the first of these settlements.

The entire population of Shalekhet comes from the same place, namely the desert Sultanate of Haban in the Hadramaut part of the former Aden Protectorate. Before it immigrated to Israel the community numbered 345 people, all of whom came to Israel, and most of whom settled in Shalekhet. In spite of the fact that in Haban they had lived in the "capital", they had very little experience of or need of social relations, co-operation and organization over and above those of the extended family. Almost to a man, they had worked as silversmiths, and since they were concentrated in one very small place, they had been dependent on a large hinterland for work, and consequently lived as itinerant hawkers. The men (those from about 13 to 50) moved from place to place constantly, leaving the women, the small children and the aged at home. The families were reunited only on Saturdays and on religious holidays and the *hamoulas* met regularly only for Sabbath prayers or during other religious ceremonies. Roles and relationships transcending the *hamoula* and pertaining to the community as a whole were even more sporadic, and were undertaken for the most part in times of trouble, when head taxes had to be paid and so forth. Although restricted in scope, the *hamoulas* served thus as the basic social and religious framework, with little interaction and contact between them. Local legend has it that once relations between the *hamoulas* were closer, but that they had deteriorated by the middle of the 19th century. Since this social cleavage still persists, it is worth a brief description. Apparently, in addition to the cumulative effects of an itinerant way of life, there were two specific reasons for the division between the groups.

The first was the evolution of different prayer rituals. None of the variations was theologically important or extensive; in fact, they related only to four repetitive points in the entire prayer book. But the subjective symbolic value of the different rituals was enormous. Supporters of the opposing versions not only stopped praying together, but also gradually withdrew from common attendance at prayer. Since "ascending to the Torah" during prayers is important both religiously and socially for orthodox Jews, a multiplicity of synagogues at which this honour could be given to as many people as possible had, in any case, been characteristic of the traditional Jewish community. At Haban, however, this trend was not only reaffirmed; it also overlapped and emphasized an already deep social division based on kinship.

The second factor was the "affair" of the ritual bath. Originally, the various *hamoulas* had used a common ritual bath, attached to the synagogue which belonged to the Hillel *hamoula*. As relations worsened, members of the competing Maatuf group proclaimed this bath ritually impure, and began to send their women to a water-pool outside the walls of the town. This was taken as an intolerable religious as well as social slight. Revenge took the form of "Peeping Toms" who disturbed the bathing, and the polluting of the pool with a dead camel. In turn, rotten fish were thrown to the Hillel bath. These acts of retribution continued until both sides finally agreed to separate, and a second real ritual bath was built, adjoining the Maatuf synagogue.

These and similar points of disagreement almost totally estranged the local kinship groups from one another. Two rival camps came into existence, each composed of one big *hamoula* and one of the two smaller lineages. This situation has been replicated in the *moshav* in Israel. The same four *hamoulas* exist and they are still organized in what can be called two systems made up of "a sun and a satellite":

System A		
Group I	Maatuf *hamoula*	38 families
Group IV	Mifi *hamoula*	8 families
Total		46 families

System B		
Group II	Hillel *hamoula*	30 families
Group III	Shamuch *hamoula*	10 families
Total		40 families

These systems cut across all the spheres of *moshav* activity. Religiously, they do not intermix. Since the Settlement Department has erected only one synagogue building in Shalekhet, additional though temporary quarters have been provided in the village club, and the two groups take turns each week at each synagogue. The authority of the Maatuf rabbi, appointed by the Ministry of Religious Affairs to serve the whole community, is not accepted by the opposing groups, whose members have often refused to permit him to officiate at their weddings and have protested the appointment in writing.

Economic interaction has also been reduced. The villagers support and utilize the necessary marketing and other facilities, but refuse to cooperate *directly* between groups. One good example, draught animals (usually mules) are often given in joint ownership to two or three *moshav* families. In Shalekhet, however, mules were given to neighbouring families from different *hamoulas* (see Map 8). The tensions which then arose affected the relationship between the *hamoulas* as a whole, and led to non-cooperation with the Settlement Department. The villagers refused for months to accept any equipment and other means of production which were issued to them, thereby considerably delaying the start of efficient farm cultivation.

The same situation exists in other spheres of social interaction; and, apart from the school, the youth club, weddings, circumcisions, etc., there is almost no informal contact between members of the different groups.

To sum up, this kind of social integration is based on the minimal over-all soli-

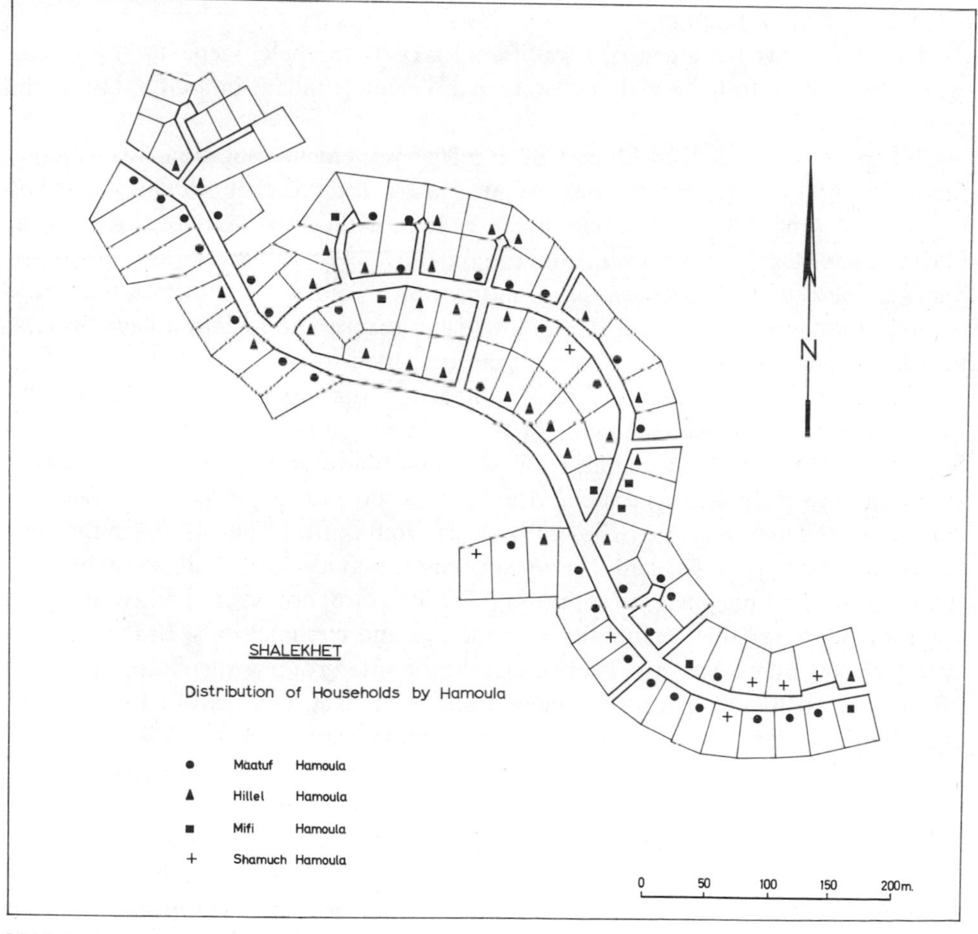

MAP 8. Shalekhet

darity of ascribed groups, solidarity which derives not from positive social preferences, but rather from lack of choice. Each of the groups described would opt for living in a homogeneous village of its own, and sees the present arrangement, at best, as a not entirely unsatisfactory substitute. In reality though, the stability of this structure is considerable. Not only is there a common cultural consensus, but the social situation is actually both familiar and reassuring. The antagonism and mutual suspicion of the various groups is sanctioned, as well as regulated, by tradition; they are, in a way the accepted rules of the game and as such, certainly preferable to the unknown conditions obtaining in the world outside. Need we say more than that not a single family has left Shalekhet since its establishment—a unique record in the history of Israel's new villages.

4. THE TRADITIONAL-HETEROGENEOUS OR "SPLIT" COMMUNITY

In contrast to the homogeneous traditional type is the heterogeneous traditional type, of which we found a vivid example in a Yemenite village in the Lakhish area, *Moshav* Savel.

This settlement had been blessed by excellent settlement conditions and regular financing and its settlers, with the aid of good instructors, reached a high standard of agricultural proficiency and development. In fact, within two years of reaching the intermediate stage, their crops brought in an above average income. But in the ten years of the *moshav's* existence, not even the most minimal social integration of the community has developed and the various factions of the population have, in fact, grown still more hostile to each other than they used to be.

Emergence of a community-wide solidarity was made impossible by the relationship between the *hamoulas,* of which there are two. But while in *Moshav* Shalekhet all the *hamoulas* came from the same place and brought with them a tradition of carefully balanced social cleavage and cooperation, in Savel the *hamoulas* came from different localities (though both are from central Yemen). From the very beginning, each group has had its own synagogue and assembly hall, so exclusively maintained that members of opposing factions are not even invited to such traditionally hospitable ceremonies as weddings and circumcisions. In the village's entire history there has not been one case of intergroup exogamous marriage, although it is common among the Yemenites, and is in fact, a mechanism for resolving inter-kinship differences. All mixed youth activities have been forbidden, and the village youth club no longer functions. Even at elementary school, there have been many instances of friction among children of the two warring groups.

This type of cleavage also occurs among other traditional groups when *hamoulas* from different places of origin are brought together. The Yemenites, however, seem particularly prone to such conflict, perhaps because their *hamoulas* have greater religious value content and are more tightly integrated. At all events, over

50 percent of the Yemenite settlers in Israel have left the villages to which they were originally assigned and found themselves more congenial places. Although, generally speaking, Yemenite Jews work hard, take well to rural life, and are quite capable of mastering the skills necessary for successful farming, they seem to find it difficult to sustain integrated and viable community life unless the composition of the community is both familiar to them and to their definite liking.

INTERMEDIATE AND MIXED TYPES

We have pointed out earlier that the "intermediate" type of community (i.e., one based on social relations somewhere in between the familistic and the contractual), and the "mixed" type of community (which embodies both kinds of relationship) appears in various forms and gradations. Both these types can, moreover, be cut across by more or less homogeneous composition of the population. *Moshav* Zimriya and *Moshav* Biyoun are examples of the "intermediate" homogeneous and the "mixed" homogeneous village respectively.

Zimriya lies in the central part of the country, which is well-populated and, on the whole, prosperous. The settlers come mainly from large Moroccan towns such as Marrakech, Fez, Rabat and Meknes with only a very small segment coming from the rural areas.[6]

When the *moshav* was first settled, divisions along kinship and residence lines formed the main basis for social identification and interaction. But even then, this pattern never really approximated the definite, exclusive and all-embracing nature of the *hamoula*, which, long before these people had immigrated to Israel, had begun to lose most of its vitality and scope. Dependence upon the in-group increased fleetingly during the initial stage of settlement and absorption, but this was largely because the settlers were so unfamiliar with the new situation which faced them. At present, there are still groupings in Zimriya which are based on kinship and place of origin and which, in a way, are more prominent than in the Western type described. But they are not paramount; interaction based on kinship or residence group membership is often cut across by other relationships (age, friendship, education, etc.) and has come to be more and more limited to family festivities, domestic help and minor loans. With development of the "associational" type of social relations, the overall co-operation and solidarity of the village community as a whole has also grown, and its structure is now similar to that we noted in Ta'amon.

Although everyone in the settlement of Biyoun comes from Tunisia, the social usages of its two segments have consistently been different, providing us with a good illustration of the mixed type. The majority group is urban in background (chiefly from the capital itself), and in Tunisia itself was already quite westernized and secularized. It was made-up chiefly of fairly young people, many of whom had received either partial or complete secondary education.[7] The second group, on the other hand, was formed by older people from small towns and villages, characterized by more traditional social and religious backgrounds and stronger kinship ties.[8]

These different social orientations and cultural backgrounds led to significant social segregation. The westernized majority encouraged a general associational pattern of interaction, but in reality very few actual links, based on criteria which would cut across the two groups, were forged. This cleavage was further emphasized by sharply differing attitudes towards religion. The traditional element, which centered around the synagogue, was very much in favour of a compulsory religious way of life, both at home and in the public sphere; and this "missionary" point of view was of course resisted by the more modern secular group. In time, however, the processes which we described in some detail in the case of Ta'amon helped everyone to arrive at a compromise in this respect, even though the consensus has been more religiously defined than in Ta'amon. Private and public spheres have thus been separated so that each household can now legitimately decide for itself how it will live, but no offence to religious propriety and ritual will be brooked outside the home. The external face of the community, therefore, is essentially orthodox.[9]

This majority group flexibility, which made it possible for the religious segment to be met more than half-way, permitted the development of Biyoun as one functioning community. The social support of the traditional group has been bestowed on the *moshav's* cooperative and administrative institutions, which are manned almost exclusively by members of the younger secular element. The same support has been given to the vocational and general (i.e. non-religious) education of *moshav* children (above the elementary level), to intensified youth activities, and so on. A pluralistic but viable social system thus evolved, in which the contradictions in social orientation and cultural background were compensated for by the *moshav's* devoted, competent and flexible leadership.

Conclusion

In the preceding pages, we have examined the extent and the manner in which different villages in Israel achieved stable social structures. We have tried to show that both the "modern" and the "traditional" type of *moshav* can attain social integration, given the condition of a culturally homogeneous background; and that this has brought to the fore the importance of a proper social selection policy. We have also seen how an initial cultural variety and distance can be bridged by determined and suitable leadership. Now we must examine the way in which these different types of solidarity relate to village organization.

NOTES

[1] The following is the distribution of the population of Ta'amon (1958–1959):

Country of origin	No. of households	%	Country of origin	No. of households	%
Yugoslavia	80	48.2	Bulgaria	2	1.2
Rumania	37	22.3	Austria	2	1.2
Poland	9	5.4	Greece	2	1.2
Israel	7	4.2	Morocco	1	0.2
Czechoslovakia	6	3.6	Tunisia	1	0.6
Hungary	6	3.6	Iraq	1	0.6
Russia	5	3.0	Unknown	3	1.8
Yemen	4	2.4			
			Total	166	99.9

[2] *Ashkenazi* ("German") Jews are descendants of Yiddish-speaking Jewish groups whose forebears lived in Central and Eastern Europe until the eighteenth century and then were dispersed throughout the world; *Sephardi* ("Spanish") Jews are descendants of Jewish communities, expelled from Spain at the end of the fifteenth century, who then lived mainly in the Middle East, the Balkans, the Netherlands, and, from the seventeenth century, also in England. There are certain specific cultural differences between these groups.

[3] Ta'amon, in fact, is the "longest" *moshav* in Israel—a prototype of the so-called "towel" or "stretched" village, established in certain new settlements which were based on the milch branch, in an attempt to put the green fodder as near as possible to the farmyard itself.

[4] The following is the composition of the population of Resissim (1958–1959):

Country of origin	No. of households	%	Country of origin	No. of households	%
Rumania	27	34.18	Iraq	1	1.26
Persia	13	16.46	Russia	1	1.26
Morocco	8	10.17	Germany	1	1.26
Turkey	7	8.87	Yugoslavia	1	1.26
Israel	6	7.99	Poland	1	1.26
Argentina	3	3.80	Hungary	1	1.26
Yemen	2	2.53	Aden	1	1.26
France	2	2.53	Belgium	1	1.26
Greece	2	2.53	Tangier	1	1.26
			Total	79	100.0

[5] The main sub-groups are: (a) the bulk of the Rumanian immigrants, characterized by a common language as well as shared traditional and elementary general education; (b) the Persians, Moroccans and Turks with similar characteristics; (c) a group made up of native Israelis, Western and Central Europeans, Argentinians and a few Rumanians, distinguished by a better general education and by the fact that they use Hebrew as their everyday language. Each of these groups has attached to itself some of the remaining families which are culturally closest to them.

[6] Composition of Zimriya by place of origin (1958–1959):

Geographic origin	No. of households	%
Large cities (Casablanca and Marrakech)	17	24.3
Provincial cities (Meknes, Rabat, Fez, Oujda, Safi)	36	51.4
Atlas Mountains	13	18.6
Other areas (Tangier, Algiers, and Iran)	4	5.7
Total	70	100.0

[7] In fact this village was the only non-European *moshav* to be consolidated by the end of 1958.

[8] Composition of Biyoun by place of origin (1958–1959):

Geographic origin	No. of households	%
Tunis and vicinity	47	60.3
Small towns and villages	31	39.7
Total	78	100.0

[9] This applies chiefly to the observance of the Sabbath and the High Holidays, and to the religious character of the village primary school.

CHAPTER 4

VARIATIONS ON AN ORGANIZATIONAL THEME: RURAL COOPERATION AND GOVERNMENT IN THE NEW MOSHAV

Introduction

The purpose of this chapter is to survey certain aspects of organization in Israel's new immigrant *moshavim*.

This type of village is intended to function within a comprehensive cooperative framework, and to maintain a system of local government charged with providing modern municipal services. The question we will discuss here is just exactly what happens when a distinct organizational form—in this case, multipurpose cooperation together with the "Westminster" type of democracy—is superimposed on a variety of populations with often entirely different traditions and aspirations.

We shall divide our discussion into three parts. First, an examination of the normative pattern or "blueprint" of *moshav* organization and some of its implications; documentation and analysis of actual organizational behaviour we observed in sample villages, in terms of the "ideal type"; and, finally, some general conclusions.

The Organizational Blueprint

In Table 25 (folding page) we have mapped the various tasks which form the *moshav* fabric, and pinpointed their organizational locus.[1] In Table 26, the administrative hierarchy is presented graphically.

From these data (although most readers, we assume, will skip the extremely elaborate list, and take our word for the information contained) it is clear that the organizational blueprint embodies very definite precepts regarding both the *functions* of village organization and its political-administrative *structure*. As far as these functions are concerned, the corporate body has control over three fundamental spheres of government—of decision-making, in terms of policy formation and coordination; provision of services; and social control. The essential features, however, are the *scope* and *intensity* of its intervention; the corporate entity is, in fact, expected to guide, regulate, and sanction all of the community—and many of the private—aspects of the *moshav's* economic, social and cultural life.

TABLE 26—Organizational Hierarchy in the *Moshav*

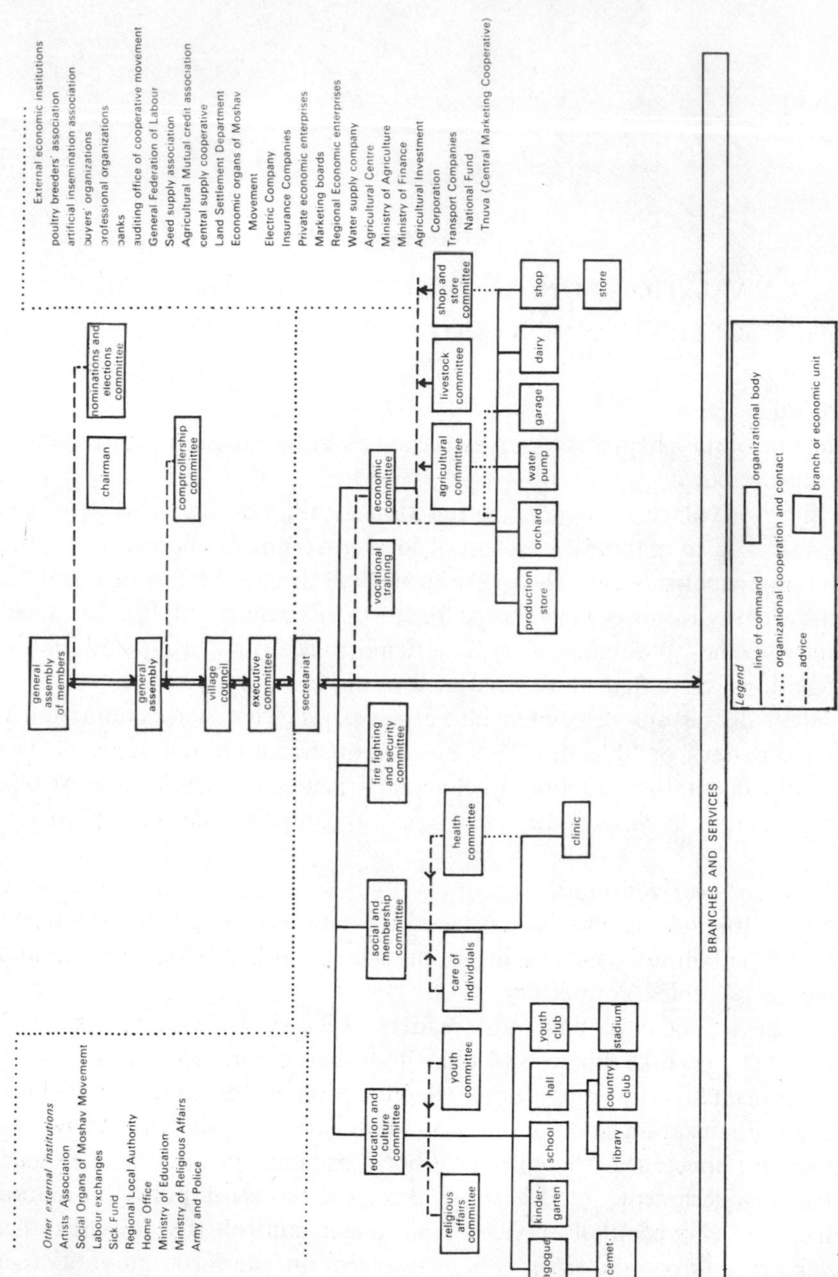

The structural norms of the system, embodying four basic organizational principles, are just as explicit. These norms are:

1. *Political autonomy, or exclusiveness,* i.e. the rule that the various organizational functions must be vested in the corporate body itself, relinquished neither to outside institutions, to externally appointed personnel, nor to any internal sub-groups.

2. *Democratic government,* in the "accepted" two-fold sense of: (a) institutions based on free elections, secret ballot, universal suffrage, and universal right to office; (b) institutions which act on the basis of majority rule, embodying free, regular change of governments and the rotation of office holders, and recognizing that they are subordinate to the general assembly of members which is the supreme legislative body in the *moshav*.[2]

3. *Rational-bureaucratic organization,* again in a double sense of: (a) rational definition of roles, division of labour and authority structure;[2] and (b) rational-efficiency and achievement-oriented-recruitment of public personnel.[2]

4. *Equality of treatment and service*—in other words a universalistic orientation towards the obligations and privileges of all *moshav* members.

To sum up, the *moshav's* organizational pattern is characterized by a comprehensive set of community goals—both cooperative and municipal;[3] which are executed by an independent, democratic political structure, and a bureaucratic-rational administrative one. In veteran villages, this system of government was nurtured by ideology and supported by homogeneous and solidary communities. Let us now examine what took place when various groups of new settlers in Israel, which lacked such characteristics, came face-to-face with this system.

Novel Forms of Moshav Organization

As our point of departure, we shall take the structural properties of the new immigrant village. The structural variations documented here are, however, analyzed in terms of community patterns and related to the ways in which the actual functions of government are fulfilled.

As we have mentioned, the *moshav's* organizational structure can be formulated in four main principles—autonomy, democracy, rationality of organization and recruitment, and universalism. If, for simplicity's sake, we think of each principle as one element of a dichotomous dimension, we get a Cartesian product of 16 possible profiles.[4] But we will only deal in any depth with three types. These types are: (a) the "normative" organization which is autonomous, democratic, rational and universalistic; (b) the "traditional" organization, which is autonomous, non-democratic, non-rational and particularistic, and (c) the "managed" organization which is heteronomous, non-democratic, rational and universalistic. Although, of course, many more theoretical possibilities exist in reality, and are, in fact, represented in this study,[5] these types seem to us to be most basic and most meaningful.

A. THE "NORMATIVE" STRUCTURE

The "normative" type of government, namely the autonomous "Western" (or modern) structure appears in our sample in three communities—Ta'amon, Zeviya, Biyoun. Ta'amon, with which the reader is already familiar, is an example.

To begin with, Ta'amon is a consolidated *moshav* which has been running its own affairs *independently almost from the beginning of its existence.* More precisely it became independent (except for certain agricultural branches) by the end of its first year, and has not backtracked since. The most prominent feature in Ta'amon's organizational pattern, however, is, without question, its *modern bureaucratic structure,* pushed to the very limits which are compatible with the egalitarianism and solidarity which ideally characterize *moshav* society.

This bureaucratic structure is given full expression in the realization of those organizational principles we discussed above, namely: (a) *the structure of public office and its division of labour which are based on rationality and efficiency:* i.e., they embody a distinct hierarchy of authority, advice and supervision, clear-cut and practical definition of the competence of the various institutions, and a strong achievement-orientation; (b) *a universalistic method of dealing with all clients.*

Table 27 schematically summarizes[6] the *moshav's* organizational bodies and their relationships and demonstrates the parallel with the "ideal" model. Of course, the pattern of specific committees is somewhat different; institutions such as the synagogue and the cemetery are missing; the poultry committee is absent (Ta'amon is a dairy farm), and so on. But it is clear that these differences stem from special local features; on the other hand, Ta'amon maintains bodies which exist only in the most rigorous, old established villages, and do not exist at all in many others. In addition to the committee, there is also a large advisory council—absent in the majority of *moshavim,* and also from the essential blueprint. Ta'amon has also special committees for internal and external affairs which are, again, not obligatory.

The spheres of activity of each of these organizational bodies are quite separate. Each has its own area of undisputed authority, and standing regulations which guide its current work. The relative importance of the various institutions is inherent in the definition of functions (the Welfare Committee, for instance, for social reasons which we touched on earlier, does not manage to fulfil a central need), and there are inevitable ebb and tide periods in tempo of committee work. But all the committees operate, meet regularly, deal with specific, well-defined matters, and not only constitute a formal part of *moshav* structure but fulfil an organic need.

The emphasis on effective organization can be felt also in the principles which govern appointment to public office. All the incumbents are qualified for their jobs; for the most part, they are the people best qualified for their particular tasks. Specialization and appropriate division of labour, in fact, is *more* prominent in this village than it is in the "model" itself, and we shall discuss this phenomenon further

TABLE 27—Simplified Organizational Chart of *Moshav* Ta'amon

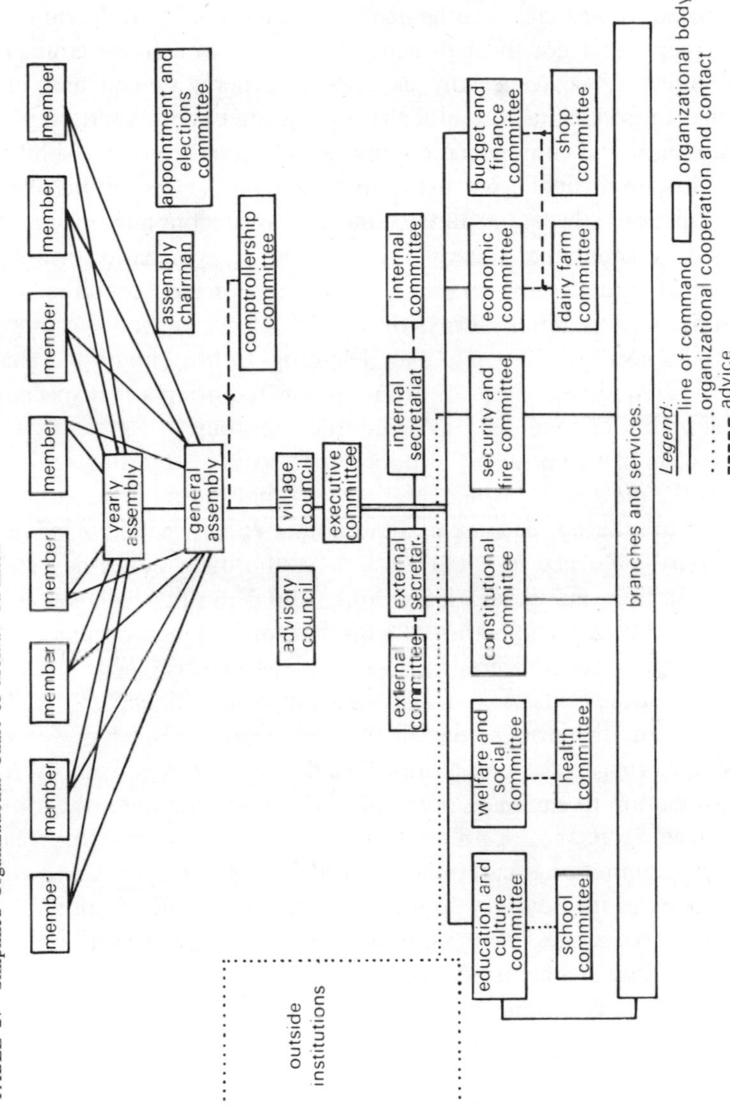

on. Here, however, it seems appropriate to quote the chairman of the council: "The general functioning (in the classical *moshav*) of village institutions is still based too much on the irrational phenomenon of non-specialization. True, the two separate spheres, the municipal on the one hand, and the economic cooperative on the other are interrelated. But each should be dealt with according to different criteria and by different experts, and not through general elections to a single council. While one sphere is more public (especially as regards general policy) and may properly be entrusted to politicians, the other is professional and should be organized as a regular economic and commercial company with shares, or some similar structures. At present the "municipal" chairman can decide, on the basis of his own judgement, budgetary matters which are purely financial and economic. The same situation holds for the economic sphere itself, where specialization, though present, is insufficient. In practice, the person chosen to serve on the Economic Committee and on the council itself is almost always the owner of a successful farm; but he may be a dairy specialist now called upon to plan field crops or fiscal matters." The chairman's attitude exemplifies the concept of economics as requiring a real specialization, and of the desirability of autonomy in economic decisions.

The principle of universalism in public matters is also strongly supported; each member of the *moshav* is treated equally. Personal integrity, honesty, and genuine commitment are the *sine qua non* of all appointments to public office. Prevention of undue external influence or "pull" is one of the main concerns of the *moshav's* supervisory institutions: separation—rarely found in other villages—is maintained between elected committee members who determine general policies, and between the salaried employees who implement these. The two secretaries—one for internal and one for external affairs—who are usually council members, in Ta'amon are non-residents, and therefore neither likely to arrogate too much power to themselves nor to be subjected to the pressure of friends and relatives from the village itself. This determination to eliminate potential abuse was once defined for our benefit as follows: "The Secretary for Internal Affairs has the committee breathing down his neck; the committee is carefully watched by the Advisory Council; the Village Council supervises the advisory council and the comptroller's committee has its eye on everyone." We witness here a complex system of managerial and public supervision, coloured by a constitutional-legalistic tinge.

In point of fact, Ta'amon has a *quasi* constitution of its own, over and above the organizational legislation of the *Moshav* Movement; when it was first established, one of its members—formerly a lawyer—was asked to study the legal problems specific to Israel and in particular those affecting agricultural settlement, and then to draw up a detailed internal constitution adapted to the village's special needs.

These uncompromising organizational principles unavoidably hampered the democratic government of the village. Most requirements associated with local democracy have been scrupulously met: free and open elections, democratic representation, majority decisions, separation of the legislative and executive branches, and the primacy of the former—all these are characteristic of the *moshav*. Moreover, these principles are in line with the village's social structure (which, as we have seen is characterized by the absence of an ascriptive or any other total crystallization) and with the settlers' own ideology. Things are different, however, as regards change of government and rotation of functions. As mentioned, these principles always contradict to some extent the rational division of labour and process of specialization. In Ta'amon, however, this phenomenon in the course of time brought about the existence of a "professional" elite whose members eventually became really qualified and began, implicitly or explicitly, to demand a monopoly of power. While the multiplicity of committees and control mechanisms helped to limit this demand somewhat, the committee posts, too, were filled by suitably qualified people, who also specialized in their particular spheres of responsibility, and the reservoir of manpower again depended on the same people who were elected again and again. Moreover, membership in committees was not a very important position. In terms of status as well as power, it was, perhaps, considered superior to that of the paid secretary, but much below that of Village Council membership. In other words, a committee member was not, either objectively or subjectively, a recognized leader, while the council members gradually evolved into a small, fairly exclusive group which *de facto* ran the village affairs by making all the important policy decisions. As we have said before, this group could certainly not be accused of poor management: its work was very successful and quite free of corruption. Also, it was constantly under the supervision of the comptrolling committee and the village assembly, both of which discharged their supervisory functions thoroughly. But even so, the power monopoly was resented. In part, this hostility was created by the frustration felt by and expressed by some of the politically inert settlers who realized that their agricultural work was considered less "important" than the public activities of office holders; additionally, at this stage, ethnic organization began to rear its head. This was initiated by the Rumanian settlers who saw power being a permanent hand-over to the Yugoslavs, even though this occurred by majority vote and was clearly good for the community and the individual settler alike. The main reason, however, was the flaw in democratic government as such. The lack of rotation in public office reinforced the already fully acknowledged personal superiority of the *moshav* elite, a superiority which became more obvious as work went on; and which, essentially, made all the democratic election mechanism seem insignificant—although it was never actually abused. Gradually the elite developed attitudes of "benevolent absolutism"; utilizing paternalistic authority through democratic channels, it began to act on behalf of the people and decide, by itself, what was good or bad for them. We were not able to follow this development in its early stages, but it was easy to see how aware the settlers were of it, and to note the sharp reactions of the non-Yugoslavs. About a year before our study got underway, a council had been elected from a group of "new" men. Unlike other previous changes in function which took place among the same members all the time, on this occasion offices were manned mainly by "opposition" members who belonged to the *moshav's* Rumanian minority. This was the result not of a "revolution" but of the voluntary standing down of members of the former council who decided not to run for office again, although they had enjoyed majority support. Their refusal had been preceded by considerable propaganda and much criticism voiced loudly by the minority. No one was accused of any concrete organizational or political mistakes, but the criticism concentrated instead on the limitations of democracy and on the subsequent non-participation in government of the broader community. The elite group, which had been managing village affairs, now gave a chance to the others, quite sure however, that the "new men" would fail, and that the "rebellious" settlers of little faith would thus be taught a lesson. This was exactly what happened. The new council continued the work mapped out by its predecessor, but was, as predicted, simply not sufficiently efficient or experienced. Its chief difficulty was in the realm of outside contacts, an inadequacy which led to all kinds of financial crises and management problems. The truth was that the previous members of the council, who had been elected *ex officio* to various regional offices, had—due mostly to their personal abilities—gained there recognition and positions of importance. Because of this they succeeded in securing development budgets, credit guarantees, improved services, and even extra support for Ta'amon. The new council members who also held such offices, lacked the qualities of their predecessors, and instead of gaining influence often clashed with other office holders. The only institution which supported the new council—and saw it as being "a more popular" body—was the *Moshav* Movement. Other bodies, and especially the chairman of the regional council, looked for ways and means, however indirectly, to restore the previous set-up. This being the situation, and the background being one of current difficulty in comparison with past success, the new people were not really given enough time or credit. Little cooperation from the old elite, plus the tension and aggressiveness of the insecure new council, combined to exacerbate matters to such a pitch that by "popular" demand the old council was finally recalled. It promptly requested a change in the electoral system, suggesting that the entire council be voted for *en bloc*. The General Assembly confirmed the collective list *in toto,* rather than any individual names, and the list was elected. The only person who objected strongly to this procedure was a member of the elite itself, who submitted a separate list with only one name on it, thus protesting the marked deviation from democratic procedure implicit in the new election.

In this way, the need for a political and managerial professionalization and specialization was exploited by the existing elite in order that its power be maintained

—and even increased. This was not, in the first instance, a matter of personal ambition; practically all the members of this group already held positions in state and public institutions above the village level. It was rather a question of emphasis on the use of rational and autonomous criteria in the management of financial and economic matters—an emphasis which contradicted but proved stronger than the very same democratic-political principles that the group itself had always upheld.

The basic social characteristics and orientation of the village were felt even more in respect to the functions of government, modifying the original comprehensive definition considerably.

It will be recalled that Ta'amon is, socially, a modern-homogeneous village, capable of achieving overall community solidarity. The modern-associational type of social integration has, however, impinged on both the *scope* and the *intensity* of its corporate activity, limiting some functions, and handing others over to various social sub-systems—as, for instance, in the transfer of welfare matters to neighbourhood clusters, which restricted a function that the organizational structure could have easily executed.

B. THE "MANAGED" STRUCTURE

The "managed" (or the "administered") village is a settlement which either cannot[7] or will not govern itself. Its administration is therefore vested in external personnel. In our sample, this type appears in three distinct variants, related to the social character of the community. Let us take up each of these forms in turn.

I. *The managed structure in a "Western heterogeneous" ("sectoral") community.* This type is exemplified for us by *Moshav* Resissim. Because of its composition, this village never evolved any overall solidarity or sense of identification with the community as a whole. Consequently, it was not capable of supporting the *moshav* institutions although *the political traditions of its inhabitants would have made this quite feasible.*

One illustration of the sort of problems which kept the village organization from functioning properly was in the sphere of marketing.

In Resissim, where dairy farming and fruit production were the main economic branches, there was no argument about the need for, and the efficiency of, organized marketing in general, or of a single marketing agency for the village as a whole. But on the level of concrete marketing policy, this became a very complicated problem, which involved everyone in long discussions within the Economic Committee and its dairy and fruit sub-committees, at the level of the council, and in the General Assembly. Questions were raised as to the marketing agency best suited for each branch; the size of payments and conditions of marketing which should be adhered to; the ratio between the amount of money which the cooperative was entitled to debit each producer's account, and the minimum amount which each farm had to be paid regardless of its balance; and so on. The differences on each such point were not very large, and were not even identified with the various groups in the village; but the very need for so much negotiation, talk and effort on every one of the three levels mentioned, made it virtually impossible to arrive at quick decisions or fast action. The trouble was the participants' inability to isolate their organizational role from their social background. Since this inability was evident only in selected situations, and since it contradicted the settlers' recognized interests, to say nothing of their better judgement, the organizational structure's ability to function was not entirely destroyed; but its efficiency was certainly impaired. Decisions were reached and appropriate steps taken, but only after enormous outlay of time and work, and long delays. As soon as this realization sank in, the village decided to change its organizational set-up. Some authority was removed from the assembly and council, especially in the area of economic policy and services, and handed over to an outside team of experts composed of two secretaries (one for internal and the other for external affairs) and the manager of the fruit branch. On the other hand, the need to give greater organizational autonomy to the sub-groups in matters requiring close contacts was recognized, and the marketing organization divided into three parts, paralleling the village's three main groups. A roof-organization, i.e., the cooperative, was retained to represent the formal-judicial interests of the village, and it determined and watched over the general "overall" interests; but within these limitations, each association or sub-cooperative was entrusted with management of its own affairs. Each such organizational framework dealt with the entire process of marketing the farm produce assigned to it; and three independent "poultry committees"[8] were carved out of the original single committee which had disintegrated. Each of these committees, among other things, was entrusted with collecting money from its members, while the internal affairs secretary was appointed to act as the liaison officer charged with transmitting the required sums of money to and from the committee. Thus it happened that a village, initially based on a system of self-government, relinquished its authority in favour of professional managers on the one hand, and its various social groups, on the other.

To sum up: Resissim's organizational structure is characterized by the following features:

1. As regards self-government there is only very limited independence. Most matters which, according to the blueprint of the independent *moshav,* are entrusted to the council, are entrusted here to outside management;

2. The concept of full democracy does not apply. The managers of the village's affairs are responsible to a General Assembly which functions properly, and are also supervised by an active control committee, but there is no division of power between the various office holders, no real elections for offices, and no rotation in office.

3. Both the structure of public office, and recruitment to it, are rational and

achievement-oriented; but limited by the trichotomic division which impairs the profitability of marketing and disperses the managerial potential.

The social factors determining the structure of the organizational web (given schematically in Table 28) of necessity limited also the *extent* of corporate activity. Resissim, like Ta'amon, had no ideology of corporate expansion or of the encroachment of the public upon the private sphere. But in Resissim the very fabric of the community served to limit noninstrumental functions, and the village organs could not contribute to social integration or to social policy.

II. *The "managed" structure in a traditional-homogeneous ("familistic") community.* We shall illustrate this type by further reference to *Moshav* Shalekhet.

The traditional patterns of social interaction, described above, affected the political organization here and the *moshav's* administration. Support of political institutions was thus given only on the condition that this would be in the interests of the *hamoula*. Furthermore, formal office in village government was either regarded as inferior to, or as directly connected with the office-holder's status within his own *hamoula*. This prevented the creation of an overly independent power elite, but it also precluded the separation of the various spheres of internal government, and creation of autonomous status scales.

The following is, in fact, the relationship between the ascribed social structure and the political system in Shalekhet: the council is staffed by each faction in turn in every alternate year; the secretariat stays in the hands of the majority *hamoula* (Maatuf), but the second largest *hamoula* (Hillel) is allowed, when it sits on the council, to choose the Maatuf member it likes best as secretary. This arrangement holds also for less important functions. The list below shows how these jobs are distributed by the *hamoulas* in Shalekhet, and demonstrates the attempt to maintain a delicate intergroup balance.

Secretary	*hamoula* I
Rabbi	*hamoula* I
Treasurer	*hamoula* II
Storekeeper	*hamoula* II
Security officer	*hamoula* IV
Border policemen	*hamoula* I, II
Worker at the Mekoroth Water Co.	*hamoula* I
Recreation director	*hamoula* II
Youth Club instructor	*hamoula* I
Cook	*hamoula* III
Teachers	*hamoula* I, II

In consequence, Shalekhet is a cooperative society in name only. This organizational form is, as we know, required by law, and the settlement authorities

TABLE 28—Simplified Organizational Chart of *Moshav* Resissim

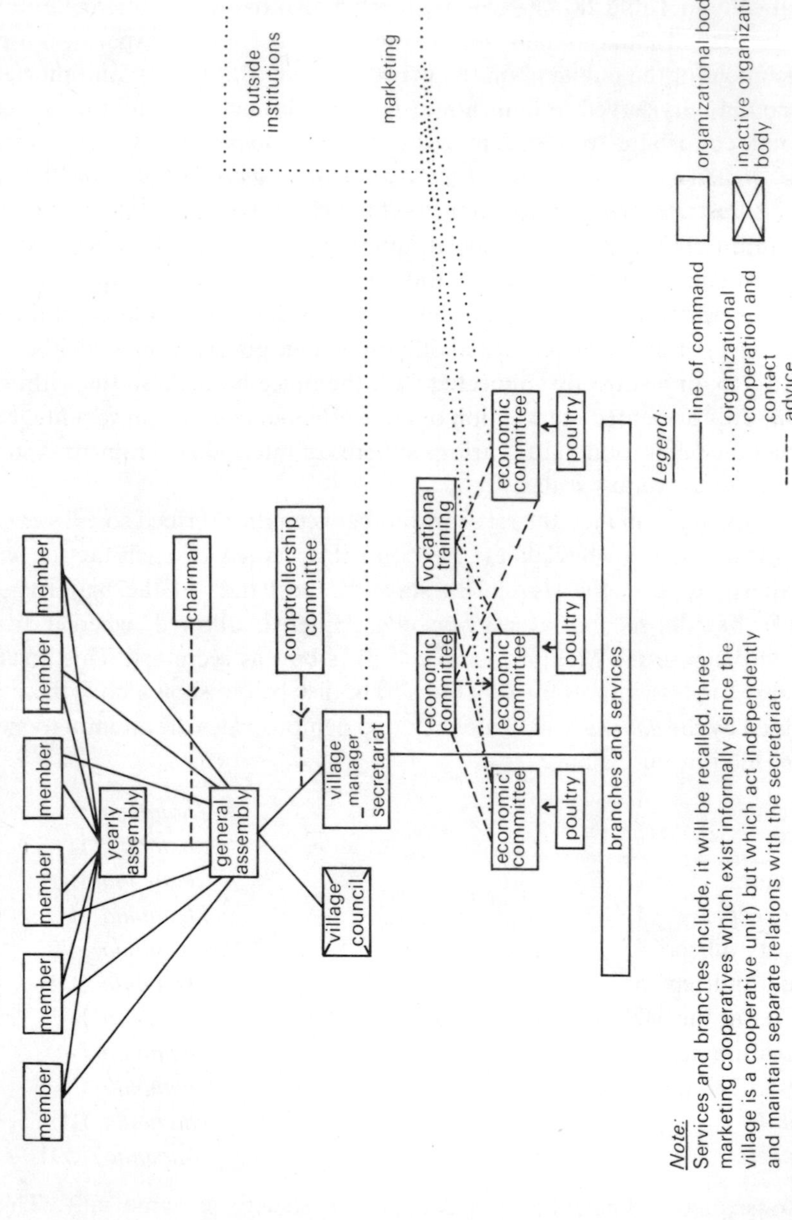

Note:
Services and branches include, it will be recalled, three marketing cooperatives which exist informally (since the village is a cooperative unit) but which act independently and maintain separate relations with the secretariat.

enforced it from the very outset of agricultural production,[9] since this kind of registered society satisfies the judicial and procedural conditions of village management. Hence, the existence of those institutions which are inseparable from the cooperative's very structure; the Annual Assembly which elects the cooperative's council, and the council itself, which is registered with the Company Register and the signature of whose members is binding. In practice, though, these bodies are only formally elected. They are not conceived of (nor run) as live institutions with real administrative functions; membership in them is viewed as a source of additional income and as a symbol of traditional, rather than modern, status which reinforces the position of the elected elders, and of the kinship groups which they represent. In fact, the council which only includes leaders of the *hamoulas,* actually reflects the *hamoula* structure perfectly. It was appointed by this structure when the "political cake" was cut and all of the village's ascriptive groups are proportionately represented in it. As a result, the councillors are men whose organizational experience and managerial know-how are very meagre and who have only partially assimilated the village structure either on the cognitive or the normative level. In this situation, the settlement authorities are still saddled with management of the cooperative's affairs which, at least on the instrumental level, have been entrusted almost entirely to the social instructor.

This does not mean, however, that the village has no organization of its own at all. Its traditional structure determines policy in certain spheres, and exercises social control in accordance with this policy. This arrangement was not initially supported or legitimated by the authorities, who tried to turn the *moshav's* institutions into *foci* of genuine public power and, at the same time, to imbue them with principles of democratic rule and bureaucratic organization. The social instructor at first hoped to staff the council with younger people who might be more malleable and more interested in progress than the older men—but failed to do so; Shalekhet's social integration and consensus were strong enough to keep the instructor from breaching the traditional structure and to maintain an alternative, or supplementary, organizational framework. A clear division of labour was arrived at between the instructor and between the traditional village institutions. Today, the village is heteronomous and outside-managed in respect to its municipal and cooperative services, economic policy and production, but "sovereign" in its social, religious and cultural arrangements.

Table 29 summarizes this division of organizational responsibility and shows the gaps in activities—some for traditional reasons, and others because of administrative or financial difficulties—which resulted from these characteristics.

This schematic division into a power dichotomy is, of course, a simplification, and only shows the situation on the level of top policy making. In reality the *hamoulas* enjoy considerable internal autonomy, which *extends over all those traditional*

TABLE 29—Division of Organizational Functions in *Moshav* Shalekhet

Task	Authority	
	Instructor	Village
General policy—goals and aims	+	+
General budgeting	+	+
Organizational structure	+	+
General welfare and advancement of public functionaries and members		+
Basic economic policy	+	+
crop-rotation	+	
composition of crops	+	
development of dry farming	+	
development and amelioration of livestock	+	
planting of poultry branch plantations	+	
Basic social policy		+
principles of recruitment and expulsion: sanctions		+
Basic educational policy		+
size and structure of school		+
participation in regional school		+
Preparation of list of candidates		+
consideration of prospective candidates		+
publication of list of candidates	+	
elections to village council		+
election to committees		+
election of council chairman		+
election of chairmen of assemblies	+	+
chairing of assembly (yearly)	+	+
chairing of assembly (extraordinary)	+	+
activation of council and committees	+	
order of deliberations	+	
population census	+	
village books	+	
care of mail	+	
care of village offices	+	
village news letter	—	—
follow-up of functionaries' work	+	+
representation of village in ceremonies	+	+
external relations	+	
tourist guides	—	—
care and hospitality for visitors	—	—
erection of public buildings	+	+
training of functionaries	+	+
allocation and roster of mechanized equipment	+	

TABLE 29 (continued)

Task	Authority	
	Instructor	Village
maintenance of public buildings	+	
herd-books	+	
special public works	+	
poultry books	+	
packing files	+	
motorized transport files	+	
collection of milk from members	+	
milk hygiene	+	
distribution of drinks	+	
central buying of supplies	+	+
pricing of supplies for sale	+	
maintenance of water lines and water	+	
evaluation of water use	+	
analysis of marketing costs	+	
veterinary care	+	
preparation of feed mixtures	+	
supply of beef stock	+	
provision of tools	+	
allocation of water quotas	+	
irrigation roster	+	
hiring of functionaries	+	+
acceptance of new members	—	—
cessation of membership	—	—
housing for public functionaries	+	
problems between individuals and council	+	
allocation of employment to members		+
arrangement for hired labour	+	+
economic analysis of individual farms	—	+
changes in taxation	+	+
problems between individual members		+
problems between members and cooperative enterprises	+	+
disciplinary problems and actions		+
employment for disabled members		+
visits to sick members		+
mutual aid		+
job rotation		+
special care for needy households		+
special tax concessions and exemptions		+
follow-up of council work		+
auditing	+	
supervision of cooperative enterprises	+	
reports to accounting office	+	
village balance sheet	+	
individual accounts	+	

TABLE 29—(continued)

Task	Authority	
	Instructor	Village
external accounts	+	
salaries	+	
taxes and welfare deductions	+	
cost accounting information	+	
production accounts	+	
suppliers' accounts	+	
income tax payments	+	
production accounts	+	
trial balance	+	
village shop accounts	+	
suppliers' accounts	+	
branch accounts	+	
general accounting	+	
reading of water meters	+	
industrial crops	+	
green fodder	—	—
vegetables	+	
buying and selling of beef	—	—
irrigation works	+	
pest control	+	
analysis of fat-content in milk	—	—
selling of consumption items	+	
selling of production items	+	
collection of agricultural produce	+	
marketing of produce	+	
storage of empty boxes	+	
grading and packing of produce	+	
work safety measures	+	
isolation strips	—	
maintenance of sheds	+	
maintenance of motorized equipment	+	
national insurance	+	
members insurance	+	
livestock and poultry insurance	+	
buildings insurance	+	
crop insurance	+	
mechanized equipment insurance	+	
maintenance of electric network	+	
current security	+	+
special security	+	+
ecological lay-out	+	+
location of fire-fighting equipment	+	

TABLE 29—(continued)

Task	Authority	
	Instructor	Village
maintenance of fire-fighting equipment	+	
planting and maintenance of public gardens, landscaping	—	—
maintenance of cemetery		+
members' gardens	+	
neatness	+	
maintenance of paths, lanes and roads	+	
sanitation	+	
equipment for kindergarten and school	+	
loans for members	+	+
contributions	+	
payments to institutions	+	
banking	+	
payments to members	+	
financial arrangements with members	+	+
payments to workers	+	
financial reports	+	
agricultural credit to members	+	+
excursions	—	—
contact with parents and pupils		+
public fêtes and holidays	+	+
educational activities for adults	+	+
library and newspapers	+	
cinema shows	—	—
maintenance of clubs	—	—
youth instruction		+
"Gadna" (military cadet training)	+	+
social gatherings	—	—
artistic groups	—	
special cultural activities	+	+
special health problems	+	
public health	+	
hygiene	+	
blood bank	—	—
contact with medical services	+	
contact with dental services	+	
convalescence for members	—	—
inoculations	+	
religious worship accessories		+
maintenance of synagogue		+
religious activities		+
funerals		+

spheres—internal matters, religious ceremonies and ritual, and welfare—which were in their province abroad.

The most interesting fact is that this situation in the meantime has been given some recognition by the instructor; a *quasi* institutionalization which is expressed by the informal establishment of a "supreme" institution for the coordination of the various functions and *foci* of power.

The organizational features of Shalekhet, seen as representative of the socially homogeneous traditional Israeli village, can be summarized as follows:

1. Division of authority, in which the instrumental sphere is given to external management, and the integrative and cultural spheres are internally managed.

2. The instrumental sphere is achievement-oriented and universalistic (though obviously non-democratic) and governed by rational methods of organization; but work is concentrated in the hands of a small staff, which must implement objectives that are divided up, in other villages, among several bodies. This imposes a very heavy burden, particularly on the social instructor and may even lead to his having to neglect proper training and guidance.

3. The spheres entrusted to the village itself are organized according to a wholly traditional scheme:

a. The village council is elected by democratic elections, but this is only a show of democracy; in reality, the list of candidates is not the result of free political activity but based on the *hamoulas*. The council is a "foreign" organizational body, whose formal pattern is quite unfamiliar to the settlers; it does not actually perform any concrete organizational tasks, also it is not involved in decisions taken elsewhere; and, to the extent that it has any public responsibility this is not to the general assembly but rather to the *hamoula* structure.

b. The council is elected on the basis of criteria which are conspicuously ascriptive.

c. The council is not guided by universalistic principles, but serves instead to confirm the existing particularistic division—albeit within the limitation of a consensus as to the political game.

The autonomous element in the village is therefore dual: partial independence of sub-units whose structure and activities are traditional; and a quasi—"collegium" recruited by co-optation of the *hamoula* elders which also essentially constitutes continuation of a non-Israeli pattern. The "collegium" manages to exert social control and to determine social and cultural policies. With the external management, it represents the "supreme" political authority of the *moshav*.

Table 30 gives us a schematic picture of this structure.

III. *The "managed" structure in the traditional-heterogeneous ("split") community.* As we saw in the case of *Moshav* Savel, the emergence of community-wide solidarity was prevented by the relationship between the *hamoulas*.

TABLE 30—Simplified Organizational Chart of *Moshav* Shalekhet

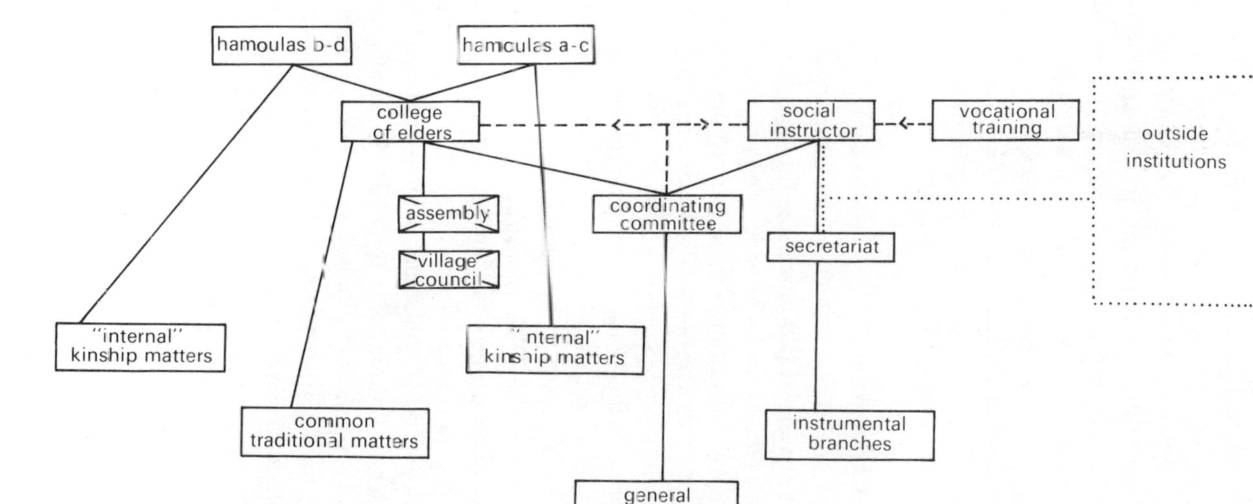

1 Internal kinship matters are, as has been mentioned, areas in the social, educational and cultural spheres which are handled by the *hamoulas* themselves—e.g. relations between kin, matters of religious ritual, welfare, etc.;

2. Common traditional branches are areas in the a/m spheres which relate to the traditional community as a whole—e.g. relations between *hamoulas*, division of functions in the village, school, etc.;

3. General dicisions are those which are taken jointly by the instructor and the village leaders (in the coordinating committee)—see table 5 above.

As long as *moshav* administration and government were vested in the absorptive team, the division between the *hamoulas* was one of withdrawal rather than of open conflict. The social instructor and his small clerical staff did all the jobs which needed interaction with and acceptance by all the settlers, thus concentrating in their hands the *moshav's* economic power and impartially allocating various resources and rewards. This, though not actually approved or ratified by the population, nonetheless commanded compliance and prevented a bitter fight over so-called spoils.[10]

In short, the organizational activity in the village was minimal, and autonomy was limited to a few internal *hamoula* matters. All the authority, which in Shalekhet was vested in the "collegium" of elders and in the coordinating committee, was deposited here in the settlement personnel. This situation holds true also for other villages in our sample, namely Kavoa, Koresh, and Levanon in the first years.

In Table 31 we elaborate on this phenomenon.

C. THE TRADITIONAL AUTONOMOUS STRUCTURE

The independent traditional village is a direct continuation of the managed traditional one. Its characteristic trait is that change of government within it is *not conditional on any change in social structure or on the assimilation of new organizational principles*; it results rather from a projection of the traditional pattern on to the organizational structure *as a whole*. In other words, the traditional lines of organization which, in the previous type, existed only in a restricted sense, now appear in all of the village institutions. The council, once basically fictitious, became the real ruling body and, with the secretariat, executes all those duties which were previously those of an external management; but its work is governed by non-democratic, ascriptive and particularistic criteria. This, by its very nature, is premature autonomous rule; and is, therefore, unlikely to succeed. But there is one very significant difference between a homogeneous and a heterogeneous traditional community. While the former can function as an instrument of policy making and social control, and meet with difficulties mainly as the provider of services, the latter is doomed to fail in all three areas.

I. *Autonomy in the homogeneous traditional ("familistic") village.* This type is represented by the *moshav* of Levanon, in its more recent period. In fact, we can say that this village achieved its independence via a "revolution", i.e., in a non-institutionalized, non-planned way—by showing the door to the social instructor. As in Shalekhet, here too, the team tried to change the principles and composition of the settlers' organization, by transferring the centre of power to the council and then staffing it with young people. But while in Shalekhet the settlers were content to oppose the situation from within, in Levanon the outside management was removed altogether (this was done by an adamant refusal to cooperate with the instructor or to continue to put the village facilities at his disposal), and the village has not accepted an instructor since.

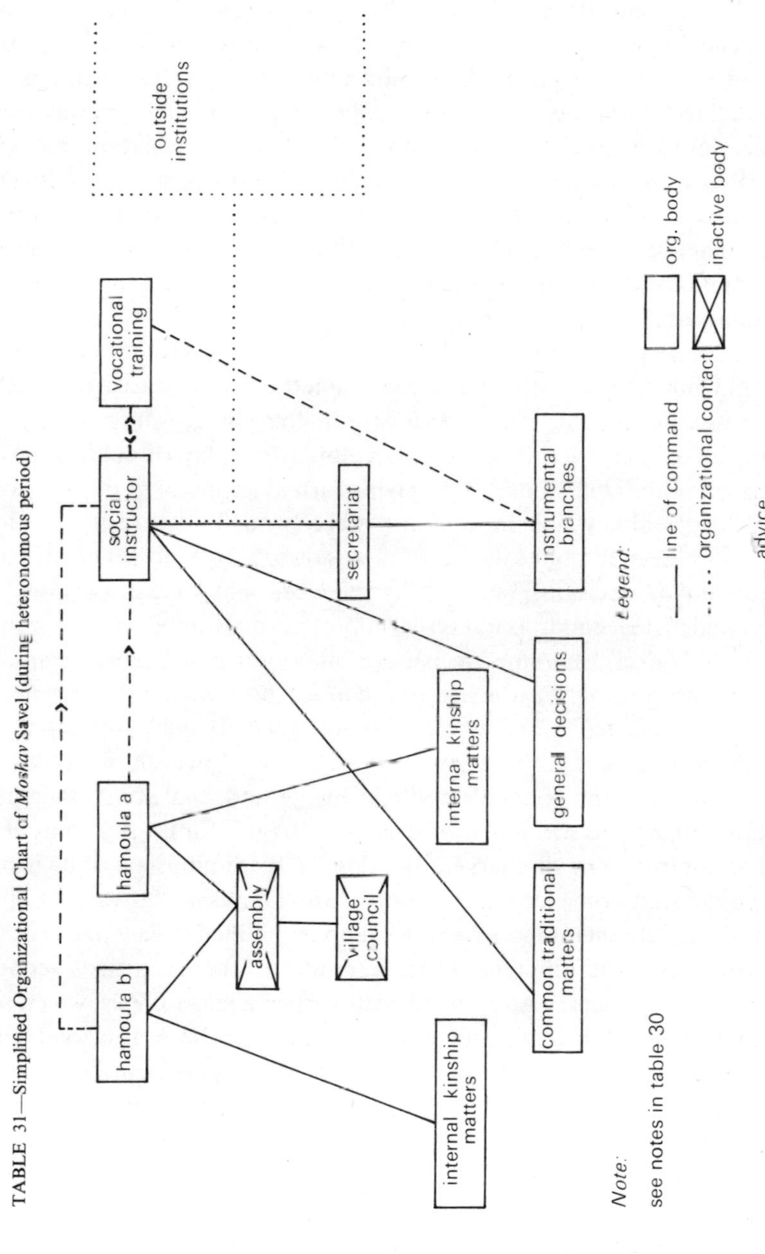

TABLE 31—Simplified Organizational Chart of *Moshav* Savel (during heteronomous period)

As a result, and owing to Levanon's social homogeneity, the following organizational web was created:

1. "Proper" organizational frameworks were limited to the barest minimum necessary. The only active institutions, in fact, were the council, the secretariat, and the farm committee (and even that happened much later)—although, on paper, other bodies existed too. Thus there was a comptroller's committee, which was required by the Registrar of Cooperatives in accordance with existing legislation, but which had been inherited from the heteronomous period and did not have any function any more; similarly a security committee, required by local conditions, was formed—but it, too, was inactive; finally, a religious committee was created but this was no more than an address for the receipt of grants and budgets from the Ministry of Religious Affairs. As a result of the fact that the *moshav* was run almost completely by the council and the secretary, and that there was no proper division of labour, specialization could not progress and no specific functions were carried out efficiently.

2. There was no genuine democratic rule in the village, since no organization existed which could either encourage or develop a free play of political power. The General Assembly contented itself with giving formal approval to the decisions of the traditional leadership, which in any case were brought before it only to satisfy *moshav* statutes. Even this official procedure was resorted to only for council elections, and general policy decisions were hardly ever brought to the assembly's notice. Obviously, under such conditions, there could be no question of responsibility to the general assembly as a "supreme" legislative body, nor could there be any effective control over the council. In practice, the council was answerable to the *hamoula* leadership which elected it and which it represented. It goes without saying that *moshav* women had no active or passive vote in it. However, since this form of government reflected the *moshav's* political image and had been validated by the settlers, its homogeneous social structure made it possible for the functions of decision making and control to be discharged. So, despite the limitations of its institutions, the *moshav* enjoyed some degree of coordination among the various spheres of activity, and the inhabitants were able to support council policy and its execution.

3. The situation was different where agriculture and municipal services were concerned. Although these matters were dealt with in a general way, which related to all the members of the particularistic group in a manner that was actually universalistic, they were not attended to in an efficient or achievement-oriented fashion. Farming and services, like other organizational matters, were entrusted to the traditional leadership. It would be inexact to say that this leadership was entirely ascriptive. It included two elderly men who had enjoyed positions of honour abroad, a religious leader, and men who had represented the Jewish community before the authorities of their country of origin, a responsibility which required certain gifts and qualifications. Status acquired by virtue of family and age was in this way mingled

with the principle of proof by performance; in the kinship framework there was also the expectation of efficient management of public affairs, based on past intellectual and political achievement. Obviously, however, such partial achievement criteria were essentially different from those now required in Israel, and this kind of qualification was quite irrelevant to the task at hand. Despite this, the leadership demanded complete control in the sphere of organization of *moshav* services and refused to hand over to the more efficient people who were being pushed by the social instructor before he left Levanon. These included graduates of agricultural schools, young men who had completed their military service, and the more experienced farmers. Failure to make use of their initiative and potential organizational ability because these lacked traditional legitimation, led to a series of crises in the village about the supply of services and the functioning of the cooperative, and the result was a sharp decline in the efficiency of marketing and purchases, the slowing down of development, financial problems, and the dwindling of the *moshav's* credit. The situation got so bad that the settlement authorities resorted to extreme measures, such as denying the right of signature to council members. Thus the situation which obtained before the instructor left was partly restored, i.e., heteronomous rule was partly reinstated through tight outside control. This situation is summarized in Table 32.

II. *Autonomy in the heterogeneous-traditional ("split") village.* As might be expected, the heterogeneous independent village faced an even more serious crisis. We described the situation of Savel, during the time that it was heteronomously managed, and we have seen that as long as the social instructor was at the helm, he was able to carry out minimal organizational functions. But the settlement authorities felt that since the village showed no signs of progress in the course of ten years, it was time to take drastic measures if organizational independence was to be promoted. In accordance with this policy, at the end of 1958 it was decided to take steps described to us as "throwing someone into the water so that he would learn to swim". The instructor was suddenly transferred from the village without the settlers' approval, and power given to the council. An organizational vacuum was created, and all corporate activity came to a stop. It was impossible for the council to adopt a common point of view; the various members and officials put forward by the two *hamoulas* invariably showed preferential treatment to their own kin; and, conversely, they received no cooperation from any one but their own allies. This not only precluded efficient administration, but also created acute tensions hitherto kept within limits by mutual avoidance. The resultant paralysis extended to all organizational decisions and led to a breakdown in the cooperative's activity and that of the municipal authority. Taxes were no longer collected regularly, the marketing mechanism was severely undermined, and the process of payments and credits with outside institutions was thrown out of kilter. In other words, the council and the secretariat showed that they could not possibly function as the main executive bodies of the

TABLE 32—Simplified Organizational Chart of *Moshav* Levanon

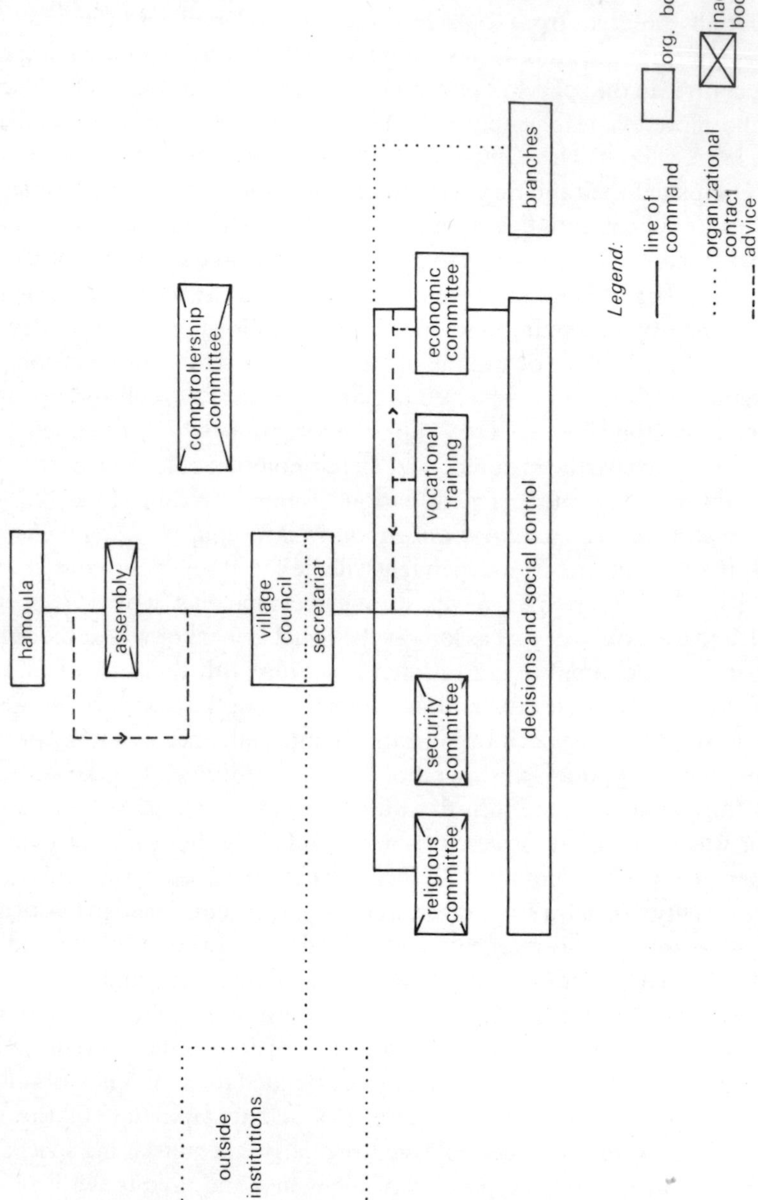

TABLE 33—Simplified Organizational Chart of *Moshav* Savel (during autonomous period)

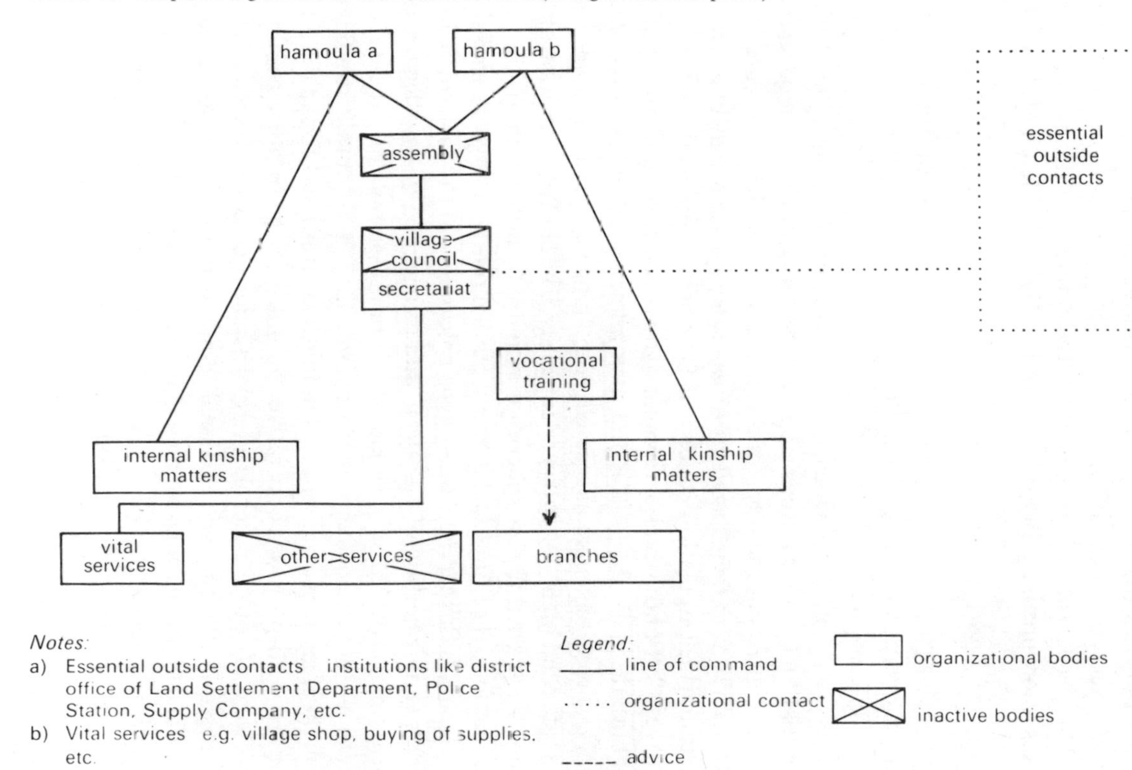

Notes:

a) Essential outside contacts institutions like district office of Land Settlement Department, Police Station, Supply Company, etc.

b) Vital services e.g. village shop, buying of supplies, etc.

moshav, and the assembly demonstrated that it could not arrive at any decisions. In fact, the only important organizational activity which went on relatively undisturbed was in the village cooperative shop (run by an outsider) and the supply store.

Table 33 shows us the situation in Savel during this period.

Since the events occurred at the end of our study, we were unable to follow them up; but later we learnt that around 1960, the community disintegrated and half of the settlers (more precisely, one of the two rival *hamoulas)* left it altogether.

Conclusion

In the preceding pages we have seen what occurs when a confrontation takes place between an ambitious scheme of rural cooperation and modern municipal government, and different social groups.

At the risk of stating the obvious, our material, we think, shows clearly the need for a differential and very cautious approach to organizational modernization and growth. This applies to the *scope* of the changes with which these rural populations are faced, as well as to their *specificity* or *uniqueness.* The *moshav* blueprint combined what were for the population concerned far-reaching innovations both in terms of cooperative effort and local government. Moreover, it set down regulations which affected both the goals themselves and their implementation. As a result, an overall framework of requirements was created, combining various areas of *moshav* life into one integrated and highly interdependent entity. The lack of separation among—and autonomy of—these different spheres of activity, with its emphasis on total change and total performance, imposed a heavy burden on the village's social resources, a burden which was further increased by the inflexibility of the pattern, by its emphasis on uniformity, its rejection of pluralism, and its negation of any "legitimate alternatives for development". Not a single village in our sample met these requirements fully; even the homogeneous western community—a "natural" candidate for the development of modern economic and political institutions—found the intensity and scope of the multi-purpose cooperative too much for it. In other communities, the problems were, of course, much greater. Particularly conspicuous was the problem of establishing an efficient and rational administration in heterogeneous social structures, and in populations which had no modern political orientations. However, by "sacrificing" political and ideological goals—namely democracy and autonomy—some of these problems were solved, as for example when external administration was relied upon almost entirely.

Of course, this is not to say that in such a case *direct* administration from above by government or public representatives is necessarily the most suitable basis for efficiency. Frequently, this kind of intervention is likely to subject the farmer to paternalistic patronage or undue bureaucratic heavy-handedness. The weight of such an intervention might be particularly felt when rural cooperation is used as a measure of agrarian reform calculated to free the farmer from dependence upon a landlord and/or a middle man, in his relations with goods, money and labour markets. Instead of these, one master is merely exchanged for another. A "congenial" pattern was the one adopted by Resissim; there, efficiency was achieved by appointing a professional manager who was responsible to and employed by the community. The idea of safeguarding the essentials of development, and at the same time attempting an "honourable" or a participant solution of course, underlies the institution of the Panchayat, as evolved, for example, in Pakistan and, more recently in Nepal.[11]

Without judging the issue—which after all each society must evaluate for itself—of what are the most suitable aims and modes of development, it is clear that the prerequisite for successful "cooperatization" and "municipalization" is a definite social pre-condition, of the sort which is not likely to be common in any developing society. A long preparatory stage, gradual introduction, and a variety of alternatives seem to be essential ingredients, if failure is to be avoided.

NOTES

1 This organizational blueprint is based on a job analysis which was carried out in two veteran established *moshavim* which can be considered as prototypical, as well as on information given by the *Moshav* Movement and the Land Settlement Department.

2 It must be mentioned that democratic and bureaucratic principles are actually, to some extent, at odds: insistence on office rotation and on the diffusion of power (as reflected in the unnecessarily large number of specific committees), can affect efficiency both in implementation and in decision making. Later on, we give a specific example of how this contradiction resolves itself in practice.

3 Needless to say, certain communal activities are optional, and differ from one place to another. Some settlements have no synagogue; others cannot afford a community centre, etc.

4 These profiles are shown on the next page. The profiles discussed here are 1, 8, and 13.

5 We analyze a "hybrid" profile of this sort in Chapter 6, where we show a change from the "traditional" pattern—namely non-democratic, non-rational (or ascriptive) and particularistic, into the non-democratic or the semi-democratic, particularistic but rational one. This may indeed represent a preferential order of change in this sphere, with each kinship group mobilizing the best people from the *moshav* point of view, and still insisting on, and ensuring their loyalty to, the in-group.

6 I.e. omitting particulars of branches and services detailed in the "blueprint".

7 Sometimes this inability is only in the eyes of the beholder and the Settlement Authority may quite unjustifiably prolong an instructor's administration.

8 For overriding technical reasons the marketing of milk continued for the village as a whole.

9 We only know of one village which is not, formally, a cooperative society: a heterogeneous village settled by people from the Atlas Mountains who couldn't agree on the election of common institutions.

10 We deal, later on, with the story of what happened when government was transferred to the village council.

11 See for instance, M. Mohsin and Pashupati Shumshere, *Some Aspects of the Nepal Panchayat System* (mimeo). A discussion of the range of "guided democracy" patterns on the local level is however, clearly beyond the present empirical context.

	A Independence	B Legitimation	C Structure and recruitment in offices	D Public service
	(a) Autonomous (b) Heteronomous	(a) Democratic (b) Non-democratic	(a) Rational (b) Non-rational	(a) Universalistic (b) Particularistic
1.	Autonomous	Democratic	Rational	Universalistic
2.	„	„	„	Particularistic
3.	„	„	Non-rational	Universalistic
4.	„	„	„	Particularistic
5.	„	Non-democratic	Rational	Universalistic
6.	„	„	„	Particularistic
7.	„	„	Non-rational	Universalistic
8.	„	„	„	Particularistic
9.	Heteronomous	Democratic	Rational	Universalistic
10.	„	„	„	Particularistic
11.	„	„	Non-rational	Universalistic
12.	„	„	„	Particularistic
13.	„	Non-democratic	Rational	Universalistic
14.	„	„	„	Particularistic
15.	„	„	Non-rational	Universalistic
16.	„	„	„	Particularistic

CHAPTER 5

ONE MAN'S MEAT: THE MOSHAV AS SEEN BY SOME OF ITS SETTLERS

Introduction

This chapter will deal with *subjective adjustment,* with the characteristic *aspirations* of various immigrant groups, and their significance in terms of the *moshav.*

Our discussion will focus on the confrontation which takes place between the attitudes and expectations of the new settlers, on the one hand and the requirements and institutions of the *moshav,* on the other; and on the sort of motivation to *moshav* life which results from this confrontation.[1]

As we showed, the *moshav* is a closely knit economic, social, political and cultural unit, ecologically concentrated and functionally highly interdependent. Fundamentally, this is a system in which most spheres of activity are rigidly defined; most of its "technical" and economic aspects have a symbolic meaning; and there are in it, consequently, only a few permissive areas. The new settler thus faces a set of concrete features and requirements, which may be spelled out more or less as follows:

1. A certain amount of insecurity about life and property;
2. Isolation from urban centres;
3. Dependence upon, and obedience to central planning and overriding national considerations;
4. A modern and intensive economy which is geared to a high level and sophisticated agricultural performance; and which is market-oriented and thus requires the ability to compete, to wait for rewards, to use credit extensively, to risk immediate loss for the sake of eventual profit and to adjust the scope and composition of production;
5. Small-holding farming which limits the extent and the rewards of entrepreneurship, in so far as it creates an inevitable reliance on self-labour (which is also manual labour), places a ceiling on development and expansion, and represents a demanding and rather harsh way of life, also associated with "peasant" status;
6. A *Gemeinschaft* community life.

A positive attitude towards these features, and the necessary motivation for adjusting to them had been provided originally by combining Zionist, Socialist and pioneering ideologies, into one—thus giving early settlers in Palestine an identification which made it possible for them to be achievement-oriented on the one hand, and capable of considerable abnegation on the other. But subsequent immigrants, particularly those that came to the country after the establishment of the State were, on the whole, lacking this complicated and unique motivation. Most of them tried instead to preserve as many as possible of the aspirations which they had brought with them from abroad. In the following pages their reaction to the *moshav* and to *moshav* life is spelled out fairly specifically and documented.

The Moshav *and the New Settler*

Taking into account the two dimensions of the motivational process (see Note 1)—that which is expected and that which is perceived—there seem to be five basic approaches to *moshav* life:

1. *"Proper", value-anchored motivation*—that is, a positive, symbolic acceptance of the *moshav* demands deriving from identification with the original ideals of Zionism, Socialism and pioneering.
2. *Alternative, value-anchored motivation*—an intrinsic identification with the *moshav,* but one based on values which differ from those that are inherent in the pattern.
3. *Positive instrumental or extrinsic motivation*—a reference to aims and objectives outside the *moshav*—that is, non-identification with the *moshav* in terms of its merits as such, and a conception of it as being a means towards other ends; but at the same time a positive evaluation of its potential relative to and as compared with other concrete opportunities and realistic alternatives.
4. *Negative instrumental or extrinsic motivation*—which is similar to the above, but different in its implications; this is based on evaluating the *moshav* as inferior to other open choices.
5. *Negative value-anchored motivation*—an orientation which sees the *moshav* as intrinsically inimical to the settler's values and as clashing with his aspirations.

Each of these types of course can apply differentially to various aspects of the *moshav.* But in our analysis we will not burden the reader with a full mapping-out of complete motivational patterns; we will try to bring out salient features, and to pin down dominant themes.

Most of our analysis is devoted to comparing, in terms of the above-mentioned conceptualization, two basic and contrasting motivational profiles—the "Western" or modern one and the traditional one. To round off the discussion, we will highlight some of the approaches and problems which are characteristic of "transitional" groups.

The Modern, Uncommitted Settler: the Moshav Viewed Extrinsically

The group with which we are now concerned is largely composed of people of modern, urbanized backgrounds. They differ, of course, in education and previous social, economic and occupational status; and there are also distinctions regarding the extent to which they come from more or less "westernized" countries, and more or less emancipated Jewish communities. But all in all their basic cultural pattern was and is rational, dynamic and secular, based primarily on the universalistic values of economic, social and political participation, and on the promotion of social, occupational and consumer mobility. Development and progress both individual and collective, constituted a central value, symbolized by economic and professional achievement. Status was accordingly spelled out in terms of income, way of life and occupation. In terms of social interaction, individualism and the free play of different motives and abilities served as a guiding image.

This group tended to leave its country of origin and immigrate to Israel for reasons that had to do with various types of push rather than Israel's pull. They came because of economic, social, religious or political pressures, which made it hard or impossible for them to achieve various personal aspirations. Their choice of Israel was, in fact, largely a matter of chance, not of deep ideological deliberation or the desire to change their way of life entirely.

The same applies, very broadly, to the general Zionist (but nonpioneering) type of immigrant—at least the one who ended up in the *moshav*. Although this kind of settler *was* motivated by national consciousness, it was general rather than specific, and applied chiefly to a desire to change his nationality rather than to a desire to change the very structure of his existence. Many survivors from the Nazi Holocaust for instance, came to Israel because they were unable to reintegrate themselves either socially or psychologically in those countries in which they suffered so terribly. Their immigration to Israel was thus motivated by a personal and a social status crisis; but it did not entail any fundamental change in the "modern", urban self-image as such. In other words, the purpose of their migration was chiefly to move into a new, more secure political setting while remaining with a familiar social, cultural and economic framework.

It was logical then to expect that the more modern the background of the settler, and the higher his general and vocational education and sophistication, the better he would adjust (at least potentially) to the entrepreneurial and dynamic aspects of farming, particularly in terms of individual initiative, responsibility and profit. By the same token, however, it was reasonable to anticipate the rejection of an ideological orientation towards personal and social pioneering, the simple life, and the artificial limitations placed on entrepreneurship; and to assume that individualism would be substituted for collectivism and equality, and *Gesellschaft* for *Gemeinschaft*. It was probable that the settler would be perturbed about manual labour and dismayed at the prospect of social and cultural isolation. His self-image, it was predicted, would include an urban occupation and way of life; and he would probably aspire to high status associated with this way of life instead of symbolic rewards.

We found ourselves in the sociologically embarrassing position of having to admit that what was reasonable was unfortunately also realistic. The villages Ta'amon and Zeviya bore out most, if not all, of these assumptions.

It will be recalled that the majority group in Ta'amon, i.e., the Yugoslavs, was made up mainly of assimilated, middle-class, professional, white-collar elements. World War II, however, had affected this group as direly as it had most other European Jewish communities. They suffered both as Jews, and as Yugoslavs who had taken an active part in the war and in the resistance movement. When hostilities ended, they tried to reconstruct their lives, to participate again in local and national activities on the one hand, and to continue cultural assimilation on the other. They were both bitterly disappointed and shocked to learn that despite their desire to adapt themselves to Yugoslavia's post-war regime, they were even farther from complete integration than they had been before the war. Not only did they feel that their Jewishness was held against them, but they found it impossible to erase the trauma caused by the catastrophe that had overwhelmed the Jews of Europe, or to go on living in places which were saturated with tragic memories and unbearably painful personal associations. The result was a strengthening of their Jewish consciousness and Zionist feelings, and their subsequent emigration to Israel. But neither their Zionism nor their emigration to Israel involved a change of outlook and aspirations. In Israel, they hoped to be able to carry on in the same occupational, economic and social patterns as before, but this time within a more acceptable and congenial social and political framework. At no time did these immigrants intend to settle in a *moshav*.

What, then, made them nonetheless do so? It is interesting that the group embarked upon its course deliberately, after much consideration, and on the basis of a wholly rational decision. It decided that settlement in a *moshav* was the quickest way to achieve economic and social absorption in their new surroundings, since they understood how protracted and difficult the process of integration was in the anonymity of city life. They also understood how hard it would be to maintain their social and professional status under these circumstances. These facts having been faced and digested, the group decided it would try the *moshav* way of life—and prepare for it properly.

Before they actually settled in the village, they set up a communal camp designed to provide them with some vocational training as well as to give all thc settlers a chance to get to know one another and to feel secure in the first stages of absorption. From the very start a deliberate effort was made to establish links between the new immigrants and the absorbing society; and for this purpose they persuaded a number of

Yugoslav farming families, long settled in Israel, to join them. All in all, their preparation for the *moshav* was realistic, somewhat detached and unemotional.

The minority group of Ta'amon (similar in this respect to the population of Zeviya as a whole) had a more prolonged period of preparation for their emigration to Israel, as well as for their settlement on the land. They came from a country which had been a center of Zionism and from which there has been a constant flow of emigrants to Palestine since the end of the last century. For most of these families, immigration and settlement in the *moshav* involved no drastic lowering of their social status or standard of living. The central feature, however, which stands out when we look at the attitudes of the settlers in *both* these villages, is their lack of any *intrinsic* commitment to the *moshav*. There is a very small minority which has formed an affective attachment to the farm and to land; a larger group which considers the place as home, and would be very reluctant to leave it. But neither group has any dedication to the way of life as such. On the contrary—they see the *moshav* as a way to acquiring a high income, an independent business and being able to retain their position as individuals. And since all the villagers feel this way, and maintain a loose rather than a tightly-knit community structure; and since they all realize that in their particular situations[2] they would be worse off in the city, they appreciate the *moshav* as being very useful to them in these respects. Agricultural success, therefore, becomes of paramount importance and the virtues of entrepreneurial initiative, responsibility and achievement—which are in any case both congenial and familiar to them—develop impressively in the *moshav*.

This is reflected in the intensification of production in *Moshav* Zeviya, as measured by the indices of (a) land utilization;[3] (b) size of dairy herds; (c) size of chicken coops; (d) cultivation ratio expressed in Standard Work Days.

Tables 34 to 37[4] show us clearly that the record far exceeds the official farm plan and begins to approximate the progress of much older villages.

These static data for the year of research (1958 to 1959) are reinforced when we review the development and increasing yields of the dairy branch between 1953 and 1959 (see Tables 38 and 39 in figures and graphs). There, the herd and its yield show an almost constant and sometimes even dramatic growth, as does the average production which compares favourably with, and sometimes surpasses, the national annual norm—for established family farms—of 4,500 litres a year per cow (or 1,125 quarterly, and 2,250 half-yearly).

Unfortunately, the settlers we interviewed (and the Village Council) were unwilling to give us precise data on their yearly income, but it is certainly much above IL 6,300 gross (before taxes)—which is the *planned* income for a farm of this type (according to 1959 estimates), the basis being the norms given in Tables 34 to 37 (i.e., 28.1 dunams of irrigated land, 100 layers, 5 head of cattle, and a total of 350 Standard Work Days).

We did learn the median net income, which is between IL 900 and IL 1,000 a

TABLE 34—Land Utilization in *Moshav* Zeviya

(a) In absolute numbers

total cultivated area according to official plan	2529 dunams
real total cultivated area	2529 dunams

(b) Distribution of farms by cultivated area

No. of dunams	*No. of Farms*
15–20	8
21–25	20
26–30	34
31–35	14
36–40	7
65–70	1
unknown	6
total	90

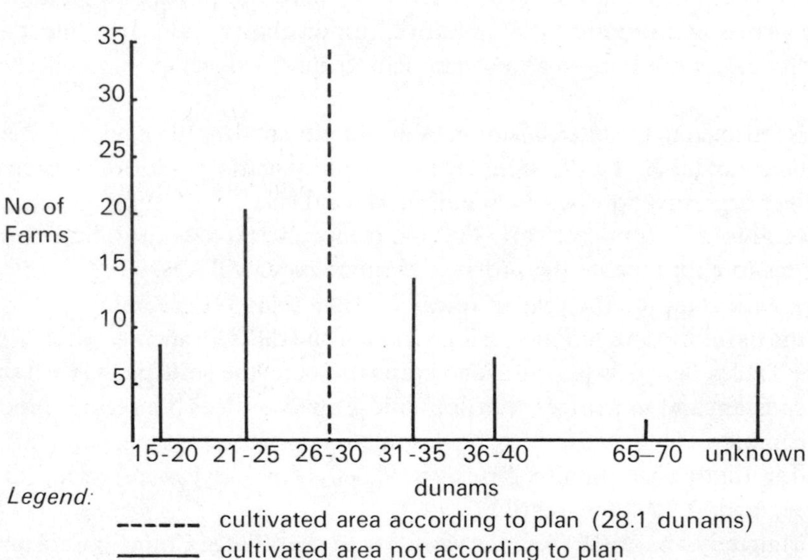

TABLE 35—Development of Dairy Herd in *Moshav* Zeviya

No. of Head	*No. of Households*
0	3
1–5	10
6–10	28
11–15	26
16–20	16
40–45	1
unknown	6
total	90

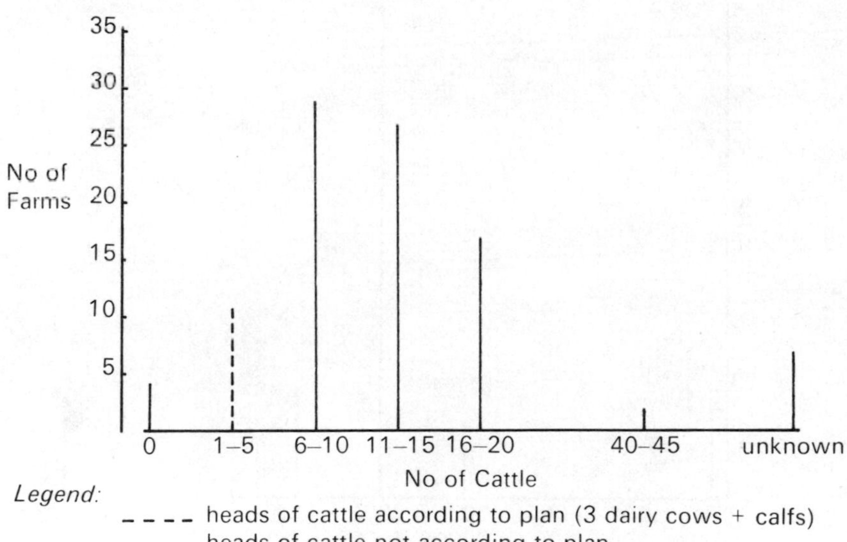

TABLE 36—Development of Chicken Coops in *Moshav* Zeviya

No. of layers	*No. of Households*
0	7
100–200	8
201–1000	2
1001–2000	6
2001–3000	50
3001–4000	9
5000–6000	2
unknown	6
total	90

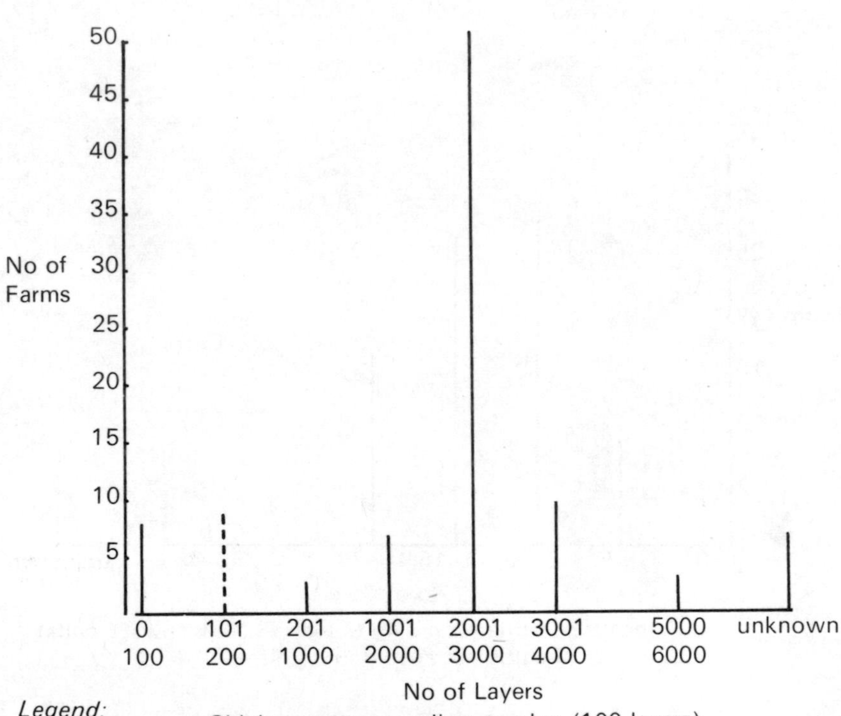

TABLE 37—Farm Activity in *Moshav* Zeviya Expressed in Standard Work Days

Standard Work Days	*No. of Households*
up to 100	18 auxiliary farms
101–200	3
201–300	8
301–400	13
401–500	13
501–600	17
601–700	6
701–800	3
801+	3
unknown	6
total	90

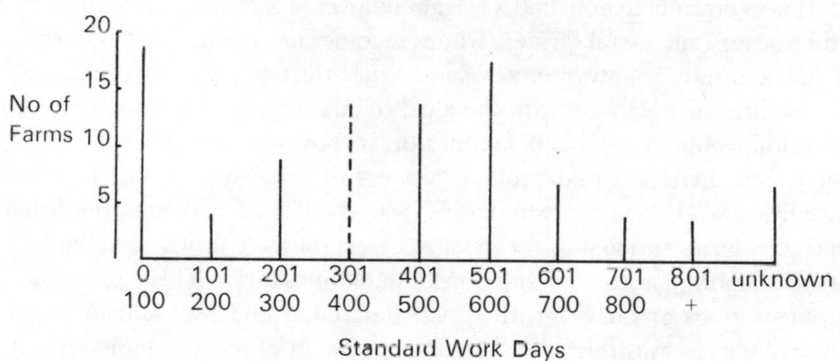

Legend:

- - - - Standard Work Days according to plan (average 350 a year)
——— Standard Work Days not according to plan

TABLE 38—Dairy Branch in *Moshav* Zeviya 1953–1959

	Households with dairy herd	Total yield in litres	Total of heads (in parentheses—milk cows)	Average yield per cow in litres*
30.6.53	71	64,158	182 (100)	641
30.9.53		65,307	197 (108)	604
30.12.53	74	69,118	199 (106)	652
31.3.54		90,500	253 (132)	685
30.6.54	78	107,440	264 (144)	746
30.9.54	78	109,700	294 (159)	689
31.3.55	84	141,260	223 (177)	798
30.9.55	80	295,900	303 (164)	1804
31.3.56	85	326,725	327 (155)	2107
30.9.56	85	391,456	408 (166)	2358
31.3.57	95	332,660	408 (163)	2040
30.9.57	86	487,484	415 (259)	3065
31.3.58	78	439,581	494 (233)	1414
30.9.58	88	583,144	524 (240)	2428
31.3.59	85	582,000	812 (275)	2117

* Averages for three or six months, as is seen from the dates.

month. It is interesting to note that a certain quarter in the village, inhabited by fairly new and not very successful farmers whose incomes are estimated at between IL 600 and IL 750 a month, is known in Zeviya as "the street of the underprivileged".

There is little patience here with the ideal of equality. Nor does anyone have any compunction about using hired labour, or withdrawing from agriculture, when necessary. But there is considerable awareness of achievement—for its own sake. Both Zeviya and Ta'amon are intensely proud of finding themselves listed in a national survey as surpassing the norms of established farms, and having been re-classified among Israel's old and consolidated *moshavim*. This commitment to a development ethos or image—with which Ballandier and McClelland might both have been happy[5]—was formulated by the chairman of the Ta'amon council as an alternative to ideological motivation: "A reform in the official ideology of the *Moshav* Movement is inevitable, since this ideology clashes with the real interests of a new and large agricultural sector. This conflict derives from the fact that, in many villages, pioneering has ceased to be the dominant motive in economic behaviour; it is, at best, one of many factors. This is a great pity, but the fact remains that rational economic drives now overshadow an ideology whose day has passed. It is therefore necessary to rescind rules which harm the settler—i.e., the prohibition on hired labour; and it is also necessary to streamline marketing and divorce it from monopolistic corporations[6] which are dominated by political influence and pressure groups. In general, this is true also of other aspects of the *moshav* life, which must be made

TABLE 39—Dairy Branch in *Moshav* Zeviya 1953–59

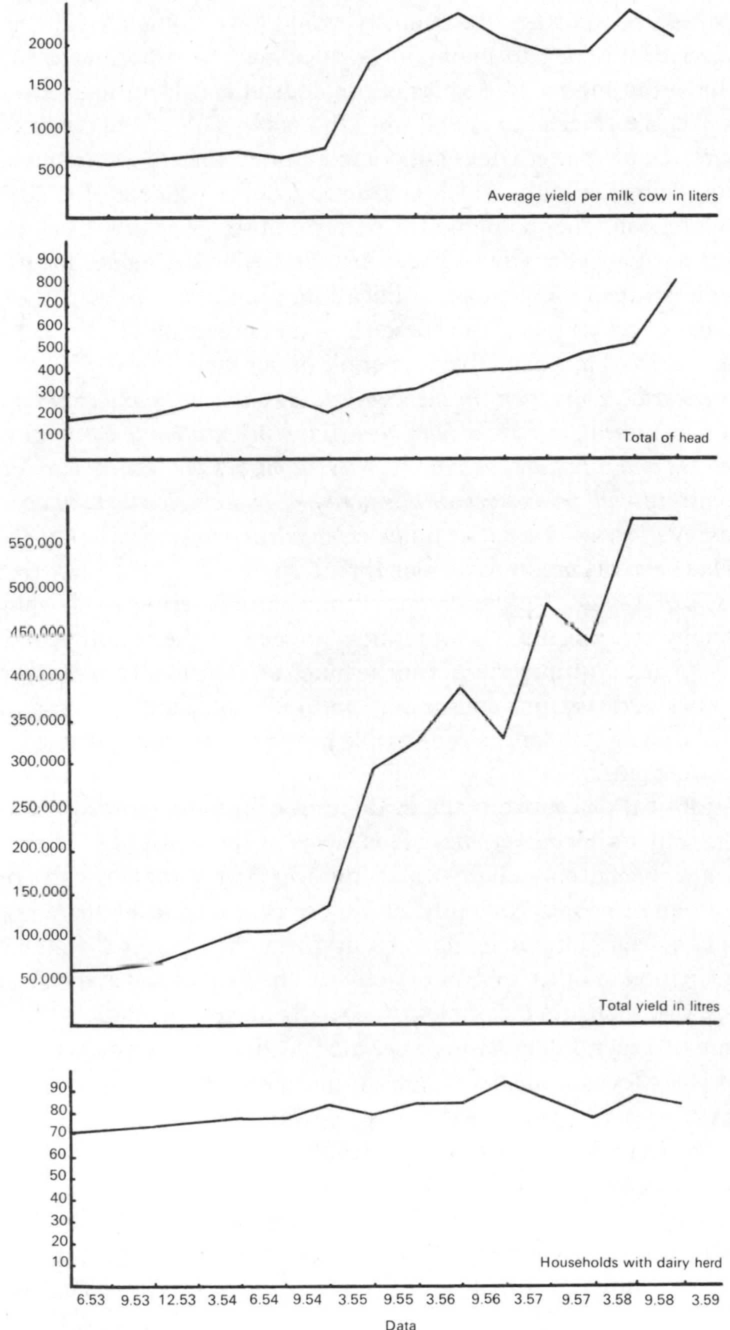

subject to professional and rational considerations." Or quoting another council member: "The situation today is that if one wanted to prosecute members for ideological crimes and apostasy, the majority would have to stand trial. The pattern which the Movement wants to maintain is calculated to subordinate productive activity and the profit motive to a series of ideological considerations: the new law which it proposes is a reversal to feudalism.[7] In many villages, and especially in the immigrant ones, the old pattern does not command that sincere emotional devotion, and the almost religious faith, which characterized the veterans. Let the veteran villages, therefore, continue to uphold the pattern, in so far as they can; the others, however, must have an alternative. There are, undoubtedly, values in the *moshav* which have not lost their vitality and justification, such as the principles of mutual aid and democratic government. But these too—and especially the former—can be improved, and rendered more suitable for people of our kind."[8]

The entrepreneurial motivation, in the two-fold meaning of maximization of profit and a sense of achievement, is thus the hard core of this orientation towards the moshav: *it induces intensive and rational economic activity; it pushes the settlers into attempting change in the institutional framework of this activity; and it helps them to accept those aspects of* moshav *life which cannot as yet be changed, and towards which their attitude is negative*. These aspects are in particular three:

a. *Hard manual labour*. Unlike certain "transitional" groups (of whom more later) who literally abhor manual labour, and who see it as the symptom and symbol of their own failures, the attitude here is not so much an emotional one as it is realistic. This kind of work is dirty, time-consuming, and inordinately demanding of people who are unused to it and no longer young; like poverty, it is "not a shame but only a damned inconvenience".

b. More intrinsically negative is the evaluation of the limitations placed by the *moshav* on the settler's *social horizons*. This is so, in the first place, in the specific sense of life in a very small community which involves intense contact with a restricted and uniform group of people. Secondly, at a more profound level, there is a feeling that small-holding agriculture, in its present form, hampers self-fulfilment and prevents participation in other spheres of activity, chiefly political and cultural ones. In other words, that it creates incomplete or socially narrow people.

c. This sense of general deprivation is related to the consciousness of *low social position*. This is so because all the people in question conceive of social status as something based primarily on occupation—professional roles being regarded among the highest on the scale and agricultural among the lowest.

All in all, then, the motivational pattern is ambivalent; as entrepreneurial scope is hardly a feature of the *moshav* as such, there is no intrinsic identification even partially; commitment depends on a delicate balance of positive and negative factors. The precise composition of this balance depends largely on the specific educational, social, occupational and cultural background of the people concerned. The higher it had been—along these dimensions—the more prone these settlers were to feel deprived, and the more likely they were to look for and find alternative channels. As is the case in most other rural settings, they were the first people to leave, and in this respect we see a negative selection process here. But those who stayed on the *moshav* are typified by a distinct reaction pattern exemplified by the "high status" Yugoslav group in Ta'amon. This group has tried to underline and emphasize—perhaps to exaggerate—the professional aspects of *moshav* agriculture, and in particular of its organizational, managerial and financial aspects. It has even unsuccessfully attempted to gain recognition as members of a semi-free profession—by creating a country-wide, general farmers' association which is independent of any political movement or party, by insisting on a high and a formal level of vocational education and training and by intensifying specialization and differentiation in production. But these were mostly symbolic manifestations. On the practical, concrete level, this group slowed down farm development, in order to devote more time to cultural, recreational and public activity and a large share of their savings went to the acquisition of city-type housing, comfort, etc. In Table 40 we have shown the differential preference, over a given period of time, of production and consumption spending in two status groups in Ta'amon—the higher (Yugoslav) and the lower (Rumanian).

These variations apart, however (and time has levelled most of them off), almost all these settlers feel thorough commitment to the *moshav* and consequently intend to stay where they are and make the best of it.

This is not so—by any stretch of the imagination—as far as their children are concerned. Although specific plans for their future also consistently vary, along the lines of preparation for academic, technical and/or white collar occupations, they almost always have nothing to do with agriculture and/or the *moshav*.[9]

In this respect, at least, the young people of the village are in complete accord with their parents. The crucial problem of this extrinsic and ambivalent attitude is, of course, that of the *moshav's* physical continuity.[10]

The Traditional Settler—a "Right" Commitment for the "Wrong" Reasons

In contrast to the groups we just examined, we will now deal with settlers of "traditional" Jewish and rural background. This very broad category includes a number of distinct cultures—the Yemenite, the Kurdish, the Atlas Mountain, and others; and we shall refer to some of the differences between them later. Broadly speaking, however, they all adhered to a traditional way of life—both in general and in Jewish terms—to a world which was static, religious and familistic, and strongly value- and integration-oriented. The fundamental image of these Jewish communities was characterized by their extreme conservatism, whose purpose was to uphold an

TABLE 40—Average Investment in Farm and Non-Expendable Consumption Items in *Moshav* Ta'amon (measured by the average expenditure of its households excluding inactive and auxiliary farms)

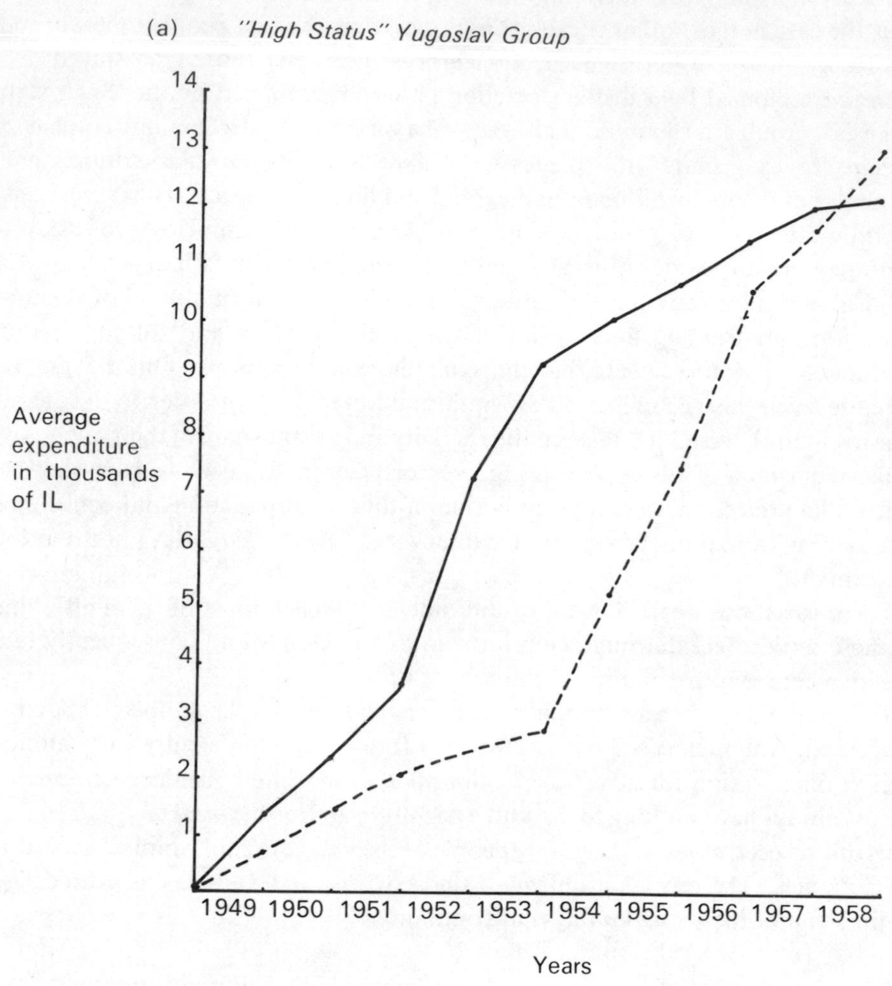

(b) *"Low Status" Rumanian Group*

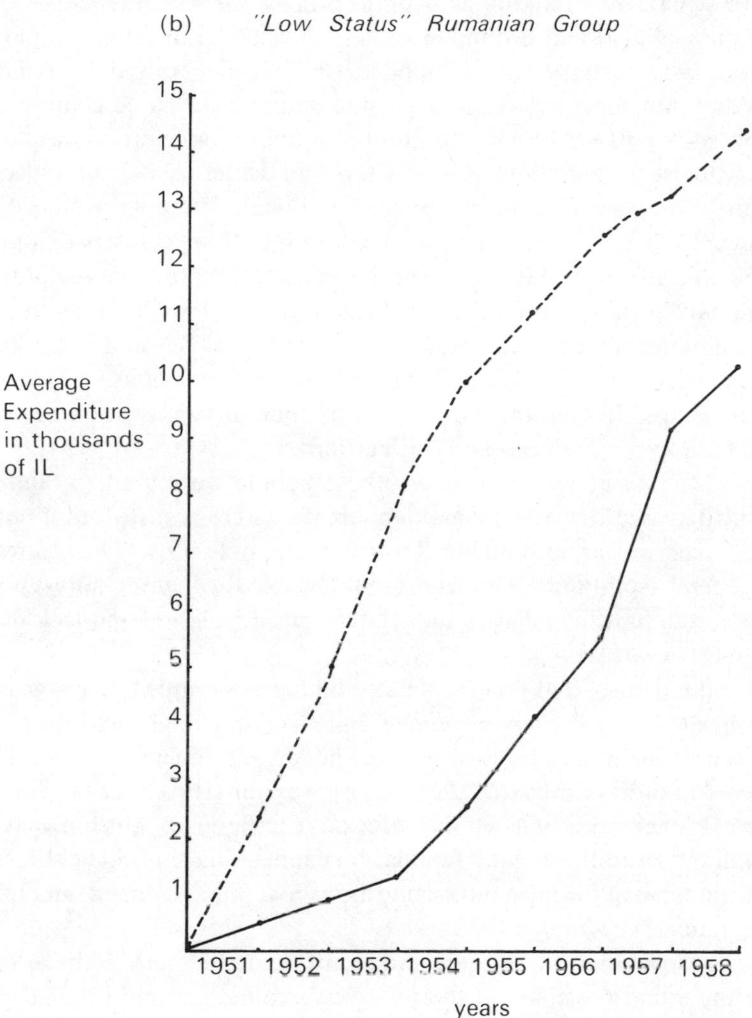

Legend:

. . . . . . investment in farm

______ consumer expenditure

Note The Rumanians arrived two years after the Yugoslavs.

existing value system, in which the present was conceived of in terms of the past, and the future significant primarily as a projection of the present. Hence the lack of autonomous political and economic values, in relation to religious and familistic ones, hence also a stratificational model which is symbolized by family, ethnic, religious and rabbinical criteria, and a vision of a kinship-based community.

The motivating power behind this group's immigration to Israel was "messianic". Like the Zionist immigration, this one too had Israel as its sole object, but the underlying drive was religious rather than political. There were 50,000 Yemenite Jews flown to Israel from Aden in the famous "Magic Carpet" operation of 1949-1950, and all believed that this was the apocalyptic "Ingathering of the Exiles". Understandably, they expected their future in the Jewish State to be idyllic, reminiscent of the biblical description of "each under his vine and under his fig tree". More specifically, it was a utopian projection, and an intensification of a basic traditional image. It was, therefore, obvious that this motivation served only to reinforce basic predispositions and expectations.

In other words—as we now know—these people were used to, and would be favourably disposed towards manual labour; they were accustomed if not to actual farming,[11] then, at least to rural life. Their standard of living was low, as was the level of their general aspirations. All this made it feasible for them to adjust positively to agriculture, to a hard life, and to the relative social isolation and lack of amenities implicit in the new *moshav*.

It was realized, also, that these settlers could have developed no image at all of the *homo economicus* and the *homo politicus* and that they might find it extremely difficult to accept the implications of modern goods and money markets. Their background could not have prepared them in any way for Israel's secular society, or for interactive frameworks transcending ascriptive criteria of kinship and ethnicity.

We shall return to the already familiar Yemenite village of Shalekhet in order to demonstrate some of the most interesting aspects of this settlement, and refer—when necessary—to other communities as well.

The basic expectation which these immigrants had of Israel was the reconstruction in it—to the extent possible—of their native surroundings and original way of life. Since in the Yemen they had lived in a small kinship-based community; and since this tradition was further reinforced by the desire to be with a familiar group in the new situation, their settlement as one unit in a *moshav* seemed, *prima facie,* to be a most "natural" solution. The more so, because their individual households at home had always been independent units of production and such autonomy was very important to them.[12] When they came to Israel, however, they were sent first to a transitional work settlement near a large city, in which they worked as casual labourers in citrus orchards or on public works. This dramatic confrontation with what they conceived to be an alien, secular and therefore hostile world, and the jarring experience and humiliation entailed in their contact with the labour exchange for unskilled workers[13] served (if we are to believe what they now recall of this period) to make the idea of settling in a village of their own a *bona fide* deliverance for them. When the *moshav* was established a year later, they started up with a vast fund of good will and dedication, and viewed the geographical isolation of Shalekhet as a boon, since it protected them from exposing themselves and their children to some of the more pernicious influences of outside society.[14]

Identification with the *moshav* through a process of syncretism also characterizes attitudes to cultivation—more specifically, to work. We have already stressed that the occupational structure of these traditional Jewish communities prepared them for hard, mostly manual (though skilled) labour. The Yemenites, however, have been found to possess a more intrinsic point of view in this respect, not only based on long usage, but rather on the concept of work as a value in itself. In retrospect, this commitment can be traced to the premium they placed for generations on consistently serious and constructive occupations—whether religious or vocational—as against any conspicuous or "frivolous" waste of time.[15] Thus "traditional" factors were substituted here for secular pioneering in the promoting of a general sober attitude towards the whole enterprise.

One is indeed tempted to discern other elements of the "Protestant Ethic" in this pattern, such as an emphasis on frugality and a drive to save.[16] In Table 41 we show investment and development in livestock branches, over and above the official plan.

TABLE 41—Farmer Initiative in Development in *Moshav* Shalekhet

(a) *Composition of "privately" bought beef herd*	
Total of milk cows	10
Total of calves	32
Number of families with milk cows	10
Number of families with calves	17
(b) *Composition of "privately" bought sheep*	
Total of sheep	149
Total of lambs	109
Number of families with private sheep-pens	44
(c) *Composition of "privately" bought goat herds*	
Total of goats	54
Total of kids	51
Number of families with private goat herds	53
(d) *Composition of "privately" bought chickens*	
Total of layers	291
Total of chicks	50
Number of families with "private" chicken coops	36

While this effort seems puny compared with the "Western" entrepreneur (as was also the case regarding the *level* of cultivation) it certainly explodes the myth of a general traditional "lotus eater" who only works as much as is absolutely necessary in order to gain the essentials of life.

This particularly pronounced pattern is the result of the specific combination of Yemenite Jewish tradition and of village integration, which reinforced motivation and made it easier to tolerate agricultural and economic reverses, which resulted from poor cultivation and market crises.

Another characteristic of this group, perhaps more general and more fundamental, is that its members had had no previous contact—either direct or indirect—with agriculture; and were therefore quite free from any rigid commitment to specific patterns of production and marketing.

The seemingly paradoxical situation in which an agricultural (traditional) background is negatively rather than positively related to development, is exemplified by *Moshav* Koresh, which was settled mainly by Kurdish immigrants from the village of Bitnor in northern Iraq.[17] Like the farmers of Shalekhet, the settlers in Koresh also expected to be able to reconstruct their native way of life in Israel. This image, however, had a more direct relationship to the *moshav,* because it was based on a *projection of contrasting farm practices and beliefs.*[18] Let us examine the concrete reflection of this projection in some of the village's actual production branches.

Agriculture—and some cottage industries—were the main source of income for the Jewish families in Bitnor. Their farms were composed mostly of fruit orchards and livestock (beef and poultry); production was static, extensive, and employed very rudimentary techniques; and the household-based economy was on a subsistence level. The few additional items required by the population were obtained in the local exchange market.

The initial confrontation of this group with Koresh had, on the face of it, all the appearances of continuity. The topography, climate and flora of the Judean Hills, the small agricultural community, and the farm based on fruit trees and livestock all combined to create a feeling of familiarity and security and to reinforce the traditional farm beliefs and patterns of behaviour.

Needless to say, all this was soon found to be illusion; the new situation in fact being fundamentally characterized by intensive, scientific cultivation, by considerable investment, and by dependence on impersonal external markets and a bureaucratic marketing organization. One example was the fruit orchards, the main branch of production in Koresh. In spite of being market-oriented, the various stone fruit trees seemed to the settlers to have the enormous advantage of being relatively stable and secure, and good for many years of fruition. In reality, however, most of the settlers were unable to command the necessary professional orientation towards new cultivation methods. In this way, for example, they have consistently refused to adopt modern systems of pruning and thinning: "We didn't do it at home and nonetheless the yield was no lower", they said, or "Here the Settlement Department destroys our trees by thinning and pruning them", and so on.

More complex, and more broadly negative, was their reaction to the development of chicken coops—another branch with which they were familiar. Here, their objections had to do with the extremely complicated management, new-fangled ideas such as immunization, selection of layers, protection of feed from birds, etc., as well as the unstable and fluctuating market. So, although initially they welcomed (and even invested in) this branch, its first crisis—compounded from poor care and low prices—resulted in its being almost entirely liquidated. The same situation, more or less, was true as regards sheep. The main points of difference which impeded the development of this branch were three:

a. Sheep-herding was considered a very low status occupation. In Bitnor, it had been done by Arab urchins, for little or no pay. Therefore, in Koresh, the settlers employed special personnel for this purpose, a process which made the small flock completely unprofitable.

b. There were many problems connected with consumption and marketing. In Iraq, the main consumer had been the household itself, and the excess yield, if any, was processed and exchanged. In Israel, the settlers found it cheaper to buy what they needed in the local shop, and it was hard for them to adjust to the high standards of hygiene required in the commercial preparation and marketing of milk and milk products.

c. The same applied to wool production, which in Bitnor had been the basis of cottage industry, but in Koresh had to be completely reorganized and maintained on a large scale in order to be worthwhile.

Altogether, these settlers lacked that flexibility which is essential for successful modern farming. Its absence expressed itself on the one hand, in their inability to develop a rational orientation to agriculture as a market branch; and on the other, in their constant reference to past practices and norms as a basis for accepting and evaluating present ones. There were, of course, exceptions related primarily to age, but it is significant that a clear advantage in this respect lies with another group in the same village, composed of Kurds from Persia, who, though socially and culturally similar, are to be distinguished by their non-agricultural background.

From these brief sketches of the polar motivational types—modern and traditional—and some of their variations, it is justified to expect that the most balanced attitudes and adjustment will be found somewhere in between, i.e., in "transitional" social groups. And indeed, in *moshavim* that fall into this very broad category, there were none of the pronounced tensions we have mentioned above; many of them have developed in a steady, continuous way. This is all so self-evident as to make the presentation of any case-study or additional documentation unnecessary. But, two important qualifications must be made. *The "transitional" type of settler seems to be most sensitive to hardships and to agricultural crises and reverses, because he lacks both the high skill and the entrepreneurial perspective of the "modern" settler, and the low aspirations and high group solidarity of the traditional ones.* The history of *Moshav* Te'ena provides us with an instructive and relevant example. The settlers of this *moshav* came from Persia, mostly from the city of Shiraz, where they had been merchants and tradesmen and were neither inclined nor trained to become farmers. Before they immigrated, they had almost no idea of conditions prevailing in Israel, and no preparation for their new way of life. Their knowledge of their new country derived chiefly from propaganda which painted a rather rosy and inaccurate picture of life in Israel generally and in the *moshav* in particular. Besides, they came to the country as individuals, not as part of an organized group, and they had neither the necessary leaders, nor the experience, which would make it possible for them to function as an organized community, especially in times of stress. On the other hand, they had some financial means of their own, were fairly well educated, and came from a culturally homogeneous and stable background.

The delicate balancing of "positive" and "negative" factors pointed up the importance of the absorptive process in general, and of the initial confrontation with *moshav* life in particular. But the first stages of their settlement in Te'ena were disappointing. They lived for two years in tin huts which were suffocatingly hot in Israel's long summer, and cold and leaky during the rainy winter. The village was favourably situated, near a main road and not too far from urban centres, but it took nearly two years before an approach road was built. Bread and water often had to be carried across the fields, sometimes two and three miles from the nearest point accessible to trucks. Installation of water pipes took a long time; internal roads, electricity and telephone took even longer. When houses were put up at last, they consisted of two tiny rooms and were uncomfortable (addition of a third room is envisaged in the blueprint but usually provided by the authorities only for new large families, i.e., at least eight members). This congestion was further intensified by the frequent presence in a household of three generations at once—aged parents, the settler, his wife and children and unmarried brothers and sisters. The sizes of the 71 households in Te'ena were as follows: 16 had from one to four members; 37 had from five to seven members; and 18 had from eight to eleven members. At the disposal of these households were 18 three-room houses, occupied by families with eight or more members; 49 two-room houses (of which two are vacant); and six one-room houses (specially built for unmarried farm-owners and young couples). It is, therefore, not to be wondered at that housing and services were the first topics of conversation in almost all our interviews with the settlers.

Against this setting, we must now examine the problem of the market conditions in Te'ena. By the time the settlers began farming (around 1952) they had already suffered severe disillusionment, the results of which are not to be underestimated. On the one hand, there had been all the material difficulties described, and on the other, a long delay in actually embarking on farming. This had been caused by lack of irrigation piping and the protracted period of hard work on building, which alternated with unemployment. Although, financially, almost all the families could afford to weather the intermittent absence of income, its effect was very detrimental to their adjustment. Five families left the village, while others lived on in a state of constant anxiety. When water was finally brought in, in sufficient volume, in 1952, the settlers threw themselves (and their meagre remaining capital) into farming with considerable enthusiasm.

The economy planned for the *moshav* was a mixed-dairy type. The first irrigated dunams were accordingly devoted to intensive cultivation of vegetables, and as soon as fodder was grown, milch cows were allocated. During this first year of farming, the settlers invested an average of IL 500 of their own into each farm and often expended as many as four Standard Work Days per family in a single working day. But when the produce was disposed of, it was found that the proceeds did not even cover the expenses. There were many reasons for this: first of all, the unskilled farming technique of the settlers, which the two preparatory years had done little to correct (an aspect dealt with in Chapter 2); secondly—and this should have been made clear from the outset—a small dairy herd could not be expected to be profitable. What made the greatest impact on the villagers, however, was a steep decline in prices which affected both branches of their economy and for which they were not compensated by any subsidy. Seen in its proper perspective, this could be regarded as a normal development hardship. In fact, the Settlement Department stepped in energetically, explained the situation in detail, and began at once to plan a new farm type for the village, what was to be known as the industrial crops farm. Judging from the later success of this type, this would have been a sound solution for Te'ena. The price collapse, however, coming at such a critical juncture and in a sensitive situation, put an effective check upon the development of the village, on its agriculture, solidarity, and self-government. Twelve families cut their losses and left. Almost all of those who remained lost faith both in farming and in official promises, so much so that they asked the Settlement Authority to arrange for neighbouring veteran settlements to take responsibility for their farms, while they, the farm owners, would continue working as paid labourers. This suggestion was offered as a permanent solution, and the Authority (which was later to perfect the managed farm system as a stage in development) rejected the request out of hand. Most of the settlers then turned to outside employment, and each household made an effort to secure at least one permanent and regularly paid job. Since in several families, one working individual constituted the entire full-time labour force of the family, the farms seemed doomed. But even those families which did have enough manpower both for farming and to do outside work were disinclined to continue investing in their farms. This state of affairs persisted in Te'ena up to the time of our study (1959), some six years after the original crises, despite the fact that the farm type had been changed, and that funds had been offered for intensive development to make up for the delay. In effect, then, the village is still in an intermediate stage, the chief reason being the reluctance of its settlers to invest, or to accept development loans, or even to devote themselves full time to agriculture. Apart from some 20 people (several of whom persist in farming not out of choice but because they have not yet been able advantageously to liquidate their dairies and are not willing to cut their losses or let the property lose its value), most of the *moshav* is not primarily agricultural (Table 42).

TABLE 42—Farming in *Moshav* Te'ena

Extent of farm development	Number of farms	Number of households having outside work also
Farm cultivated and developed according to plan	13	7
Dairy farm, taken care of but awaiting liquidation	8	8
Farm partially cultivated half or two-thirds	26	15
Farm less than half-cultivated or neglected	24*	14
Total	71	44

* In two of these farms, the settler is a social welfare case, incapable of regular work.

A similar phenomenon of marking time, or even of regression, is evident in other spheres of *moshav* life. As we said before, these settlers came to Israel and Te'ena as individuals, and without any recognized leaders. Nevertheless they succeeded in evolving both a stable social structure and an active, able and devoted elite group (which was, in fact, largely responsible for the fact that the village weathered the initial shock of confrontation). Now, however, the *moshav* is in a state of apathy: it is still a social entity, but the common denominator on which it is based is of a very low order. The regular *moshav* institutions are maintained but there is little motivation fot the assumption of any public responsibility; the secretary is an outside official, and there is no active group, eager or capable of initiating any changes. All this, despite the fact that the economic situation is still below the settlers' expectations, whether they are employed outside or whether they cultivate their farms. As is already clear, none of these complex situations are the sole, or even the predominant, result of a single factor. In Te'ena, too, responsibility cannot be attributed solely to the causes we have mentioned; it may be traced also to demographic structure, to admitted preference for lighter work, to new social conditions introduced with the coming of the second group of settlers and the resulting challenge to established leadership, etc. This, however, in no way invalidates the analysis made, and the facet we have discussed here is of major importance.

On the other hand, "traditional" Jewish groups seem to be particularly vulnerable to feelings of status insecurity, perhaps because they come from places where a so-called Jewish problem exists: namely where Jews were neither completely secluded from, nor completely accepted by, the surrounding society. In such places Jews faced insoluble conflicts: they were expected to be loyal to the nations among whom they lived, but were discriminated against by the very people who demanded this loyalty; they were encouraged to acquire an education and to accept the values and way of life of their surroundings, but they were denied social acceptance and status, even when they did live up to the most exacting standards in all these respects. Such immigrants come to Israel in the hope that all problems of status and identity will be automatically resolved there. Their willingness to put up with any new status insecurity is, therefore, minimal. (With the exception of those who manage to turn their quest for identity into a comprehensive social ideology and come to Israel as members of organized social movements. But there have been few immigrants of this kind since the establishment of the State in 1948).

In this respect, there seem to be crucial differences between two distinct segments of the transitional population—those which may be labelled as "stable" or the gradually modernized, as opposed to the "unstable".

Contrasting patterns of this sort are exemplified by two distinct Jewish groups in former French Morocco.

a. The first pattern was found chiefly in provincial towns with old Jewish communities: Meknes, Fez, Rabat and Oujda. Their crucial characteristic was that the general and internal process of modernization they underwent was *moderate, gradual, integrated, and carried over a span of several generations*. Thus, though trades and crafts remained the main Jewish occupation, these became specialized and increasingly based on vocational training. Since the overall markets and finance had grown and become partly modernized, the Jews—so intimately connected with them—of necessity increased their own economic and commercial horizons and understanding. *Pari passu* with these tendencies, general education—though still chiefly on the elementary level—was introduced, both by the French authorities and by metropolitan Jewish voluntary associations. Consequently, while the standard of living of the broad Jewish strata was low, and political and social acceptance limited, mobility aspirations began to make themselves felt, and economic and vocational status criteria were introduced. By the same token, social relations started to transcend the narrow ascribed frameworks of kinship, locality and ethnicity; elders and religious leaders lost some of their dominance over the community. A new leadership, change- and modernization-oriented, began to develop. Not less significant was the fact that this new elite functioned together with the more traditional one. The two strata both restricted and complemented each other, so that one was not too hasty, while the other adjusted more smoothly to the idea and the facts of change, and, this being the case, there was relatively little social discontinuity or disorganization. Also in this way, no inordinate mobility aspirations, liable to undermine adjustment and confidence, were generated. *All in all then, there was a basic security of status and identity, which was conducive to acceptance of change.*

b. In contradistinction to the balanced transitional group, there emerged the "unsuccessfully modernized" elements of the developing and the cosmopolitan centres of Casablanca and Marakesh. Formally speaking—i.e., in respect to indices such as education, exposure to communication, etc.—the level of westernization of those people was, in many respects, similar to (if not more advanced than) the group we described above.

But there was an immense difference in the smoothness, speed, and framework in which this process was carried out. The Jews in question were, in fact, of immediate traditional rural or semi-rural origin, not more than one generation removed from this background: their immigration to urban centres was, moreover, usually on an individual basis and the transition involved them, on both counts, in sharp cleavage, a great discontinuity, and keen insecurity. Leaving the frameworks of origin as membership and reference groups, they evolved a strong orientation to the culture and society of the colonial power. But the status symbols which they acquired—outward appearance, dress and language—remained only external in the main and even usurped. The reasons for this were evident: here was a confrontation between a group which—though possessed of an elementary education and at home in a modern urban civilization—was, nevertheless, native and of a low socio-economic status, and between a colonial framework which by definition was exclusive and which represented an upper social stratum.

This discrepancy, however, did nothing to modify the nature, or lower the level, of their expectations. On the contrary, these aspirations became, as it were, their main psychological anchor in an otherwise rootless situation. And while they slid to marginal positions in the social, economic and the public spheres, they still identified themselves ritually with a high urban status and way of life. *In other words, the process of change involved the breaking-away from traditional frameworks and orientations, but did not entail a reintegration either within the European or the indigenous local Jewish communities.* Their social isolation and anomie thus became pronounced, and served to further strengthen the gap between expectation and achievement, and these Jews came to Israel inadequately prepared to face change, or particularly any deviation from the ritually-adhered-to image. Their status anxiety and crisis of identity expressed themselves in relation to the *moshav,* in literal abhorrence of manual labour, agriculture and rural life. The *moshav* was absolutely rejected, and the erstwhile settlers left, almost *en masse,* often to take up residence in urban slums.[19]

Conclusion

The foregoing discussion documented two basic, contrasting motivational patterns which were characteristic of different attitudes towards *moshav* life. The patterns dealt with by and large parallel the findings and the conclusions of a host of other, earlier studies—so much so that these very brief sketches were considered sufficient to evoke a whole familiar picture. However, precisely because of this familiarity, and the danger of generalizing from it too facilely, some of the facts bear repetition.

The use of such ideal-type constructs as "traditional" and "modern" is of a positive value only if it does not inhibit the search for and discovery of significant variations. Comparative analysis, in any case, demands sacrifices in the depth and sophistication needed for treating any of the individual units observed, and the level at which the general would be tempered with the particular must be determined in terms of aim and subject matter. However, care must be taken that the price, in terms of inevitable mistakes and over-simplifications, is not too great.

Just as important is the qualification that the reference to polar types is not taken to imply that they necessarily constitute extreme points of an ordered sequence. Although we hesitate, following Miner,[20] and a host of more recent studies,[21] to add yet another cautionary remark, it does seem clear that any concept of social change and modernization as a linear process of a "traditional-modern continuum" (visualized either as one scale, or as several dimensions moving in association)—is a simplistic one. It is not only that different structural, demographic and cultural indices may vary independently; but also, and possibly chiefly, that the "transitional" society is qualitatively as well as quantitatively set apart from both these extremes. It has its own specific social elements and structures; and, also, specific problems and susceptibilities. It has been demonstrated that "similar" transitional groups significantly differ in their orientation to, and potential for, sustained change (or, more specifically, in their reactions to change and crisis), and that these differences are associated, apart from anything else, with the very nature of the process of modernization. The crucial importance of basic security of status and identity in change processes generally, and in the matter of adjusting to—*and making the best of*—downward mobility in particular, is most dramatically emphasized when the crisis among the transitional immigrants is compared with the reaction of the "Western" settler. The latter, secure in his long middle-class "tenure", is willing to consider and even accept manual labour when circumstances so dictate; while those immigrants whose fathers (or they themselves) had only recently been workers, and who had just started the upward climb, were completely unable to tolerate any reversion in this respect.

This, perhaps, is the essential meaning of modernity—not that there are no traditions, but that *a free interplay* is permitted between legitimated customs and new factors; the situation itself is given a chance to convince and convert.[22]

NOTES

1 We have employed the concept of motivation here in the specific sense of the extent to which there is readiness to assume the *moshav* role, according to its specified requirements. This readiness has both qualitative and quantitative aspects, the first representing the composition of those motives in the light of which the role is either assumed or rejected; and the second, their strength. It is determined in relation to two levels of orientation: the level of the desired (or the hoped-for rewards); and the cognitive level, i.e., perceiving the *moshav* as it really is and evaluating it in relation to other openings—a distinction roughly equivalent to Kurt Lewin's expected and perceived milieu.

2 Agriculture is subsidized, and commands considerable, easy development credit; for people who have no professions or capital, there are, as a result, very few if any, equal economic opportunities.

3 Land utilization is the least significant index, since development is limited by the total of available land. However, not a single dunam lies fallow; and advantage is taken by neighbours who rent inactive parcels of land. (The less active farms, by the way, belong to demographically-unbalanced households, which lack sufficient manpower—see Chapter 1).

4 Data previously published in a case study of Zeviya: T. Horowitz, *From Gemeinschaft to Gesellschaft—a New Type of Moshav* (in Hebrew), (Jerusalem, Department of Sociology, Hebrew University, 1962).

5 See: G. Ballandier, "Comparative Study of Economic Motivation and Incentives in a Traditional and Modern Environment", *International Social Science Bulletin,* 1954 and O.C. McClelland and J.W. Atkinson, *The Achievement Motive* (New York, Appleton-Century-Crofts, 1953).

6 The reference is to *Tnuva,* the marketing cooperative of Israel's General Federation of Labour.

7 The reference here is to a proposed Bill (1958) which would permit village councils and the *Moshav* Movement to take legal sanctions against non-conforming settlers. Its provisions (it has not yet been passed) concern membership in the *moshav;* possession of *moshav* property by a non-member, and expulsion of a *moshav* member. The items which caused the most violent debate are those concerned with the cessation of membership in a *moshav.* The proposed law demands expulsion under the following circumstances:

(a) The member has a farm but does not work it, or is a member of a farming family under section (3) of article 171, and does not cultivate the farm, and this without the permission of the *moshav* General Assembly as set out in article 172 (a), or by breach of the conditions of permission granted by the Assembly, this body's decisions being final.

(b) The member regularly neglects his farm without sufficient cause.

(c) The member deliberately damages property or equipment intended to facilitate settlement and received from the Settlement Authority or the *moshav* itself.

(d) The member disturbs the peace either by overt violence or by threatening this, and who has been found guilty by an authorized court, or after this law has been passed, by a special court.

(e) The member lives permanently outside the *moshav,* without permission of its General Assembly, as under article 172 (a), or by a breach of any of the conditions granted by the Assembly.

(f) The member fails to fulfil those obligations laid down in the *moshav's* regulations defined as compulsory for all members, the breach of which is accepted as grounds for cessation of membership.

8 An analysis of the Ta'amon political elite, in relation to which these statements are more significant, can be found in Chapter 3.

9 Of 30 fathers interviewed in the two villages, only six wanted their children to continue on the family farm, or in rural life in general.

[10] Of course, this situation may change. Children who are still young now may become more attached to the *moshav,* or may—when faced with the irrevocable decision of letting a prosperous enterprise decline—have second thoughts, particularly in a situation of general national economic recession. Regional planning and development are likely to help by providing rural elite positions (see: D. Weintraub and O. Shapiro, "The Role of Rural Organization in Rural Development in Israel", *Sociologia Ruralis,* Vol. V, No. 3 (1965). Last, but not least, there may be some modification in the agrarian structure of the smallholding settlement itself. Discussion of these points is clearly beyond the scope of this book, and in any case could hardly invalidate our analysis.

[11] In some orthodox Moslem communities, particularly in Yemen, Jews were not allowed to own land, and maintained themselves, as did Jews in mediaeval Europe, mostly by exchange of various services with the surrounding society.

[12] The salience of this pattern in the Yemenite group can be observed even in third generation immigrant youth, for whom running a small family business still seems the most worthwhile plan for the future.

[13] The Jews in the Yemen were mostly skilled artisans. This particular group were all silversmiths—a highly respected occupation (see for instance: H. Scott, *In the High Yemen* (London, J. Murray, 1942)).

[14] Such intensity of motivation, though, is rare—primarily because transplantation of entire "organic" communities has been the exception rather than the rule. For further details, see Chapter 6, "Kinship Structure and Modernization."

[15] The Yemenites' idea of recreation was that of a clearly integrative or religious nature. Also symptomatically, they had a negative attitude to the irresponsibilities and the moratorium of childhood. Children assumed adult responsibilities, occupational and religious, very early in life—much earlier, in fact, than was customary in other groups which religiously symbolized maturity by the *rite de passage* of the *Bar-Mitzvah* at the age of 13. The Yemenites were the only traditional Jewish group which did *not* observe this ceremony—obviously because, in practice, the responsibilities it symbolized had already been assumed.
See, for example, S.O. Goitein, *Jewish Education in the Yemen as an Archetype of Traditional Jewish Education,* in C. Frankenstein, ed., *Between Past and Future* (Jerusalem, The Henrietta Szold Foundation for Child and Youth Welfare, 1953).

[16] During the first year in Israel—namely that of occasional labour in the transitional work settlement each household was able to save, and invest in its farm, the sum of approximately IL100 (then equivalent to £100). This pattern of saving and investment has continued.

[17] The data are based on O. Shapiro, *Moshav Koresh* (mimeo, Hebrew), (Jerusalem Land Settlement Department, 1959).

[18] Although, as we have mentioned, Jews in Moslem societies were not allowed to own land, in some places chiefly in Iraqi Kurdistan and in the Atlas Mountains in Morocco—certain informal arrangements existed, which actually permitted some Jews to make their living from farming. This was true also of the Iraqi Bitnor group. Such arrangements were various: land could be rented, or held as security against loans; or a farm might be cultivated in partnership—the Arab providing land and most of the labour, and the Jew participating via "capital"—i.e., the livestock. Cases of this sort—though chiefly as part-time farming, rather than as primary occupations—have been documented even in the Yemen—e.g. in the village of Geddes. See S.D. Goitein, *Portrait of a Yemenite Weavers' Village,* (New York, Conference on Jewish Relations, 1955).

[19] The author once talked to the head of this kind of family (from Baghdad) which had literally suffered pangs of hunger for six years because he had refused to accept public works employment. He said, "But how can I do such shameful work *publicly?*"

[20] H. Miner, "The Folk-Urban Continuum", *American Sociological Review,* Vol. 17, (October 1952).

[21] See for example:
G. Beaumert, and E. Lupri, "New Aspects of Rural-Urban Differentials in Family Values and Family Structure", *Current Sociology,* Vol. 12, No. 1, (1963/64);
Herbert Kotter, "Changes in Urban-Rural Relationships in Industrial Society", *International Journal of Comparative Sociology,* Vol. 14, No. 2, (1963);
R.E. Pahl, "The Rural-Urban Continuum", *Sociologia Ruralis,* Vol. VII, No. 1, (1967);
E. Lupri, "The Rural-Urban Variable Reconsidered", *Sociologia Ruralis,* Vol. VII, No. 1, (1967).

[22] The fact that many "Western" settlers were not ultimately convinced by the *moshav* is irrelevant in this context and is the result of the existence of competing alternatives, which fitted in more closely with their expectations. Recent developments in Israeli society lend special importance to this point. One such change, associated with, or intensified by the transition to statehood, relates to the prevalent status criteria. During the pre-state *(Yishuv)* period, a particular type of status, best represented by political leaders and pioneers, was accorded the highest prestige. More specifically, the criteria associated with highest status were public activity and participation in some kind of cooperative or collective movement. The income of people who enjoyed this status was typically low, and considered unimportant. By contrast, other status configurations—such as the urban "middle class"—were rated much lower. Recently, new values, and elites embodying them, have emerged, chiefly professional, governmental and entrepreneurial. These new elites have increasingly become the foci for competitive reference, as well as targets of mobility aspirations. As a result of this and other processes, the pioneering settlement is no longer—or to a much lesser degree— a symbol of the ultimate values of society. This development significantly limits the 'missionary' success of *moshav* ideology, especially in respect to the "modern" immigrant, whose urban status-image might be reinforced by the general tendencies described.

PART TWO

In this part of our book we will try to refine some of our earlier findings, study the continuing processes of change, and evaluate future trends. The analysis now presented relates to two main topics, to each of which we have assigned two chapters:

The first deals with traditional kinship in the process of modernization, with emphasis on lineage and family respectively; the second concerns itself with the aspirations and future plans of the younger generation, and with the significance of these for the *moshav,* paying special attention to general orientation to change and to specific educational, occupational and social patterns, and expectations.

An additional chapter sums up the village developments in figures, showing the range of variability which they present. All data in Part II were collected from 1963 to 1964.

CHAPTER 6

KINSHIP STRUCTURE AND MODERNIZATION

Introduction

Our purpose in this chapter is to analyze those social factors responsible for the striking difference in development and modernization of two neighbouring villages located in the mountain district near Jerusalem (see map opposite). Of particular interest is the fact that both these villages have virtually identical farming and market conditions, population, and extension service; i.e., they resemble each other in exactly the areas to which variability in development is so frequently traced. We have, therefore, a sort of a laboratory situation, making it possible for us to examine systematically the effect of structural social factors on development and modernization. The analysis falls into four parts: first, we shall describe the similarity of background and setting of both villages; next, we shall show how divergent are the roads each has taken; we shall then try to link this divergence with differences in kinship structure; and finally trace the historical processes responsible for the crystallization of contrasting kinship patterns.

Background and Population

The *moshavim* of Erga and Zafrira are situated in the Jerusalem area, some two miles apart. Their climate, topography, soil, market situation, and general facilities are much the same. Their economies are equally based on the mixed mountain type of agriculture and comprise the same production branches. In both villages, each settler was allocated the same amount of land[1] and water. Both *moshavim* were established at the same time, and settled by immigrants from Kurdistan—people with one culture of origin, similar occupational and educational backgrounds, and identical motivations for immigration to Israel, to say nothing of twin attitudes to agriculture and rural life. Erga numbers 43 households, and Zafrira 70.

Their essentially shared heritage is also reflected in their similar demographic pattern, as regards marriage, fertility, and mortality. They are alike also in respect to distribution of their manpower and age-composition (see Appendix 1).

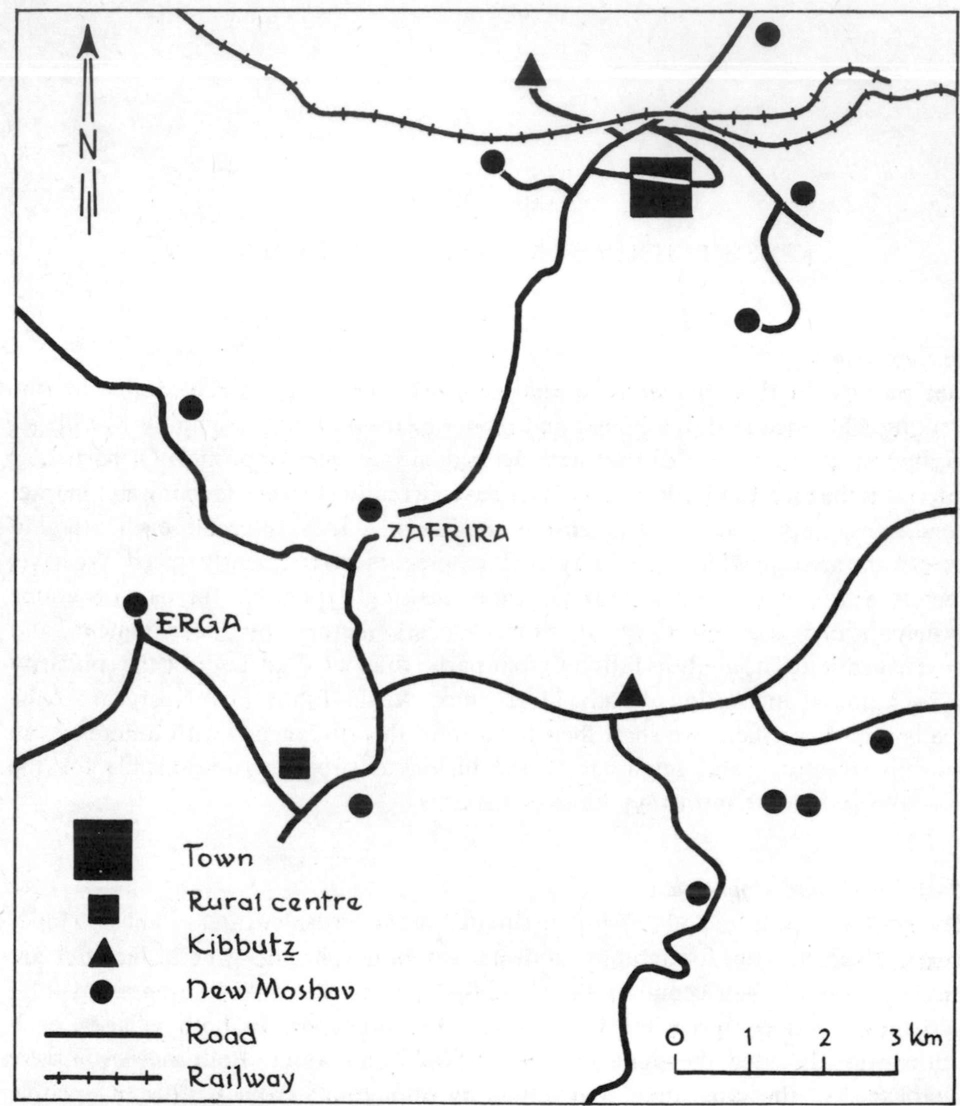

MAP 9. Location of Erga and Zafrira

Economic, Political, and Social Development

The differences in economic, political, and social development of these villages stand out against the similarity of their physical characteristics, cultural and communicative backgrounds, and demographic features. Let us briefly compare each of these areas in turn (fuller data are given in Appendix 2).

1. ECONOMIC DEVELOPMENT

A. *Cultivated area.* While in Erga, the maximum cultivated area is 14 dunams with two-thirds of the farms not exceeding 10, in Zafrira most of the farms are larger, two-thirds of the households cultivating an area of from 20 to 24 dunams.[2]

B. *Number of Standard Work Days required on the farm.*[3] The average number of yearly Standard Work Days in Erga is 122.4, while in Zafrira it is 241.4—or almost twice as many.

C. *Level of proficiency in farming.*[4] The farmers' proficiency was graded on a scale 0 to 100. While the average level of skill in Erga was 31, in Zafrira it was 55. Moreover, whereas in Erga only 19 percent of the population achieved a score higher than 40, and none exceeded 53, in Zafrira over half the population scored more than 50, the highest score being over 70.

D. *Gross farm income per household.* This index was based on the settlers' testimonies, and is not, therefore, entirely reliable.

While in Erga not one family was found whose farm brought in an income of more than IL2,000 per year, in Zafrira 45 percent of the households boasted at least this income. Since the great majority of Erga settlers, and some of those in Zafrira, supplement their farm income by outside work, we computed the overall income per family, and found that, while in Erga 83 percent of the families declared an income of less than IL2,000, in Zafrira only 34 percent earned so little. In short, while some of the indices we used are crude, they demonstrate quite vividly how very great the economic gap is between the two *moshavim*.

2. POLITICAL DEVELOPMENT

Local government in the two villages, primarily the two central political institutions—the Nominations Committee and the Village Council—is also very different.

The Nominations Committee is charged with the drawing up of a list of candidates for council election, but in most established villages this work extends to the canvassing of the various factions and pressure groups, in order that the most acceptable candidates be selected on the broadest possible basis. But in Erga nominations are decided by the two basic political groups, each one representing a combination of two kinship networks.[5] Each group submits a list of five names from its membership, and then votes for this list *en bloc*. There is no exchange of ideas, and no attempt at adjustment and accommodation; the political process is limited to the struggle for the "floating" votes and the ballot is obviously collective. The council represents one political group rather than the village as a whole, and it is not either generally supported or legitimated by the *moshav* as such.

In Zafrira the active nominations committee is composed of members of the three largest kinship groups. Its terms of reference are also kinship-oriented, and it functions among the kinship-based political units. There is, however, a prior adjustment of interests as well as of personalities, and the final list of candidates includes as many groups as possible, and is voted for on an individual basis. Council members are in this way elected directly and represent the entire village, rather than just one political unit in it.

The difference between the two villages is also reflected in the structure and functioning of the council. As seen in Chapter 4, the *moshav* council is a central administrative body, responsible for all municipal and cooperative services, and thus the focal point of political struggle. In Erga, the council is elected by a small majority which is controlled by one of the two political cliques or coalitions between two kinship groups. Frequent shifts in the allegiance of the "floating" voters make it impossible for any one political group to plan or implement any long-term programme. The council cannot run proper municipal or economic services or undertake any real responsibility for the welfare of the village as a whole, because the candidates are nominated only on the basis of kinship seniority, not on the basis of their ability. The council, being founded on a narrow, ascriptive basis, tends primarily to advance the interests of the in-group. Political office is seen in terms of particularistic obligations and the reinforcement of the traditional status of kinship elders. The situation became so serious that outside people were appointed to many decision-making positions on the council by the Land Settlement Department in order to exclude various vital administrative jobs from the sphere of political conflict. This arrangement, of course, further minimized the participation of the settlers in their own government. In other words, the organization of Erga still resembles the situation documented in other villages in the first stage of the research, five years earlier.

In Zafrira, the five-man council has, over a number of years, managed to reconcile some of the various political interests, including two members from the largest kinship network, and one each from three other groups. In this way four of the six groups are "in", i.e., there is representation of over 80 percent of the electorate in the council. Its universalistic orientation is also significant: once elected, members rise above considerations of kinship and really get down to promoting the welfare of the *moshav* itself.

This orientation has been accompanied by changes in the criteria for election to and, consequently, in the composition of the council. Until 1958, members were elected, as in Erga, on the basis of traditional status, but since then kinship groups have started to nominate those members best qualified to manage village affairs. Initially, the younger people were given specialized jobs below the decision-making level; but having proved themselves in these fields they were given positions of greater responsibility (such as the secretaryship of the village), while the elders retained the headship of the council and most of the seats. Gradually, the younger generation assumed a higher proportion of the formal offices, while the traditional leaders kept their prestige within the kinship group, providing the still-needed legitimation of economic and political activities, and preserving traditional values. Friction over these changes has been cut to a minimum by drawing a line between public and private spheres, the solidarity of the family, the deference accorded to parents and elders, and the acceptance of religious obligations on household and community levels.

The institutionalization of youth in the leadership elite of Zafrira is reflected in the different ways in which the two villages regard the appointment of younger people to various posts: their chances of reaching leadership positions stand at 23 percent in Erga and 63 percent in Zafrira.[6]

3. SOCIAL DEVELOPMENT

Erga and Zafrira also differ considerably in the extent of their social modernization, in the sense of the "unfreezing" and differentiation of traditional frameworks of interaction. These differences are reflected in the varying friendship networks of the two *moshavim* arrived at with the help of a sociometric questionnaire, which asked each settler to name his two best friends.[7] Examination of these charts (see Figs.1,2) shows that in Erga there are two main groups, which largely coincide with the basic political division of the village into two "coalitions" of kinship networks and that each group is subdivided into two clusters. Table 43 gives the population distribution of Erga by kinship,[8] friendship, and political affiliation,[9] and shows how strongly traditionally imbedded political criteria influence the choice of friends: for example, all nine of the members of friendship group 1 belong to political group 1; only four—two in friendship group 2 and two more in group 4—have friends who are not affiliated with their political group. This connection between personal friendship and kinship-based political commitment not only reflects a congealing of the undifferentiated traditional structure, but is also a further obstacle to village unity. Any change in the political setup[10] is likely to disrupt friendships and, conversely, each personal quarrel turns into a political crisis.

In Zafrira, on the other hand, there are seven friendship groups which are unrelated to any other grouping. Table 44 shows that there is no significant connection between the kinship frameworks (and the political units identical with them) and personal friendship; members of the same kinship network belong to different friendship groups; and every friendship group includes people from various kinship units.

The contrast is just as striking with regard to relations among the different friendship frameworks. As shown in the sociograms, most friendship groups in Zafrira are linked by a system of outwardly oriented sociometric stars,[11] of which there are two in almost each of the friendship groups. The more popular of these usually gives his

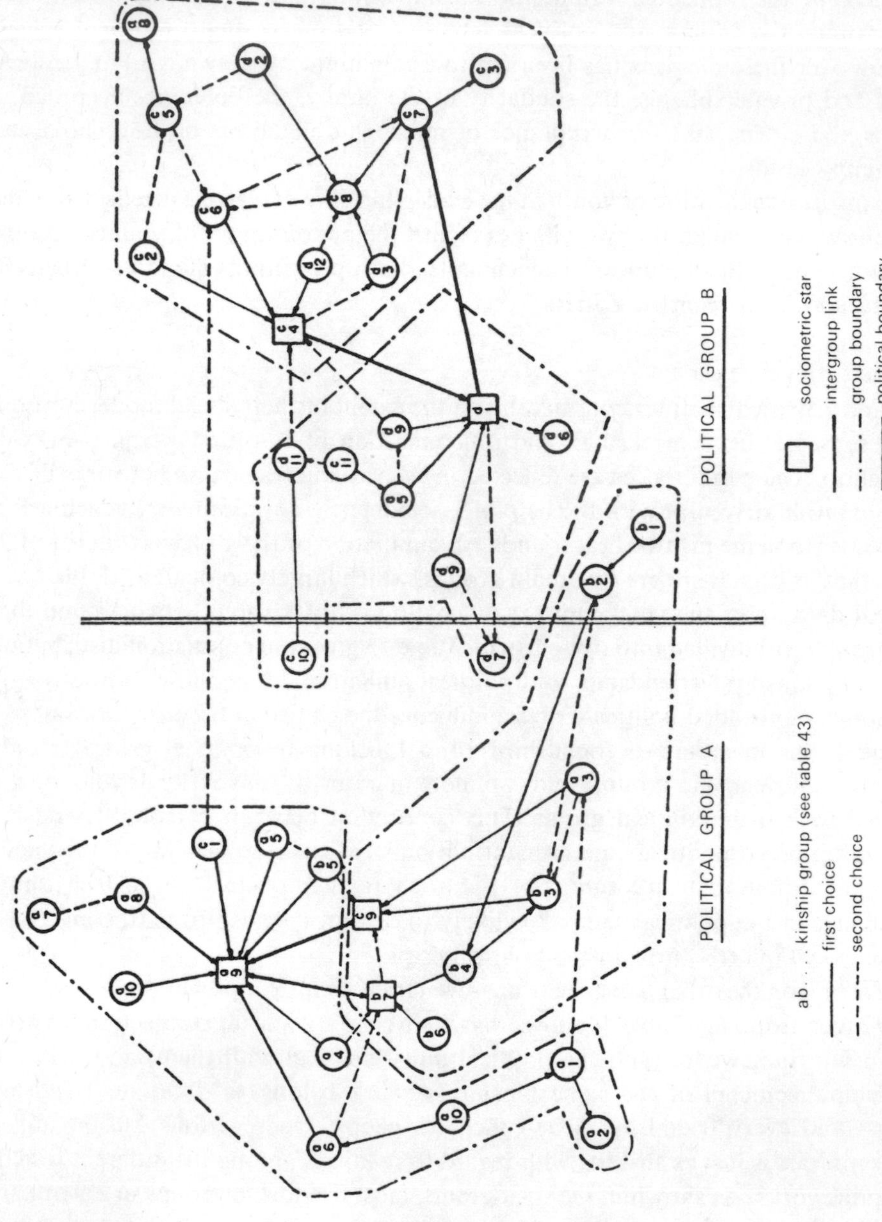

FIGURE 1. Sociogram of Friendship in Erga (first two choices)

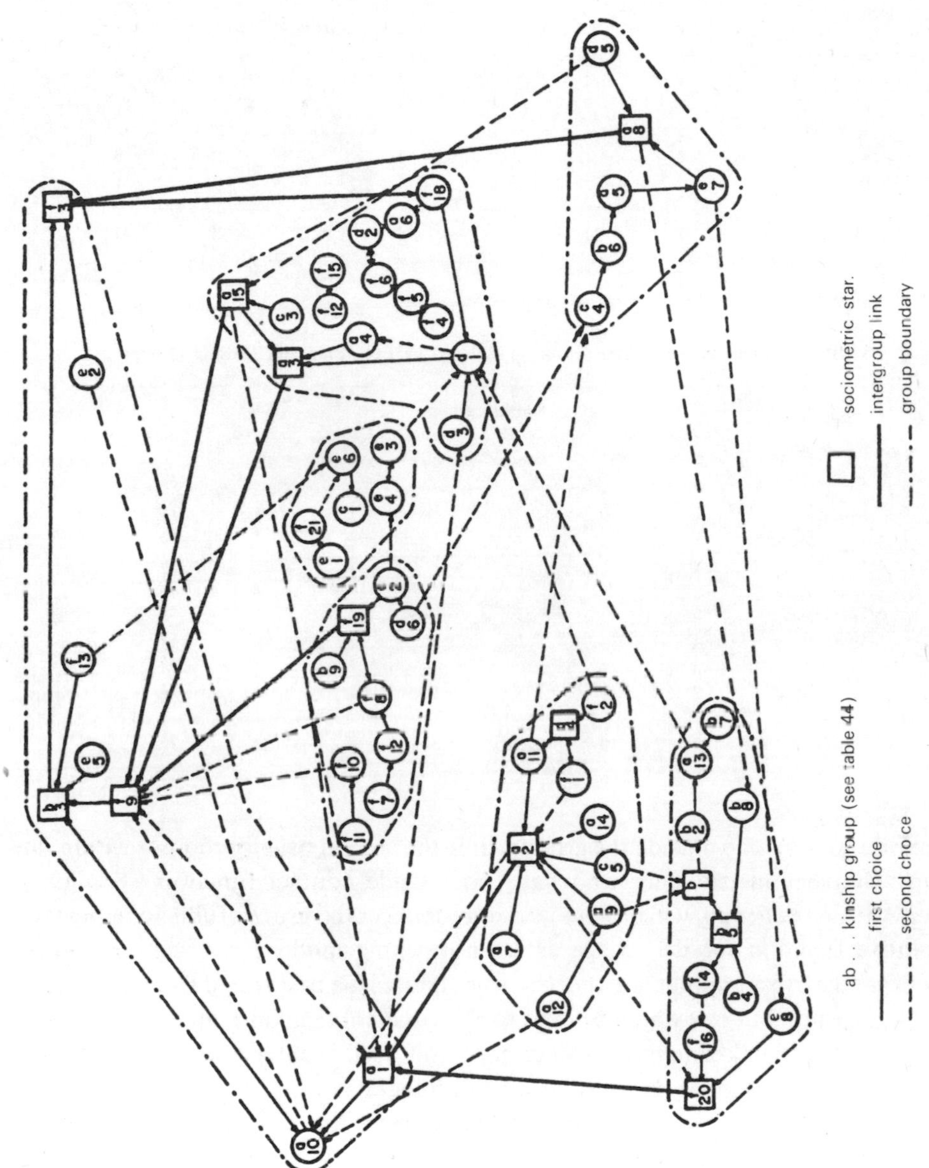

FIGURE 2. Sociogram of Friendship in Zafrira (first two choices)

TABLE 43—Farmers in Erga (including Isolates) by Friendship, Kinship and Political Groups

Friendship group	Kinship group					Political division		
	a	b	c	d	Total	Group I	Group II	Total
1			2	7	9	9		9
2			7	4	11	9	2	11
3	9	1	1	1	12		12	12
4	1	6	1		8	2	6	8
Isolates				1	1	1		1
Total	10	7	11	13	41	21	20	41

TABLE 44—Farmers in Zafrira (including Isolates) by Friendship and Kinship Groups

Friendship group	Kinship group						Total
	a	b	c	d	e	f	
1	1	6	–	–	1	3	11
2	6	—	1	1	–	2	10
3	2	1	1	1	1		6
4	—	1	1	1	–	6	9
5	—	—	1	–	4	1	6
6	4	—	1	3	–	6	14
7	2	1	–	–	2	3	8
Isolates	2	1	–	2	–	1	6
Total	17	10	5	8	8	22	70

first choice to someone outside the group, while the second usually chooses within the group. The sociometric stars who have no outside contact function as solidary leaders within the group, while those who interconnect the groups fulfil an important integrative function for the village as a whole along modern, associational lines.

In Erga, the most popular sociometric star chooses his best friend from a different friendship group, but one which belongs to the same political unit. Since the political units are not interlinked here, and since each unit itself is subject to changes caused by the "floating" element, there is no overall integration.

We have traced briefly, through selected aspects, the differences in economic development and political and social modernization between the two villages. Seen against their uniformity of background and setting, and forming within the short span of ten years, this contrast seems nothing short of amazing. Part of the explanation for it can probably be found in the mutual reinforcement and cumulative nature of the changes. But feedback mechanisms cannot account for the initial differences, nor can they be automatically maintained. It is suggested therefore that the different kinship structure of Zafrira, reinforced by a more homogeneous group composition provided this basis and has served ever since as the backbone of the *moshav's* development. Since the significance of social homogeneity for culturally similar traditional immigrants has already been documented in respect to such villages, we will focus attention mainly on the kinship structure, and mention the associated factor only when clarity so demands.

The Kinship Structure of Erga and Zafrira

As we have already said, the "traditional" Jewish community—to which the Kurdish Diaspora belonged—was organized in a highly familistic way, and the family unit determined social interaction and the division of labour. This pattern was characterized by a very strong attachment to kinship and territorial groups, by limitation of social interaction to these groups, and by an unwillingness to "cooperate" with outsiders. The basic framework of this type was, it will be recalled, the *hamoula,* that is, the Mediterranean patrilineal and patrilocal lineage. In their country of origin, members of the Kurdish *hamoula* usually formed a neighbourhood group (which sometimes involved an entire village), membership in this case implying the obligation to give economic help, hospitality, political support, and general protection to other members. These bonds did not require communal or cooperative arrangements in production, and the individual households (usually comprising the extended family) were the units of production and consumption, as well as of socialization. Status, however, was determined primarily by the importance of the *hamoula* and by the member's position in it. The *hamoula* was usually endogamous, and often had a special prayer version and synagogue and thus engendered an intense loyalty that easily overrode any other affiliation.

As seen earlier (Chapter 3), familism as a value, and as a pattern of social organization, continued after immigration to Israel, and fitted in "naturally" to the small community pattern, even being reinforced by the crisis of migration and the greater scope of activity in the *moshav*. The structural integrity of the kinship units, however, was sometimes impaired during the process of settlement. As a result, the original criterion of membership—direct patrilineal descent—became blurred and *quasi-hamoulas,* representing the familistic principle but permitting ties by marriage and territorial cliques began to emerge. Erga and Zafrira differ considerably in this respect, the one having a more "simulated" or modified kinship structure, the other a more "organic" one.[12]

These kinship systems in each of the two villages, which may be seen in chart form in Appendix 3, were analyzed with reference to three specific characteristics, assumed to represent "organic" continuity; these are the "density" of the network, or the extent to which it is based on close blood ties (father-son, sibling, uncle-nephew, cousins, grandfather-grandson), or else on distant or marriage ties;[13] the historic memory of the members; and the size of the units themselves.

In Table 45, we see that the kinship network in Zafrira is much denser than in Erga; 76 percent of the relationships are close blood ties, as against only 49 percent in Erga. Moreover, in Erga only one out of four groups has a hard core of close blood ties, while in Zafrira this is true of five out of six groups.

TABLE 45—Kinship Networks in Erga and Zafrira According to Type of Tie (Based on Adult Male Population)

Erga			Zafrira		
Group	Type of tie		Group	Type of tie	
	Close blood tie	Distant or by marriage		Close blood tie	Distant or by marriage
a	7	3	a	16	1
b	3	4	b	8	2
c	5	6	c	5	—
d	5	8	d	4	4
			e	6	2
			f	14	8
Total	20	21	Total	53	17
Percent	49	51	Percent	76	24

The historic memory of the two villages, as expressed in the number of generations mentioned and how far back names of lineal ancestors could be recalled, was much stronger—by as much as 30 percent—in Zafrira. This memory tends to be related to the density of the network, so that it may be a corollary of the higher intensity and salience of the closely knit group. In any case, in Zafrira it reinforces the "organic" continuity of the units.

The same trend exists with regard to the relative size of the kinship groups in the *moshavim*: Erga is characterized by four more or less equal groups, while in Zafrira there are two units that are appreciably larger than the others, and which form a natural nucleus of authority.

These factors are of considerable relevance in terms of political organization. Neither in Erga nor in Zafrira are there divisions based on ideology, policy, or economic interests; the political struggle deals with power and prestige, and alignment tends to be vertical, corresponding to kinship lines.[14] But its extent and nature differs significantly in the two communities. In Erga there are two political units, each based on a coalition of two kinship groups. This identity, however, is incomplete, since the coalition is between closely blood-related nuclei, while the households attached by marriage, or by distant relationship, are "floating" elements, courted by everyone. Thus, ties which are not "dense" or "organic" form no politically binding criteria: of 22 adults remotely related to their kinship networks, 12 crossed family lines in their political choices during the year of our research. On the face of it, the situation seems to be one of greater flexibility, with the "floating" vote preventing hardening of the political structure along rigid ascriptive lines. In reality, though, the "unattached" traditional households are incapable of giving loyalty to one group for a prolonged period of time and constantly change sides. The situation is aggravated by the heterogeneity of origin of the Erga *hamoulas*,[15] so that political stability is never achieved, and there is no basis for any concerted community action.

In Zafrira identity between political affiliation and kinship is complete: each of the six networks constitutes a political unit, which includes both close and distant kinship ties. There is thus a qualitative difference between the structural effect of the "organic", closely knit kinship system and that of the loosely knit one: the first holds marginal members together, while the other does not. Moreover, this greater internal cohesion keeps the networks from becoming intransigent, thanks to the existence of a dominant social group and to their homogeneity of origin. The solidarity of the component units in this way is associated with over-all village unity. It would thus appear that as long as ascription remains the decisive element of social organization, "organic" kinship networks and homogeneous social composition are able to constitute a positive force for the integration of the community, and for its crystallization at a high level of activity and efficiency.

The apparent paradox lies in the fact that the strong kinship units of Zafrira, while upholding traditional organization, do not strengthen resistance to innovation and change. On the contrary, it is this integrated kinship-embedded political system that produced more modern political behaviour and greater social differentiation. This process seems to have come about mainly via two interrelated mechanisms.

1. *Conditions facilitating the emergence of young leadership within the traditional framework.* The leader of the younger generation in Zafrira—the most vocal and gifted of its members—was located strategically within the central extended family belonging to the *moshav's* largest *hamoula*. By staying within the kinship framework, accepting its authority and drawing upon its legitimation, and by the successful performance of his own functions which enhanced the *hamoula's* status, this young man has gained the support of the whole *hamoula* for his election as the first fairly youthful chairman of the council. Since then, he has won the support of other kinship groups and considerable personal popularity,[16] all of which reinforced his position within his kinship unit. Undoubtedly, some of the credit must go to his own personality and qualifications. But even the most competent and charismatic candidate

could not have succeeded without specific structural conditions, which let secondary innovating elites become effective and gain the support of a central traditional group.

This particular blend of kinship-embedded political organization, on the one hand, and achievement and universalism in elite selection and government, on the other, has played a crucial role in the development of a balanced process of modernization, and has prevented the emergence of new factions and demands which the new elite might have been unable to meet.

2. *Differential toleration of change.* In contrast to Erga, the "dense" kinship networks of Zafrira were able to absorb and to secure the political loyalty also of distantly related households. An inverse situation obtained in respect to social interaction, and friendship outside the *hamoula* was characteristic of the stronger rather than the weaker system. It would appear that this derived from the greater structural flexibility of the "organic" group which was more capable than the "simulated" one of co-existing with competing patterns of organization. In other words, an assured core of real loyalty allows the group, as it were, to "unfreeze" or release part of the commitments due to it, while the lack of such a core hardens resistance to any innovation.

Table 46 pinpoints this structural difference. Here, the population of each community is divided into those who are close blood relations to their kinship groups, and those who are merely distantly related, or related by marriage, to them. In Erga each friendship group contains a nucleus composed of close relatives who choose friends within the nucleus. In Zafrira, on the other hand, even those who are centrally located in the kinship system are free to choose their friends from outside it.

We must now take a brief look at some of the historical factors responsible for the crystallization of different kinship structures and compositions, in both villages.

TABLE 46—Population of Erga and Zafrira by Type of Tie to Kinship Group and Choice of Friends

Choice of friends / Type of tie to kinship group	Erga			Zafrira		
	Outside kinship group	Within kinship group	Total	Outside kinship group	Within kinship group	Total
Close blood relations	3	16	19	22	19	41
Distant or marriage ties	9	10	19	9	6	15
Total	12	26	38	31	25	56

The Background: Some Earlier Social Processes

The most significant difference in the histories of the people of these two villages is that, before they came to Israel, the settlers in Zafrira already constituted a group—

though a loose one—whose members knew each other, shared common experiences and had a common purpose. Although the various *hamoulas* lived in different localities and are thus different in this respect from those in a village like Shalekhet, they all came from Barazani's district in Iraq, were all involved in his abortive rebellion of 1945, and together fled in order to escape persecution by local sheikhs. When they learned of the establishment of the State of Israel in 1948, they assembled in Baghdad, clustering there around the leading *hamoulas* for nine months, and then together, were flown to Israel.

The settlers of Erga, on the other hand, came from different regions, did not know each other beforehand, and were thrown together by chance. They included 32 immigrants from various parts of Iraqi Kurdistan, and a large minority of 11 Turkish Kurdish families. This minority group was integrated, but the majority was divided against itself. From the point of view of systematic analysis, the clue to the situation is that the factor of selection and village composition was left to chance—and this, in the context of the social, cultural, and ethnic heterogeneity of all the immigrant groups to Israel and the disorganization inevitably associated with migration. It was thus quite by accident that a relatively homogeneous and cohesive nucleus composed of "organic" networks was sent to Zafrira, and that Erga, by contrast, was filled up piecemeal by Turkish and Iraqi Kurds as well as by some Moroccans (who left later). The greater heterogeneity of origin was thus accompanied by greater fragmentation of settlement.

The situation created in Erga actually dovetailed, initially, with the official "melting pot" policy of absorption, which aimed at quick integration of different groups of origin. Afterwards, because of social crises in many villages, this policy was abandoned in the *moshavim* themselves and attempted at a regional level. For existing villages, however, it was by then too late to make any changes, short of complete upheaval. Nor was there as yet any real understanding among policy makers of the significance of social homogeneity for a "traditional" population; and when the Moroccans left Erga, it became, by Settlement Authority criteria, socially uniform. In a situation like this, nothing could be done by the settlers themselves; the village was much too small to prevail on any one group to leave in order to create greater political stability, and there was no natural nucleus around which the settlers could reorganize themselves. In Zafrira, however, a similar situation could be and was resolved. Here, too, the first group of settlers did not fill all the farm units in the village, and the Settling Authority sent in "reinforcements". The newcomers, composed of one *hamoula* and fringes, were strangers to the original settlers and did not integrate well within the village. There was constant trouble with them, and the presence of a "militant" minority, which refused to accept the "rules of the game", was very disruptive. This situation culminated in an all-out fight (to the point that firearms were used) following which most of the "active" intruders left the *moshav*. The vacant farms were then reallocated to sons of farmers, the population being strong and large enough to resist introduction of another batch of new settlers, and the social fabric was mended.

It seems, then, that the following historical factors favoured Zafrira over Erga: (1) previous acquaintance and interaction abroad, (2) some signs of early organization around dominant and organic groups, and (3) selection by rejection and ejection during the early years of settlement.

General Remarks

In the foregoing analysis, we have examined the place of kinship structure in development and modernization processes in two ostensibly similar agricultural villages in Israel.

The data refine and extend earlier findings on the confrontation of traditional groups with the *moshav*. In Chapters 3 and 4 we have seen that a basic integrity of the traditional social structures was initially a necessary condition for adjustment to the new reality, and for the corporate activity of the group as such. Here we observe that this association may be maintained beneficially even when the process of change is intensified and maintained. We have learned that traditional patterns can be used to facilitate modernization through social integration, regulation of mobility, and mobilization of resources for new policies and goals. Of critical importance in this respect is the demonstration that a traditional "lag"—or structural discrepancy in development—may be functional for efficiency of the system and its continued and orderly change.[17]

The question arises whether traditional patterns, which can be incorporated into the processes of modernization, should be encouraged to do so; i.e., what is the balance of profit and loss in taking into account traditional patterns? Put simply, the argument is between possible loss of speed and possible gain in social continuity. Our study suggests one criterion at least for a generally valid conclusion, namely, the *type* of modernization which is attempted. When modernization is individually oriented—as it is in industrialization and urbanization—the "atomization" and dispersion of traditional structure seems to be indicated. But when change refers to a total community—as represented by the cooperative village—some adherence to traditional structures as units of interaction seems essential.

In formulating these conclusions, though, one important caution must be borne in mind. The data presented refer to certain developments which occurred within the kinship unit, and to some mechanisms which related these to the modernizing community. The analysis has thus been largely structural or formal, and does not do justice to the internal processes underlying the situation we studied—to the tensions, the differences and the sense of loss which were inevitably generated, nor to the personal and interpersonal adjustments which have come into being as a response to these. Some of these processes, though on the level of the family rather than of the wider kinship group, form the subject of our next chapter, and hopefully they will, in part, fill the gap.

NOTES

1 Each farm was given six dunams ($1\frac{1}{2}$ acres) of arable land under irrigation, excluding fruit orchards which were cultivated by the village as a whole (12 dunams were reserved for further development) and ten sheep. Sheep pens and chicken coops (the latter to be developed on individual initiative) were provided as part of a long-term loan scheme.

2 Size of farm is a good measure of development and innovativeness since (see above) each unit has a built-in reserve allowing the farmer to expand as fast as he can increase his ability to farm more land. Additionally, he can also rent plots from less active neighbours—something that was indeed done in Zafrira though not in Erga.

3 In this index, the annual agricultural production in all branches is expressed in the workdays required according to established norms. The measure, while related partly to the size of the farm, is not the function of it; it reflects also the intensity of cultivation of any given area, as well as livestock development; and it is significant here too when the size of the farm is controlled. Because of a similar farm composition, there is little bias due to heavily manpower-loaded branches.

4 The grading of the farmers was done by a panel of experts on the basis of a questionnaire and observed performance. Data included a sample of activities in a sample of crops (and livestock) within each branch. The skill expended on each operation was defined against generally established norms relating to timing, quantity and quality. The degree of skill was then weighted according to the importance of the crop within the farm type (so that proficiency in a marginal crop would not be given undue place) and according to the real value of the activity for the success of the crop.

5 This structure is explained fully below, and the exact relationship between it and between the political system is traced.

6 Based on a survey of all heads of households in the two villages—70 in Zafrira and 43 in Erga.

7 Friendship groups were defined on the basis of sociometric connections—each group consisting of a network of first and second choices (of one person and by one person). In case of membership in more than one group by this criterion, (a) first choice determined over second choice, (b) the person was placed in the group to which he had more sociometric ties.

8 Operationally, the kinship groups were defined on a twofold basis:
(a) self-identification by households as belonging to one group.
(b) nomination by key informants. There was *complete* agreement between the two criteria, and not a single case of dual membership in these terms, so that kinship status was quite objectively and subjectively clear.

9 For determination of political groups see Note 14.

10 That is, a shift in the allegiance of the "floating" votes.

11 Identified by the number of choices received.

12 The term "organic"—even though in quotation marks—is not a very happy choice in this context, but we used it for want of a better word. Clearly, the process of migration and confrontation with the *moshav* has meant a break in continuity for all groups of this kind, and they are all reconstituted entities. The difference lies in the nature of the reconstituted entity, that is to say, the extent to which it approximates or reconstructs an earlier pattern. "Organic" here means thus "neo-traditional" rather than strictly continuous.

13 As pointed out above (Note 8), each kinship group represented a clearly identified entity. Within this entity, each individual was considered to have a kinship tie with every other member of the group.

Initially, these ties were classified into three types: (a) close blood relations (as defined above); (b) distant blood relations—that is, blood ties of a degree not defined as close (e.g., third cousins); and (c) relations by marriage. However, analysis of data showed that the latter was insignificant, and we grouped all ties not of the close blood-tie type as "distant or by marriage".

14 In establishing the political units of the villages, we made use of informants who classified all adult males according to their political affiliation; of participant observation in elections and general meetings; and of direct questions. There was full agreement among all our sources of information, reflecting a clearly articulated structure. This structure only includes males—because, although the *moshav* constitution calls for universal suffrage, in "traditional" *moshavim,* women are excluded from direct participation in the political game.

15 Kurdistan, of course, is divided among Russia, Persia, Turkey, and Iraq. The settlers in Erga come from different regions in Turkey and Iraq, while those in Zafrira come from the same part of Iraq.

16 In the 1962 elections, he won by 77 percent of the votes. A similar process has accompanied the rise of the secretary—a member of the second largest group—elected by 67 percent.

17 This apparent paradox, though regarding industrial modernization, was documented by M. Levy, "Contrasting Factors in the Modernization of China and Japan", *Economic Development and Cultural Change* (October, 1953). Generally similar lines were pursued, also, in some earlier Israeli studies on problems of absorption of immigrants. See chiefly S.N. Eisenstadt, *Absorption of Immigrants* (London, Routledge & Kegan Paul, 1954); and "Patterns of Economic Adaption of Oriental Immigrants in Agricultural Settlements in Israel", in *Essays on Sociological Aspects of Political and Economic Development* (The Hague, Mouton & Co., 1961).

APPENDICES TO CHAPTER 6

APPENDIX 1. Demographic Characteristics in Erga and Zafrira

TABLE 47—Distribution of Manpower in Agricultural Households in Erga and Zafrira

Manpower	Erga		Zafrira	
	Number of households	Percent	Number of households	Percent
1 or less standard workers (insufficient)	13	31.0	25	37.3
$1\frac{1}{4}$–$1\frac{3}{4}$ standard workers (meeting requirements)	27	64.3	37	55.2
2 or more standard workers (excess agricultural)	2	4.7	5	7.5
Total	42	100.0	67	100.0
Unknown	1		3	
N	43		70	

Note: The categories of insufficient, sufficient, and excess manpower are computed in relation to the requirements of a Standard Planned Farm in Erga and Zafrira. Calculation of the total number of workdays required, their seasonal curve, and breakdown by skill and manual effort show 1.3 standard workers to be optimal manpower for cultivating the available farms, and the actual manpower of the household was determined by weighting its members by sex, age, physical fitness, and other duties (such as schooling for children, and child-rearing for mothers), as specified in Chapter 1.

TABLE 48—Age Distribution Among Farm Owners in Erga and Zafrira

Age group	Erga			Zafrira		
	Number of farmers	Percent	Cumulative	Number of farmers	Percent	Cumulative
20–25	7	17.5	17.5	9	13.64	13.64
26–30	8	20.0	37.5	14	21.18	34.82
31–35	6	15.0	52.5	12	18.18	53.00
36–40	3	7. 5	60.0	8	12.12	65.12
41–45	2	5.0	65.0	7	10.61	75.73
46–50	2	5.0	70.0	4	6.06	61.79
51–55	3	7.5	77.5	5	7.57	89.36
56–	9	22.5	100.0	7	10.61	99.97
Total	40	100.0		66	99.97	
Unknown	3			4		
N	43			70		

APPENDIX 2. Economic Development in Erga and Zafrira

TABLE 49—Distribution of Farms in Erga and Zafrira by Net Area Under Cultivation

Dunams	Erga			Zafrira		
	Number of farms	Percent	Cumulative	Number of farms	Percent	Cumulative
0– 4	15	38.5	38.5	1	1.6	1.6
5– 9	15	38.5	77.0	2	3.2	4.8
10–14	9	23.0	100.0	9	14.5	19.3
20–24				11	17.7	37.0
20–24				38	61.2	98.2
24+				1	1.6	99.8
Total	39	100.0		62	109.8	
Unknown	4			8		
N	43			70		

Note: The net area under cultivation includes all crops grown during the year under consideration, on both regular and temporary (i.e. rented) plots, and accounts for the land utilization ratio.

TABLE 50—Distribution of Farms in Erga and Zafrira by Yearly Standard Days

Standard Days	Erga			Zafrira		
	Number of farms	Percent	Cumulative	Number of farms	Percent	Cumulative
0– 49.9	7	24.2	24.2	2	3.3	3.3
50.0–99.9	8	27.8	51.8	2	3.3	6.6
100.0–149.9	5	17.2	69.0	8	13.1	19.7
150.0–199.9	1	3.4	72.4	9	14.8	34.5
200.0–249.9	5	17.2	89.6	10	16.4	50.9
250.0–299.9	2	6.3	96.5	15	24.6	75.5
300.0–349.9	1	3.4	99.9	7	11.5	87.0
350.0–399.9				4	6.6	193.6
400.0–				4	6.6	100.2
Total	29	99.9		61	100.2	
Unknown	14			9		
N	43			70		

TABLE 51—Distribution of Farmers in Erga and Zafrira by Level of Agricultural Know-how

Degree of skill	Erga			Zafrira		
	Number of farmers	Percent	Cumulative	Number of farmers	Percent	Cumulative
10–19	1	3.8	3.8	1	1.69	1.69
20–29	10	38.5	42.3	3	5.07	6.75
30–39	10	38.5	80.8	4	6.76	13.52
40–49	3	11.5	92.3	16	27.04	40.56
50–59	2	17.8	100.1	15	25.35	65.91
60–69				6	10.14	76.05
70+				14	23.66	99.71
Total	26	100.1		59	99.71	
Unknown	17			11		
N	43			70		

TABLE 52 Distribution of Gross Farm Income (Before Taxes) in Erga and Zafrira

IL per year	Erga			Zafrira		
	Number of farms	Percent	Cumulative	Number of farms	Percent	Cumulative
500	12	42.86	42.86			
500–999	11	39.28	82.14	4	7.47	7.47
1000–1499	4	14.28	96.42	9	16.67	24.14
1500–1999	1	4.54		17	31.48	55.62
2000–2499				20	37.04	92.66
2500+				4	7.47	100.13
Total	28	99.96		54	100.13	
Unknown	15			16		
N	43			70		

Note: This table is based on declared income and therefore is not entirely reliable. Unwillingness to answer questions about income is also responsible for the high percentage of "unknowns".

APPENDIX 3. Kinship Networks in Erga and Zafrira

CHARTS 1–4—Kinship Groups a, b, c and d *Moshav* Erga

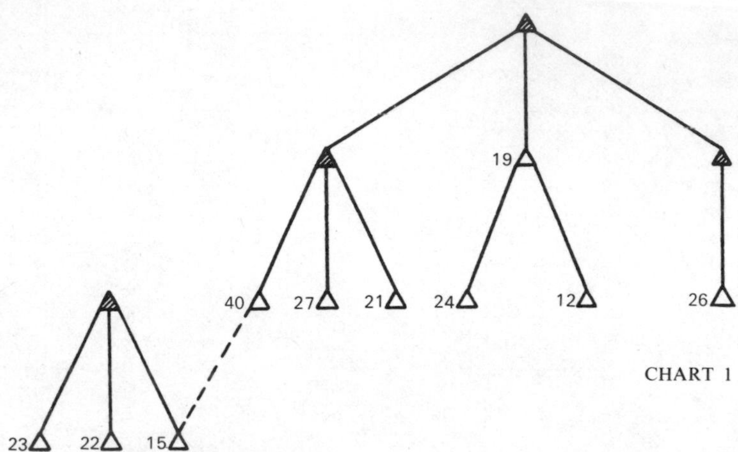

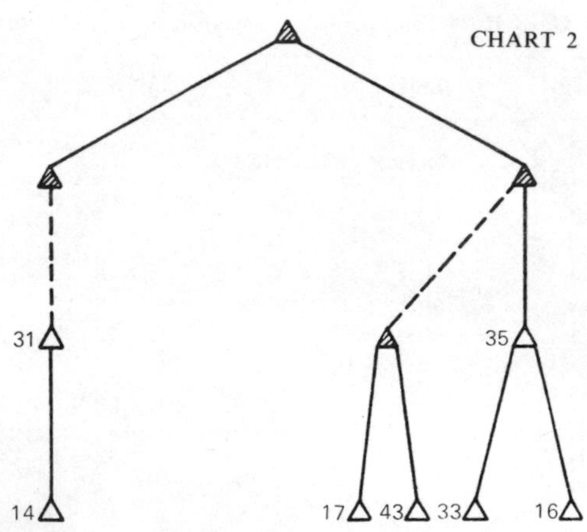

Blood ties
Ties by marriage
Deceased
Numbered triangles signify farm owners.
farm owners.

CHART 3

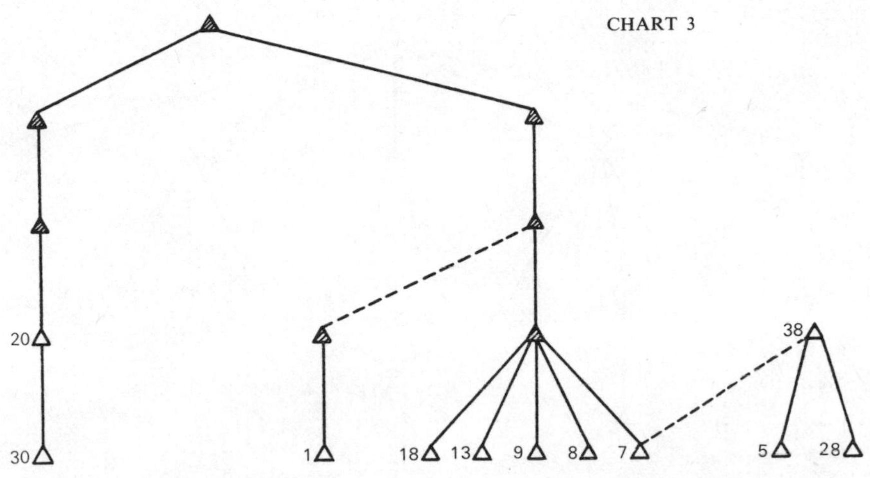

CHART 4

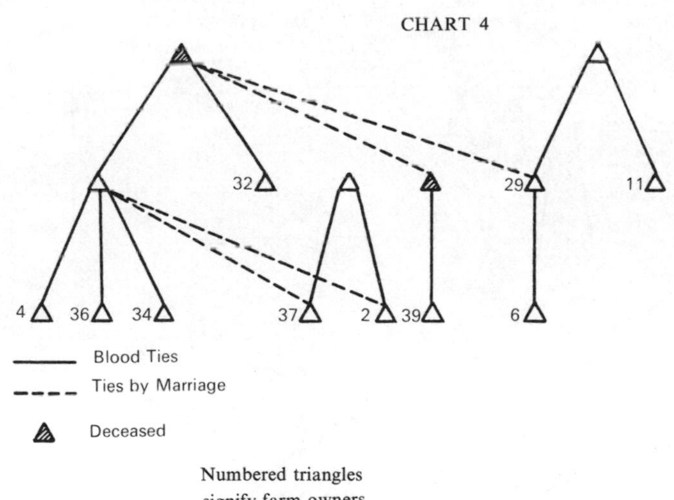

Numbered triangles signify farm owners.

CHARTS 5–10—Kinship Groups a, b, c, d, e, f in *Moshav* Zafrira

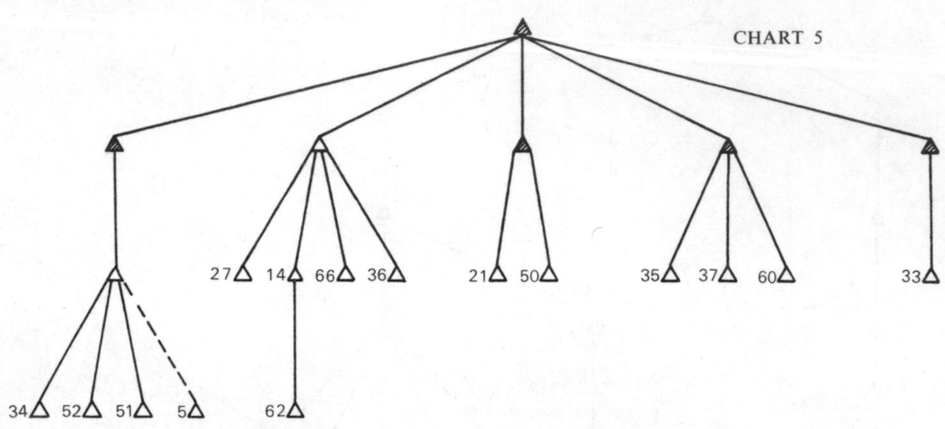

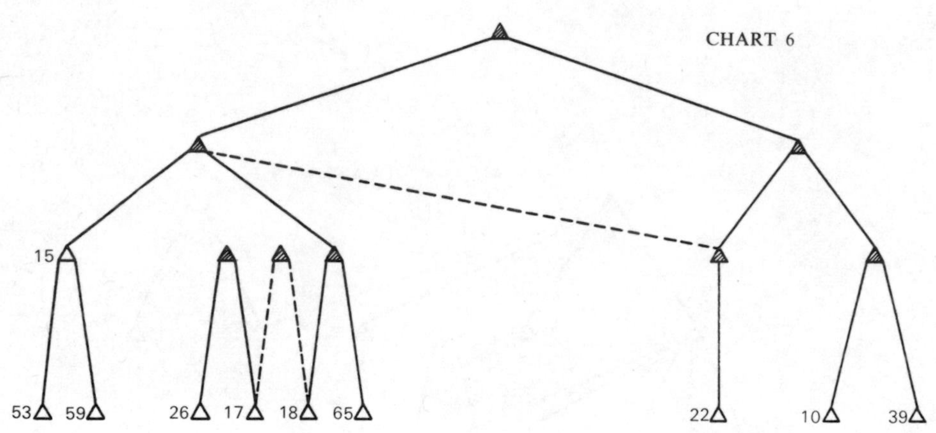

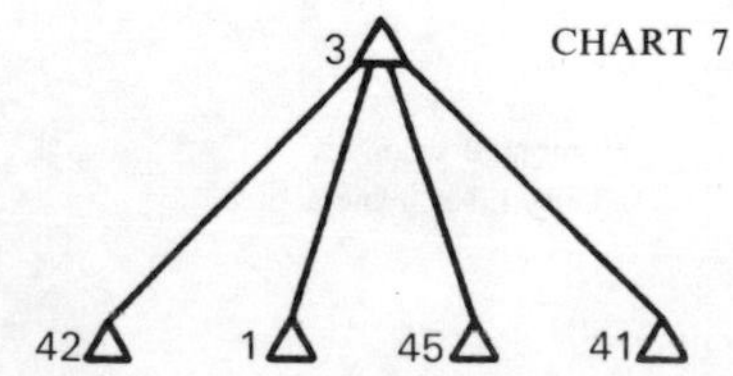

Blood ties

Ties by marriage

Deceased

Woman Farm-owner

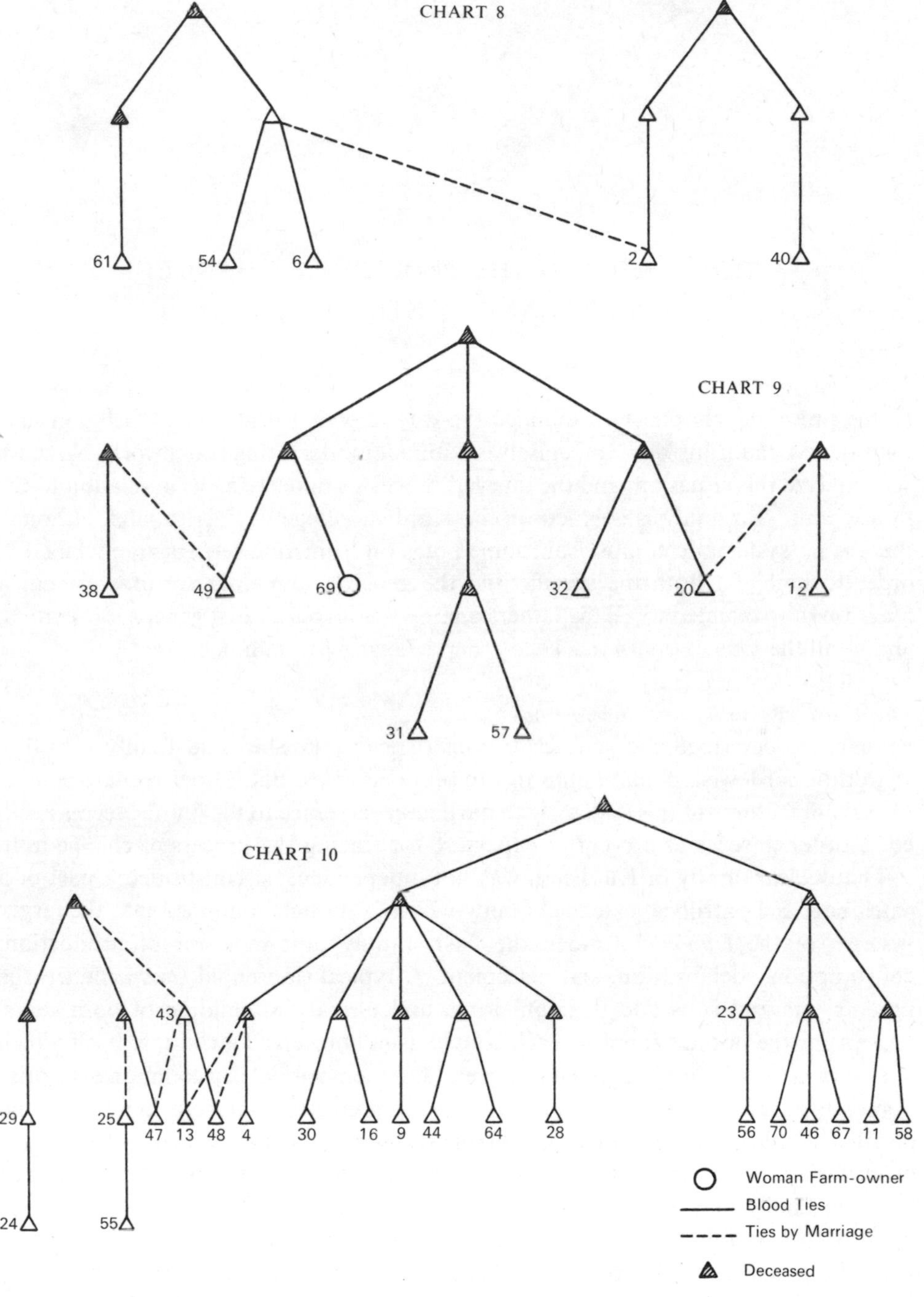
CHART 8
61
54
6
2
40
CHART 9
38
49
69
32
20
12
31
57
CHART 10
43
23
29
25
47
13
48
4
30
16
9
44
64
28
56
70
46
67
11
58
24
55
Woman Farm-owner
Blood Ties
Ties by Marriage
Deceased

CHAPTER 7

THE FAMILY IN THE PROCESS OF CHANGE: CRISIS AND CONTINUITY

Introduction

In the preceding chapter we examined the way in which traditional kinship groups maintained and transformed themselves within a modernizing framework. Now, we will analyze this situation, and the internal processes underlying it, in relation to the family unit. Our analysis is based on the Kurdish village of Zafrira, and, although there is no systematic comparison, some notes on Yemenite settlers are included in order to highlight both the specific and the general. Our data are drawn from a questionnaire directed to all the fathers among the *moshav's* first generation settlers, and to all the sons in the 14 to 24 age group who still live at home.

The Kurdish Family and the Moshav

Earlier, we described the general characteristics of kinship and family structure of traditional Jewish communities in Moslem countries, but a brief re-statement of the salient features of this system, with particular reference to the Kurds, seems needed in order to serve as a point of departure for tracing the process of change in it.

The nuclear family in Kurdistan was not independent: it constituted a part of a patrilineal and patrilocal extended family which (although combined into the larger systems of the *hamoula*) formed the basic family unit in terms of production, consumption, socialization, and placement. A typical household thus included the parents, married sons and their offspring, and unmarried children of both sexes. Except for the poorest families, each couple usually received a room to itself which later served the whole nuclear unit as it grew. The men worked in a common enterprise —mostly in agriculture, as itinerant workers, or as craftsmen (chiefly in weaving and metal)—and these occupations passed from father to son. The women's share in the productive process was limited to some cottage industries. The standard of living was low, the family had few material possessions, and their clothing was very simple. Most of their income went on food which (unlike that of the Yemenites) was plentiful and wholesome, and played an important part in the well-being of the family.

All earnings were pooled together under the exclusive direction of the *pater familiae* (possibly in consultation with other adult members). Corporate organization extended also to the internal workings of the household, namely to the work of its women. Young wives participated in the general work of the entire household: all these tasks, whether marketing family produce, buying food, or cleaning, were communal. The eldest wife of the head of the family allocated the various tasks and supervised them. The woman's position was rendered permanently insecure by virtue of Jewish religious law which gives the husband the right to unilateral divorce. By making his wishes known in the presence of a rabbi, and handing over whatever sum of money was agreed upon in the marriage contract (the *ketuba*), he could send his wife back to her parents without assuming responsibility for her support, and at the same time could keep all the children. The converse, on the other hand, was impossible: the husband had no obligation whatsoever to grant his wife a divorce, and, moreover would usually refuse to do so, since by agreeing to divorce he committed himself to pay off the marriage contract. An unhappily married woman then could only escape her marriage by running away to her parents, and remaining separated from her husband without being able to remarry, unless she converted to Islam, in which case her former marriage was annulled. Under such circumstances, she could marry again, but her status as a Moslem woman was not more secure than it had been when she was a Jewess.

In the Kurdish community, marriage—especially for women—took place very early, usually at or soon after puberty, around the age of 14 (somewhat later than among the Yemenites where the average age of marriage for girls was 10 to 12). These marriages were often consummated before the girl was sexually mature, and she frequently had her first babies before she was sufficiently developed physically. In this context we are not concerned with the effect of such customs on maternal or infant mortality rates; the important point here is that the woman thus passed from the authority of one man to that of another before she was an adult herself. Marriage was invariably arranged by the family, and the bridegroom was sometimes already married,[1] and much older than his bride, who could do nothing to reverse the harsh paternal decision. Cases of resistance did occur, but they were considered shameful. More important still, there was nothing that a rebellious daughter could possibly do on her own, either economically or socially.

The bridegroom, if he was young, was also subject to paternal authority. Nevertheless, he usually had greater opportunities for expressing his own feelings about the projected marriage. Besides, unlike the girl, he was free to leave his parents' home for another locality, a circumstance which considerably reduced his parents' ability to force him into a marriage he did not want. The marriage contract (preferentially *hamoula* endogamous) was usually arranged on a barter basis between two fathers with the help of a marriage broker called in by the interested party. These arrangements included such points as the sum of the brideprice (usually paid in money), the amount to be paid after consummation of the marriage, and the extent of the gifts to be bought for the bride (i.e., her dowry). Sometimes, the father of the bride had second thoughts after the bargain was struck, and then took considerable pains to discover a more suitable match for his daughter. When this happened, he offered compensation to the jilted groom, or else gave the girl away clandestinely, thus creating a *fait accompli*.

The birth rate in the Kurdish Jewish family was high, but so was mortality (particularly during infancy) since sanitary conditions were poor and medical care almost totally absent. In child rearing, however, great love and devotion were lavished on young children by the entire household.[2] Life's slow and even rhythm, the leisurely pace at which household chores were performed and the security of family members in their roles, all encouraged mothers to be patient and relaxed with the children, whose material needs were all taken care of, and whose frustrations were few and far between. The pattern of socialization, among other factors, thus laid down the basis for the high solidarity characterizing the Kurdish family, and especially the nuclear unit within the larger system.

By contrast, the intellectual potential of children was very much neglected; they were seldom spoken to except about elementary and essential matters, and not encouraged to ask questions or develop their vocabulary and powers of conceptualization and abstraction. This stemmed from and reflected the general lack of appreciation of scholastic and spiritual achievements which characterized this community. The socialization of Kurdish children was carried out almost entirely within the family set-up. There was some formal education outside the family, in which the younger boys received religious instruction and were taught the elements of reading, but this was available only for a few years, while the girls attended no such institutions at all. The level of education was thus conspicuously low, most of the men—and all of the women—being illiterate. Religious learning—which enjoyed such high esteem among Yemenite Jews—was not considered important among the Kurds, and the young men were not encouraged to become proficient in the Scriptures and the Talmud. Religious taboos, laws and rules of conduct were rigidly observed and passed from generation to generation, but this observance tended to be largely ritualistic, and was based on tradition and custom rather than on knowledge or internalized values. The religious role-holders were not endowed with qualities of "spiritual leadership", their part in community was small, and their status was lower than that enjoyed in similar groups.

Obviously, immigration to Israel and settlement in a *moshav* substantially undermined the social legitimacy and viability of this traditional family pattern, irrespective of whether its values continued to be salient for the group itself. The most general effect of the confrontation was, undoubtedly, *the loss of familial functions,* and those of the extended unit in particular, to other institutions, in such areas as socialization, education, placement, care of the sick, etc. Take, for example, the sphere of education. As a result of compulsory schooling in Israel, there has been a decline in the educational role of the Kurdish Jewish family. Vocational training has been completely transferred to specialized agencies (even the instruction given on the farm itself is, for the time being, mainly entrusted to the absorptive team); and the same is true, of course, of general education. It is only as regards religious education that the family has retained some of its functions; but even here the school has taken over much of what used to be parental prerogative.[3] Fathers may still teach sons some religious texts and examine their progress fairly closely, but the Bible is now taught differently, at school, by a teacher whose training and status are higher than those of the fathers. In many cases the teacher is a woman, especially in the lower grades. All these changes have had several effects: a) they have diminished the close relationship between children and parents and the amount of time they spend together; b) they have shifted the main focus of social interaction and the primary frame of reference of the young people to school and to other new social frameworks; and c) they have undermined the authority structure of the family. This process has been aggravated by the parents' frequent inability to perform even those functions which are still within their province, and of which on principle they might approve, such as taking part in school affairs or helping the children to do their homework.

A further discrepancy with the background results from the formation of youth groups. The period of "moratorium", it is true, is not very long in the *moshav*. Except for those children sent to boarding schools (usually agricultural), most young men enter the production process at a very early age. Since this work is carried on inside the family, it strengthens family interaction and serves to counteract the processes we have just mentioned. On the other hand, youth culture in general, and youth movements in particular, are an integral feature of the Israel scene, over and above the grade structure of the schools themselves. The reasons for this probably lie in cultural differences between parents, the majority of whom are immigrants to Israel, and children, who grew up in Israel. As a result, the experience of *moshav* youth, even after elementary school, is quite different from that of their parents; some of these youngsters spend a few years in agricultural boarding schools, all go into the army, and most are also—for a while, at least—members of a youth movement. All this tends to crystallize village youth into a distinct social stratum, with its own attitudes, interests and way of life.

This process of attrition affecting functions, as well as traditional practices in areas still entrusted to the family (e.g., child care) is, of course, universal and an extensively studied phenomenon,[4] and needs no further documentation by us. It is of interest, however, that the *moshav's* agrarian system has reinforced this trend through enforced *structural nuclearization,* required by the very nature of the smallholding and of the house—both of which are designed for the single unit. It is true, of course, that the *moshav* does lend itself to what has been called "the modified extended family"[5]—and we can see many instances of mutual help between parents and children, and among siblings (to a lesser extent also among more distant blood relations), in terms of loans and household chores, as well as actual partnership on the farm. But for the traditional extended family, this is only partial reconstitution, the backbone of the original structure having been irrevocably severed. The *moshav* similarly affects the *traditional allocation of family roles on the basis of age and sex*. The requirements of the farm—as well as of village administration—place a premium on modern vocational skills and orientations, thus inverting the intergenerational balance; and the same holds for the place of women who had no economic standing of their own at all in Kurdistan. They were, of course, responsible for homemaking, and worked at weaving and cheese making, selling products which were not intended for home consumption. But these were very rarely—if ever—the household's main economic activities nor its chief source of income, which was earned by the men in the family at quite different crafts. Consequently, the division of labour on the basis of sex was complete. Even in the agricultural households that existed among Kurdish Jews, women were not allowed to work outside the house, and the large number of men in the extended family, plus some hired labour, made possible the extensive and simple cultivation of even relatively large plots. The intensive *moshav* farm, on the other hand, requires the participation of wives in the productive process, particularly during peak seasons.

This encroachment by women upon the male preserve is further strengthened by those other economic aspects of the village which we discussed above. On the one hand, part of the village marketing is done not through the *moshav* cooperative, but "on the side" in a nearby town or city. This applies chiefly to such produce as eggs, especially when the poultry runs are still small, or when cash is badly needed, and is an activity carried out almost exclusively by women, as it was in Kurdistan. But there, the market was closer to home, and these transactions were invariably controlled by the elders of the extended family. In Israel, however, each household acts independently, and sends its own representative to market. As a result almost all the wives or grown-up daughters are in direct contact with outside economy and, in this area at least, must use their own judgement. On the other hand, their status is enhanced by new consumption patterns. The variety of household goods is much greater in Israel and they are not produced by the household itself. Some of these purchases must be made outside the village, and are expensive (e.g., gas ranges and refrigerators). Furthermore, many of these household items are recognized status symbols, all of which broadens the scope of women's social contacts and strengthens their authority within the family itself.

These changes are further reinforced by legal provisions which drastically alter traditional patterns of courtship and marriage. In Israel the minimum legal ag[illegible] marriage (except in very special cases) is 17 years. At this age the Kurdish girl [illegible] Israel is already mature, and knows her way around. She has been outside the home and has mixed both in general society, and in the society of boys. While in Kurdistan the bride sometimes would make the acquaintance of her bridegroom for the first time just before the marriage ceremony, here both sexes meet much more freely and frequently. In consequence, the prospective couple know each other well and are able to make their own choice. Additionally, they can both work and leave behind them not only the parental home but also authority. Similar processes affect the legal status of wives; polygyny—practiced among the Kurdish and other Eastern Jewish communities abroad—is illegal in Israel, and there have also been far-reaching changes in the application of Jewish divorce laws. Although in Israel, too, marriage and divorce are governed by the same strict religious laws, and administered by rabbinical courts, their practice is much more equitable, and wives have acquired what amounts to actual equality. In matters of alimony and maintenance, there is also recourse to civil courts.

The Kurdish Family in the Moshav

In the preceding section we briefly traced factors which impinge upon the traditional Kurdish family when it confronts a modern social and agrarian setting. We have seen that this confrontation, of necessity, undermines the original pattern, by affecting its structure, functions and practices, and differentially exposing its generations to new communication. The strain, inherent in this process of social change, has been shown to lead to internal disorganization;[6] and the familiar picture of family disintegration—with its corollaries of deviance, apathy or aggression—might logically have been expected in Zafrira; the more so, since the situation there combines the stress of migration and induced modernization, and the transition involves the sort of pressure which telescopes significant changes into a very short space. *But the accepted stereotype does not hold, and the family in Zafrira—although much changed in character—continues to function as a viable unit—able to adjust itself to, and accommodate the situational stress.* In the following discussion, we will document some features of the solidarity and integration of this nuclearized family in Zafrira.

1. ACCEPTANCE OF CHANGE BY FATHERS

The first interesting aspect of family life in Zafrira from the point of view of adjustment to change is the extent to which heads of families—i.e., the representatives of the "traditional order"—accept and legitimate new arrangements in the scope and structure of their authority and in allocation of roles.

a. *Decision-making in the productive sphere.* Of a total of 50 respondents, only nine heads of households insisted on sole responsibility in this respect; in 23 families, the father saw himself as the head of the farm, but institutionalized regular consultations with his wife or children; in 11 cases, the wife was accepted as an equal partner in decision-making; while in seven, the complete take-over by a grown-up son was recognized.

b. *Decision-making in the sphere of consumption.* In this area, the father has surrendered his status to an even greater extent. Of 63 cases, only eight fathers persisted in holding on to total authority; in 40 instances both parents are accepted as a decision-making unit; in three households, the entire family is consulted on these matters; while in seven others consumption is handed over entirely to wives.

c. *Wives in occupational activities.* In answer to the question "How do you feel about your wife working on the farm, or outside it for a salary?" 26 out of 63 respondents showed a positive attitude, although all of them with one exception, preferred their wives to work on the family holding. 37 offered negative replies, but their reasons were, in 35 cases, pragmatic and not really value-oriented—namely that their wives couldn't possibly manage to fulfil their obligations at home, if they also worked in the field. Two interviewees only objected on explicitly traditional grounds, saying that "This is not the custom among our people", and "Woman's place is in the home."

d. *Education*. Here we asked "Would you agree to your son (or daughter) leaving home in order to study in a (secondary) boarding school?" To this question (administered as an index to attitude both to modern secondary education, and to children leaving the family household, control and supervision) 42 of 56 respondents answered positively with regard to their sons, and 26 gave a positive answer in respect to their daughters.

e. *Placement of the second generation.* Willingness to relinquish traditional control and grant considerable autonomy to children was revealed in answers to our question "How will you decide on the choice of an occupation for your son?". Only 16 of 64 respondents maintained an essentially traditional view: ten said that the father should first consult the family and then decide on his own, while four suggested that the father should present several alternatives, on the basis of which a joint decision could be reached. By contrast, 21 fathers thought that a joint decision should be reached in reference to preferences or alternatives offered by their sons, while 27 wanted to leave the matter entirely up to their sons.

Our instruments were, of course, not subtle enough for us to be able to measure psychological nuances, and we hesitate to say to what extent these opinions reflect internalized changes, and whether they were based on motivation of "guilt" or of "shame". But the data would seem to indicate that these fathers are prepared to accept changes in the family system, appropriate to the new way of life, and that in most cases they are ready to go part of the way—if not all of it—towards implementing these changes.

2. ACCEPTANCE OF TRADITIONAL CONTINUITY BY SONS

A crucial feature of the families we studied was that although the fathers are (by and large) willing to accept unfamiliar internal arrangements, and thus meet the expectations of their role partners, their sons are as anxious to do the same in reverse—i.e., to maintain family solidarity even when it goes hand in hand with traditional continuity. This is reflected primarily in safeguarding the father's status (even when his opinions are not necessarily accepted), and in the sharing of life experiences.

a. *Acceptance of parental authority*. Two questions—on fact and attitude—were first put this way: "Generally speaking, how are decisions made in your family?"; and "Is this method satisfactory to you?". Of a total of 21 respondents, 12 said that decisions on major issues rested with the father, while nine told us decisions were reached jointly, after discussion, and on the basis of common agreement; not one of the people who answered our questions expressed dissatisfaction with the situation, or said that conflict or disagreement had stemmed from the pattern of decision-making adopted by the family.

A related question was "Do you think it is very important to obey your parents?". This was a closed question to which four different answers could be given: a) A son should always obey his parents; b) A son must be careful not to offend his parents, even if they do not always understand him; c) A son ought not to offend his parents, but in important matters he should act according to his own judgement; and d) A son should always act according to his own judgement.

Of 20 responses, 12 made the first choice, two the second, five the third and only one the last.

b. *Family communication*. A high degree of family sharing was exhibited in answers to the question "Do you usually consult members of your family about your personal affairs? If so, who, in particular?" Of 21 young men interviewed (with more than one indication allowed), 20 said they talked things over with their fathers, 12 said they asked advice of both parents, eight talked to older brothers, and four to other members of the family. As can be seen, *all* respondents (with the exception of one who was an orphan) consulted with their fathers, with exchange of opinion extending also to other people in the household.

c. *Keeping within the family orbit*. A distinct preference was shown for retaining proximity to the family at the expense of occupational advantages. To the question: "If you were offered a choice between a job in the neighbourhood of your family and a better job elsewhere, which would you prefer?", distribution of the 21 responses elicited was as follows:

15—would prefer to live in the same neighbourhood as their families, even if this meant earning a smaller salary themselves;
2—wanted to live near their families but not to give up the better paid job;
4—were not anxious to live near their families.

This "meeting of minds"—and the reciprocality of expectations in the two generations—is brought into yet sharper focus when we compare attitudes *within* the family unit.

For this purpose, we analyzed matched pairs of fathers and sons about two critical family issues constituting potential sources of intergenerational conflict.

a. *Mate selection.* In 13 families, we compared the desired pattern of mate selection of fathers and sons, according to five categories: 1) Lineage; 2) Parental decision; 3) Sons' choice from among parental candidates; 4) Sons' decision after consulting parents; 5) Sons' sole and independent decision. The responses we got showed 11 instances of complete, or almost complete, identity—all in favour of choices 4 and 5—namely, the free selection by the sons with, or without, consulting their parents. Only in two cases did we get contrasting views—liable to lead to tension and conflict—the attitude of the fathers being traditional-authoritarian (choice 1 and choice 2), while that of the sons was individualistic (choices 4 and 5).

b. *Religious observance.* Responses to our questions about religious observance were matched in 16 households, in respect to four specific areas: 1) observance of Jewish dietary laws *(Kashruth)*; 2) smoking on the Sabbath; 3) travelling on the Sabbath; 4) daily prayers in synagogue.

The four categories differ in their implications in respect to the family system. Differences with regard to the first two categories are apt to create tensions within the family, as their observance, or non-observance, reflects on its daily life. As for the third category, a member of the young generation who does *not* observe it, causes no serious social disruption in the family (although, of course, it may upset his parents to know that he travels on the Sabbath). The same is true of the fourth category—daily prayer, which is regarded as a personal matter and not a family ritual, and has little to do with its life-style.

Interestingly enough, the distance between fathers and sons reflects this differential relevance to the preservation of family solidarity and avoidance of tension in it. In the first two categories, the differences in observance were notably small. Of 16 pairs of responses concerning food taboos, 15 showed father and son to be equally observant, while only in one instance the son was less observant than his father. In respect to smoking on the Sabbath (in relation to which we could match only ten responses), there was an equal degree of observance. But the differences were much more pronounced in the remaining categories. Of the 15 pairs of attitudes to travelling on Sabbath, only eight were of equal observance; while in respect to daily prayer, identity existed only in five of 13 sets of answers.

All in all, then, the sons seem to be characterized by identification with family values, and attachment to its members—thus reflecting a high degree of family solidarity. This is striking, since in other areas the younger generation has quite obviously moved away from its parents. The differential change is not immense, and, as we shall see later, the young men of Zafrira have by no means developed really "modern" conceptions, attitudes or aspirations. At the same time, almost all of them (there were two exceptions) have received at least partial elementary education; and all consistently exhibit more sophisticated and more rational public orientations. Nor are the sons unaware of these differences. In reply to our question "How do you consider yourself to differ from your father?" they mentioned aspects which cover the main areas of life. We quote these in order of precedence:

a. They (the sons) know Hebrew better and know more about conditions in Israel.

b. They have a more developed sense of citizenship, are eager to join the army, and ready to volunteer for security tasks.

c. They are better educated.

d. They have more experience and know-how in agriculture, and are better farmers.

e. They are more interested in recreation, movies, sports, trips, etc.

f. They are anxious to succeed and be progressive in farming and in other areas of life.

g. They are more acculturated to Israeli standards of dress, manners, behaviour, cleanliness.

h. They are more secular than their fathers—who are devout.

i. They are better able to plan, and to calculate.

It is clear that the fathers, and the tradition which they represent, are, in many respects, no longer models or normative references; and the positive orientation to the family as a group thus requires *segregating or separating membership and solidarity from reference behaviour*—thus allowing the one to function without the other.

Some of the mechanisms which make this possible are the topic of the following pages.

The Why and the How

The preceding analysis has shown that most Zafrira families seem to be weathering the trials and tribulations of their confrontation with a new setting. This is being achieved through the willingness of fathers to accept changes in the family system, and by the parallel desire of their sons to enable them to maintain their sense of integrity and personal security. Not unimportant in this respect is the separation of the family from other spheres: sons divorce the internal position of their fathers from their relative inferiority to them elsewhere, while the fathers disregard "deviations" of the sons (e.g. religious non-observance) when these do not directly bear upon the family as a group.

Both partners, in fact, are geared to maintain unit solidarity, so that mutual expectations are respected and do not, in most cases, transcend the bounds of permissiveness. As a result, the process of change is regulated by tolerance of the system, and is made easier, smoother and less ridden with psychological difficulties for all concerned.

The purpose of this section is to try to account for this integration in terms of three sets of factors: the predisposition of the population, the specific institutional characteristics of the *moshav,* and the special features of Zafrira as a community.

1. One vital element in the process described is undoubtedly the strong solidarity prior to their migration of the units we examined. This is so in a twofold sense. On the one hand—as we saw above—the nuclear unit in Kurdistan had been bound, within the extended family, by an especially strong sense of attachment, so that nuclearization in the *moshav* meant a less severe break than would otherwise have been the case. On the other hand, the family institution in the country of origin had not yet begun to undergo the crisis of change, and it thus arrived in Israel intact, secure and unaffected by any earlier disintegration, and was therefore in a better position to act in the new reality.

No less important for adjustment, and especially to secularization, was the fact that the value or religious content of the Kurdish family had been poor and relatively not internalized. It is doubtless due to this that the older generation managed to tolerate the kind of religious deviance which did not directly affect the family itself. The contrast here with the reaction of Yemenite families is vivid. The latter—richer in value content—had a broader basis of identification and an even stronger solidarity. But this solidarity made Yemenite Jews who came to Israel more resistant to, and far less tolerant of the process of value change and secularization, and when intergenerational differentiation did appear, it more often than not led to sharp tension and deep conflict.

2. Turning to situational factors, a crucial role, of course, is played by the institutional pattern of the *moshav* as such, which stresses the importance of the family as the unit of production. The family actually constitutes the basis of life here, its viability is an *a priori* condition of success; and the individual has to make his way in cooperation with it. The family farm thus legitimates family solidarity also in new, "modern" terms.

3. Zafrira, however, also has a *specific* advantage as a community, in that its social fabric consists, as we have seen, of viable kinship systems. Those systems have maintained much of their traditional family solidarity, and at the same time they also sustained processes of development and modernization, so that there existed here what Moore and Feldman call "cumulative retroactive change"[7]—namely, a stochastic process in which traditional elements support successful change, which in turn transforms and strengthens the former.

Conclusion

In these pages we have examined a group of "traditional" immigrant families, whose institutions were undermined by new conditions and requirements, but which were able to adjust without any pronounced social crisis or disintegration. This successful accommodation was related to the nature of the religious tradition which these families had maintained and transmitted, and which was essentially ritualistic, heteronomous and divorced from centres of high culture (in the Redfieldian sense); and also to the fact that they faced the novel situation as highly solidary and well-integrated units. No less important, however, was the structure of the change situation, and the framework and conditions of the confrontation—which represented a measure of continuity, and made possible a gradual process of transition.

NOTES

1 Polygyny was practiced chiefly among the richer and more important families, and constituted a status symbol. At the same time it also compensated for the relatively faster ageing process of women in this society.

2 See chiefly: D. Feitelson, "The Socialization of the Young in the Kurdish Community" (Hebrew), *Megamoth,* Vol. 6, No. 4, (1955).

3 Israel has two types of public school: the "State" schools and the "State Religious" schools. The latter—in which most of the new "traditional" immigrants enroll their children—include a great deal of religious instruction taught by modern teaching methods.

4 For a general analysis, see, for example, W.F. Ogburn and M.P. Nimkoff: *Technology and the Changing Family,* (New York, Houghton Mifflin, 1955).

5 E. Litwak, "Geographical Mobility and Extended Family Cohesion", *American Sociological Review,* Vol. 25, (1960).

6 The references are legion—the earliest and perhaps still the best known being: W.I. Thomas and F. Znaniecki: *The Polish Peasant in Europe and America,* (New York, Dover Publications, 1958) (second edition). For a general analysis, though, see, for instance, K. Davis, "The Sociology of Parent-Youth Conflict", *The American Sociological Review,* No. 4, (1940); Albert A. Bloch: *Disorganization—Personal and Social,*(New York, Alfred A. Knopf, 1952); and Robert E.L. Faris, *Social Disorganization* (Chapter 10—"Family Disorganization"), (New York, The Ronald Press, 1948).

7 Wilbert E. Moore and Arnold S. Feldman (eds.): *Labour Commitment and Social Change in Developing Areas,* (New York, Social Science Research Council, 1960).

CHAPTER 8

THE YOUNGER GENERATION—COMMITMENT TO THE MOSHAV, ORIENTATION TO CHANGE, AND MODERNIZATION

Introduction

In the last two chapters, we analyzed trends of development in the new *moshavim* in terms of the traditional kinship group and the traditional family; and we saw that, under certain conditions, both these frameworks are capable of internal modernization while still maintaining their solidarity, and that they thus can—at least initially—sustain the growth of village institutions and society and of household activities.

The purpose of the discussion which follows is to examine the future of the *moshav* from the point of view of the younger generation. We observe thus the scope of this generation's general commitment to the *moshav,* namely the extent to which it on the whole favours the *moshav* way of life, and would—if practicable—carry on in it in preference to other available openings. We then attempt to trace some basic social characteristics of those in favour of the *moshav* and those who do not wish to continue in it.

This analysis is threefold. First, it sets out to analyze the relationship, in different groups of farm youth, between personal preference for staying in rural life or leaving it, and between degree of openness and sensitivity to general processes of change in society. It was hypothesized that the existence of such an orientation to social change should influence the individual's future plans by promoting a positive motivation for occupational enterprise and social mobility as against routine and continuity; and that it would thus be associated with the choice of the *moshav* as a way of life not directly or uniformly, but depending upon the situation of the farm and the village. In cases in which this situation represented an economic challenge and an opportunity for social mobility, positive orientation to change in society should promote preference for staying; and conversely, where farming meant occupational routine and social continuity, the same attitude to change should be conducive to leaving.

Second, we examine differences in the distribution of orientation to change *among* the groups, in terms of the extent of social modernization the respondent's group of origin had undergone.

Third, differences in orientation to change *within* groups of similar background are analyzed.

Framework of the Study

The framework within which orientation to change was identified and traced is the *stratificational models held by the* moshav *youths.* Such a model—or conceptual scheme of how society is ordered—is a focal point in every individual's image of his social universe and a basis for his fundamental world picture. Analysis of stratificational models, undertaken in a variety of ways and from many points of departure, has occupied a central place in most studies concerned with social adjustment and mobility, occupational choice, and many other topics. We examined one specific aspect or group of factors: *the extent to which the stratificational model is essentially open, flexible and differentiated.* The selection of this particular focus was guided by the assumption that the visualization of the stratificational system in terms of its pluralism and accessibility is a fundamental dimension in the individual's conceptualization of his society and that it reveals whether this society is conceived of as dynamic and mobile. Thus the greater the openness, differentiation, and flexibility of the stratificational system in the youth's eyes, the stronger will be his inclination to attempt new and challenging things; and his attitude to farming will be influenced by what it offers in this respect.

The presence of the abstract qualities representing a basically dynamic and mobile conceptual pattern was sought through the examination of the *structural properties of the model.*[1] Attention was not given to the concrete or substantive nature of the social strata or positions visualized, but rather to the type of the basic components or categories in terms of which stratification is seen to be structured, and to the degree of variety and fluidity characterizing their configurations. Four sets of structural variables were examined in this connection:

1. *The number and the institutional spread of major social positions, which are conceived of as conferring social status and included in the model.*

2. *The number of the stratificational criteria according to which these positions are evaluated.*

The *scope* of both positions and criteria referred to was taken to be indicative of the number of the *alternative ways* for the acquisition of social status deemed legitimate by the individual. However, emphasis on criteria would give a stronger orientation to the *means* required for the maintenance of social status, and thus to *performance*; whereas preoccupation with positions might represent primarily a stress on personal *rewards.* In other words: both conceptions are assumed to be associated with a basic achievement orientation: the first, however, stands for *achieving* in itself—the other for its *end-product*. Or, in economic terms, the distinction is between emphasis on *producing* and an emphasis on *consuming,* the first being possibly more closely associated with enterprise.

3. *The extent to which the major social positions included in the model are conceived of mainly in terms of occupations, or in terms of social properties* (e.g. rich/poor, educated/uneducated, etc.). This factor, too, reflects a distinction between producing and *doing* something as against *being* something.

4. *The extent to which the model is polarized or gradated* (i.e. whether it contains an intermediate stratum (or strata), including a variety of positions which are distinct but link up below and above; and which represent, presumably, an image of several accessible ladders, enabling gradual but significant progress). This factor therefore interprets the stratificational structure in terms of its actual mobility potential.

These abstractions will become clearer, it is hoped, when seen in terms of the questions asked, and of the answers anticipated and obtained. Two consecutive open-ended questions served as the basis:

a. Into how many groups or strata do you think the Israeli society is divided, and what are they? (arrange them from highest to lowest).

b. On what basis or according to what criteria is this division founded?

The following are some examples of actual answers and of the way such answers were translated into the analytical variables:

I. Answer to question a. (5 strata):

1. Engineers, doctors, lawyers, artists, large industrialists;
2. Civil servants, teachers;
3. Shopkeepers, merchants, manufacturers;
4. Skilled tradesmen, mechanics, technicians, farmers;
5. Non-skilled workers.

Answer to question b.:

"according to education, income, and importance for society."

Variables 1, 3, and 4, namely, number of major social positions in different institutional spheres; character of these positions (occupational or non-occupational); and the gradation of the model—were culled from the first question. Variable 2, number of stratificational criteria, was obtained from the second one.

This "model" was thus classified as follows:

1. Containing positions in many institutional spheres. This was so as the answer refers distinctly to a) various "technical" free professions (law, medicine, construction); b) non-professional cultural sphere (teachers, artists); c) public administration; d) various economic roles in the sphere of production and marketing (industry, agriculture, trade).

2. Referring to many criteria: the model mentions 3 (education, income, service).

3. Occupationally oriented—it refers clearly to occupational categories or strata.

4. Gradated: contains intermediate strata, each of which has a variety of distinct positions.

A contrasting example is:

II. Answer to question a. (3 strata):

1. Rich
2. Medium
3. Poor

Answer to question b.:

"according to wealth".

Such a "model" would obviously be classified as:

1. containing few positions;
2. containing only one criterion;
3. non-occupational;
4. non-gradated.

(The examples given present two diametrically opposed profiles, but this was not always the case, and answers may be "positive" along one dimension and "negative" along others).

To re-state: the relationship we set out to establish between structural properties of stratificational models representing sensitivity to social change and choice of family farming as a way of life is not a specific one, but inherent in a more general nexus. That is to say, variability in the openness, flexibility, and differentiation of stratificational conceptions is not taken to influence a choice among concrete alternatives as such; it is assumed to be relevant rather in a situation implying a choice between doing something new and challenging, or else continuing on the beaten track. In our particular case: in groups of youth for whom the *moshav* represented continuity, routine, and the road of least resistance, the presence of a model embodying a variety of positions and criteria, an occupational emphasis, and gradation, would mean the rejection of such a way of life, and the preference for something different. Conversely: among those for whom family farming meant a more "revolutionary" option, a greater reversal of conditions, such a model would be related to staying in settlement.

The population of the study was designed for the examination of the problems posed, without actually tracing the motivational mechanisms involved. The population thus included four *moshavim*. First, we had the familiar village of Zafrira, settled, as the reader will remember, by new immigrants from Iraqi Kurdistan in 1951. This group came from a "traditional" background, both in regard to the surrounding Kurdish society, and the Jewish community itself. This was a setting mainly familistic, religious and largely divorced from any modern secular education (general or vocational), and from processes of change and development. The economy in the country of origin of these villagers was essentially static, stagnant, undeveloped and technologically rudimentary, and they lived on extensive subsistence farming, or on semi-skilled trades and cottage industries such as weaving, the products of which were sold on the local exchange market. Socially, they were an ethnically and religiously closed unit, in fact, an underprivileged caste. Within these general bounds, moreover, the small kinship groups—the *hamoulas*—constituted the basic unit of interaction, and often the entire social horizon of their members. The political horizon of the Kurdish Jewish community was also narrow and restricted. Political consciousness was undeveloped, and participation in political life was limited and haphazard. In the Kurdish region (an isolated and practically semi-autonomous area in Iraq) government on all levels was based on traditional tribal organization and the separation of "church and state" was only beginning. There was little "citizenship" in the modern sense, especially as regards minorities, whose members had second-class status. Jewish public activity was thus limited to traditional-particularistic settings, without democratic processes of government, and without bureaucratic processes of administration.

While these characteristics have recently begun to change (see Chapter 6) we assumed that for the people of Zafrira, the *moshav*—with its intensive, developing, and market-oriented economy, multipurpose cooperation, and modern municipal government—would, given their educational and occupational background (see below), constitute a greater objective challenge in terms of social demands and occupational enterprise than employment in such openings as semi-skilled trades, building, and public works and life in urban semi-slums into which the majority of the Kurdish immigration has gravitated.[2] Consequently, staying in the village would here be associated with openness, flexibility, and differentiation of stratificational conceptions.

At the other end of the sample was Karmon, a modern village of veteran European settlers, established in 1930 by one of the founding fathers of the *moshav* movement, and among the most developed and successful settlements in the country. Here the young generation was brought up on intensive family farming and within a modern institutional framework; and the *moshav* was thus taken to stand for the tested, the familiar, and the secure—a way of life sanctioned by both ideology and habit. Indeed, it represented no objective challenge: the farms were already intensified almost to the limit of their capacity, and further initiative was subject to agrarian and normative limitations; and scope for enterprise was thus largely limited to varying the crop rotation and to changing a Ford tractor for a Ferguson. Here an image of a "dynamic" and a "mobile" stratificational system should be associated with leaving rather than with staying.

Representing the "middle" of the sample there were two "transitional" villages, Hazan and Yaron, also settled in 1951, by immigrants from Tripolitania and French Morocco respectively. Of the two groups, the second came from a more modernized background: its communities of origin were of a more urban character (such cities as Fez, Marrakesh and Casablanca, as against provincial Libyan towns) and industrialized; they had a greater degree of occupational variety and specialization; they possessed a larger measure of secularization—educational and cultural—and they were characterized by a higher emancipation and social and political participation. However, in spite of these differences of degree (to be taken up later) the *moshav* represented for both groups a new but not a novel range of economic and public activity: one not essentially contrasting to other available openings in terms of social mobility and enterprise. Their stratificational conceptions were, consequently, expected to show no consistent relationship to a positive or a negative choice; and these two villages were thus adopted as controls.[3]

To re-state: in Zafrira, in which we assumed *moshav* life to mean entrepreneurship and social mobility, openness, flexibility, and differentiation of stratificational conceptions should be positively related to preference for staying in the village. In Karmon, for whose youth *moshav* life meant the occupationally routine and the socially static, the same properties of the stratificational model—that is, the same high openness to social change—should be associated with plans for leaving; while in Hazan and Yaron—for both of which the *moshav* was neutral in terms of enterprise and mobility—there should be no significant relationship between the two factors.[4]

As can be seen from the above thumbnail sketch, the four groups of settlers come from institutional backgrounds representing basically different stages of social modernization: from the traditional Kurdish community of Zafrira, through the "transitional" communities of Tripolitania and Morocco (with the second group more westernized than the first), and up to essentially modern Karmon. And this design should enable us to examine also the second and third problems posed, and to see in what way does the institutionally defined process of modernization correlate with individual openness to change.

Within each village, all male youths in the 17–24 age group were interviewed. However, since the entire population comprised 152 youths (30, 50, 36 and 36 in the respective villages), at best only tentative results could be expected, indicating trends rather than stating firm facts; and the study is thus to be considered a pilot project.

Future Plans—Character and Crystallization

The most striking feature of the data we obtained are the vast differences among the four villages as regards attitude to the *moshav* as a way of life. Commitment to it is high in the ideologically-oriented and established settlement of Karmon (with a positive attitude at 33.3 percent, negative or an ambivalent attitude at 42.7 percent and unknowns at 24.0 percent) and in the traditional community of Zafrira (with a positive attitude at 40.0 percent, a negative or an ambivalent attitude at 53.4 percent and unknowns at 6.6 percent); but it decreases sharply in the two transitional populations (in Hazan, 24.0 percent view the *moshav* positively, 70.0 percent negatively or ambivalently, and 6.0 percent are unknown, while in Yaron only 14.0 percent are in favour of this way of life, and 86.0 percent are either against it or ambivalent about it). This reinforces our earlier findings which showed that the more advanced the immigrant group is, the more likely are the villages to be faced with the problem of continuity; and these findings are, of course, in line with general trends of rural exodus, especially among young people, as has been reported in many countries, irrespective of their socio-economic systems.[5]

Of special interest, however, is the distribution of attitudes towards the *moshav* along the various dimensions of orientations to change.

The findings were not always on the level of proper statistical significance, but give evidence of a clear and consistent trend in line with the reasoning of the study. Table 53 presents the essential data on the differential stratificational conceptions of the four groups, and on the relationship between these conceptions and future plans as regards life in the *moshav*.

1. *Number of stratificational positions.* This factor stands in a clear relation to future choice in the two extreme groups (although this relationship is largely asymmetrical); a relatively greater scope of position characterizes the "stayers" in the first village, and the "leavers" in the fourth; but does not vary significantly in the intermediate ones. The relationship is reinforced when differences between *average* number of positions conceived of by the two categories are examined.[6]

Zafrira: Stayers > Leavers—0.8
Hazan: Stayers < Leavers—0.2
Yaron: Stayers < Leavers—0.1
Karmon: Stayers < Leavers—1.7

2. *Number of Stratificational Criteria.* The relationship between the nature of the stratificational model and individual bend towards social mobility and enterprise is maintained, even more strongly, also in this aspect—there being an inverse (but again asymmetrical) relationship between stayers and leavers in the "traditional" and the veteran *moshavim.* The same applies also to differentials in averages—that is, in the average number of criteria mentioned in the various villages by "stayers" and "leavers" respectively:

Zafrira: Stayers > Leavers—0.9
Hazan: Stayers = Leavers
Yaron: Stayers < Leavers—0.2
Karmon: Stayers < Leavers—1.8

3. *Occupational versus non-occupational positions*—the same trend.

4. *Polarization of Model.* Though the broad tendency persists, it is weaker; and this predictor is more promising in the "traditional" village than in the "modern" one.

TABLE 53—Stratificational Models and the Place of the Moshav in Future Plans
(a) In Absolute Numbers

Stratificational conceptions	Future plans	Zafrira: Attitude to *moshav* Positive	Negative	No.	Ambivalent[3]	Unknown	Total	Hazan: Attitude to *moshav* Positive	Negative	No.	Ambivalent[3]	Unknown	Total	Yaron: Attitude to *moshav* Positive	Negative	No.	Ambivalent[3]	Unknown	Total	Karmon: Attitude to *moshav* Positive	Negative	No.	Ambivalent[3]	Unknown	Total
Stratificational positions[1]	Few	8	10	18			18	7	14	21	3		24	3	12	15	2		17	8	2	10	6		16
	Many	8	2	10			10	4	17	21			21	1	13	14	1		15	4	5	9	3		12
	Total	16	12	28		2	30	11	31	42	3	5	50	4	25	29	3	4	36	12	7	19	9	8	36
Stratificational criteria[2]	Few	10	9	19			19	6	22	28	1		29	3	10	13	2		15	5	0	5	3		8
	Many	6	0	6			6	5	10	15	2		17	1	16	17	1		18	6	7	13	4		17
	Total	16	9	25		5	30	11	32	43	3	4	50	4	26	30	3	3	36	11	7	18	7	11	36
Occupational structure of positions	Non-occup.	4	9	13			13	3	10	13			13	3	12	15	2		17	7	1	8	3		11
	Occup.	12	3	15			15	9	20	29	3		32	1	13	14	1		15	5	6	11	6		17
	Total	16	12	28			28	12	30	42	3	5	50	4	25	29	3	4	36	12	7	19	9	8	36
Polarization of model	Pol.	7	10	17			17	10	14	24	2		26	2	7	9			9	7	2	9	5		14
	Grad.	9	2	11			11	2	18	20	1		21	3	19	22	5		27	5	5	10	4		14
	Total	16	12	28		2	30	12	32	44	3	3	50	5	26	31	5		36	12	7	19	9	8	36

Notes: [1] Dividing point: up to 2, and 3 or more; [2] Dividing point: up to 2 and 3 or more; [3] Ambivalent those who would consider village life but definitely not farming;
[4] Unknown: includes those who have not yet made their future plans.

(b) Proportion Positive to *Moshav* by Stratificational Conceptions

Moshav	Stratificational conceptions / Future plans	Stratificational positions		Stratificational criteria		Occupational structure of positions		Polarization of model	
		Few	Many	Few	Many	Non-occupational	Occupational	Pol.	Grad.
Zafrira	Proportion positive	.44	.80	.53	1.00	.31	.80	.41	.82
	N*	18	10	19	6	13	15	17	11
	a**	−.36		−.47		−.49		−.41	
	z	2.09		−4.12		2.99		2.46	
	p (level of significance)	p ⟨.05		p ⟨.01		p ⟨.01		p ⟨.05	
Hazan	Proportion positive	.33	.19	.21	.33	.23	.31	.42	.10
	N*	21	21	28	15	13	29	24	20
	a**	+.14		−.12		−.08		+.32	
	z	.48		.83		.05		1.39	
	p (level of significance)	Not significant		Not significant		Not significant		Not significant	
Yaron	Proportion positive	.20	.07	.23	.06	.20	.07	.22	.14
	N*	15	14	13	17	15	14	9	22
	a**	+.13		+.17		+.13		+.08	
	z	1.05		1.30		1.05		.05	
	p (level of significance)	Not significant		Not significant		Not significant		Not significant	
Karmon	Proportion positive	.80	.44	1.00	.46	.87	.45	.78	.50
	N*	10	9	5	13	8	11	9	10
	a**	+.36		+.54		+.42		+.28	
	z	1.73		3.91		2.19		1.33	
	p (level of significance)	p ⟨.10		p ⟨.10		p ⟨.05		Not significant	

* Excluding respondents with unknown or unclear future plans.

** The Coleman effect parameter, indicating the amount and direction of causal effect of the independent variable (Stratificational Conceptions) on the dependent variable (future plans). In the present context, a equals the simple percentage-difference (Coleman, 1964). (James S. Coleman: *Introduction to Mathematical Sociology*, The Free Press of Glencoe, 1964, Ch. IV.)

The data thus show that openness, flexibility and differentiation in stratificational models, as measured by their structural properties, are significantly related to preference for change as against preference for continuity. In this way, the enterprising and the mobile in the two extreme villages (that is, the "stayers" in the one and the "leavers" in the other), are characterized by a greater openness in *all* the aspects proposed for consideration.[7]

The four structural indices examined differ among themselves in their predictive strength—the number of stratificational criteria being most salient in this respect. This special significance of criteria lends support, it seems, to our assumption that this factor is associated with an emphasis on a "means of production" conception as against a "rewards and consumption" one; and thus is particularly relevant to an active orientation to change.

We must now go a step further and consider the nature and the significance of the patterns in which the various dimensions of the model appear and become combined.

Table 54 summarizes the ratio of the different stratificational conceptions in the four *moshavim* representing different stages of social modernization.

TABLE 54—Distribution of Dynamic Stratificational Conceptions in the Four Villages (in percentages)

Stratificational conceptions / Village	1.	Many positions	2.	Many criteria	3.	Occupational positions	4.	Gradation of model
	N		N		N		N	
Zafrira	30	35.70	30	24.00	28	53.58	30	39.30
Hazan	50	46.70	50	37.00	50	71.10	50	44.70
Yaron	36	46.90	36	54.50	36	61.70	36	75.00
Karmon	36	42.90	36	68.00	36	79.60	36	50.00
Range of variability		11.20		44.00		26.02		35.70

As may be seen from this table, the clearest distinction is between the most traditional village and all the others—Zafrira being consistently lowest in all respects and exhibiting the smallest measure of orientation to social change. However, the range of variability of the specific measures in the differently modernized groups is far from uniform, running from 44.0 percent between lowest and highest in the second column (criteria) to 11.2 percent in the first (positions). Number of positions is thus either more tenuously related to modernization or—as is more likely—constitutes a dimension changed early in the process, in consequence of which substantially similar proportions throughout refer to and differentiate between several social positions in various institutional spheres. Of interest is also column 3 (occupational emphasis): while its range of variability within the process of modernization is greater—26.02—it begins on the highest level, hinting that an occupational image of stratification is the rule rather than the exception. Stratificational criteria again emerges as most salient—supporting the assumption that it is an individual mechanism most closely associated with and reflecting general processes of development and change.

Another glance at Table 54 brings out a further feature of interest. We see that the variable of criteria alone maintains fully linear progress in association with stages of modernization, while in the others this order is broken. The village of Hazan significantly precedes the one after it in column 3; Yaron advances over Karmon in column 4; while column 1 demonstrates the "irregularity" of both Hazan and Yaron overtaking Karmon. Of course, this evidence, if suggestive, is tenuous; but additional considerations allow us to state the course somewhat more forcibly. These considerations refer to the differential relations *between* the various stratificational conceptions within the four groups. Table 55 presents the relationship in the sample villages between scope of stratificational criteria (evidently the focal variable) and each of the other aspects analyzed.

The relationship between the different dimensions is much stronger at the two extremes than it is in the middle. At the initial and at the advanced stages of modernization, the "dynamic" dimensions are consistently associated, forming a balanced profile; in the middle, by contrast, variation is much more independent. This is thus both a horizontal and a vertical "staggering" of the stratificational model, and the two indicate a definite tendency towards "pattern disruption", setting the transitional middle apart from its predecessors and followers alike; a disruption which affects the personal world picture internally, and at the same time dissociates it from the institutional indices of modernization. This shows, on the individual level, what has recently been becoming increasingly clear on the societal level, namely, that any conception of modernization in general as a linear process along one "traditional-modern" continuum is a simplistic one. Clearly, the functional significance of such a structural "disruption" or dissociation of components, previously—and subsequently—forming a more coherent pattern, varies from situation to situation. Thus the quality of a differential "unfreezing" or "traditional" ways of thought may denote a greater flexibility, a capacity to move in leaps and bounds—each aspect as it were untrammelled by its fellows. Conversely, the inconsistency involved may lead to anomie, strain and disorganization of identity, and predisposes towards extreme sensitivity to failure. The conditions under which either of the two effects is likely to predominate are obviously beyond the scope and the data of the present discussion, (though we will offer some ideas on the function of the family in this respect later on). What is suggested, however, is that the *pattern* of the imbalance or the nature of the lagging components, might in itself be of considerable importance

TABLE 55—Relationship between Model Dimensions

Other dimension	Criteria	Zafrira			Hazan			Yaron			Karmon		
		Few	Many	Total	Few	Many	Total	Few	Many	Total	Few	Many	Total
Position	Few	13	1	14	16	7	23	7	8	15	8	8	16
	Many	6	5	11	12	9	21	7	9	16	2	11	13
	Total	19	6	25	28	16	44	14	17	31	10	19	29
Occupational emphasis	Non-occupational	10	2	12	9	5	15	4	6	10	7	7	14
	Occupational	9	4	13	19	11	30	10	11	21	3	12	15
	Total	19	6	25	28	16	45	14	17	31	10	19	29
Gradation	Polarized	12	1	13	15	7	22	6	7	13	7	6	13
	Gradated	7	5	12	13	9	22	8	10	18	3	13	16
	Total	19	6	25	28	16	44	14	17	31	10	19	29

	G	Z	P	G	Z	P	G	Z	P	G	Z	P
Positions	0.83	2.22	5%	0.26	0.85	Not significant	0.05	0.15	Not significant	0.69	1.94	10%
Occupational emphasis	0.37	0.82	Not significant	0.02	0.06	Not significant	0.15	0.39	Not significant	0.60	1.69	10%
Gradation	0.79	1.98	5%	0.19	0.62	Not significant	0.03	0.019	Not significant	0.66	1.97	5%

in this respect. A particularly valid distinction might thus be between a profile in which a *means-production orientation* led the shift, and one in which it was a drag upon the others.

Turning now to the problem of factors responsible for differential modernization *within* each group or village, we see what determines the range of development of modern stratificational images among people of the same "traditional" or "transitional" background. Two social mechanisms were closely examined in this respect: familism (that is, family identification and solidarity);[8] and, by way of contrast, modern communication.[9] The finding which stands out most, when we look at Zafrira, Hazan and Yaron,[10] is that the two factors do not operate as might have been expected, and that they behave differentially in each one of these villages.

Tables 56 to 58 picture the situation. Perhaps the first striking feature is the *simi-*

TABLE 56—Zafrira—Stratificational Models in Relation to Familism and Mass Media

Stratificational models	Familism and mass media	Familism						Exposure to mass media					
		Low		High		Total		Low		High		Total	
		N	%	N	%	N	%	N	%	N	%	N	%
1. Stratificational positions	Few	6	35.3	11	64.7	17	100.0	5	27.8	13	72.2	18	100.0
	Many	1	10.0	9	90.0	10	100.0	3	30.0	7	70.0	10	100.0
			25.9		74.1		100.0		28.6		74.1		100.0
	N	7		20		27		8		20		28	
	Unknown					3						2	
	Total					30						30	
	G=				0.66						0.05		
	Z=				1.44						0.05		
Level of significance					Not significant						Not significant		
2. Stratificational positions	Few	6	33.3	12	66.7	18	100.0	5	27.8	13	72.2	18	100.0
	Many	0	—	7	100.0	7	100.0	2	25.0	6	75.0	8	100.0
			24.0		76.0		100.0		26.9		73.1		100.0
	N	6		19		25		7		19		26	
	Unknown					5						4	
	Total					30						30	
	G=			1							0.07		
	Z=				1.75						0.13		
Level of significance					0.10						Not significant		
3. Occupational structure of positions	Non-occupational	6	46.2	7	53.8	13	100.0	4	30.8	9	69.2	13	100.0
	Occupational	1	7.1	13	92.9	14	100.0	3	20.0	12	80.0	15	100.0
			25.9		74.1		100.0		25.0		75.0		100.0
	N	7		20		27		7		21		28	
	Unknown					3						2	
	Total					30						30	
	G=				0.44						0.28		
	Z=				0.35						0.67		
Level of significance					Not significant						Not significant		

TABLE 56— (continued)

Stratificational models	Familism and mass media	Familism Low N	%	High N	%	Total N	%	Exposure to mass media Low N	%	High N	%	Total N	%
4. Polarization of model	Polarized	6	35.3	11	64.7	17	100.0	5	29.4	12	70.6	17	100.0
	Gradated	1	10.0	9	90.0	10	100.0	3	27.3	8	72.7	11	100.0
			25.9		74.1		100.0		28.6		71.4		100.0
	N	7		20		27		8		20		28	
	Unknown					3						2	
	Total					30						30	
	G=				0.66						0.05		
	Z=				1.44						0.12		
Level of significance					Not significant						Not significant		

TABLE 57—Hazan—Stratificational Models in Relation to Familism and Mass Media

Stratificational models	Familism and mass media	Familism Low N	%	High N	%	Total N	%	Exposure to mass media Low N	%	High N	%	Total N	%
1. Stratificational positions	Few	18	78.2	5	21.8	23	100.0	7	26.9	19	73.1	26	100.0
	Many	7	36.8	12	63.2	19	100.0	3	14.3	18	85.7	21	100.0
			59.5		40.5		100.0		21.2		78.8		100.0
	N	25		17		42		10		37		47	
	Unknown					8						3	
	Total					50						50	
	G=				0.72						0.37		
	Z=				0.72						0.6		
Level of significance					0.01						Not significant		

TABLE 57—(continued)

Stratificational models	Familism and mass media	Familism						Exposure to mass media					
		Low		High		Total		Low		High		Total	
		N	%	N	%	N	%	N	%	N	%	N	%
2. Stratificational criteria	Few	14	48.3	15	51.7	29	100.0	8	27.6	21	72.4	29	100.0
	Many	11	68.8	5	31.2	16	100.0	3	18.8	13	18.2	16	100.0
			55.6		44.4		100.0		24.5		75.5		100.0
	N	25		20		45		11		34		45	
	Unknown					5						5	
	Total					50						50	
	G=				−0.40						0.24		
	Z=				1.32						0.73		
Level of significance					Not significant						Not significant		
3. Occupational structure of positions	Non-occupational	10	83.3	2	16.7	12	100.0	5	41.7	7	58.3	12	100.0
	Occupational	15	45.5	18	54.5	33	100.0	4	11.4	31	88.6	35	100.0
			55.6		44.4		100.0		19.1		80.9		100.0
	N	25		20		45		9		38		47	
	Unknown					5						3	
	Total					50						50	
	G=				0.71						0.69		
	Z=				2.25						2.29		
Level of significance					0.05						0.05		
4. Polarization of model	Polarized	19	76.0	6	24.0	25	100.0	7	26.9	19	73.1	26	100.0
	Gradated	6	35.3	11	64.7	17	100.0	3	14.3	18	85.7	21	100.0
			59.5		40.5		100.0		21.2		78.8		100.0
	N	25		17		42		10		37		47	
	Unknown					8						3	
	Total					50						50	
	G=				0.70						0.37		
	Z=				2.63						1.06		
Level of significance					0.01						Not significant		

TABLE 58—Yaron—Stratificational Models in Relation to Familism and Mass Media

Stratificational models	Familism and mass media	Familism						Exposure to mass media					
		Low		High		Total		Low		High		Total	
		N	%	N	%	N	%	N	%	N	%	N	%
1. Stratificational positions	Few	11	64.7	6	35.3	17	100.0	5	26.3	14	73.7	19	100.0
	Many	14	93.3	1	6.7	15	100.0	1	6.3	15	93.7	16	100.0
			78.1		21.9		100.0		17.1		82.9		100.0
	N	25		7		32		6		29		35	
	Unknown					4						1	
	Total					36						36	
	G=				0.76						0.68		
	Z=				1.95						1.56		
Level of significance					0.10						Not significant		
2. Stratificational criteria	Few	9	60.0	6	40.0	15	100.0	3	20.0	12	80.0	15	100.0
	Many	17	94.4	1	5.6	18	100.0	2	10.5	17	89.5	19	100.0
			78.8		21.8		100.0		14.7		85.3		100.0
	N	26		7		33		5		29		34	
	Unknown					3						2	
	Total					36						36	
	G=				−0.83						0.36		
	Z=				2.40						0.77		
Level of significance					0.05						Not significant		
3. Occupational structure of positions	Non-occupational	8	66.7	4	33.3	12	100.0	5	38.5	8	61.5	13	100.0
	Occupational	17	85.0	3	15.0	20	100.0	1	4.5	21	95.5	22	100.0
			78.1		21.9		100.0		17.1		82.9		100.0
	N	25		7		32		6		29		35	
	Unknown					4						1	
	Total					36						36	
	G=				−0.47						0.85		
	Z=				1.21						2.57		
Level of significance					Not significant						0.01		

TABLE 58—(continued)

Stratificational models	Familism and mass media	Familism						Exposure to mass media					
		Low		High		Total		Low		High		Total	
		N	%	N	%	N	%	N	%	N	%	N	%
4. Polarization of Model	Polarized	9	60.0	6	40.0	15	100.0	4	30.8	9	69.2	13	100.0
	Gradated	16	94.1	1	5.9	17	100.0	2	9.5	19	90.5	21	100.0
			78.1		21.9		100.0		17.6		82.4		100.0
	N	25		7		32		6		28		34	
	Unknown					4						2	
	Total					36						36	
	G=			0.92						0.61			
	Z=			3.29						1.57			
Level of significance				0.01						Not significant			

larly high ratio of exposure to mass media which is maintained in all the three villages (standing at 71.4, 77.8 and 82.9 percent respectively). Perhaps when such communication is truly accessible, even the relatively traditional group cannot resist it. However, it appears that while one can often bring horses to water and even make them drink, the drinking has very different effects. Thus it is primarily in the most modernized group of Yaron that modern communication is consistently associated with all of the dimensions of modern stratificational images analyzed; in Zafrira, on the other hand, it is essentially irrelevant. In other words, in order for such communication to have real impact, certain predispositions are necessary: and these are not acquired early in this process. *What Zafrira has is the security of familiar primary groups*; and this village is not only understandably highest in familism (74.1 percent) but it also shows a palpably *positive* relationship between this characteristic and between open stratificational conceptions. The truth of the matter is probably that the security found in the traditional family is a prerequisite for development of new, possibly more "adventurous" orientations; and that those who have lost their sense of belonging to the group, but who have not yet lost their *need* for it, are thrown upon themselves and the safety of the familiar.

This finding strikingly parallels, of course, that described in Chapter 6 on the level of community structure, and in reference to lineage. The reader will recall that the interpretation we offered there for this same phenomenon was that the fundamental security of the strong traditional framework allows the unfreezing of "loyalties" and commitments or of traditional patterns of behaviour in other spheres; this interpretation seems to hold here also on the level of individual orientations.

In Yaron, however, this kind of familism is already drastically shrunk, and it appears in only 21.9 percent of the respondents. Moreover, here its relationship to openness of outlook is seen (although the numbers are minute) to be inverse—traditional group solidarity being associated with narrow and rigid stratificational horizons.

Clearly, then, modernizing individual world images is a very complex process, in which traditional elements provide the initial sustenance but then must recede at exactly the right time. Such a critical and delicate point in time is, perhaps, seen in Hazan, where the scope of stratificational positions, their structure, and the polarization of the model appear to be positively related to both familism and mass media, while the scope of stratificational criteria is negatively related.

This last—namely the inverse relationship between familism and stratificational criteria—seems to be particularly significant, set as it is against a background in which almost half of the population is still family-oriented. It exemplifies therefore a condition of a potential "breakdown" in modernization on the personality level, residing in a dependence upon a traditional social unit *although this unit is no longer able to sustain modernization*.

Conclusion

In our study we examined future plans of farm youths in Israel in regard to preference for change or for continuity. We saw that this fundamental dimension of individual aspirations crystallizes in reference to a general orientation to change, as represented by the basic structural properties in terms of which the stratificational system is conceptualized. The properties of the individual stratificational "model" which were analyzed in this connection were the "spread" of status criteria and positions, the extent to which these positions were seen as mainly occupational, and the degree to which social strata were considered internally varied as well as ascending in a gradual way. The interpretation offered for the relationship between these conceptions and a bent for personal push lay in the assumption that they reflected, each in its own way, a picture of society visualized as essentially open, differentiated and flexible. It seems that while the spirit of enterprise and mobility, as against a spirit of routine and continuity, have here been spelled out in terms of attitude to a specific type of family farming, the significance of the findings is wider and represents a general mechanism in the subjective evaluation and the assumption of social roles.

The data also show that stratificational conceptions are related to the process of social modernization. Two factors in particular have emerged in this connection. First, the relative paucity of open, differentiated and flexible models in the traditional group throws some light on the problem of scarce entrepreneurship in many developing societies. More precisely, it explains a little of the lag that often exists between the creation of objective entrepreneurial opportunities, and the taking up of these opportunities by the "average" person. Second, individual modernization, like the institutional, is a complex process, going on a variety of tracks and combining into a variety of patterns.

It was also seen that "stable" individual modernization is related to the extent to which the traditional family recedes and hands over to other reference frameworks in a balanced, "graceful", and controlled way. That is to say, the extent to which its basic structure and solidarity neither disintegrate precipitously, nor linger too long. It is for this reason, surely, that modernization—at least as far as individual world pictures are concerned—was not found to be either directly or causally related to modern communication (or exposure to mass media). It appears, in fact, that the broadening of communicative horizons becomes effective in this respect only when and if certain preconditions are met.[11]

To round off the discussion, something more directly relevant to rural settlement must be said. The truism that life—and therefore also agriculture—means many things to many men, has been spelled out here in terms of the continuator and the mobile person. In this respect, the reference to a specific pattern—to the *moshav*—can be made to apply, though of course, with varying implications, to all and any type. This does not mean that orientation to change can or should be equated with the good, or even the functional; and groups, societies, and circumstances (and, obviously, politicians) can combine to dictate conserving and keeping existing tradition rather than changing it. However, if agriculture is not to become the backwater of development, it must be capable of continuously attracting and sustaining change. This lesson is clear in regard to the inherent flexibility of land tenure, ecological structures, etc; it appears to be no less true in respect to human motivation. If rural life is kept institutionally static, and so made to appear stagnant, an accelerated process of "negative" selection is inevitable; and farming will be regarded as fit only for the "traditional"; i.e. incapable, beyond a given point, of sustaining enterprise and entrepreneurship.

NOTES

[1] While not a common focus in stratificational research, it has been employed, for example, in the following:
Elizabeth Bott: "The Concept of Class as a Reference Group", *Human Relations,* No. 3, (1954);
Samuel B. Hammond: "Stratification in an Australian City", in *Readings in Social Psychology,* Swanson *et. al.* (New York, Holt & Co. 1952);
M.S. Martin: "Some Subjective Aspects of Social Stratification", in David V. Glass (ed.), *Social Mobility in Britain,* (London, Routledge & Kegan Paul, 1952);
John L. Haer: "Empirical Study of Social Class Awareness", *Social Forces,* No. 2, (December, 1957)

Also:

Moshe Lissak: *Occupational Trends of Urban Youth in Israel* (Hebrew), unpublished Ph.D. thesis, Jerusalem, 1963.

2 Nor is the *moshav* unique in constituting a homogeneous ethnic community—these exist in many immigrant urban quarters, and are, in fact, characterized by a greater scope for maintaining the "traditional" way of life.

3 The reader may well wonder why in this connection we did not follow up the villages studied in the first phase of our project—which would have certainly added to the picture, and lent it a more dynamic dimension. The answer is that the problems of some of the new studies—such as those reported in this and preceding chapters—required designs into which none of the previous *moshavim* could be fitted. Not less important was our feeling that we might well have used up their fund of goodwill and our own welcome: it is easy to imagine—from the variety of the topics tackled—how long the individual interviews were, how many hours we spent with the public office-holders and functionaries, and how many days were devoted to participant observation. In any case, we had no desire to transplant to these villages the popular image of the Navaho family—supposedly composed of two parents, three children and a Harvard anthropologist.

4 As may be seen, the design is not elaborate or sensitive enough to allow us to distinguish between challenge in terms of enterprise and in terms of social mobility, and both Zafrira and Karmon are relevant (positively and negatively) in terms of the two factors together.

5 See, for instance, Boguslaw Galeski: *Chlopy i zawod rolnika* (Peasants and Farming as an Occupation), (Panstwowe Wydawnictwo Naukowe, Warszawa, 1963); or Ian Tauber, *Kdo zije na vesnicy* (Who Lives in a Village) (Nakladatelstvi Ceské Budějovice, 1965).

6 Though in Yaron, the number of those who said they wanted to stay on is too small for comfortable comparison (5).

7 It is worth repeating that the distinction made here is between those who are, as it were, *inwardly constrained* to change, and those who are not; this does not mean, of course, that the "stayers-on"—or those who are not change-oriented—will not "deviate" from "tradition" under certain pressures; nor that those who are potentially mobile will always necessarily have realistic or realizable aspirations.

8 The need for family support was established on the basis of the young man's desire to go on living in close proximity with the family, in preference to otherwise more advantageous alternatives (such as a higher income, a better standard of living, a higher level of organization and services).

9 Measured by exposure to mass media.

10 The problem area discussed here was not relevant, of course, to the "securely" modern, European village of Karmon.

11 For a causal interpretation of the place of mass media in change, see chiefly: D. Lerner, *The Passing of the Traditional Society*, (Glencoe, Illinois, The Free Press, 1959).

CHAPTER 9

THE YOUNGER GENERATION—PATTERNS OF VOCATIONAL CHOICE, GROUP MEMBERSHIP, AND REFERENCE

Introduction

In Chapter 8 we dealt chiefly with the commitment of the young generation to the *moshav*, and how this commitment is related to a basic orientation to change. Now we shall look into the specific occupational aspirations and plans of these young people, see their social characteristics in terms of membership and reference frameworks (in and out of the *moshav*), and examine the significance of these aspects for the *moshav* itself, and for relations with the wider society.

The analysis is carried out in the same four villages and these two chapters together give us a broad picture—even though unfortunately it was impossible significantly to cross-tabulate the different sets of factors: the numbers were too small and there was a relatively high percentage of unknowns in some of the tables. The data thus refer again to the 14 to 24 age group in Zafrira, Hazan, Yaron and Karmon —representing, as will be recalled, traditional, transitional and modern (veteran) groups of origin. The study population is 30, 60, 39, and 32 families respectively in the four *moshavim,* or a total of 161, being the same (with slight variations, resulting from absences during parts of the extended interview period) as that which we analyzed previously. Here, however, the analysis distinguishes between the 14 to 18 age-group, and the 19 to 24 age-group (including 39 and 72 young people respectively). The idea is to reflect the fact that while the younger group was still largely in a "moratorium" or preparatory stage, and had received most of its education in Israel, the older one was already on the labour market, and had (at least as far as the new immigrant families were concerned) grown up mainly in its countries of origin. Our presentation thus compares the characteristics of these age-groups, those of the three immigrant villages (Zafrira, Hazan and Yaron) with the veteran one (Karmon), and those of the traditional immigrant village (Zafrira) with the two transitional ones (Hazan and Yaron).[1]

The sample villages were chosen, it will be recalled, as groups coming from societies at different levels of modernization; and the same trend was represented in respect to the *specific* backgrounds of the families involved in terms of the fathers' education and occupation. Tables 59 and 60 summarize these backgrounds.

While all of the immigrant groups come largely from non-agricultural settings, almost none of them have urban "middle-class" backgrounds—educational or

TABLE 59—Distribution of Fathers' Education

Village \ Education	Illiterate		Traditional-religious education: Up to 4 years		5 – 8		9 – 12		Modern-general education: Up to 4 years		5 – 8		9 – 12		13 +		Total		unknown
	N	%	N	%	N	%	N	%	N	%	N	%	N	%	N	%	N	%	N
Zafrira	14	77.78	–	—	–	—	–	—	1	5.55	1	5.55	1	5.55	1	5.55	18	99.98	5
Hazan	3	9.09	1	3.03	1	3.03	2	6.06	5	15.15	18	54.54	1	3.03	2	6.06	33	99.99	7
Yaron	2	6.25	1	3.12	9	28.12	1	3.12	3	9.38	8	25.00	5	15.63	3	9.37	32	98.98	—
Karmon	—	—	–	—	1	3.44	6	20.69	–	—	6	20.69	14	48.27	2	6.89	29	99.98	—
Total	19	16.97	2	1.77	11	9.82	9	8.04	9	8.04	33	29.47	21	18.75	8	7.14	112	100.00	12

Note: The total in this and in the following table is less than the population of young people (161), since some interviewees are the sons of the same father, and some fathers are deceased (few details being known about them).

TABLE 60—Distribution of Fathers' Occupation

Village \ Occupation	Rabbi, religious teacher or functionary		Teacher, clerk medical orderly		Semi-skilled traditional artisan		Hawker, petty trades-man		Farmer		Small shop-keeper		Total		Unknown
	N	%	N	%	N	%	N	%	N	%	N	%	N	%	N
Zafrira	–	—	2	14.28	10	71.44	–	—	2	14.28	—	—	14	100.0	9
Hazan	1	5.0	2	10.0	8	40.00	2	10.0	1	5.00	6	30.0	20	100.0	20
Yaron	—	—	2	9.09	9	40.91	2	9.09	1	4.55	8	36.6	22	100.0	10
Karmon	—	—	2	6.89	—	—	—	—	27	93.11	—	—	29	100.0	—
Total	1	1.17	8	9.41	27	31.77	4	4.70	31	16.47	14	36.48	85	100.0	39

occupational. In fact, the three immigrant populations have a low occupational and educational status of origin, whether religious or secular, but the level of both increases from the traditional to the transitional society. Thus in Zafrira the mode was that of semi- or unskilled traditional artisans (e.g., weavers, cobblers, cheese-makers) who had no formal education at all; in Hazan, both traditional and modern schooling—though not high—was already common, while the main occupations included petty tradesmen and small shopkeepers; in Yaron, finally, the occupational structure was by and large the same, but it was combined with a somewhat higher educational standard.

In Karmon, by contrast, the youth was born into modern educated families, *ideologically committed to farming*—all the fathers having come to the country and voluntarily settled on the land as pioneers a whole generation ago, most of them fresh out of school. It is against these backgrounds that the occupational plans and social characteristics of the *moshav* second generation can best be understood.

Occupational Plans and Aspirations

In examining the processes of occupational placement, a few basic data on the educational standards of the study population will perhaps be helpful. From the total of Table 61 we get a general idea of the educational picture.

About 30 percent of the group have not yet completed their education (including 29.0 percent who are still in secondary schools, and a fragment—1.0 percent—attending institutes of higher learning). Of those whose education is finished, only 11 percent have less than an elementary education, 24 percent have finished elementary schools (with some additional courses or evening classes), 15 percent have some secondary schooling, while about 20 percent have a complete secondary-vocational or academic education. On the whole, this is an encouraging picture: 65 percent of the children in these *moshavim* have a partial or a complete secondary education—in a population which is entirely rural, and composed largely of immigrants from traditional colonial societies. Significant differentials are evident, though, in a breakdown by village and by age.

The difference between the two groups is negligible among those who are still studying (about 3 percent higher in the established village); otherwise, however, the contrast is great. In Karmon, no one has only elementary education, or less than that; and almost no one has incomplete secondary schooling, or vocational secondary education in general: and the norm is complete secondary-academic education. In the immigrant villages, on the other hand, 46 percent have only an elementary education—either complete or incomplete; 12 percent have had some secondary schooling; 11 percent have a certificate of matriculation; and of these the proportion of vocational as against academic students is much higher. This table illustrates, of course, only the expected and the commonplace—deficiencies inherent in back-

TABLE 61—Education by Village and by Age-group

Education / Age-group and village	Incomplete elementary		Complete elementary		Complete elementary and additional courses		Incomplete secondary		Complete vocational secondary		Complete academic secondary and studying in institute of higher learning		Still studying in secondary schools		Total	
	N	%	4	%	4	%	N	%	N	%	N	%	N	%	N	%
Zafrira	16	53.30	7	23.30	1	3.00	2	6.00	—	—	—	—	4	13.40	30	100.0
14–18	4	26.27	6	40.00	—	—	1	6.66	—	—	—	—	4	26.67	15	100.0
19–24	12	80.00	1	6.66	1	6.66	1	6.67	—	—	—	—	—	—	15	100.0
Hazan	2	3.30	14	23.30	10	16.70	14	23.30	2	3.30	2	3.30	16	26.80	60	100.0
14–18	—	—	8	21.63	2	5.40	9	24.33	1	2.70	1	2.70	16	43.24	37	100.0
19–24	2	8.70	6	26.09	8	34.79	5	21.74	1	4.34	1	4.34	—	—	23	100.0
Yaron	—	—	6	15.40	2	5.20	6	15.40	7	17.90	3	7.70	15	38.40	39	100.0
14–18	—	—	5	21.75	—	—	2	8.70	1	4.34	—	—	15	65.22	23	100.0
19–24	—	—	1	6.25	2	12.50	4	25.00	6	37.50	3	18.75	—	—	16	100.0
Total in 3 villages	18	13.90	27	20.97	13	10.10	22	17.00	9	7.00	5	3.90	35	27.13	129	100.0
14–18	4	5.33	19	25.33	2	2.67	12	16.00	2	2.67	1	1.33	35	46.67	75	100.0
19–24	14	25.93	8	14.82	11	20.17	10	18.52	7	12.96	4	7.40	—	—	54	100.0
Karmon	—	—	—	—	—	—	3	9.40	1	3.10	18	56.30	10	31.20	32	100.0
14–18			—	—	—	—	1	7.10	—	—	3	21.43	10	71.43	14	100.0
19–24	—	—	—	—	—	—	2	11.00	1	5.56	15	88.34	—	—	18	100.0
Total	18	11.20	27	16.10	13	8.10	25	15.50	10	6.20	23	14.30	45	29.00	161	100.0

ground and immigration can hardly be overcome in one generation even under conditions of sustained educational effort, characteristic of Israel's society. The importance of original background in this respect is further emphasized by the perceptible differences between the three immigrant villages; educational achievements correspond, by and large, to the extent of social modernization in the country of origin, with Yaron ahead, and Zafrira well behind.[2]

No less decisive (and equally to be expected) is the influence on education of the age-group itself. The table points clearly to the advantage held by those who came to the country at a younger age, and it shows, furthermore, that this factor is especially strong in the traditional group.

However, from the point of view of the present discussion, the salient feature of this data is surely that, subject to differences which are due to background, most of

TABLE 62—Occupational Choice by Village and Age-group

Occupational choice / Age-group and village	Farming		Crafts and trades		Technical		Driving		Clerical		Teaching		Regular army		Commerce (own business)		Academic		Still undecided		Total	
	N	%	N	%	N	%	N	%	N	%	N	%	N	%	N	%	N	%	N	%	N	%
Zafrira	16	53.3	2	6.7	7	23.3	—	—	2	6.7	—	—	—	—	1	3.3	2	6.0	—	—	30	100.0
14–18	6	40.0	1	6.7	5	33.3	—	—	1	6.7	—	—	—	—	—	—	2	13.3	—	—	15	100.0
19–24	10	66.6	1	6.7	2	13.3	—	—	1	6.7	—	—	—	—	1	6.7	—	—	—	—	15	100.0
Hazan	17	28.3	5	8.3	20	33.4	5	8.3	2	3.3	1	1.7	—	—	5	8.2	4	6.7	1	1.7	60	100.0
14–18	7	18.9	4	10.8	16	43.3	3	8.1	2	5.4	1	2.7	—	—	1	2.7	2	5.4	1	2.7	37	100.0
19–24	10	43.5	1	4.3	4	17.4	2	8.7	—	—	—	—	—	—	4	17.4	2	8.7	—	—	23	100.0
Yaron	7	17.9	5	12.8	10	25.7	1	2.6	1	2.6	1	2.6	2	5.1	2	5.1	7	17.9	3	7.7	39	100.0
14–18	2	8.6	3	13.1	8	34.8	—	—	—	—	—	—	2	8.6	1	4.3	4	17.5	3	13.1	23	100.0
19–24	5	—	2	—	2	—	1	—	1	—	1	—	—	—	1	—	3	—	—	—	16	100.0
Total in 3 villages	40	31.0	12	9.2	37	28.7	6	4.6	5	3.9	2	1.5	2	1.5	8	6.2	13	10.1	4	3.1	129	100.0
14–18	15	20.0	8	10.7	29	38.7	3	4.0	3	4.0	1	1.4	2	2.6	2	2.6	8	10.7	4	5.3	75	100.0
19–24	25	46.3	4	7.4	8	14.8	3	5.6	2	3.7	1	1.8	—	—	6	11.1	5	9.3	—	—	54	100.0
Karmon	11	34.4	—	—	1	3.1	—	—	1	3.1	4	12.5	—	—	—	—	5	15.6	10	31.2	32	100.0
14–18	4	28.6	—	—	1	7.1	—	—	—	—	2	14.2	—	—	—	—	3	21.5	4	28.6	14	100.0
19–24	7	38.9	—	—	—	—	—	—	1	5.6	2	11.1	—	—	—	—	2	11.1	6	33.3	18	100.0
Total	51	31.7	12	7.4	38	23.7	6	3.7	6	3.7	6	3.7	2	1.2	8	5.0	18	11.2	14	8.7	166	100.0

Note: Farming also includes some auxiliary agricultural occupations—such as rural extension work; crafts and trades include (by order of priority) smithery, shoe-making, building and construction, carpentry, and hair-dressing; technical occupations refer to (by order of priority): mechanics (including motor and aero-nautical), electronics, instrument making, draughtsmanship and surveying; driving is presented as a special category because, while being a "modern" trade, it is one which requires little vocational training and general education; academic occupations refer chiefly to a variety of professions in humanities and social science (such as literature and economics), to engineering and to law.

the non-modern groups either have, or are acquiring, an educational basis which will let them compete for a variety of modern occupational openings. We must now see just how this potential is translated into actual occupational choice.

1. OCCUPATIONAL CHOICE

The totals of Table 62 summarize occupational choice (or occupational plans of youth which is still attending school) in the four villages which we have grouped into ten categories.

Though the range of choices is wide, agriculture, blue-collar work and the free professions are emphasized, showing that this population can be characterized by two basic socio-economic features: a) *occupational modernization* as reflected in the high rate of essentially "modern" choices (skilled trades, technical and academic); b) *occupational productivization*[3] as reflected in the low incidence of commerce and white-collar work.

When we compare Karmon and the three immigrant villages we have a more strongly differentiated picture.

The most prominent difference brought out by the table is the much higher proportion of the "undecided" in Karmon, apparently related to the longer period of preparation or "legitimate" moratorium in this group. In the other *moshavim,* by contrast, the choice is much more decisive, and made earlier in life.

As to the contents of this choice, the youth of Karmon concentrates on farming, free professions and teaching—with 34.4 percent, 15.6 percent and 12.5 percent respectively; while in Zafrira, Hazan and Yaron, technical occupations are a very high second at 28.7 percent with *blue-collar occupations* (that is, technical together with trades and crafts) standing at 38 percent. So, in the less "modernized" villages, there is a greater flexibility and a wider range of prospective occupations.

These characteristics hold also in each of the three villages, although there is a difference as to the choice of farming. Thus 53.3 percent of the youth of *moshav* Zafrira selected farming, as opposed to 23.3 percent and 17.9 percent in Hazan and Yaron respectively; while Yaron is relatively more academically-oriented. Otherwise, though, the prominent position of blue-collar occupations is basically the same. Slightly sharper distinctions, by contrast, are exhibited between the two age-groups, especially in the immigrant villages. These differences extend primarily to the *relative* place of farming and blue-collar work: in the younger group, the salience of the first diminishes and of the second increases. Another difference is in the greater emphasis on commerce in the 19 to 24 category (more than 4 to 1). *The greater vocational "modernization" and "productivization" of the 14 to 18 group, however, is not associated with a higher level of aspiration in terms of an academic orientation and/or with white-collar jobs—which in both of these categories are moderate.*

By and large, then—while farming is chosen by both veteran and new immigrant youth—there is much less polarization among the less "modern" or non-European population, and greater variety—representing a higher potential in "intermediate" or "middle-range" primary occupations. The finding that young people who come from modern, prosperous, and educated families, and who can therefore pick and choose their careers, generally do not prefer blue-collar jobs is, of course, too commonplace for comment. But it is significant that other groups do have a positive attitude to these occupations and view them as an entirely feasible alternative to farming; thus education here is used to serve, rather than to by-pass, technical opportunities. Table 63 shows in fact that, except in the extremes, the *level* of education *per se,* is not strongly associated with the area of choice (the extremes being a nexus of low education with agriculture, and of academic secondary education with the professions).[4]

We must now turn to the aspirations which underlie and clarify these vocational plans.

2. OCCUPATIONAL MOTIVATION

We get some inkling of the mechanisms which influence these patterns of choice when we look at the *criteria* on which occupational choices are based, or the anticipated *rewards.*

The bases of choice obtained[5] can be grouped into six broad categories:

1. *Relative ease (or simplicity), physical comfort and cleanliness*—combining such answers as: "one should choose an occupation which is easy and comfortable"; "not for money or anything, only most comfortable"; "relative physical ease"; "work which is not too difficult, out of the sun"; "quiet and healthy occupation".

2. *Income and economic security*—including, for example: "a lot of money"; "work is chosen for money, for a living—a good occupation is one which gives a good income"; "assurance of regular employment"; "continuity of employment"; "an assured living"; "economic security, profitability, returns on work and investment".

3. *Independence and mobility*—e.g.: "independence in work"; "work which affords independence"; "independence, without a boss, without instructions from above"; "a possibility of change when desired".

4. *Interest, personal fulfilment, development of potential*—as for instance: "one should take a job one loves even if it earns little money, rather than a job which brings a lot of money but one doesn't love it"; "interesting, fitting one's inclinations and character"; "a job which will provide interest and fulfilment"; "an occupation which will give internal satisfaction, from which one can learn"; "an occupation which will suit one's abilities"; "an occupation giving a sense of satisfaction with a job well done".

5. *National service and ideological fulfilment*—mentioning such factors as:

TABLE 63—Occupational Choice by Educational Level in Immigrant Villages

Education \ Occupational choice	Farming	Trades and crafts	Technical	Driving	Commerce (private business)	Clerical	Teaching	Regular army	Academic	Un-decided	Total
Incomplete elementary	12	—	3	—	2	2	2	—	—	—	19
Complete elementary	8	3	9	1	2	—	1	—	1	1	26
Complete elementary + courses	6	2	3	1	—	—	—	—	—	—	12
Incomplete secondary	3	5	7	3	3	—	—	—	—	1	22
Complete vocational secondary	4	—	1	—	1	—	—	1	1	1	9
Complete academic secondary	—	—	—	—	—	—	1	—	4	—	5
Still in secondary school	7	2	14	1	—	3	—	1	7	1	36
Total	40	12	37	6	8	5	4	2	13	4	129

"service to the country"; "importance for the State"; "a contribution to society"; "work which will be useful to society and to the State"; "an occupation which is useful and productive".

6. *Prestige*—and specifically macro-societal prestige (rather than prestige in small groups) referring to replies of the following kind: "work which serves to achieve prestige in society"; "appreciation in society"; "an occupation which is prestigeful in society"; "an occupation which will give high social status".

In the totals of Table 64 we see which factors—in the opinion of the young men themselves—*generally* (or optimally) ought to be taken into consideration when occupational choices are made.

Three rewards are considered the most legitimate—material benefits (including income and security), the chance for personal fulfilment or what may be termed "ego expansion" and—to a lesser extent—work that is easy or comfortable to do. All in all, however, there is a wide range of criteria or of positive occupational attributes,

TABLE 64—Criteria for Occupational Choice by Village and Age-group
(Multiple mention, weighted by priority)

Criteria / Village and age-group	Simplicity comfort and cleanliness		Interest, fulfil-ment, develop-ment potential		Indepen-dence and mobility		Income and economic security		Prestige		National service and ideological fulfil-ment		Total	
	N	%	N	%	N	%	N	%	N	%	N	%	N	%
Zafrira	31	19.3	26	16.2	5	3.1	74	45.9	16	9.9	9	5.6	161	100.0
14–18	13	15.3	17	20.0	1	1.2	39	45.9	8	9.4	7	8.2	85	100.0
19–24	18	23.7	9	11.8	4	5.3	35	46.2	8	10.5	2	2.6	76	100.0
Hazan	40	12.4	84	26.0	17	5.3	149	46.1	17	5.3	16	5.0	323	100.0
14–18	27	14.0	47	24.4	11	5.7	85	44.0	15	7.8	8	4.1	193	100.0
19–24	13	10.0	37	28.5	6	4.6	64	49.2	2	1.5	8	6.2	130	100.0
Yaron	16	7.1	64	28.6	3	1.3	111	49.6	17	7.6	13	5.8	224	100.0
14–18	11	8.5	33	25.6	0	—	68	52.7	11	8.5	6	4.7	129	100.0
19–24	5	5.3	31	32.6	3	3.2	43	45.7	6	6.3	7	7.4	95	100.0
Total in 3 villages	87	12.3	174	24.5	25	3.5	334	47.2	50	7.0	38	5.4	708	100.0
14–18	51	12.8	97	23.6	12	2.9	192	47.1	34	8.3	22	5.3	407	100.0
19–24	36	11.9	77	25.7	13	4.3	142	47.3	16	15.4	16	5.4	301	100.0
Karmon	7	3.6	66	33.9	9	4.6	94	48.2	9	4.6	10	5.1	195	100.0
14–18	3	3.6	28	33.3	2	2.4	46	54.7	4	4.8	1	1.2	84	100.0
19–24	4	3.6	38	34.3	7	6.3	48	43.2	5	4.5	9	8.1	111	100.0
Total	94	10.4	240	26.6	34	3.7	428	47.4	59	6.5	48	5.4	903	100.0

without one dominant theme. It is also meaningful that *both prestige (or relational) and symbolic (or expressive) rewards are marginal.* This perhaps explains why "intermediate" occupations not significantly associated socially with either, have been given such a central place.

The table also shows that the more "modern" the groups are, the less important relative ease of effort, cleanliness and physical comfort become, while individual fulfilment is increasingly stressed. Otherwise, however, *the pattern is fairly constant,* being only slightly differentiated according to village or age-group. Thus, *although levels of education and of aspirations differ from group to group, the basic occupational values are much the same.*

A very similar picture is seen when we examine occupational values not abstractly, but in terms of the *actual* choices made—that is, the real reasons or the motives given for these choices.[6] These reasons reflect the advantages which are attributed to various occupations, as well as their drawbacks, and thus represent the overall balance of anticipated rewards, benefits and the *price which the interviewee is willing to pay for these.* First, let us examine the general structure or composition of these reasons and try to find out which specific traits are considered positive and which are seen as negative. This kind of "map", of course, will not give us the "ultimate" occupational levels of aspiration, because the attributes of the vocation chosen obviously do not always correspond to what one really most wants, but it will provide us with an insight into what is in general regarded as an occupational asset or as a liability.

Table 65 shows the pattern of positive occupational traits in all four villages, arranged in categories which correspond, on the whole, to those mentioned "in the abstract".

Here, too, the same three rewards stand out; once again, there is a wide, and similarly structured, range of values, with no dominant theme—showing us that actual aspirations can be achieved in a number of ways. The main distinction between "objective" and "personal" evaluation is that here physical comfort, cleanliness, and independence play a higher role, and economic rewards a lower one than should "ideally" be the case.

Examining the data by village we again find consistent differences.

It is not uninteresting that the veteran village is not noticeably higher when it comes to ideological fulfilment or "expressive" expectations—and it shows that while the ideals or the "virtues" of settlement and productivization are still practiced, they are no longer preached. In the new villages, young people are clearly more satisfied with "unassuming" rewards, which relate to the technical aspects of work; to say nothing of the emphasis on material advantages. In Karmon, by the same token, pride of place is given to individual fulfilment. On the face of it, this motivation is the most open, since it does not either limit or define the characteristics of the vocation itself.

TABLE 65—Composition of Rewards of Chosen Occupations by Village and Age-group (Multiple mention weighted by priority)

Rewards / Age-group and village	Simplicity, comfort and cleanliness		Interest, personal fulfilment, development of potential		Independence and mobility		Income and economic security		Prestige		National service and ideological fulfilment		Others		No rewards mentioned		Total	
	N	%	N	%	N	%	N	%	N	%	N	%	N	%	N	%	N	%
Zafrira	17	36.9	6	13.0	5	10.9	12	26.0	1	2.2	2	4.4	1	2.2	2	4.4	46	100.0
14–18	7	29.1	4	16.7	1	4.2	6	25.0	1	4.2	2	8.3	1	4.2	2	8.3	24	100.0
19–24	10	45.4	2	9.1	4	18.2	6	27.3	—	—	—	—	-	—	-	—	22	100.0
Hazan	35	25.9	23	17.0	24	17.8	42	31.3	6	4.5	4	3.0	1	0.7	-	—	135	100.0
14–18	20	26.7	9	12.0	14	18.7	23	30.7	5	6.6	3	4.0	1	1.3	-	—	75	100.0
19–24	15	25.0	14	23.9	10	16.7	19	31.7	1	1.7	1	1.7	-	—	-	—	60	100.0
Yaron	7	8.6	33	40.8	4	4.9	17	20.9	6	7.4	13	16.6	1	1.2	-	—	81	100.0
14–18	4	9.3	15	34.9	1	2.3	11	25.6	2	47	9	20.9	1	23	-	—	43	
19–24	3	7.9	18	47.4	3	7.9	6	15.8	4	10.5	4	10.5	-	—	-	—	38	
Total in 3 villages	59	25.5	62	23.7	33	12.6	71	27.1	13	5.0	19	72.	3	1.1	2	0.8	262	100.0
14–18	38	24.4	42	26.9	16	10.3	42	26.9	6	3.8	10	6.4	2	1.3	-	—	156	100.0
19–24	2.1	19.8	20	18.9	17	16.1	29	27.3	7	6.6	9	8.5	1	0.9	2	1.9	106	100.0
Karmon	2	4.6	18	41.9	7	16.3	7	16.3	3	7.0	4	9.3	2	4.6	-	—	43	100.0
14–18	1	6.2	8	50.0	2	12.4	3	18.7	1	6.3	1	6.3	-	—	-	—	16	100.0
19–24	1	3.7	10	37.0	5	18.5	4	14.8	2	7.4	3	11.1	2	7.4	-	—	27	100.0
Total	61	20.1	80	26.3	40	13.1	78	25.6	16	5.2	23	7.5	5	1.6	2	0.6	305	100.0

In practice, however—as we shall see—it can be realized only in very selected occupations, and is thus really oriented to rather narrow and specific vocational channels. This high motivational selectivity is further highlighted by the substantial concentration of expectations in one category—which recalls a similar feature in the pattern of choice (Table 62)—and which contrasts strongly with the "spread" of alternative choices and satisfactions in the less "modernized" and lower status groups. Also, among the "veteran" youth, concrete rewards exceed what they themselves consider to be "proper", while among the other groups, the actual aspirations are lower than the "ideal". This shows us that the self-image of the socially modern, higher status group can become relatively "closed" and one-sided: it is, then, not oriented to new occupational openings and new channels of mobility, and might thus be insensitive to and lag in competing for new roles and opportunities under novel conditions.

The table also shows us that—as was true before—there are consistent but not considerable differences among the new villages. These differences are associated with background and range along the "traditional-modern" dimension—Yaron being the closest to Karmon in this respect, while Zafrira is the farthest from it.

By contrast, there are *no* important differences at all between the two age-groups, signifying that while they have, as we have seen, distinct patterns of occupational choice, these patterns are motivated by essentially similar ambitions.

The motivational pattern is also reflected in the negative vocational attributes mentioned, which can properly be grouped into categories paralleling, by and large, the positive factors.

1. Complicated demands, difficulties, physical discomfort
2. High investment required
3. Lack of economic security, and low income
4. Lack of autonomy
5. Lack of interest or personal fulfilment
6. Low prestige.

As can be seen from Table 66, the drawbacks are, indeed, largely the obverse of the rewards, the main negative emphasis being on difficult, uncomfortable or dirty work. Also of interest is the equally high proportion of answers which do not mention drawbacks.

When we compare Karmon with the three other villages we see that the main difference lies in the factor of personal fulfilment, the lack of which plays an important role in Karmon, though it is negligible elsewhere.

Here again, the factor of individual fulfilment, or the job's intrinsic interest is the main dividing line between the two categories of *moshavim*. In this respect, the internal differences between the new villages are smaller, but again Yaron minimizes the importance of the demands of work and of its economic rewards.

Once more we find no startling differences between the age-groups showing that the basic criteria according to which occupations are evaluated, are determined, in the first instance, by background, even though the occupational preferences themselves are different.

So, much, then, for occupational values in general. We must now see in what way these values are specifically related to actual vocations; and determine the concrete balance of the rewards in terms of which they are perceived and chosen.

Table 67 (folding page) presents the overall distribution of occupational advantages and draw-backs, attributed to these chosen vocations (because of the complexity of the data, they are not cross-tabulated).

Those who choose agriculture as an occupation conceive of it primarily in terms of personal independence (38.3 percent), with income at 21.9 percent being second, and interest and physical comfort running a close third and fourth (15.0 percent and 13.3 percent respectively). By contrast, considerations of prestige and ideological

TABLE 66—Composition of Drawbacks of Chosen Occupations by Village and Age-group (multiple choice)

Drawbacks / Age-group and village	High requirements, hardships, discomfort		Lack of interest and fulfilment		Lack of autonomy		Lack of economic security, low income		Low prestige		High investment required		No drawbacks		Total	
	N	%	N	%	N	%	N	%	N	%	N	%	N	%	N	%
Zafrira	9	31.1	—	—	—	—	7	24.1	—	—	1	3.4	12	41.4	29	100.0
14–18	5	29.4	—	—	—	—	3	17.6	—	—	1	5.9	8	47.1	17	100.0
19–24	4	33.4	—	—	—	—	4	33.3	—	—	—	—	4	33.3	12	100.0
Hazan	27	45.0	1	1.7	—	—	10	16.7	—	—	4	6.6	18	30.0	60	100.0
14–18	15	45.5	1	3.0	—	—	4	12.1	—	—	—	—	13	39.4	33	100.0
19–24	12	44.4	—	—	—	—	6	22.2	—	—	4	14.8	5	18.6	27	100.0
Yaron	10	29.5	1	2.9	1	2.9	2	5.9	—	—	2	5.9	18	52.9	34	100.0
14–18	6	33.3	—	—	—	—	1	5.6	—	—	—	—	11	61.1	18	100.0
19–24	4	25.0	1	6.3	1	6.2	1	6.2	—	—	2	12.5	7	43.8	16	100.0
Total in 3 villages	46	37.4	2	1.7	1	0.8	19	15.4	—	—	7	5.6	48	39.1	12.3	100.0
14–18	26	37.9	1	1.5	—	—	8	11.9	—	—	1	1.5	32	47.2	68	100.0
19–24	20	36.4	1	1.8	1	1.8	11	20.0	—	—	6	10.9	16	29.1	55	100.0
Karmon	7	28.0	7	18.0	—	—	4	16.0	1	4.0	1	4.0	5	20.0	25	100.0
14–18	3	30.0	4	40.0	—	—	2	20.0	—	—	—	—	1	10.0	10	100.0
19–24	4	26.7	3	20.0	—	—	2	13.3	1	6.6	1	6.7	4	26.7	15	100.0
Total	53	35.8	9	6.1	1	0.7	23	15.5	1	0.7	8	5.4	53	35.8	148	100.0

fulfilment are conspicuously low here, making it quite clear that farming is not thought of in terms of its societal values or importance. *Thus, while this choice represents an objective or a functional process of productivization, the process is not motivated by values "proper" to it—i.e. those of personal and social pioneering, or "productivity"*. In fact, the very attributes of agriculture appear to be, on the whole, similar to those of commerce (or private business) in general, where autonomy and income are also the most salient factors (although in reversed importance). In other words—the image of the farm as being primarily a *family "business" is gradually becoming the accepted motivational pattern among the* moshav *youth.*

This applies especially to the second generation of the immigrant settlers, as is clearly shown when the three villages are examined separately (Table 68, folding page).

Here, the choice of farming is associated with independence in 45 percent of the answers, while income and easy work stand at 22.5 percent and 20 percent respectively; interest and personal fulfilment are, however, entirely marginal. This configuration is, in fact, conspicuously similar to the choice of a privately run business and to business only—in which personal fulfilment is also not expected and prestige and ideology are lower than in other vocations, with the categories of autonomy and instrumental rewards combining to 95.4 percent. The same is true regarding anticipated disadvantages (although the numbers are here too small for any confident statement): and the entrepreneurial aspects of risk and high investment stand at 67.8 percent in farming, and at 50 percent in commercial business. *This picture seems of crucial importance if we are to understand the basis of these occupational choices. By showing that entrepreneurial risks are considered a price worth paying for entrepreneurial gains, the picture also shows that the emphasis on family enterprise here is not just a matter of the continuity of the first generation's traditional petty trade (as seen in Table 60) a continuity in which the kind of the occupation changes but not its nature; instead, it is actually a far more modern, market-oriented concept.*

Trades and crafts, driving, and clerking all represent another distinct category in terms of rewards; in all three, ease and comfort, plus a high income, are the main features, but are accompanied also by considerations of personal fulfilment, as well as by a general "value judgement" (status where driving and clerking are concerned and awareness of the importance, from the point of view of service to the country, in the area of trade and crafts). All in all, the three occupations relate primarily to "modest"—instrumental and material—attributes, but promise other rewards.

Of special significance, however, is the fact that the intrinsic factors of personal fulfilment, as well as value considerations are much higher in trades and crafts than they are in clerical work—proving not only that the modern "middle range" occupations are more salient in this group than the white-collar ones (Table 62), but also that they are conceived of as richer in content and in promise. This picture is further reinforced by the profile of technical occupations in which fulfilment already plays the most important part. These occupations, in fact, constitute an "intermediate" link before the major category of academic choice, which is characterized primarily by personal identification with the vocation, a lesser emphasis on actual conditions of work and income, and somewhat greater stress on national service and ideology, as well as on social prestige. It is also interesting to see the similarity, in this respect, of military service and non-farming rural vocations, which combine a considerable measure of personal fulfilment together with high prestige and ideological orientation, respectively. Indeed, rural non-farming work seems to have a secondary core of "service"—with a quarter of the answers mentioning some form of ideological fulfilment. In this respect, it gives way only to teaching, which—at 50 percent—is a "service" occupation *par excellence.*

This picture remains essentially the same when specific villages and age-groups are compared with slight changes in the proportions along the lines of our earlier findings.[7]

The paucity of "service" orientations, and their concentration in selected occupations also typifies the established *moshav*, as does the essentially entrepreneurial conception of farming. The main difference here is that personal fulfilment or "ego expansion" dimension is considered relevant to agriculture, both positively and negatively. In Karmon, though (Table 69, folding page), the pattern is also much more polarized and focused; and the three major vocations (farming, academic and teaching) all represent primarily the rewards of personal fulfilment.

To sum up, in all these groups, the "normally" modern "farmer" conception of agriculture is dominant—signifying a change from the ideological background of the "veteran" youth and from the traditional background of immigrants. In other respects, though, the differences between the two are considerable—with Karmon emphasizing fewer and higher occupations and rewards, and the three villages of Zafrira, Hazan and Yaron showing a greater spread and diversity, a trend to intermediate occupations, and much more modest personal aspirations.

These findings are of some importance in terms of the *moshav*, and its relations with society as a whole. But we must postpone their interpretation or evaluation, in order first to examine these aspects also as regards social frameworks and images.

Membership and Reference Groups

In the preceding sections, devoted to occupational plans and motives, we examined *individual* characteristics and aspirations. Now we must locate the *moshav* youth in its *social context* and see how the various villages differ in 1) their youth groups, and 2) the relative salience of ethnic as against general frameworks, as reference groups in each.

1. YOUTH GROUPS

An examination of the friendship patterns of the four populations, presented in the following sociometric charts[8] and their accompanying table (70), shows that there are considerable differences between the villages in respect to two interrelated dimensions; *the character of the youth groups formed, and their scope.*

As can be seen, in Zafrira the friendship network is generalized and amorphous, does not form itself into cohesive age and education-homogeneous "cliques", and does not transcend the community bounds. *Relations with peers, in other words, are narrow in scope and not clearly differentiated from other relationships, showing that age-group organization is secondary here.* This finding is well in line with the picture we obtained previously on the salience of kinship frameworks in this group, and in particular the solidarity of its families; which can now be seen as indeed unaffected in the main by any clear intergenerational division, despite the considerable gap in the

TABLE 70—Summary of Friendship Patterns, Measured Sociometrically

Pattern variables / Village	Number of distinct groups	Age homogeneity (average)	Educational homogeneity (average)	Family homogeneity (average)	Family choices	Network intensity	Group cohesiveness (average)	Outside linkage
Zafrira	2	53.1%	—	27.2%	44.8%	3.5	5.9%	10'7%
Hazan	6	97.3%	68.7%	15.2%	23.3%	3.1	15.5%	29.6%
Yaron	5	96.9%	85.0%	7.39%	6.1%	3.9	27.2%	51.3%
Karmon	11	100.0%	94.9%	3.9%	3.6%	3.5	—	40.5%

Notes:

Number of distinct groups: in Zafrira the number given is two, because the bulk of the choices given—almost 80 percent—form one amorphous mass, and cannot really be considered a group (although it is, of course, taken into account as a unit of analysis in computing the following indices).

Age homogeneity of groups: calculated on the basis of the percentage of people in the same age-group (14 to 18 or 19 to 24) in each framework; it refers to respondents and to those non-respondents whose age was known to us.

Educational homogeneity of groups: calculated on the basis of the percentage of people of the same educational status (i.e. whether they are still studying or not) in each framework; here, only respondents are taken into account, since there is no precise information in this respect on non-respondents. (This variable is irrelevant in Zafrira, where only four out of 30 respondents were still in school).

Family homogeneity of groups: computed according to the percentage of relations bound by friendship in each group; here, both respondents and non-respondents figure.

Family Choices: signify the number of links directed to relatives, either within or without a group boundary.

Network intensity: refers to average number of choices per respondent.

Group cohesiveness: means the proportion of reciprocated choices in each group.

Outside linkage: measures the ratio of choices outside the community in thê total choices made by respondents.

In Karmon a high proportion of respondents were unwilling to name their friends[9] (8 out of 32); for this reason, interpretation here is less secure, especially as regards mutual choices. We think in fact that this may account for the lack of mutual choice obtained in our chart for this village.

education, attitudes and sophistication of parents and children. By contrast, in Hazan, Yaron and Karmon, age-mates form themselves into integrated and differentiated sub-groups, and there are also numerous links outside the community. More specifically, *in these three villages, friendship patterns are more distinct and better differentiated, more age-homogeneous, more salient and less parochial.* These aspects are, of course, directly related to longer years of study, and to the fact that part of this educational process takes place in non-local schools; over and above this, however, *the data indicate that age-groups tend to crystallize when familistic orientation and division of labour lessen.*

This conclusion supports thus the well-known hypothesis of S.N.Eisenstadt on the

FIGURE 3. Friendship in Zafrira

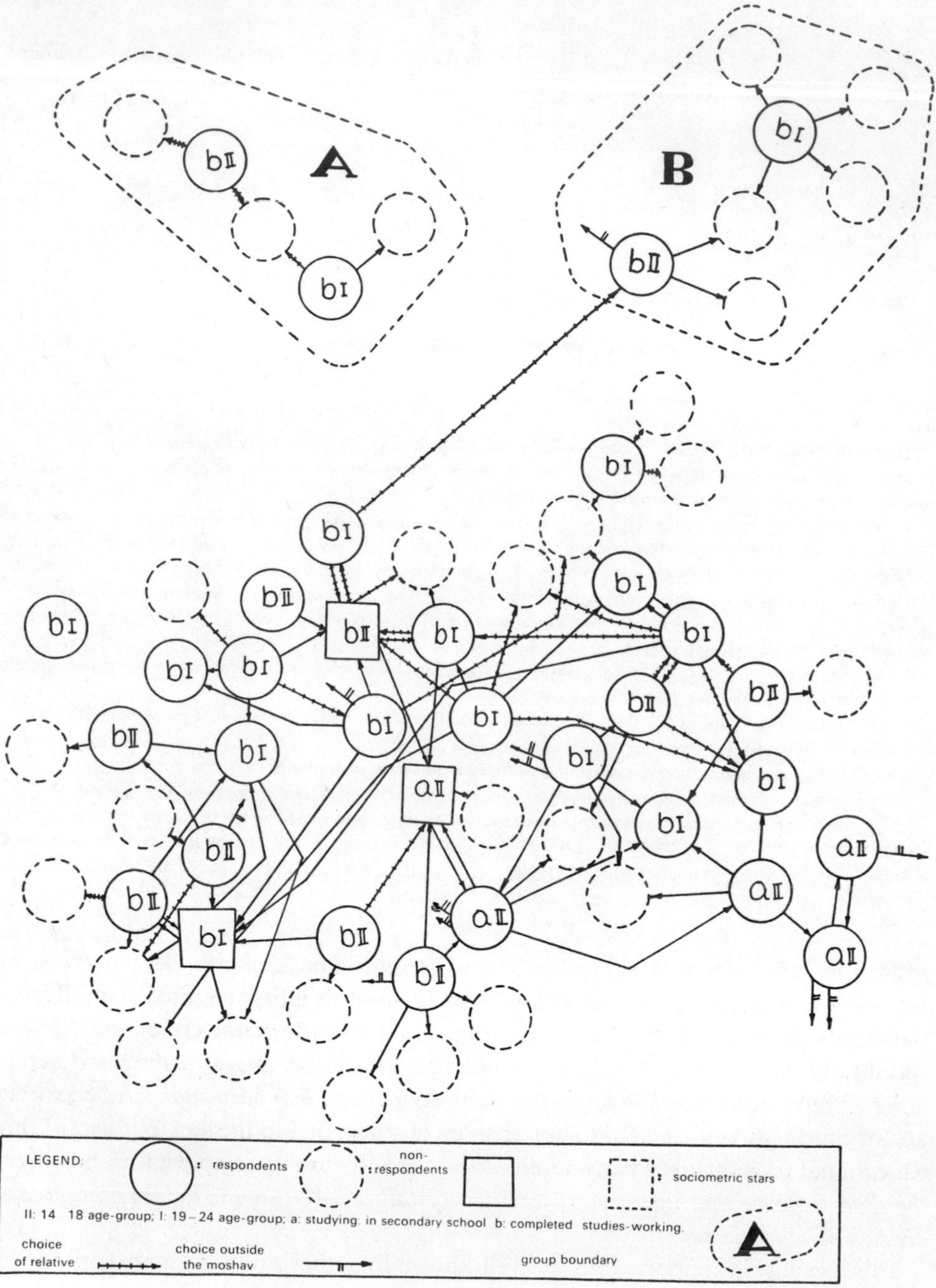

FIGURE 4. Friendship in Hazan

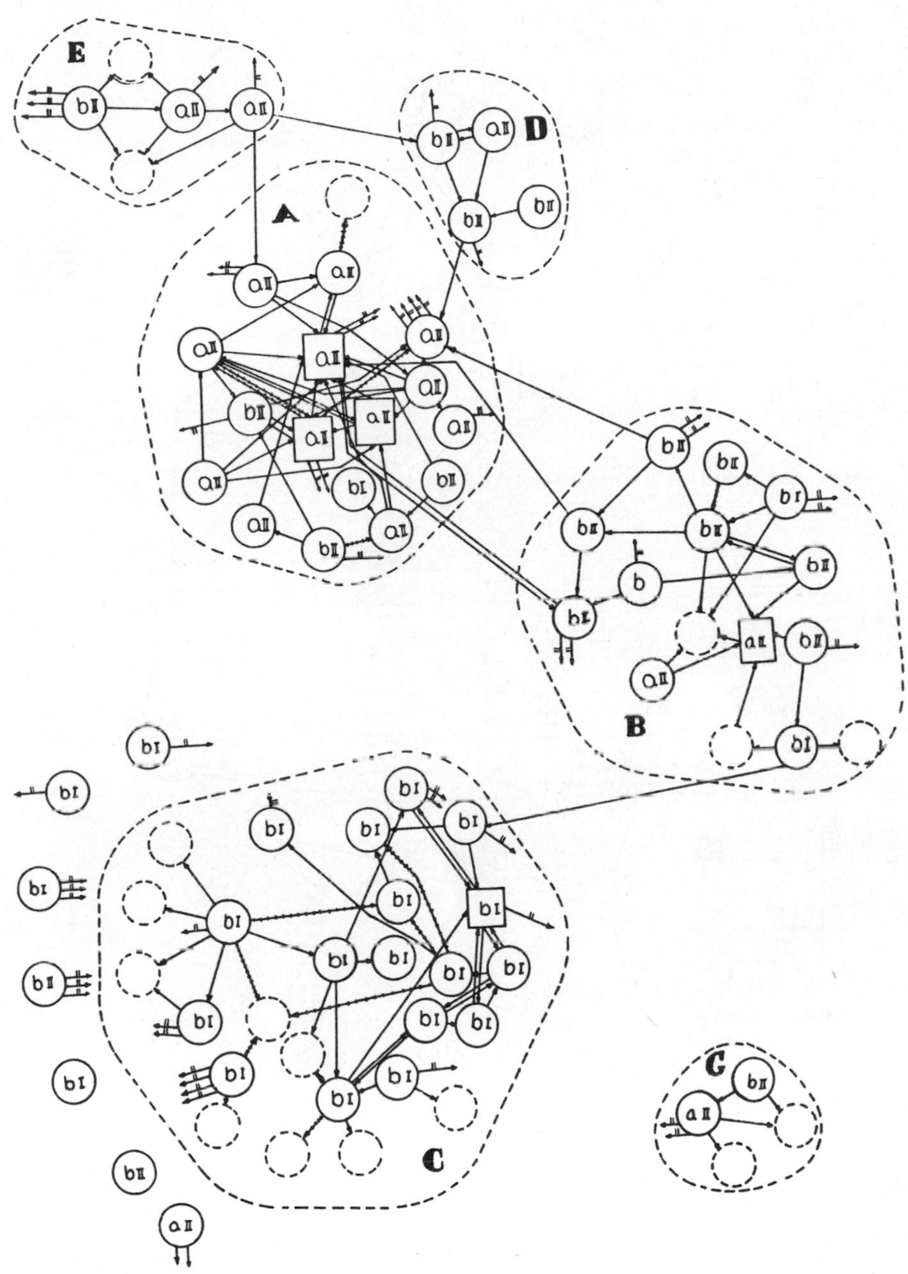

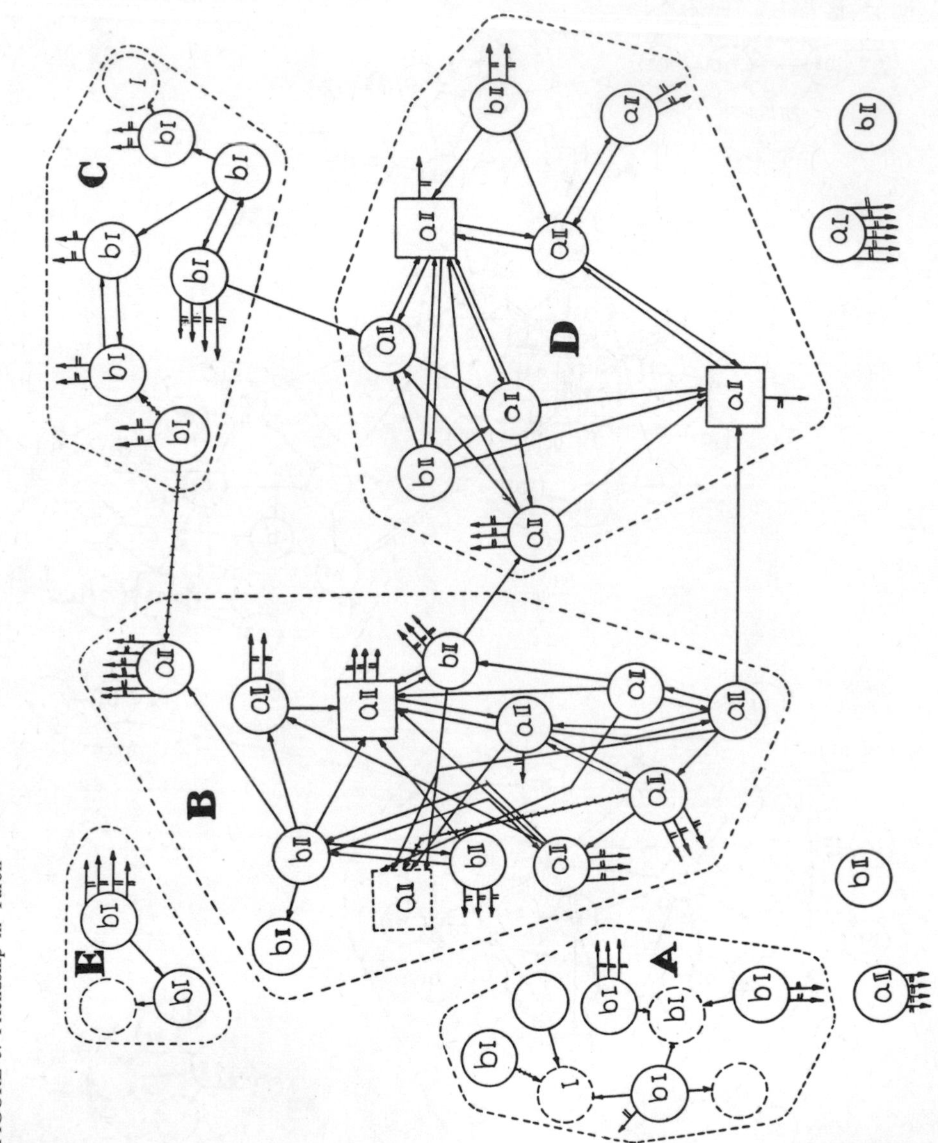

FIGURE 5. Friendship in Yaron

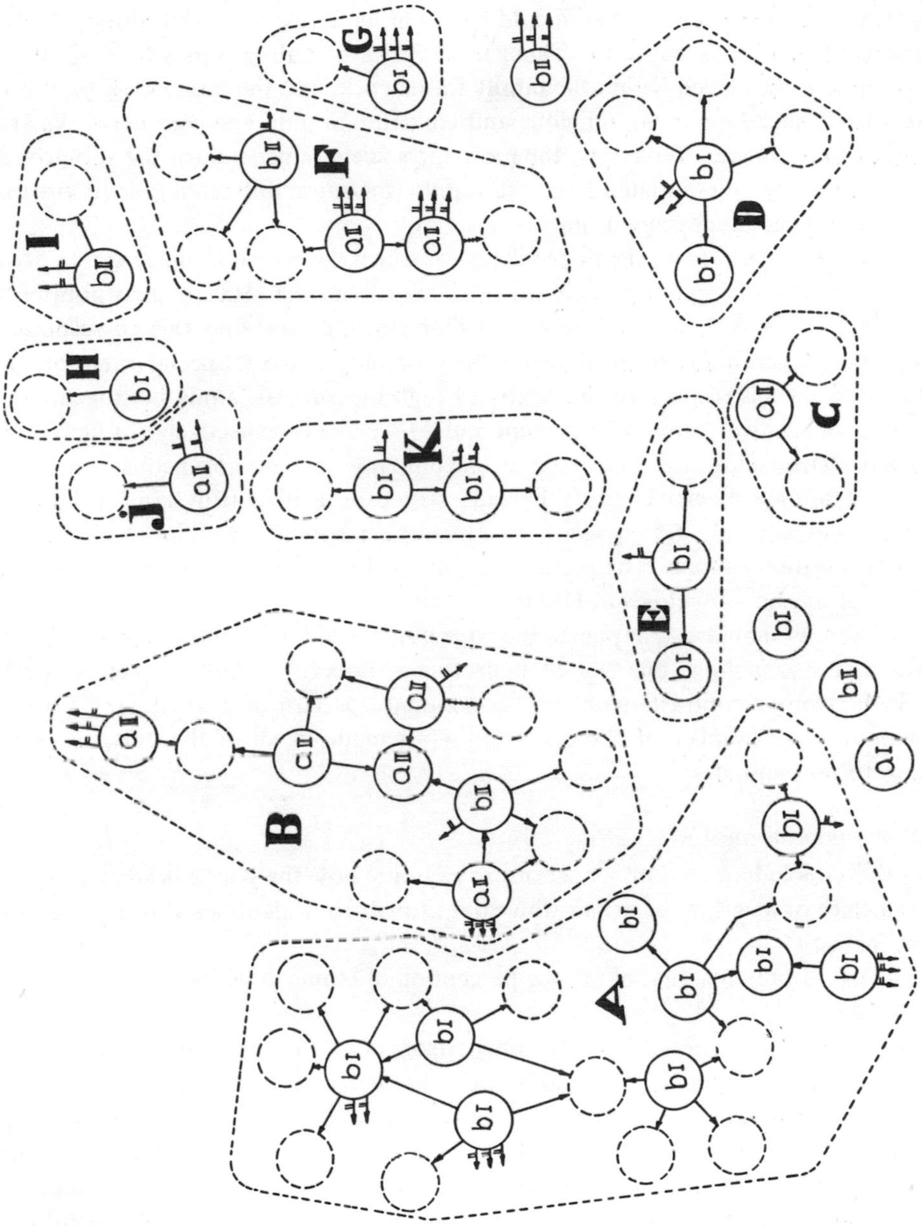

FIGURE 6. Friendship in Karmon

role of age-peer relations as mechanisms of socialization.[10] Eisenstadt suggests that the place and structure of such age-groupings in society varies in relation to the extent to which the orientations that a child learns in its family fit in with those which are expected of him as an adult. Thus, in societies or sub-groups where adult roles continue to be played within the family framework, and the framework itself serves as a basic social, political, religious and educational unit, age-peer networks are of minor importance. Conversely, the more the society in general (or the sub-group) is institutionally differentiated from the family, the more outstanding is its organization along age-homogeneous lines.

The differences *among* the three villages in which the principle of age-group organization plays an important role are also worth noting. Hazan incorporates this principle on a consistently lower level than does Yaron; and this corresponds to a greater degree of familism, shown in the preceding chapter. Special attention might be given, in this respect, to the relatively high measure of family homogeneity and choice of relatives here—15.2 percent and 23.3 percent respectively. In fact, family-based friendships in this village accompany age-homogeneous ones, thus documenting a special kind of "hybrid" structure, neither truly kinship-based nor truly associational—which seems to represent a special transitional phase in the modernization process. The picture we obtained on a group level again fits in with the findings on individuals in Hazan.

Attention should also be paid to the large number of small "autonomous" cliques in Karmon—something one would expect of "modern" relations, and something which strongly contrasts with the "communal" pattern in Zafrira. As to why the *same* average number of choices—3 to 4—is made in all of the villages—we can hazard no opinion.

2. REFERENCE GROUPS

In this concluding section, we set out to examine how the young *moshav* generation conceives of its group of origin; the extent to which it identifies with it; and how it evaluates it.

Table 71 presents, first of all, the perception of ethnic differences in Israeli society in general.[11]

Clearly, ethnic perceptions are much stronger at the two extremes—the "traditional" and the "modern"—and weaker in the transitional "middle", probably reflecting a defence mechanism of an ambivalent and sensitive group. This interpretation is reinforced when we look at identification with the ethnic community (Table 72).[12] It is thus evident that Karmon, while perceiving ethnic differentiation, considers ethnic identification as largely irrelevant to itself: over 50 percent of the answers do not refer to such identification at all, and none admit to it fully; Zafrira, by contrast, has a considerable measure of positive feeling for the ethnic community;

TABLE 71—Perception of Ethnic Differences by Village and Age-group

Perception / Age-group and Village	Perceptible differences exist between ethnic groups		Ethnic differences exist only in the old generation		There are no differences along ethnic lines		Total		Unknown
	N	%	N	%	N	%	N	%	
Zafrira	17	68.0	6	24.0	2	8.0	25	100.0	5
14–18	9	75.0	3	25.0	—	—	12	100.0	3
19–24	8	61.5	3	23.1	2	15.4	13	100.0	2
Hazan	27	48.2	20	35.7	9	16.1	56	100.0	4
14–18	16	48.5	12	36.4	5	15.1	33	100.0	4
19–24	11	47.8	8	34.8	4	17.4	23	100.0	—
Yaron	13	40.6	17	53.1	2	6.3	32	100.0	7
14–18	8	44.4	9	50.0	1	5.6	18	100.0	5
19–24	5	35.7	8	57.1	1	7.2	14	100.0	2
Total in 3 villages	57	50.4	43	38.1	13	11.5	113	100.0	16
14–18	34	50.7	27	40.2	6	9.1	67	100.0	8
19–24	23	50.0	16	34.8	7	15.2	46	100.0	8
Karmon	20	68.9	5	17.2	4	13.9	29	100.0	3
14–18	10	71.4	3	21.4	1	7.2	14	100.0	—
19–24	10	66.7	2	14.3	3	2.0	15	100.0	3
Total	77	54.2	48	33.8	17	12.0	142	100.0	19

while Hazan and Yaron are of two minds—showing affinity to both ethnic and Israeli youth at the same time. Here, there are *no* significant differences between the older and the younger group, (the first is perhaps a shade less conscious of ethnic distinctions, but somewhat more closely identified with the ethnic community). This is not as strange as it sounds, and is probably due to the fact that the educational edge of the 14 to 18 year old category is balanced by the greater integration in society of the 19 to 24 year old one, as a result of the higher proportion in it of those young people who are already working and those who have completed their military service. This being so, this youth is bound to forge ahead in time even though the data testify again to a steady, "controlled" process of change and acculturation, without any abrupt internal discontinuities.

Attitudes towards the group of origin are given substance when we observe the characteristics attributed to it by the young generation (Table 73, folding page).[13]

The first thing that strikes us here is that both in Zafrira and Karmon negative ethnic characteristics are negligible—at 6.1 percent and 6.3 percent respectively;

TABLE 72—Ethnic Identification by Village and Age-group

Identification / Age-group and village	Identity with my ethnic community		Identity with the young generation by ethnic community		Identity with Israeli youth in general		Identity with both ethnic and Israeli youth		Total		Un-known
	N	%	N	%	N	%	N	%	N	%	
Zafrira	6	23.1	5	19.2	11	42.3	4	15.4	26	100.0	4
14–18	3	23.1	2	15.4	7	53.8	1	7.7	13	100.0	2
19–24	3	23.1	3	23.1	4	30.7	3	23.1	13	100.0	2
Hazan	1	1.8	5	9.3	25	46.3	23	42.6	54	100.0	6
14–18	—	—	3	9.7	16	51.6	12	38.7	31	100.0	6
19–24	1	4.3	2	8.7	9	39.1	11	47.9	23	100.0	—
Yaron	2	6.1	3	9.1	17	51.5	11	33.3	33	100.0	6
14–18	—	—	1	5.6	10	55.6	7	38.8	18	100.0	5
19–24	2	13.3	2	13.3	7	46.7	4	26.7	15	100.0	1
Total in 3 villages	9	8.0	13	11.4	53	46.9	38	33.7	113	100.0	16
14–18	4	6.0	8	11.9	33	49.3	22	32.8	67	100.0	8
19–24	5		5		20		16		46	100.0	8
Karmon	—	—	1	7.1	11	78.6	2	14.3	14	100.0	18
14–18	—	—	—	—	7	87.5	1	12.5	8	100.0	6
19–24	—	—	1	16.7	4	66.6	1	16.7	6	100.0	12
Total	9	7.1	14	11.0	64	50.4	40	31.5	127	100.0	34

both the traditional-Oriental and modern-European village seem secure as regards their ascribed status. Hazan and Yaron, by contrast, emphasize ethnic drawbacks to the extent of 29.0 percent and 26.8 percent exhibiting some anxiety in this respect. The picture is also consistent when we check the differential contents of the profiles of the four groups: the traditional *moshav* stresses as positive features such as religious observance, traditions and folklore; the modern *moshav* underlines intelligence and interest, Israeli roots, and education; while the two "transitionals" combine both sides, each less intensively. Of interest also are the differences between Hazan and Yaron; the former gives prominence to the "normal" drawbacks of the less modern (nos. 14 and 15 at 20.3 percent together); Yaron, on the other hand, chiefly expresses specific ethnic features—its emphasis on no.13 (lack of discipline and irresponsibility) reflecting sensitivity about the stereotype—common to Israeli society —of the Moroccan immigrant, as unruly, hot-tempered and aggressive.

No less significant, however, are the features which are shared by all four *moshavim* (though in different degrees). These are: integrity, good character and generosity,

TABLE 74—Ethnic Characteristic which may Contribute to the Creation of Israeli Culture

Village \ Qualities	Sensitivity, generosity, love of man		Patriotism, law-abidingness, industriousness		Culture, appreciation of education		Good character, simplicity, modesty of requirements		Religious observance, traditions		Wholesome and happy family life		Social life, hospitality, joy of life		Holidays and rituals		Dress, special dishes, dances		Israeli qualities		Daring		Nothing special		Total	
	1		2		3		4		5		6		7		8		9		10		11		12		13	
	N	%	N	%	N	%	N	%	N	%	N	%	N	%	N	%	N	%	N	%	N	%	N	%	N	%
Zafrira	2	2.8	1	1.4	—	—	8	11.1	4	5.6	15	20.7	8	11.1	9	12.5	24	33.4	—	—	—	—	1	1.4	72	100.0
Hazan	6	5.8	5	4.9	7	6.8	6	5.8	9	2.9	12	11.7	6	5.8	11	10.7	31	30.1	2	1.9	—	—	14	13.6	103	100.0
Yaron	7	8.9	6	7.6	2	2.5	3	3.8	12	15.1	9	11.4	8	10.1	10	12.7	15	19.0	1	1.3	—	—	6	7.6	79	100.0
Karmon	—	—	6	16.7	8	22.2	1	2.8	—	—	1	2.8	1	2.8	—	—	4	11.1	7	19.4	4	11.1	4	11.1	36	100.0
Total	15	5.0	18	61	17	5.6	18	6.1	25	8.5	37	12.5	23	7.8	30	10.2	74	25.2	10	3.3	4	1.2	25	8.5	290	100.0

wholesome family life, diligence, adaptability and patriotism, elements of folk-culture, common language.

These are indeed the universals which are usually attributed to rural society and they show a basically shared self-conception, underlying differences between transitional and modern and between age-groups.[14] This conception of the good life also constitutes the major asset which the immigrant youth feels their own communities can contribute to the creation of genuine Israeli culture[15] (Table 74).

While emphasis differs, Zafrira, Hazan and Yaron all seem to be sure that they can strengthen Israeli culture by wholesome personal and family characteristics, as well as enriching it via their folklore. *In other words, ethnicity here is not based on narrow traditionalism but rather on what may be termed general human virtues, on the one hand, and on cultural pluralism* (in the specific sense of the term) *on the other*. Karmon too, would like to contribute its "rural" qualities; but these are less salient, and are accompanied by characteristics presumably representative of modern Israelis in general—as education, grass-root local qualities, and daring.

Conclusion

Our purpose in this chapter has been to report on the differential features of the younger generation in four *moshavim* as regards their occupational choice and aspirations, membership groups, and reference patterns. We have shown that these villages present a meaningful picture in terms of differences in social and family background, a picture internally consistent, as well as consonant with our earlier findings on the relatively steady and "controlled" process of change in the *moshav*. These regularities, however, by no means signify any far-reaching or rigid continuity with the groups of origin in those areas we examined. *On the contrary: they show a high degree of flexibility and change, which indicates a considerable potential of integration in the institutional openings of society; this is especially seen among the immigrant youth, which legitimates a variety of mobility channels and goals.*

This pattern seems to be of immense importance in the context of development (communal and general) since it contrasts strongly with what is, in many other societies, a crucial problem of sustained modernization: namely, *the imbalance between academic and technical schooling and choice.*

In the majority of cases, this imbalance is undoubtedly due largely to societal backwardness as such—namely, to the relative paucity of requirements or openings for the technologically trained, and to the strong emphasis which must be placed at first on the building-up of central elites and of a basic institutional structure.[16] Elsewhere, however, the situation is due not to the lack of economic opportunity and demand, characteristic of the "take-off" stage, but rather to specific social obstacles to supply, in other words, a function not of under-development but of misdevelopment; and in this sense the findings on comparable groups in Israel are of interest.

The example of the development of modern Greece may serve to illustrate our point. One feature which has struck students of modern Greek history (after achievement of independence from the Ottoman Empire in the 1820's) is the central place held by traditions and past values in the new state. These traditions, seen as symbolic of national regeneration, are epitomized in the "gymnasium"—a secondary academic school which stresses classical studies, in accordance with the traditional Greek humanistic ideal and the spirit of the Greek Church. These schools have been shown, generally, to impede institutional creativity and innovativeness in Greek society.[17] More specifically, they promote rigid and narrow patterns of vocational aspirations and mobility, oriented mainly to white-collar, and chiefly to civil-service employment. Research carried out in the rural sector shows that the situation has persisted even after the 1959 Greek educational reform, and that though the reform introduced new types of secondary schools—technical, vocational and agricultural—academic secondary education continues as the main object of ambition.[18] In fact, most parents and children alike are slow to value modern "intermediate" skills, or to accept blue-collar, catering and other careers, on which the growth of their local economy in general and rationalization of agriculture both depend. On the contrary: the Greek farmer's son, when he finishes school, joins a large group of intellectuals who exert pressure on the government by demanding creation of new administrative posts—thus contributing either to the inordinate growth of a very cumbersome and costly public bureaucracy, or to the creation of an essentially unemployable intelligentsia.

Thus in the process of Greek modernization, there have come into being highly polarized and one-sided mobility patterns, which "by-pass", as it were, the middle ranges of the occupational spectrum without any "objective" justification either in terms of income or of employment opportunities.

Similar gaps between educational and vocational aspirations, and placement have been documented in various periods of other developing regions—notably Brazil,[19] Ceylon,[20] Egypt,[21] Ivory Coast[22] and till recently French Canada.[23] This is not so in Israel; which is the more surprising, on the face of it, because Israel is a rapidly developing country, with open mobility channels and a high premium placed on achievement. Of course, Zionist ideology, and in particular the Zionist pioneering movements, put a high value on manual labour, and on productivization (i.e. inversion of the traditional Jewish occupational pyramid). This ideology, however, was mainly agriculture-oriented; and, in any case, as we have seen for ourselves in the preceding chapters, most of the population described comes from a background alien to Zionism in general and to pioneering ideology in particular.[24]

A general value transformation, brought about in the course of early settlement, is thus too facile an explanation for the phenomenon noted. Three major factors may provide at least a partial answer:

The lack of "high traditions", governing occupational structure and mobility, which may be inimical to occupational diversification and modernization but which are carried into the central value system of the modernizing society. These traditions may be "humanistic" (as in Greece), military, caste, ideological, or even others; and from this point of view, it is precisely the attenuation of the pioneering ideology in Israel,[25] with its narrow agricultural interpretation of productivization, which may, paradoxically enough, have been partly responsible for occupational diversification and growth. Sons of new immigrants to the country—even those settled on land—in fact grew up in an ideological and social climate which was still strongly in favour of "productivization", but no longer wholly oriented to one specific occupational area and to rigid rural continuity.

The long-established "respectability" and viability of vocational schools in the country, originating in agricultural institutions and branching out to other areas. In Greece, for example, formal vocational programmes were only introduced in 1959; while in most colonial societies, though such curricula were introduced earlier, they were limited and too often "tainted" by association with the colonial administration.[26] In Israel, however, the first vocational (agricultural) school was opened in 1870, and vocational education, freeing itself from early one-sided tutelage, could at the same time retain status and public support.[27]

Allocative and communicative mechanisms. The realistic evaluation by rural youth of employment opportunities was, no doubt, considerably influenced by mechanisms of communication and placement, which link the rural sector (or periphery) to central markets and processes. As we saw, in Israel the rural village is connected to a dense institutional and interpersonal network, ranging from teams of resident instructors in each *moshav,* to frequent and informal contacts with urban centres. In Greece, by contrast—and certainly in less developed countries—this linkage is sparse (in Crete, for example, there is one rural extension worker for every 30 villages); and main-value communication, as well as information, depends thus mainly on family channels and formal bulletins. Moreover, in Israel both vocational education and varied labour markets are brought "down" to the village level; much of the schooling is done in regional institutions,[28] and regional development schemes provide for rural centres which offer the population a variety of blue-collar and other opportunities.[29] Social control, in other words, *is maintained through a system of secondary local centres.*

In effect, then, the situation described in Israel is due to the existence of a strong modern centre which hands down policy, guidance and resources, acting upon less modern social groups;[30] groups which have not yet developed the high, specific aspirations to be found in the modern village of Karmon, for instance. To what extent can this balance be maintained in a context of continuing demographic modernization, remains, of course, to be seen.

The process of modernization of the rural "periphery" is also reflected in group membership and reference patterns. These patterns show a clear trend as regards the relationship between traditional identification and societal participation, and are in line with our findings on traditional and transitional groups.

NOTES

1 Even though the data do not always allow complete cross-tabulations.

2 The regularity is maintained when we compare the data to a European immigrant village—Ta'amon—familiar to us from the first part of this book. Though it was not systematically included in the research on the second generation, we ran "a fast check" on this particular topic, obtaining the following distribution:
elementary or incomplete secondary education—none; still in secondary school, or already finished secondary education—100 percent. The educational career, then, is here even more prolonged than in Karmon.

Unfortunately, our population is too small for a significant analysis of internal differences within each group—i.e., according to the overseas education and occupation of parents in Hazan and Yaron —in services and white-collar jobs. This inversion—as is well known—was one of the fundamental and from the point of view of inheriting the farm.

3 That is, inversion of the traditional Jewish occupational pyramid which in many countries of the Diaspora was characterized chiefly by concentration in trades and commerce and—in modern societies —in services and white-collar jobs. This inversion—as is well known—was one of the fundamental values of the Zionist movement and, in particular, of the various settlement movements. See for example, D. Weintraub, M. Lissak and Y. Azmon, *op. cit.*

4 Even this relationship is possibly spurious, since it obtains mainly in Zafrira, where education is lower, and is interwoven with other factors.

5 Elicited in response to the question: "What do you consider to be most important in your choice of an occupation? Arrange these considerations in order of priority". (Instruction to the interviewer: First ask the open-ended question, then order of priority).

6 Based on the question: "What do you think are the advantages and what are the drawbacks of the occupation you have chosen?"

7 A composite table—or two tables—showing this, seemed too unwieldy to include—especially in a chapter already overloaded with numerical data.

8 Based on a sociometric questionnaire, in which each respondent was asked to name his best friends. In the sociograms, all the choices are taken into account, without order of priority.

Friendship groups were defined on the basis of sociometric connections—each group consisting of a network of choices of one person and by one person (in respect to non-respondents, we gave only passive choices of course). With membership in more than one group by this criterion, the person was placed in the group to which he had more sociometric ties. In the few cases in which two respondents were equally connected to two otherwise distinct groups, the boundary was defined arbitrarily.

9 The reason given for these refusals was that the question encroached on intimate personal matters. It is possible that members of the pioneering veteran villages, based on the ideal of intensive *Gemeinschaft* and equality, are particularly sensitive to problems and manifestations of the crystallization of sub-groups, which cut across the community. This happened, for instance, during our research in Israel's collective settlements—*kibbutzim.*

10 See S. N. Eisenstadt: *From Generation to Generation: Age Groups and Social Structure.* (Glencoe, Illinois, The Free Press, 1956).

It is interesting to note that a similar finding was obtained also in an analysis of third-generation families in an Israeli town. Here, the more amorphous and less integrated youth groups in an ethnically homogenous Yemenite neighbourhood contrasted with those of European youths. See Elihu Katz and Avraham Zloczower: "Ethnic Continuity in an Israeli Town", *Human Relations,* Vol. 14, No. 4, (1961).

[11] Elicited by the close-ended question: "Do you feel that there are perceptible ethnic differences in Israeli society?"

[12] Based on the close-ended question: "To which of the following groups do you feel closest?"

[13] Based on the open-ended question: "What are the special characteristics of your ethnic community?"

[14] See note 7.

[15] Based on the open-ended question: "What qualities do you think your ethnic community can contribute to the creation of genuine Israeli culture?"

[16] For a general statement of problems of modernization see, for example, S.N. Eisenstadt: *Modernization—Protest and Change,* Foundations of Modern Sociology Series, (Englewood Cliffs, New Jersey, Prentice Hall, 1966). For analysis of a concrete case of this kind see, for example, Philip Foster: *Education and Social Change in Ghana,*(Chicago, Illinois, The University of Chicago Press, 1965).

[17] See Bert F. Hoselitz: "Tradition and Traditionalism", in *Sociological Aspects of Economic Growth,* (Glencoe, Illinois, The Free Press, 1960); and "Tradition and Economic Growth", in Ralph Braibanti and Joseph J. Spengler (eds.), *Tradition, Values and Socio-economic Development,* (Durham, North Carolina, Duke University, 1961).

[18] See chiefly: *Crete Development Plan—1965–1975,* (Tel-Aviv, Agridev (Israel Agricultural Development Company), 1965).

[19] See, for example, Frank Bonilla: "Brazil", in James S. Coleman (ed.), *Education and Political Development,* (Princeton, New Jersey, Princeton University Press, 1965).

[20] Chiefly, Bryce Ryan: "The Dilemmas of Education in Ceylon", *Comparative Education Review,* IV, No. 2, (October, 1960).

[21] See, for example, Malcolm H. Kerr: "Egypt", in James S. Coleman, *op. cit.*

[22] Remi Clignet and Philip Foster, *The Fortunate Few,* (Chicago, Illinois, North Western University Press, 1966).

[23] Eg., Mason Wade, "Social Changes in French Canada", in Braibanti and Spengler, *op. cit.*

[24] For details, see Appendix and S.N. Eisenstadt, *Absorption of Immigrants, op. cit.*

[25] See chiefly: S.N. Eisenstadt, *Israeli Society, op. cit.*

[26] See for example: Philip Foster, *Education and Social Change in Ghana, op. cit.,* pp. 112–178;
James S. Coleman (ed.), *Educational and Political Development, op. cit.,* on Indonesia, Nigeria, and Tunisia;
Social Change—The Colonial Situation, Emmanuel Wallenstein, (ed.), (New York, I. Wiley, 1966, pp. 301–380);

James S. Coleman, *Nigeria—Background to Nationalism,* (Berkeley, California, University of California Press, 1958, pp. 113–141).

[27] See: S.N. Eisenstadt, *Israeli Society, op. cit.*

[28] See, for example, T. Honig Parnass: *Village Youths who Received Training in Agricultural Schools,* (Jerusalem, The Henrietta Szold Foundation, 1959), and also note 10, Chapter 2.

[29] For an examination of rural centers, see: *Regional Cooperation in Israel,* (Rehovoth, Settlement Study Centre, 1966); and D. Weintraub and M. Shapiro: "The Role of Regional Organization in Rural Development in Israel", *Sociologia Ruralis,* No. 3, (1965).

30 In this respect, the similarity to development in Japan is striking—this country having established, at the beginning of the century, some 240 technical schools and some 1000 elementary "continuation schools", through which mainly rural manpower was trained and channeled into a variety of industrial, commercial and agricultural occupations.

See, for instance, William W. Lackwood, *Economic Development of Japan,* (Princeton, New Jersey, Princeton University Press, 1954, Chapter X).

CHAPTER 10

A CROSS-CUT OF DIFFERENTIAL DEVELOPMENT

Introduction

In preceding chapters, we have traced several of the social processes which took place in Israel's new villages over a period of roughly ten years and have observed the very different lines along which these various villages have developed.

In this chapter, which is more of a survey than an analysis, we will document these differences quantitatively. More precisely, we hope to present an overview, as it were, of the range of variability in the growth of the *moshav* in those areas where its blueprint calls for uniformity. The picture is limited: it relates mainly to the household and the farm, and is based on data obtained in only six villages (Karmon, Zafrira, Yaron, Hazan and Erga, the five settlements we studied during the second phase, and Ta'amon, which we revisited by way of a follow-up of the second generation, and where we surveyed a partial sample). Even so, the findings are suggestive—especially since they include very different types of *moshav*—traditional, transitional and modern immigrant villages and, for comparison's sake, also a "veteran" one.

All data refer to 1963/64.

The Diverging Paths

1. SOURCES OF LIVING IN THE SAMPLE VILLAGES

As we have mentioned previously, the planning of the new *moshavim* was based on agriculture as the sole source of income and the only occupation of the household. The statistics (Table 75) bring out the extent to which reality falls short of this ideal image in all the villages of our sample. Even in the veteran settlement (No.1 in the tables), which is closest to the pure *moshav* ideology, only 61.1 percent of the households are exclusively agricultural; and when we sort out those employed by the village, there are still 23.6 percent of families with other sources of income. At the other extreme—in village No. 6—only 7.6 percent are farmers pure and simple.

This departure from the normative pattern becomes even more sharply focused when we consider the extent of farming versus other work as the *main* source of

TABLE 75—Distribution of Sources of Income

Village / Source of income	1 (Karmon) N	1 (Karmon) %	2 (Zafrira) N	2 (Zafrira) %	3 (Ta'amon) N	3 (Ta'amon) %	4 (Yaron) N	4 (Yaron) %	5 (Hazan) N	5 (Hazan) %	6 (Erga) N	6 (Erga) %
Farm only	44	61.1	31	46.3	19	43.2	23	33.8	21	23.6	3	7.6
Other work only					8	18.2	8	11.8	9	10.1	1	2.4
Farm and employment by the village	7	9.7	7	10.4	2	4.5	7	10.3	12	13.5	4	9.5
Farm and public activity	4	5.6	2	3.0	—	—	1	1.5	2	2.3	1	22.4
Farm and hired agricultural work*	—	—	12	17.9	1	2.3	9	13.2	5	5.6	7	16.7
Farm and other work	17	23.6	12	17.9	14	31.8	17	25.0	35	39.3	22	52.4
Farm and welfare, insurance, etc.	—	—	3	4.5	—	—	3	4.4	5	5.6	4	9.5
Total	72	100.0	67	100.0	44	100.0	68	100.0	89	100.0	42	100.0

* Hired agricultural work means work in fruit orchards which belong to the *moshav* and are cultivated as a whole.

TABLE 76—Distribution of Main Source of Income

Village / Main source of income	1 N	1 %	2 N	2 %	3 N	3 %	4 N	4 %	5 N	5 %	6 N	6 %
Farm	68	94.1	43	67.1	19	43.2	29	42.7	24	27.0	6	14.3
Other work	2	2.8	20	29.9	21	47.7	36	52.9	64	71.9	30	71.4
Unknown*	2	2.8	4	6.0	4	9.1	3	4.4	1	1.1	6	14.3
Total	72	100.0	67	100.0	44	100.0	68	100.0	89	100.0	42	100.0

* This category also includes households which strike an even balance between farming and other incomes.

income.[1] In Table 76, we see that in four of six villages, it is other employment that provides the financial mainstay for the family.

In fact, it is only in Karmon that an almost total dominance of farming is maintained; it is still the main economic branch in Settlement No. 2; but declines steeply from 42.7 percent in No. 3 to 14.3 percent in No. 6.

2. FARMING ACTIVITY—FARM SCOPE AND SIZE

Since the land held by each settlement is divided into equal smallholdings, all the settlers have the same chance of development and no great economic differences are created. In our villages,[2] however, this aim is not translated into practice. There are settlers with no cultivated plots at all, others who farm areas far larger than those allotted to them.[3]

Table 77 shows us that in the second village (predominantly agricultural) the principle of equality is fairly well adhered to, but in other villages, the range of variability is considerable, largely paralleling employment outside the farm (see above). Thus settlements No. 5 and No. 6 have the biggest number of non-agricultural sources of income, the greatest variations in cultivated area. No less extreme are the differences between villages, and the average area cultivated in settlement No. 3 is four times greater than in No. 6.

TABLE 77—Distribution of Cultivated Land among Farm Units (in dunams)

Differences \ Village	2	3	4	5	6
Average farm area	17.89	23.45	12.95	14.58	5.80
Variability	17.61	109.65	38.85	119.76	13.38
Coefficient of variance	0.23	0.45	0.48	0.75	0.63

Size of farm, as such, is obviously not an adequate measure of farming activity, because it reflects neither livestock nor intensity of cultivation. However, the differences persist also when the more exact index of Standard Work Days is used. Table 78 shows that in villages No. 4 and No. 5, most farms are small (concentrated in the first quartile); in No. 6 the first and second quartiles are equal; while in No. 1, No. 2 and No. 3 there are the largest number of big farms (two upper quartiles) and there, distribution is most even.

When we compare these findings with those on main sources of income, we find, as could be expected, that they are related: where there is a marked tendency to earn a living outside the farm, there is also a tendency to farm in small units. Conversely, the more agriculturally-oriented a village is, the greater the number of larger farms on it and the more evenly are they distributed.[4]

All in all, it is clear that substantial variations exist in, and among, the sample villages as regards the place of agriculture in the economic activity of their households, and the scope and intensity of farming itself. The same is true as regards income and standards of living—which are also aspects that the normative pattern would keep on a reasonable level and within a reasonable range of variability.

TABLE 78—Distribution of Standard Work Days (by quartiles, in %)

Standard Work Days \ Village	1*	2	3	4	5	6
I Quartile	14.0	8.3	24.1	55.3	50.7	35.5
II Quartile	17.3	33.3	44.9	32.1	30.6	34.5
III Quartile	53.1	41.7	24.1	7.2	12.0	13.8
IV Quartile	15.6	16.7	6.9	5.4	6.7	17.2
	100.0	100.0	100.0	100.0	100.0	100.0
N	64	60	29	56	75	29
No farm	4	3	8	7	9	8
Unknown	4	4	7	5	5	5
Total	72	67	44	68	89	42
Average			317.9	156.8	144.1	116.5
Standard deviation		1054	1509	1244	1093.4	780.5
Coefficient of variance		0.47	0.47	0.78	0.76	0.67

* For technical reasons, the Standard Work Days in this village were computed in a different way. Only internal comparison is thus significant, and no average standard deviation and coefficient of variance are given.

3. INCOME AND STANDARD OF LIVING

a. *Income.* Our discussion of incomes will be in two parts: a) farm income; and b) total income. The material is based on interviews with the population itself, not on objective information, which limits its scope and reliability and also accounts for the great number of unknowns—since we encountered considerable reluctance to answer this question.

The data in Table 79 show that in villages No. 4 and No. 5, and to a lesser degree in village No. 6, there is a concentration of low farm incomes in comparison with villages No. 2 and No. 3, in which distribution is closer to normal. Thus, low farm income is quite expectedly concentrated whenever there is a high ratio of non-agricultural employment.

Table 80 makes clear that in spite of the distribution of farm income within each village, there is a significant relation everywhere between farm income and source of income: high farm incomes characterize those who live solely off the land. This changes only slightly when we compare farm income to the *main* source of income: except for village No. 3 (in which farm income is evenly distributed between agriculture and other sources), there is a significant relationship between these two variables.

The picture becomes blurred, however, when we compute total income (Table 81).

TABLE 79—Distribution of Farm Income (by quartiles, in %)*

Farm income differences \ Village	2	3	4	5	6
I Quartile	25.9	26.9	58.8	64.8	42.8
II Quartile	31.5	46.2	35.3	16.7	39.3
III Quartile	37.0	19.2	3.9	13.0	14.3
IV Quartile	5.6	7.7	2.0	5.5	3.6
	100.0	100.0	100.0	100.0	100.0
N	54	26	51	54	28
No farm	3	8	7	9	3
Unknown	10	10	10	26	11
Total	67	44	68	89	42
Average	1378	2485.5	1379.2	1193	1378
Standard deviation	737.5	1321.5	1097.2	1052	7.37
Coefficient of variance	0.53	0.53	0.79	0.88	0.53

* The quartiles are computed separately for each village according to distribution of incomes. In village No. 1 proportion of refusals to answer was so high as to render the material worthless. Consequently, we give only the division of households into three categories of income, as calculated by the village secretariat.

Village No. 1	Low income	26.4%	
	Medium income	41.7	
	High income	31.0	100.0
N			72

Additional sources of income diminish the differences and make the distribution more normal—within each village and among all of them. Also, in all of the villages, income is now concentrated in the second quartile. Of some significance, though, is the relationship between total income and the main source of income.

Table 82 indicates that high total income is a feature mainly of households which live mainly from outside employment, although in villages No. 5 and No. 6—where this kind of employment is relatively widespread—the result is less pronounced.

b. *Standard of living*. Table 83 gives two-fold data on the standard of living in our sample villages: 1) household equipment acquired at some point in the settlers' life in the *moshav*; 2) actual state today. The difference between the two gives us the standard of living at time of settlement.

First of all, the table shows great differences in the "starting point" of the various villages: in villages No. 3, No. 4 and No. 5 (but especially in No. 3), several settlers started with a substantial standard of consumption, while in villages No. 2 and No. 6

TABLE 80—Distribution of Farm Income According to Source of Income*

Village and source of income / Farm income	2			3			4			5		
	Farm only	Farm +	Total	Farm only	Farm +	Total	Farm only	Farm +	Total	Farm only	Farm +	Total
Low	11	18	29	2	8	10	8	26	34	6	36	42
High	17	6	23	12	3	15	11	3	14	10	2	12
N	28	24	52	14	11	25	19	29	48	16	38	54
No farm			3			8			7			9
Unknown			12			11			13			28
Total			67			44			68			89
x^2		6.68			8.77			12.6			21.3	
df		1			1			1			1	
$p <$		0.1			0.01			0.001			0.001	

* Village No. 1 is omitted since its income is almost entirely from the farms.
Village No. 6 is omitted because only three people's income is almost entirely from farming.

TABLE 81—Distribution of Total Income* (by quartiles, in %)

Village / Total income	2	3	4	5	6
I Quartile	22.6	33.3	16.1	13.7	10.0
II Quartile	67.7	50.0	57.1	49.3	73.3
III Quartile	6.5	13.9	16.1	20.5	10.0
IV Quartile	3.2	2.8	10.7	16.5	6.7
	100.0	100.0	100.0	100.0	100.0
N	62	35	56	73	30
Unknown	5	8	12	16	12
Total	67	43	68	89	42
Average	2217	4526.7	3150.4	3287.7	1764.3
Standard deviation	973.2	1064.95	1436.5	1357.94	575.5
Coefficient of Variance	0.44	0.46	0.45	0.41	0.33

* Village No. 1 is omitted since its income is almost entirely from the farms.

TABLE 82—Distribution of Total Income According to Main Source of Income* (in %)

Total income (in 1000 IL) / Main source of income	2			3			4			5			6		
	Farm	Other	Total	Farm	Other	Total	Farm	Other	Total	Farm	Other	Total	Farm	Other	Total
Low	78.4	21.6	100.0	54.2	45.8	100.0	55.9	44.1	100.0	23.4	76.6	100.0	23.1	76.9	100.0
High	52.0	48.0	100.0	33.7	66.8	100.0	22.7	77.3	100.0	23.4	76.6	100.0	17.6	82.4	100.0
	67.8	32.2	100.0	47.3	52.7	100.0	42.9	57.1	100.0	23.3	76.7	100.0	20.0	80.0	100.0
N	33	29	62	17	19	36	24	32	56	17	56	73	6	24	30
Unknown			5			7			12			16			12
Total			67			44			68			89			42
x^2		2.23			2.39			6.0							
df		1			1			1							
p <		0.02			0.5			0.02			Not significant			Not significant	

* Village No. 1 is omitted since its income is almost entirely from the farms.

TABLE 83—Distribution of Standard of Living (in %)*

Village / Standard of living	1. Acquired during settlement					2. Actually today				
	2	3	4	5	6	2	3	4	5	6
N	67	44	68	89	42	67	44	68	89	42
1	3.0	13.8	4.5	7.9	28.6	3.0	—	3.0	3.4	16.7
2	20.9	16.0	23.9	24.7	79.0	20.9	4.6	14.9	16.8	73.8
3	71.6	34.1	38.8	33.7	2.4	71.6	47.7	41.8	37.1	9.5
4	4.5	36.3	32.8	33.7		4.5	47.7	40.3	47.7	—
	100.0	100.0	100.0	100.0	100.0	100.0	100.0	100.0	100.0	100.0
Average	7.21	7.36	7.75	7.83	2.95	7.21	0.45	8.51	8.91	3.50
Standard deviation	2.01	4.01	3.81	4.44	1.52	2.01	2.90	3.65	4.21	1.53
Coefficient of variance	0.28	0.54	0.49	0.57	0.51	0.28	0.31	0.43	0.47	0.44

* Standard of living (from low to high) is measured by ownership of scaled consumption items (e.g. gas or electric ranges, refrigerators, washing machines, solar or other water heaters, cars, etc.). The first village is not relevant in this context: it exists for over 30 years, and in any case, most consumer equipment is centrally purchased and standardized.

everyone started off practically at zero. Taking a look at Part 2 we see that differences between the villages still persist today; and that there is also considerable internal variability. At the same time, it is interesting to note that the variance in Part 2 is less —although only slightly so—than that in Part 1, which indicates a certain tendency for differences between neighbours to diminish over a given period of time. (This, alas, is not indicative of economic position but rather of conspicuous consumption at the expense of productive effort: in all villages except in No. 5, there is an inverse correlation between standard of living and actual income).

In preceding pages, we have briefly sketched certain objective differences which exist in and among our villages, in respect to just those aspects of life concerning which the *moshav* pattern presupposes uniformity. We have seen that the range of variability —i.e., of departure from the blueprint—is considerable; and that it embraces occupational and farming patterns, income and standard of living. The picture can be rounded off by examining the extent to which these objective differences are subjectively reflected; that is, whether they give rise to a perception of stratificational polarization in the villages, and if so, to what extent.

This perception was analyzed along two dimensions: economic and prestige. Let us take up each in turn.

The respondents were asked, first, to place themselves in one of four ranges of farm-income, and in one of three ranges of total income.

The findings (Tables 84 and 85) are generally similar to the objective data above; neither table shows perception of a polarized structure, but both reflect a differentiated one. As for total income, this structure is, by and large, dual, composed of two

TABLE 84—Self-Classification in Respect to Farm Income (in %)

Self-classification \ Village	1	2	3	4	5	6
High income	31.4	1.6	13.9	—	2.5	1.2
Medium income	59.8	35.5	50.0	28.4	21.0	25.9
Low income	8.8	54.8	22.2	48.9	41.3	33.3
No income	—	8.1	13.9	22.6	35.0	29.3
	100.0	100.0	100.0	99.9	100.0	99.7
N	102	62	36	51	80	27
No farm	4	3	8	7	9	8
Unknown	—	2	—	10	—	7
Total	106	67	44	68	89	42

TABLE 85—Self-Classification in Respect to Total Income (in %)

Self-classification \ Village	1	2	5	4	5	6
High income	22.0	—	2.7	3.2	1.1	—
Medium income	65.0	41.6	75.7	51.6	54.7	36.0
Low income	12.9	58.4	21.6	45.2	44.2	64.0
	99.9	100.0	100.0	100.0	100.0	100.0
N	100	65	37	62	86	25
Unknown	6	2	7	6	3	17
Total	106	67	44	68	89	42

adjacent categories: high and medium in the first village, and medium and low in all of the others. The picture with respect to farm income is not quite the same, either in terms of the extent of the perceived differentiation or its nature. The first village is seen by its members as being dualistic, with the emphasis again on high and medium incomes. In other words, there are the good "standard" farms—in this case, the majority—and a large minority of excellent ones, as well as a smaller number of laggards. Of the other settlements, No. 3 is the only one in which classification in medium farm income is modal. Elsewhere, there is a tendency towards lower self-perception—although No. 2 is closer to No. 3 in this respect.

As already mentioned above, villages No. 1, No. 2 and No. 3 are more farm-

TABLE 86—Self-Classification According to Prestige* (in %)

Self-classification \ Village	1 N=106	2 N=67	4 N=68	5 N=69
4	4.7	40.1	22.0	14.3
3	38.7	38.8	41.0	33.7
2	3.8	7.5	11.4	24.4
1	2.8	—	7.3	2.2
Does not know	12.2	13.4	5.7	2.2
Unknown	37.7	—	11.4	22.2
Total	99.9	99.8	99.8	100.0

* from high to low.

TABLE 87—Self-Classification According to Prestige by Self-Classification According to Farm Income*

Self-classification by farm income \ Self-classification by Prestige	2			4			5		
	High	Low	Total	High	Low	Total	High	Low	Total
High	12	9	21	5	7	12	30	10	40
Low	12	20	32	8	23	31	10	12	22
N	24	29	53	13	30	43	40	22	62
Unknown			14			23			27
Total			67			66			89
x^2	Not significant			Not significant				5.41	
df								1	
p <								0.02	

* Village No. 1 is excluded because—as can be seen above—the vast majority of those who classified themselves according to prestige, placed themselves in only one category—i.e. in the second.

oriented, and it would thus seem that the tendency towards farming is reflected in a more optimistic self-image.

Our data on prestige are only partial, since, due to a technical slip, the relevant questions were not asked in villages No. 3 and No. 6. But, Table 86 is still interesting.

Considerable differences are shown between the villages. No. 4 and No. 5 perceive a more differentiated stratificational structure according to prestige than do the other two. Both distinguish three strata (assuming a cutting point of 10 percent); village No. 2 sees two strata; while village No. 1 refuses, essentially, to acknowledge any stratificational differences—a fact in line with the egalitarian ideology of the *Moshav*

Movement (and also with similar difficulties referred to in Chapter 9 in respect to sociometric questions).

These findings fit in with Table 84 (self classification in respect to farm income), where the differentiation in villages No. 1 and No. 2 is also relatively smaller. Table 87 examines this relationship, and demonstrates that while the relationship between the two factors is statistically significant only in one village, the tendency is much the same in all three. The same tendency was obtained when we examined the relationship between self-classification according to prestige, and self-classification according to total income. In other words, there is evidence—though it is only tentative—that not only is there a perception of differences in social status in these villages, but that this perception reflects the perception of economic differences.

Conclusion

The developmental variability in and among our sample villages is, then, considerable; but the importance of the finding is not so much the fact itself, as its projection against the background of the *moshav,* or its idealized blueprint. This pattern was conceived of as being uniformly valid and generally enforceable in all the new settlements. It was supported by the moral, ideological, communicative, organizational and economic power of the *Moshav* Movement and of the Land Settlement Authority. Seen in this light, the actual differentiation is most significant. For while it is, no doubt, due partly to objective circumstances—and chiefly to inequalities in production factors[5]—one glance at the tables included shows that this factor leaves much unexplained; the more so since intensification of cultivation and good crop planning can overcome most of these difficulties. The great variability found therefore underlines the paramount need for differential planning and development, so that different social predispositions and processes are taken into account. As a lesson in agrarian development, if nothing else, this is a crucial one.

NOTES

1 Main source of income is based on farmers' own declarations, checked out against farm and employment records.

2 No data are available on village No. 1.

3 This was done through private rent-agreements with neighbours, and sometimes even outside the village.

4 This relationship is significant at the level $p < 0.01$. At the same time, it is—luckily for the sociologist—only partial, and considerable differentiation persists when source of income is constant.

5 The veteran village—No. 1— is thus the best endowed and the most uniform of the six; settlement No. 4 has several plots which are unfit for cultivation; while villages No. 2, No. 5 and No. 6 have not always been able to develop their vegetable and industrial crops fully for lack of water.

CHAPTER 11

GENERAL REMARKS

In the foregoing chapters we have examined some of the social problems and issues of the new immigrant *moshav* in Israel, dwelling first on its static aspects, and then on more dynamic ones. Our analysis has been mainly comparative and adoption of this focus has now and then caused the sacrifice of depth for breadth, as well as depriving the reader of a live picture of these villages as they really are. The proper thing to have done would have been to present the material (or large parts of it) also in case-study form; but we felt that to do this might make the book too cumbersome. We hope only that some three-dimensional images—especially of the European village of Ta'amon and the Yemenite village of Shalekhet—will nevertheless have emerged.[1]

To round off the discussion, we bow to the ritual of concluding remarks. These remarks are not by way of evaluating the *moshav* settlement scheme; the reader must make up his own mind about that from the data we have presented. Our purpose is rather to weave together some of the more generalized strands on modernization and development which have emerged in the course of the analysis. Before we do so, however, let us make a few comments on certain specific features of Israel's rural development. Four major characteristics appear to distinguish the situation here from that in other developing countries:

1. Rural development in Israel is carried out within a relatively modern and stable institutional framework.

2. The rural sector has never been isolated from, or dominated by, the urban one; on the contrary, rural elites have occupied a central position in the political, economic, and value systems of the country.

3. Owing to historical circumstances, Israel is able to invest more capital and more skilled manpower into rural development than most other developing countries have been able to permit themselves.

4. The traditional communities, now undergoing a process of change in Israel, are made up of immigrants who have uprooted from their native surroundings and resettled in pre-planned, already established villages. Their background is not one of long territorial continuity, and while this fact may possibly affect their integration, it also may lower their resistance to change. These traits are of enormous significance for the nature, and the possible rate, of modernization and development in general,

and in respect to many of the specific points we have made. For example, "de-democratization" of a village may be a purely local measure in a society whose political democracy, in general, is stable and secure; otherwise, its implications may be much more fundamental and widespread.[2]

Despite these reservations, however, the internal problems of developing rural communities in Israel seem not to be of an essentially parochial nature; and therefore certain general conclusions may be drawn from the material presented here. *Perhaps the most generally salient point of the study is the basis it provides for the empirical clarification of the often used but much abused concepts of "traditional" and "modern".*

Indeed, few sociological ideas have had such a powerful appeal for, and such a strong hold over comparative social analysis as the concepts of "traditional" and "modern". In fact, the use of these concepts—whether implicit or explicit, and whether under these or other names—has pervaded sociological literature for more than half a century. This dominance, moreover, has been true of all levels of analysis—from the societal, through the specific institutional, to the group and individual one. Of course, traditional-modern conceptualizations have differed widely in their focus, their range and their theoretical sophistication. There are thus "grand" theories—both macro- and micro-social—which emphasize basic "roof typologies" or central themes, dimensions and factors—among them classical ones such as Weber's ideal types of legitimation, Durkheim's organic and mechanic division of labour, Toennies' *Gemeinschaft and Gesellschaft.* Redfield's folk-urban model; and more recently, Parson's pattern variables, Almond's structural differentiation, Deutsch's mobilization, McClelland's achievement motivation, and Pye's associational sentiments.[3] There are, then, "middle-range" theories (in the sense of offering formulations of more delimited scope and generality), e.g. Apter's mobilization, consociation and modernizing autocracy models of the developing political systems.[4] And there are, finally, more operational or diffuse approaches, which embody rather "lists" of specific characteristics or traits—as for instance the work of Benvenuti on farmers, and of Frankenberg on communities.[5]

However, all these conceptualizations, no matter what their theoretical range and focus, and irrespective of the great differences among them as regards their substantive propositions, seem to possess two fundamental features in common. They all spell traditional and modern chiefly in terms of institutional elements and properties, and of their socio-demographic and socio-psychological indices; and they attempt to analyze the societies they study in terms of reality ordered both in time and in space, and embodying universal patterns of organization. Thus, armed with basic tools of sociological analysis and with a "larger" vision, these theories have undoubtedly provided some of the most incisive insights and some of the most powerful comparative analyses into broad social phenomena.

Recently, though, increasing doubts have been voiced concerning the continued validity and empirical utility of such traditional-modern conceptualizations. This is so in several aspects. A fundamental controversy has, of course, long raged concerning the utility of all ideal-type constructs as such—a problem thus inevitably involving most of the conceptual schemes mentioned. More directly, though, and irrespective of the problems of the Weberian type of analysis in general, strictures have been made at various traditional-modern antitheses specifically suggesting that they are culture-bound (or Western-biased)[6] and that they imply an idea of an ordered progress from one type of social (or personality) structure to another. This latter has, of course, been applied chiefly to the older, "monistic" and total theories, which—while focusing on different "first principles"—all essentially viewed the relationship between traditional and modern societies in terms of a nonreversible and an inevitable change between two poles.[7] Present day theorists, however, are also not exempt in this respect—and while they emphasize less any single factor or dimension, and while they pay more attention to the transitional or intermediate patterns, they have nevertheless also been shown to think too much in terms of patterned dichotomies, or of sequential social development.[8]

As will be recalled, "classical" traditional-modern conceptualization served as the point of departure also in the present study, but under very special empirical circumstances. The context in which this conceptualization was used was, in fact, one of a crash settlement scheme, embodying a rich variety of groups about which little or nothing was known, and which were in a situation of induced change. Clearly, in circumstances of this particular kind, the immediate purpose of sociological research had to be the rapid application of a broad and fundamental taxonomy with the help of which the diverse communities could be classified and analyzed in relation to the *moshav*—so that some differential modes of settlement in it could be evolved, before the margin of irreversibility was reached. The commonly employed concepts of "traditional" and "modern" were adopted as such an analytical tool—a tool ready at hand, and at the same time sufficiently generalized and operational to fit the case; and we set out to analyze the predispositions of the different groups of origin as regards traditional and modern elements, precisely in terms of basic patterns of institutional spheres, and their major socio-demographic indices. Or, more properly, since we were concerned not with macro-sociology of the societies of origin in relation to Israel as a whole, but rather with adjustment to the specific requirements of the *moshav,* we selected those institutional characteristics in the immigrants' background which we deemed most relevant to such an adjustment on group and individual level—in terms of manpower and consumption, vocational know-how, social integration and solidarity, village organization, and motivation.

And indeed, the broad findings of the study showed clearly *the continued utility of the concepts used—namely of traditional and modern patterns in terms of basic proper-*

ties of institutional spheres and their socio-demographic aspects—for rapid and broad sociological identification calculated to explain fundamental patterns and to prevent major strains and planning mistakes.

However, the further we moved away from the crude and static analysis of the initial confrontation between major immigrant types and the moshav, *into an analysis of closer social groups, and into an examination of differential processes of social change, and the more we paid attention to the problems of the "transitional" middle, the more did the reference to structural or institutional traditional and modern aspects alone prove a liability rather than an asset.* This was so not only as regards obvious cultural and other differences cutting across levels of modernization, and chiefly among distinct ethnic groups from Oriental countries, and among socio-economic groups from Western countries. Rather, the concept as such proved intrinsically of limited validity, and in some respects actually misleading.

To begin with, there seems to be a fundamental distinction between traditional and modern aspects in static terms of respective institutional and socio-demographic properties at a given point, and between characteristics of groups and societies as regards change over time. This is so, most broadly speaking, in respect to processes of social change in general; and, as seen in the Appendix, already from the beginning of our research we were aware that over and above any structural typologies, and to some extent cutting across them, were distinct factors associated with capacity to change, and not least among them the variables which Eisenstadt's researches on absorption of immigrants had shown to be of crucial importance for adjustment and development.[9] More specifically, however, a vital difference has been found to exist between traditional and modern aspects in static terms of respective institutional and socio-demographic properties, *and between traditionalism and modernity as a way of becoming, in terms of the capacity to modernize*—this capacity being defined on the societal or group level as the potential of continuously absorbing and initiating change which is not in the nature of secondary institutionalization, but transcends the existing institutional patterns,[10] and on the individual level, as the allowing of a free interplay between existing commitments and new terms of reference. Of course, ability to modernize as defined here is not unrelated to the institutional (and motivational) structure as such: its nature will delimit the range and speed of innovation, which may at any stage be "properly" assimilated and institutionalized, and some of its concrete arrangements (such as farm inheritance by one heir)[11] themselves constitute modernizing mechanisms *par excellence*. The two, however, are not identical, and modernity and traditionalism in the present sense may differentially characterize otherwise comparable populations at all levels. We thus found groups which were similar as regards their formal institutional and socio-demographic background, in respect to such characteristics as family structure, education, economic sophistication, achievement orientation, exposure to mass communication and political participation, but which nevertheless differed considerably in their confrontation with the *moshav*, that is, in their ability to allow interplay with and absorb the novel economic and social requirements, and to develop with them. It was, unfortunately, difficult clearly to distinguish empirically between determinants of social change in general and those of modernization in its specific sense. Groups capable of modernization, however, were found to constitute a distinct profile, characterized by both social and cultural factors. Among the first of importance were chiefly security of status, solidarity of primary frameworks, ability of a group to mobilize new leadership, and the temporal "balance" and orderliness of previous processes of change. (An example of crucial differences in this respect could be seen, it will be recalled, in two contrasting patterns exemplified by two Jewish groups in former French Morocco.) Among the latter, crucial for capacity to change were aspects relating to the transformative potential of values and ideologies. We thus saw, for instance, that the nature and extent of value internalization is focal in this respect; and that the "traditional" Kurdish group, whose religious culture was based relatively more on shame than on guilt, found it consequently easier to secularize than the more autonomously learned Yemenites.

Of course, the scope, requisites and significance of modernity as against traditionalism in promoting change and modernization vary from one situation to another; but it is an essential element in *all* processes of ongoing growth and development, initial and advanced, while being inherent in or assured by *no social pattern as such*—even one already modern in institutional (or motivational) terms. This is so in two respects. First, growth and development are not the properties of any specific institutional configuration but may be achieved in a variety of patterns; and we observed processes of sustained change in villages in which *moshav* institutions were differentially modified by settler traditions. The idea of structural or institutional variability, consonant with continuous development, is generally accepted as regards agrarian elements and forms which are recognizably Western. Not so, however, in respect to non-Western patterns, and it is precisely there that the legitimate range of such variability at different levels of modernization should be studied and taken into account.

Secondly, achievement by any agrarian pattern or specific unit of a significant level and rate of social and economic development, does not automatically ensure further capacity to modernize—that is, to change, innovate and grow. In other words, sustained modernization is not a self-perpetuating process, secure once certain conditions are met, but rather in constant need of transformative mechanisms, such as those mentioned above; and failing these, subject to breakdowns and stagnation. In fact, our data show such phenomena of impeded modernization and development not only in the initial dramatic confrontation with the novel situation of settlement, but also after a period of successful adjustment and consolidation, and often long after Rostow's supposed "take-off into sustained growth".[12] These findings on the group or micro-level, distinguishing between traditional and modern profiles of institutional and socio-demographic characteristics and between traditionalism and modernity, in terms of an ongoing process of innovation and change, are thus in line with data recently presented on the societal or macro-level.[13]

Another issue raised by our study is the relationship between traditional and modern patterns in time—a relationship often conceptualized in terms of a continuum. As our data show, this conceptualization, though a very convenient heuristic device for broad typologies and comparative analysis, is misleading in at least two important respects; it implies the inevitability of overall institutional change in one direction, and it is associated with an image of a linear process in which all the dimensions move more or less together along one scale, or in association. In reality, though, specific institutional and socio-demographic factors may vary independently, combining into a variety of profiles and temporal "tracks" of change; and such differential time sequences have enormous significance for the nature of the modernization process. We thus found, it may be recalled, that in the early stages of modernization carried out in traditional rural communities, the persistence or "lag" of the viable traditional family and kinship unit has a positive effect on economic, social, and political development—its stability and solidarity allowing and regulating, as it were, the free "unfreezing" of commitments in other spheres. Again, such group data on the significance of time sequence in modernization processes parallel patterns of overall change: as, for instance, the importance for smooth modernization in historical England of the fact that "modern" political rules of the game and a "modern" political centre developed here *before* general politization and participation, thus possibly preventing their premature swamp by demands—a situation so often characteristic of developing nations today.

This and more—institutional factors not only may vary independently in time, and not only are they—as seen above—distinct from, and do not automatically assure, continuous change; but also, and perhaps chiefly, the "transitional" society is qualitatively as well as quantitatively set apart from both the polar extremes. It has its own specific social elements and structures (such as a particular blend of particularism and universalism and of ascription and achievement in social organization), and also specific problems and susceptibilities. Because of its very position in the process of change, in the course of which different aspects are likely to change differentially, it is in fact characterized by a relatively greater disruption in its social, motivational and cognitive patterns hitherto and subsequently forming a more consistent whole; by coexistence, together, of conflicting elements and criteria; and, consequently, by greater sensitivity to failure.

Both points made—on the differential meaning of traditional and modern and on the non-linearity of their relation in time—lead us to another crucial reservation, namely that in some respects the supposedly "opposing" institutional traditional and modern patterns are not quite as mutually exclusive as has often been believed, and that not only can they coexist under certain conditions, but that they may even reinforce each other in the process of change and development. And conversely, the dissolution of a traditional social structure or institution does not necessarily assure the succession of a more modern pattern. In other words, any approach to the place of tradition in the process of development must be differentiated functionally and temporally rather than formal and uniform, and it is necessary, in each process of modernization, to analyze the various traditions of social groups so as to distinguish in their make up and composition basic significances, positive and negative, for different stages and "tracks" of development. These significances fall, it seems, into four major types:

a. Predispositions or traditions which can be—at least in certain periods and patterns—mobilized for development (whether directly or indirectly), through processes such as syncretism, utilization of group loyalties, etc. A positive evaluation of work and productivity in traditional Yemenite culture may be remembered as a relevant example within this context. In the same group, we found also—it will be recalled—another element vital to economic growth, namely the ability to develop a drive or motivation for achievement and entrepreneurship. True, this group did not develop any innovative or creative enterprise, one which promoted new symbols and roles and broke open new areas of activity. But as regards everyday or "routine" entrepreneurship, even during the first year of settlement these immigrants saved and formed capital, invested and interacted with modern money, goods and labour markets. These drives, it appears, had been dormant or suppressed under the frozen economy and society of Yemen, but could be and were mobilized on confrontation with new conditions. A similar situation exists on the level of group organization, notably as regards mobilization of traditional kinship frameworks for capital formation, as a basis for cultivation partnerships, and sometimes as a foundation for village cooperation and government.

Both findings are thus similar to those which have been documented elsewhere, e.g. on entrepreneurship and mobility among African farmers (especially in the cocoa area)[14] and economic activities in Indonesia.[15]

b. Predispositions or traditions which are irrelevant to, or unimportant for the main goals of development, and in particular for the creation of a growing economy and a stable community. This in two respects:

The ideological level of promoting pluralism, and allowing for a range of cultural and social variability in areas which do not directly affect the above-mentioned aims. And, the more direct or instrumental level, of reducing tensions by postponing changes which are not immediately vital, irrespective of the extent of pluralism expected as the "final" product. It is obvious that an immense communicative effort must be made to diffuse such primary factors as modern economic orientations, new methods of cultivation, and proper village and cooperative organization. Separating these from the transformation of customs and traditions in dress, cooking habits, or ornamentation, that is, from the attempt at total acculturation, would undoubtedly remove one unnecessary obstacle to orderly development.

c. Elements which might impede the development and modernization process, but which can be "attacked" or altered with relative "impunity" or in isolation, that is without affecting social and individual identity.

Our findings thus show that considerable and unanticipated potential exists in this respect among various traditional groups. For example, they may be capable, ahead and irrespective of other cultural change, of rapid assimilation and use of abstract norms of a kind which had been completely alien to them. Indeed, such a basic discipline as a rigorous sense of time was found, as seen in Chapter 3, to be easier to learn than we had supposed. This is not to deny the validity of the customary antithetical image of a traditional and a modern concept of time; the one is religious/agricultural, the other wholly mechanical; the one is present-bound, the other has a long perspective. But the transition from one to the other—at least, on the level of understanding and observance—does not necessarily involve (or may even be divorced from) Time as a basic component of reality, embodying fundamental or primordial images underlying culture and personality. It may indeed "merely" imply learning a new cognitive skill.

d. Finally, traditions actually likely to slow down development, and which must be handled with great care, lest their premature destruction do damage. The integration of the traditional primary group is this kind of factor, both in respect to individual security and to the possibility of corporate action.

Thus, tradition as such is not inevitably inimical to certain stages of development, and may sustain and regulate it, in this way preventing a "rampant" change which cannot be assimilated. And conversely: modern patterns as such are not necessarily functional in this respect. On the one hand advanced "modern" trends of motivation and way of life may obviously be inimical to rural culture and to agriculture in general, to certain types of farm enterprise and to branches which may be economically rational but at odds with new work and leisure patterns. And on the other hand, "modernity" in the sense of capacity for sustained change may "degenerate" into "modernism", or change for change's sake, and become—like "traditionalism"—a pathology of modernization and development. In other words, the relationship between modern features and agrarian development is not linear but curvilinear.

To restate—these categories of tradition and modernity cut across formal institutional and socio-demographic classifications, and are not absolute and intrinsic but relative to patterns of development and social growth and their problems. Thus, their differential significance and salience in actual situations is bound to vary and change:

a. according to the setting and "track" of development, and the extent to which the process is regulated, gradual, orderly and smooth;

b. according to the stage of development in which a given group finds itself;

c. and according to the transformative capacity of the group.

In this connection two general conclusions or "cautions" on the need for a differentiated approach to social characteristics in terms of "traditional" and "modern" may be formulated:

1. A warning against the "witch hunt" syndrome, characterizing primarily (but not only) the impatient policy maker—even when he is not under the special pressure of time and circumstance that has characterized settlement in Israel. This pattern conceives of tradition as indiscriminately inimical to development and modernization, and maintains that all traditional elements must be sought out and firmly subordinated to (if not actually eliminated by) the modern agrarian system.

2. In contrast to the "witch hunter" there is the "obstacle hound". He is more often than not an anthropologist or a community developer (although sociologists are not immune in this respect) who also views tradition as an obstacle to development—but one to be respected rather than to be swiftly and abruptly removed. Mention is made here not of the intrinsic value of any culture, but of a spirit of total *functional* adoration, approaching each cultural and social system as a balanced, interdependent and fully integrated whole, in which a change of any one item may pull down the whole social fabric.

To sum up. In the preceding pages we have examined empirically the value and the heuristic utility of traditional-modern conceptualizations. As we have seen, the "classical" conception in terms of institutional characteristics organized in universal patterns, has constituted a powerful analytical tool in imposing a basic, even if crude order on a heterogeneous and unfamiliar population. In the examination of processes of change, however, and in respect to "transitional" groups, such a conception—with its formal structural basis, and its underlying idea of a linear, regular and irreversible progress—is helpless, and often actually misleading.

This does not mean, though, that the very concept of traditional and modern is as such applicable only to static or polar situations; and that we can only speak of a diversity of processes of social change without recognizing in them any logic in these terms. On the contrary—traditional and modern in terms of modernization as a specific process of change, and in terms of modernity as a specific way and condition of becoming, are crucial concepts in comparative analysis. And while these concepts lend themselves much less easily to neat categorical classifications, they are no less significant for that.

When we speak of a differential conception of traditional and modern, therefore, we mean to set it up against any formal unidimensional analysis in general, and specifically against both the "pressure cooker" and the "pepper pot" (a stew with a particularly long simmering process) approaches to modernization. This being so, a flexible development pattern capable of such differentiation is obviously a fundamental condition of development. Not that an endless number of potential variations can, or should, be incorporated into any programme. We are not blind to the fact that conditions (political, ideological, economic, or "simply" those resulting from a lack of qualified manpower) often combine to dictate a uniform design, to which populations must adjust as best as they can. But there is no reason at all why—just as any physical planner worth his salt will design a farm or a village so that further mechanization, intensification and redevelopment can be incorporated—a social perspective of change, or diversity in motives and modes of organization, should not be recognized as well.

Another suggestion, related to change processes, concerns the extreme sensitivity to failure which characterizes individuals and groups undergoing a process of accelerated and induced modernization. In particular, we have seen how susceptible to reverses are those people who have just crossed over the threshold of adopting a new activity and a new set of norms and expectations. This phenomenon appears to bear directly upon one of the basic dilemmas in development ideologies and policies: namely, whether the emphasis should be placed on steady consolidation, or on dramatic spurts—where advances are made, as it were, without safeguarding the rear. We certainly do not presume to refer to the relative merits of the two patterns from the economic point of view.[16] *Our data, though, suggest that one might well be particularly wary of the risks of failure involved in the "great leap forward" vision, whenever the stability of the institutional structure and the security of the modernized units are not well established.* The Jewish community in Palestine, it is true, always practiced a "dynamic" approach,[17] and in retrospect, this seems to have been fully justified during a period in which the two conditions we have just mentioned were essentially met. But this is much less so now, as regards the immigrant settlement scheme, where at least the second factor has often been absent.

The dangers for continuous and sustained development, and overall social integration, of the failures of projects due to their "conspicuous" or over-extended nature, seem to be especially great in a "dual" society where—as described here—reverses affect distinct groups or strata which are comparatively less developed and less advantageously placed.[18] As we saw, the *moshav* is *potentially* an area of activity in which such groups can—given the necessary conditions—chalk up considerable advances rather rapidly, comparing (and competing) much more favourably in this respect than in other areas of the industrial society. Demonstrable success here, through concentrated effort, might conceivably—even if limited in scope—reduce consciousness of *relative deprivation,* while demonstrable failure may reinforce this. It seems indeed as if development, like justice, must not only be done, but must be manifestly done.

NOTES

[1] If not—and surely for their own sake, in any case—reference should be made to more lively texts, most notably to A. Weingrod's *Reluctant Pioneers,* (Ithaca, New York, Cornell University Press, 1957). Forthcoming (1970) is also O. Shapiro's *Rural Sociology in Israel,* including, *inter alia,* case-studies by sociologists of the Land Settlement Department.

Last and least—the villages of Ta'amon and of Levanon have themselves been written up in D. Weintraub and M. Lissak, *Some Social Problems of New Immigrant Smallholders' Cooperative Settlements in Israel,* Jerusalem, 1962 (mimeo).

[2] This is not, of course, to propagate the supremacy of political democracy as such, but rather to state a relationship.

[3] See chiefly: T. Parsons, *The Social System,* (Glencoe Illinois, The Free Press, 1951); M. Levy, *The Structure of Society,* (Princeton, New Jersey, Princeton University Press, 1951); G.A. Almond, "A Functional Approach to Comparative Politics", in G.A. Almond and J.S. Coleman (eds.), *The Politics of the Developing Areas,* (Princeton, New Jersey, Princeton University Press, 1960); K. Deutsch, "Social Mobilization and Political Development", *American Political Science Review,* Vol. 55, No. 3, (September, 1961); L. Pye, *Politics, Personality and Nation Building—Burma's Search for Identity,* (New Haven, Connecticut, Yale University Press, 1963).

[4] E.g. D.E. Apter, *The Gold Coast in Transition,* (Princeton, New Jersey, Princeton University Press, 1955); *The Political Kingdom in Uganda,* (Princeton, New Jersey, Princeton University Press, 1955).

[5] B. Benvenuti, *Farming in Cultural Change* (Assen: Van Gorcum, 1962). R. Frankenberg, *Communities in Britain—Social Life in Town and Country,* (Harmondsworth, Penguin Books, 1966).

[6] R.N. Bellah, (ed.), *Religion and Progress in Modern Asia,* (Glencoe, Illinois, The Free Press, 1965).
R.T. Holt and J.E. Turner, *The Political Basis of Economic Development,* (Princeton, New Jersey, A. Van Nostrand, 1966)
S.N. Eisenstadt, *Modernization: Protest and Change,* (Englewood, New Jersey, Prentice-Hall, 1966).

[7] See, for instance, discussions of the Redfieldian concept in:
H. Miner, "The Folk-Urban Continuum", *American Sociological Review,* Vol. 17, (October, 1952).
E. Lupri, "The Rural-Urban Variable Reconsidered", *Sociologia Ruralis,* Vol. VII, No. 1, (1967).

[8] S.N. Eisenstadt, *Absorption of Immigrants,* (London, Routledge and Kegan Paul, 1954).
C. Geertz, *Pedlars and Princes—Social Change and Economic Modernization in Two Indonesian Towns,* (Chicago, University of Chicago Press, 1963).

[9] See chiefly: S.N. Eisenstadt, "The Process of Absorption of New Immigrants in Israel", *Human Relations,* Vol. V, No. 3, (1952), pp. 223–245; "Institutionalization of Immigrant Behaviour", *Human Relations,* Vol. V, No. 4, (1952), pp. 373–395; "Analysis of Patterns of Immigration and Absorption of Immigrants", *Population Studies,* Vol. VII, No. 2, (1953), pp. 167–180; and *Absorption of Immigrants,* (London, Routledge and Kegan Paul, 1954).

[10] This distinction may, of course, be partly traced to Shils and Hoselitz' "tradition versus traditionalism" (see: Edward Shils, "Tradition and Liberty: Autonomy and Interdependence". *Ethics,* Vol. XLVII, No. 3, (1958), pp. 160–161; and Bert F. Hoselitz, "Tradition and Economic Growth", in: Ralph Braibanti and Joseph J. Spengler (eds.), *Tradition, Values and Socio-Economic Development,* (Durham, North Carolina, Duke University Press, 1961, pp. 57–82). Both, however, chiefly emphasize the negative aspect—that is, "traditionalism" as an obstacle, but not "modernity" as a positive condition; also,—as we have seen—the variables making up this dimension are in our study somewhat different.

[11] In Israel, as in historical Britain, such a pattern of inheritance obviously not only prevents fragmentation and thus promotes development, but it also serves as a broader social mechanism of modernization through channelling surplus rural population to new enterprises, and by integrating the rural sector in the society at large.

[12] Compare also with S. Deshen, "Case of Breakdown of Modernization in an Israeli Immigrant Community", *Jewish Journal of Sociology,* Vol. VII, No. 1, (1965), pp. 63–91.

[13] See chiefly: S.N. Eisenstadt, "Breakdowns in Modernization", *Economic Development and Cultural Change,* Vol. XII, No. 4, (July, 1964).

[14] See chiefly: P. Hill, *The Gold Coast Cocoa Farmer,* (New York, Oxford University Press, 1956).

[15] C. Geertz: *op. cit.*

[16] The dilemma has indeed been raised primarily by economists: see for example, G.M. Meier (ed.), *Leading Issues in Development Economics; Selected Materials and Commentary,* (New York, Oxford University Press, 1964).

[17] See D. Weintraub, M. Lissak and Y. Azmon, *op. cit.*

[18] In the sense in which Israel is developing characteristics of a dual society, in terms of educational, occupational, economic, political and other differences between veterans of European background, and new immigrants mainly from Mediterranean countries, see: Judah Matras, *Social Change in Israel,* (Chicago, Illinois, Aldine, 1965); S.N. Eisenstadt, *Israeli Society,* (New York, Basic Books, 1967).

APPENDIX

Immigration & Social Change.

Dov Weintraub
& Associates.

Manchester University Press, 1971.

——— . ——— . ———

APPENDIX

THE CONCEPTUAL FRAMEWORK OF THE STUDY

As was seen, the problem which this study set out to investigate was essentially that of induced social change and acculturation, resulting from, and inherent in a situation of immigrant absorption. It was a situation embodying a crash settlement scheme, in which research results were required rapidly before the margin of irreversibility was reached, and we thus focused our attention on two foci or priorities—a "primary" and a "secondary" one. Of these, the first consisted of applying a fundamental taxonomy with the help of which the diverse communities could be identified in terms of the congruities and incongruities inherent in their confrontation with the *moshav;* while the second embodied factors modifying and refining such basic patterns, and significant in terms of adjustment to and the overcoming of the gaps and tensions created.

BASIC TAXONOMY

In order to arrive at a basic classification of the settler populations we proposed to utilize the *institutional characteristics of their backgrounds,* translated into the situation of the *moshav* through the *concept of role and role analysis.* That is to say, the problem studied was re-defined *as the differential patterns of assumption and performance of the role of the* moshav *settler by people from different institutional backgrounds.* Two major assumptions underlay this approach:

1. The role is clearly a basic analytical unit both of individual behaviour, and of social structure through which their interaction can best be studied.

2. The role is a most appropriate empirical tool for comparative analysis. On the one hand, it is a generalized concept with universal significance and applicability, and one capable of precise operationalization. On the other, it is a system of action, bound to reflect the differential impact of the various structural and individual factors mentioned. Role-analysis is thus a tool with inherent heuristic properties, and especially valuable in the study of new and changing situations. Strangely enough, it has not yet been applied, to the best of our knowledge, to problems of

rural settlement and for this reason, we have given it some prominence here.[1] A more detailed paradigm of the role as we conceive it may, perhaps, make the point clear.

A role is a pattern of action organized in a system of input-processing output, normatively defined, designed for one actor, and fulfilling a specific social function.

In accordance with this definition, the role is obviously a composite structure which includes the following components or variables:

1. OUTPUT—a. to society—that is, the function of the role within the division of labour, in terms of type, quantity, quality, and the recipient (or client);

b. to the actor—the status or balance of rewards provided, in terms of level, composition and relative position;

2. PROCESSING (or contents)—namely, the tasks, activities and actions via which the output is obtained in terms of contents, time, place and role-complements (partners and objects);

3. INPUT—that is, the resources (including sanctions) commanded and used, in terms of type, quality, quantity and the source, or supplier;

4. NORMS—that is, the normative injunctions governing the above-mentioned components;

a. those pertaining to the expected nature and the permitted variability of the output (to society and to actor);

b. those defining the activities proper to the role;

c. those determining the composition and interchangeability of legitimate resources;

d. those laying down the proper suppliers of these resources and their interchangeability.

This paradigm makes possible formulation of the research problem in very detailed operational terms.

1. Spelling out clearly and exactly the actual requirements of the situation with which the new settler is at once faced.

2. Defining the areas and the extent of "proper" and "improper" role performance, i.e. of actual implementation of the normative pattern, of changes in relation to it, and of changes in it.

3. Tracing these changes to their potential origins:

a. the normative specifications themselves, which may be self-contradictory or vague;

b. the disparity between normative expectations and the resources actually provided by the suppliers designated in the norms; a disparity which may be due to high and inflexible demands and/or to paucity of resources.

We intended to concentrate on two major aspects of the conceptual formulation:

namely, on patterns of role assumption and performance, and on crystallization of different role-patterns as a function of the confrontation of initial normative requirements with differential supply of resources. Our research thus focused on the analysis of the resources and the suppliers both explicit and implicit in the social definition of the *moshav*; we then traced—in terms of the basic model suggested above—the actual provision of these resources, as we had postulated them in respect to different immigrant groups and absorptive situations.[2]

The first step in the actual implementation of this design was, therefore, through examination of the pattern or the basic blueprint of the *moshav* (explicit and implicit), in terms of the output demanded of the settler, the resources through which this output was expected to be realized, and of the normative restrictions placed on their supply and utilization. Since these elements are generally described in the introduction, and then discussed in depth in the various chapters which follow, we shall omit them here. However, basic assumptions, culled out of our preliminary analysis, are useful in understanding subsequent conceptualization:

1. The analysis showed that the means through which the settler's role was supposed to be implemented could be formulated in terms of a "basket" or a profile of *seven basic resources:*

a. general adaptive (e.g. basic ecology and security conditions);
b. material (that is, land, water, capital,[3] and rate of exchange;[4]
c. manpower;
vocational (that is, skill or proficiency);
e. social-interactive (namely, the ability to interact with individuals, groups and formal frameworks, in order to acquire and retain a sense of personal security, and a general integration of the community, capable of sustaining its institutions);
f. organizational (that is, calculated to regulate village policy making, allocation of resources, and supervision);
g. motivational.[5]

2. These resources, according to the blueprint, are essentially of two types:

a. those which are external to the actor, i.e. which belong to the absorbing society (and include the general-adaptive conditions and material resources);
b. those which belong to the actor (in any of his roles) and to his group (and include manpower, know-how, social interaction, organization and motivation).

We concentrated mainly on that aspect most relevant to the social characteristics of the settlers, rather than on the general conditions of (or the resources supplied by) the absorbing society. The problem areas we selected for study were essentially, then, the five most closely associated with the settlers as the suppliers of resources. The design of our research thus rested on the assumption that *analysis of the "predispositions" or determinants controlling the structure of these suppliers,* would make possible to predict, or explain their "role behaviour" *when confronted with the moshav.*

Proceeding, then, from the *moshav* pattern, we postulated first of all a set of independent predispositional variables, determining the character of the immigrant settler in his present capacity as supplier of resources.

Broadly speaking, each of these factors appears on three descending levels—the general-social (i.e. the overall institutional structure of origin); the sub-group (i.e. which pertains to secondary or sub-cultural variations within the overall pattern); and the individual or idiosyncratic. In this study, we have disregarded the chance (from the sociological point of view) variations inherent in the latter, and have concentrated on the first two factors. In the present context, however—for the sake of brevity—we shall pay attention chiefly to the overall social level, mentioning the other only in passing.

1. *The Family Structure*

The supply of manpower in the *moshav* was intended to be vested in the individual household. That is to say, it would depend upon the demographic structure of the unit—as reflected in the number of its members, their distribution by generation, age and sex, and their fitness for work. Our assumption was that—excluding secondary factors—this demographic structure would have been determined primarily by the *institutionalized family pattern in the country of origin.* This pattern was taken here to be the function of two factors:

a. the character of the family unit itself (whether nuclear or extended);

b. its fertility.

In practice, these variables might certainly appear in a wide spectrum of profiles; two fundamental patterns could, however, be postulated:

I. The "modern Jewish" pattern of a nuclear family, which features relatively late marriage, monogamy, and planned parenthood;

II. The "traditional Jewish" family which is an extended unit, made up of three to four patrilineal and patrilocal generations, and characterized by high fertility resulting from early (and often polygamous) marriage, and an absence of birth control.[6]

2. *The Economy of Origin*

The know-how accumulated by the immigrant settler was to be the primary source for supplying this means. We assumed that—over and above differences of class, type and level of occupation, and education—this accumulation is the function of the *economy of origin;* this economy having determined the broad occupational structure of the given society, its required vocational levels, and the vocational training it provided. The nature of this economy could be expressed in two factors:

a. the extent to which it was dynamic (namely, its rate of growth and diversification);

b. the nature of the economic activity, and chiefly the extent of industrialization, the character and scope of the market, and the state of the financial system.

It was thus possible to expect two following polar profiles:

I. The developed and developing economy, with a high degree of industrialization, extensive markets, and a complex financial system. The functioning of these factors (although not necessarily definition of their goals) is determined here primarily by rational criteria, stemming from the economic sphere itself; and is subject to a comprehensive network of commercial laws.[7] These features also involve a broad spectrum of occupations, especially of occupations requiring vocational as well as general education. The economic tendencies described inevitably doomed some of the traditional Jewish occupations, chiefly tradesmen and artisans; and this phenomenon, which affected entire strata, further impelled the immigrants to become integrated in the general process. They have been absorbed—if at all—only to a very limited extent in the new industries; but they have successfully occupied positions in other spheres requiring education, training and specialization, notably commerce and services, banking and finance, and white collar work and the free professions.

II. The underdeveloped economy, based chiefly on agriculture, with industry either absent or in its infancy. The technological level and requirements are low, production is poor, and market and money systems limited. For lack of capital and of entrepreneurship, this economy is static; the range of its occupations is narrow and they are usually transmitted from father to son; and especially marked is the absence of those occupations which, in the developed economy, constitute the middle class.

Despite the agricultural nature of the economy, there were few Jews in farming; on the whole, they maintained themselves chiefly through exchange of services with the surrounding society.

3. *Society of Origin*

The *moshav* pattern clearly meant that the "resource" of social interaction was supposed to draw upon the solidary structure that had been evolved by the settlers. It was postulated that (beyond secondary variations in class, community, etc.) this structure resulted ultimately from the *fundamental pattern of social relations in the country of origin*. That is, it was determined by:

a. the scope of the groups constituting the main frameworks of interaction;

b. the extent to which they were ascriptive.

These components again form two basic types of predispositions:

I. A pattern characterized by a widening of social horizons and membership groups. Along with nuclearization of the family and limitation of its size and functions, there is correlative growth in the scope of activity and contacts of the individual—which has now come to include professional, cultural, as well as many other frameworks. This phenomenon, in turn, results in a closer and more direct relationship with the overall social structure, and the diffusion of solidarity over and above the immediate primary group or groups, via various interlinking spheres.

II. A narrow and ascription-based pattern, usually limited to the primary group and based on the criteria of kinship and place of origin on the one hand, and on religion and ethnicity on the other. The extended family and the lineage group are the main social frameworks here, within which, generally speaking, social relations are carried out and determined.

4. *Political Organization in the Country of Origin*

The settlers themselves were charged with maintenance of the *moshav's* organizational and administrative structure and their ability to carry out this responsibility properly depended, it was assumed, on the character of the *political institutions—both national and local—in their country of origin,* and, more specifically on three aspects:

a. the extent of politization of the given society;
b. the extent to which government was democratic;
c. the extent to which administration was bureaucratic.

These variables can, of course, combine into a variety of forms. But two polar patterns can be postulated:

I. The modern, national, secular structure in which the regime is oriented to wide strata of the population, activates them and brings about the politization of society. The citizen here is the basis of the modern state, and of modern local government, and his political and personal status is secured by universal equal rights. The emancipation—i.e. the granting of full civic rights to Jews—introduced them to this political game, both as electors and as elected. This political activity transcended the framework and organization of the traditional Jewish communities, and promoted universalistic patterns of behaviour on national and local levels. The bureaucratic type of administration, so characteristic of modern organization, served to introduce discipline, rules of procedure and management, and the use of general-rational rather than personal or group behaviour patterns.

II. In the traditional polity, on the other hand, government is in the hands of a small group. Political consciousness is underdeveloped and participation in political life is limited, sporadic, and lacking permanence. The State—in fact, government on all its levels—is religious, and the separation of church and state has only begun. There is, obviously, little room for "citizenship" in the modern sense, especially as regards minorities, whose members are second-class citizens. True, the Jews are accorded religious autonomy and the right to community organization; but are not admitted to political activity proper, on any level. Their public activity is thus limited to traditional-particularistic settings; and contact with the overall structure is based on the awareness of belonging to a different and distinct society. The community in this case is the main organizational entity which embodies ascriptive and particularistic relations, without any democratic processes of government or bureaucratic administration. Of course, modes of such an administration develop in this type too but they are confined chiefly to central government and virtually closed to Jews; in any case, this kind of administration only absorbs a small number of people, and the social demands made upon it and issuing from it are also small.

5. *Value System in the Society of Origin*

It was taken for granted that the supply of motivation as a role resource is determined fundamentally by the actor's anticipated balance of rewards. For our purpose this was assumed to reside in the actor's basic self- or status-image, as developed in the course of his socialization. The development of such an image inevitably depends, to a large extent, on sub-cultural (and individual) variations.[8] On the overall level, however, we proposed tracing it to the *basic conception of reality and the "vision of the good life" which obtained in the society of origin*. It was not our intention, of course, to include all of the immensely complex aspects of a cultural ethos, and reference was made only to three selective sets of variables:

a. 'Primordial' images, namely images and beliefs which underlie the basic concepts of, and attitude towards, social and natural reality. We focused attention in particular on two images which we regarded as most relevant:

I. The dimension of activity-passivity, that is, the extent to which the individual is believed capable of affecting his environment and reaching expected goals.

II. The nature of the time conception—namely, the range of the temporal perspective which guides planning and activity, and the character of the time-unit, whether it is mechanical, or religious, or rooted in agricultural seasons and natural phenomena, etc.

b. Basic human images, i.e. the vision of the ideal man. Here we bore down on legitimation of differential activity in various institutional spheres, and it was expected that the image would emerge of the *homo economicus* and the *homo politicus*, as against the *homo religiosus* and *homo familiaris*.

c. Basic social images, namely the vision of the good society, chiefly in terms of its stratificational image. This image would express the differential legitimate levels and methods of achieving the "proper" way of life—that is to say; the nature and hierarchy of the status criteria; the distributional scheme, or number, size and type of expected status positions and strata; and the legitimate or the anticipated relationship between these strata—and in particular as regards mobility. The acceptance of the settler's status as against any other legitimate status was seen as depending largely upon this factor.

As before, two basic types of orientation, which combined all of the images mentioned, were hypothesized:

I. The rational, dynamic, and secular pattern, based primarily on the universalistic values of economic, social and political participation, and on the promotion of social, occupational and consumer mobility. Development and progress, both of the individual and of society, constitute a central value, symbolized primarily by economic and professional achievement. Status accordingly is spelled out in terms of income, way of life, and occupation.

II. In strong contrast to the pattern mentioned above, we have the traditional spiritual world—both general and Jewish—which is static, basically religious and familistic, and strongly value- and integration-oriented. The fundamental image of this Jewry is characterized by an extreme conservatism, intended to maintain existing values. In it, the present is conceived of in terms of the past; while the future is significant primarily as a projection of the present. Hence, the subordination and the lack of autonomy of political and economic values, in relation to religious and familistic ones, and a stratificational image embodying kinship, ethnic, and rabbinical criteria.

To sum up, we assumed that the nature of the actor's status image as supplier of role-motivation would correlate most significantly, first of all, with the basic societal values he acquired in the course of socialization in his country of origin, and secondly, with relevant sub-group variations, which have to do with class, occupational category and level of education. But since the situation we studied was one of migration, we decided to include an additional dimension, i.e. the specific motivation which guided the settler in his decision to immigrate to Israel. More precisely, we assumed that this motivation might modify both the salience and the applicability of basic images in relation to the projected new situation.[9]

The most significant orientation, in this respect, is of course the "pioneering" motivation, which means a whole new set of goals, superimposed upon the broad social background, and modifying it. Specifically, it would denote implementing the values which underlie cooperative or collective agricultural settlement in Israel. It should, therefore, constitute a directly positive motivational predisposition towards the *moshav*. But among the bulk[10] of immigrants who were destined to settle in the new *moshavim,* this motivation was rare, and when it existed, it was limited chiefly to a few organized youth groups. Quantitatively, therefore, we assumed that it was not of real empirical significance in terms of this work.

A much larger group was made up of "ordinary" immigrants, people who had left their country of origin because of various types of "push" rather than due to the specific "pull" of Israel. Their immigration was the result of economic, social, religious or political pressure, which deprived them of the possibility of achieving various aspirations, essentially based on old and familiar images. Their choice of Israel, in fact, was a result of a combination of circumstances of rational, but not of ideological deliberation. Thus, the image of the *moshav* as a future way of life was even less relevant. This type of migration characterized large European groups in the main.

The same applied, in broad terms, also to the general Zionist (non-pioneering) type of migration—or at least as far as agriculture and the *moshav* were concerned. These immigrants, though motivated by national consciousness, were driven to migrate—at least in the post-war years—chiefly for general rather than specific reasons, and wanted to change their nationality rather than their way of life. Immigration to Israel was therefore motivated for them by personal and social status crisis and did not involve any or much fundamental change in the Western, urbanized status image as such. Their purpose was to transfer themselves to a new setting while continuing to live as they had done before.[11]

The "messianic" immigration, characteristic of traditional communities, saw migration to Israel as the apocalyptic "ingathering of the exiles". This immigration, like the Zionist one, had Israel as its sole object, but was religiously motivated. It was, in other words, an utopian projection and a magnification of a basic religious and familistic image, now believed to be realizable; if anything, this motivation tended to reinforce basic predispositions; and perhaps to even increase, at least initially, the shock of confrontation with reality.

All in all, the various kinds of motive power prevalent among the actual groups of immigrants could hardly be expected to modify significantly the basic images socialized in their different societies. The diagnostic value of their motivations might rather lie in the fact that they focused, or reflected intensively, specific crises of aspirations which existed in different backgrounds. They pointed up the area, or the areas, in which there was a clear discrepancy between values and between institutional openings or allocative mechanisms. These areas could be presumed to contain the most salient, or rather most sensitive expectations for the future, and might, consequently, also indicate exactly where the trouble was likely to lie in the adjustment to the *moshav*.

These, then, were the variables assumed to determine directly the settlers' predispositions as suppliers of specific resources. Theoretically, they could be combined into an immense number of concrete profiles. Recent sociological thinking, however, assumed that institutional characteristics are not autonomous or independent of each other,[12] but that they constitute single aspects of whole structural types, each type representing a specific configuration. We accepted this assumption in broad outline, at least as regards the polar types, and expected thus to be able to identify and to confront two basic profiles:

a. the "modern-Western" profile, characterized by the planned nuclear family, the developed and developing economy, broad social horizons, a universalistic and bureaucratic governmental structure, and a change-oriented, economically-dominated and secular culture;

b. the "traditional-oriented" combination, featuring the large and extended family, a static and agricultural economy, narrow and ascribed social frameworks, a non-democratic, non-bureaucratic political system, a religious-familistic orientation.

In these terms the basic general hypothesis of our study was that *both extreme structural types of predispositions—the "traditional" and the "modern"—would, each in its own way and in its own time, be found to contradict the requirements of the settler role.*

To take the "traditional" pole first. This kind of immigrant is used to manual labour, and his family, more often than not, possesses ample manpower. He is brought up, if not to farming itself, then at least within the framework of rural life. He comes from a low standard of living and has a low level of personal aspirations. All this helps him to adjust positively to agriculture as an occupation, to initial hardships, both physical and otherwise, and to the relative social isolation and lack of facilities implicit in the new *moshav*.

At the same time, this settler possesses no image of the *homo economicus* and the *homo politicus,* of the sort that underlies modern economic and municipal frameworks. He lacks the ability to master the complex skills and scientific requirements of contemporary farming, or the attitudes and frame of reference which are implied by modern marketing, financing and development processes. Finally, his social pattern has not prepared him for interactive frameworks transcending the narrow ascriptive criteria of kinship and ethnic origin.

Conversely, the more modern the settler's background, the higher his general and vocational education, the deeper his faculties of scientific thought, and the firmer his grasp of and agreement with the principles of modern economic practice. The professional side of *moshav* farming, in some aspects actually, and in others potentially, presents no overwhelming problem for him. He is anxious to implement the political and administrative pattern of the *moshav* with its criteria of universalism and performance; and he is capable of establishing social interaction with a wide variety of people quite unrelated and previously quite unknown to him.

On the other hand, this settler can be expected to reject an ideological orientation towards personal and social pioneering, to be disinterested in the "simple" life, to chafe under the artificial limitation placed on entrepreneurship, and to prefer greater individualism and *Gesellschaft* for *Gemeinschaft*. He is likely to shrink from agriculture as a vocation, from manual labour, and from the social isolation and cultural provincialism of the new village. His self-image is bound to include an urban occupation and environment; and he will inevitably aspire to a high status based on this way of life rather than on solidary and symbolic rewards. It is in the "transitional" society, therefore, that the "best" averages of structural predispositions in all spheres can be expected.

It might be useful to map out schematically the distribution of the structural types mentioned among the main Jewish communities of origin.[13] This distribution

(Table 88) is projected from highly incomplete data, inexact and verbal rather than numerical. No precise details, however, are available.[14]

MODIFYING OR "DYNAMIC" FACTORS

Cutting across the basic institutional factors and modifying them, we postulated three sets of variables. These variables, too, may appear on any of the three levels mentioned: namely, the general, the subgroup, and the individual. Our study, however, has taken into account only the earlier two, while this summary concentrates primarily on the first.

A. *Socio-dynamic factors*

Under this heading reference was made to social factors which determine group or individual ability to change. Use was made, in this respect, of general research on immigrant absorption carried out by the Department of Sociology of the Hebrew University from 1949 to 1952 under the direction of Prof. S.N. Eisenstadt. This work dealt with a similar absorptive situation and immigrant population; and it served in large measure as the point of departure for our study.[15] This work developed a model in which personal and social absorption of immigrants is viewed, among others, as a function of their capacity for change—this capacity being influenced by social conditions in their country of origin and upon migration, in terms of a) the

TABLE 88—Distribution of Structural Types in Main Areas of Origin

Area of origin	"Traditional" communities	"Transitional" communities	"Modern" communities
Central & Eastern Europe			
Poland	—	Villages and part of urban communities	Majority of urban communities
Hungary	—	,, ,,	,, ,,
Rumania	,, ,,	,, ,,	,, ,,
Czechoslovakia	—	,, ,,	,, ,,
America			
U.S.A.	—	Small minority	Large majority
Argentina	—	,,	,,
The Balkans			
Yugoslavia	—	Villages and part of urban communities	Majority of urban communities
Bulgaria	—		
Greece	—	,, ,,	,, ,,
North Africa			
Morocco	Atlas Mountains and other areas	Communities in provincial cities (Fez, Marakesh, Rabat, etc.); part of Casablanca community	Chiefly part of Casablanca community

TABLE 88—(continued)

Area of origin	"Traditional" communities	"Transitional" communities	"Modern" communities
Algeria	Small minority	Communities in provincial cities; part of Oran and Algiers communities	Large segment of Algiers community; part of Oran community
Tunisia	The island of Djerba; small minority in other communities	Communities in provincial cities; part of Tunis community	Part of Tunis community
Libya and Tripolitania	The "Cave Dwellers"*; small minority in other communities	Communities in provincial cities; majority of Tripoli and Benghazi communities	Small minority in large cities
Middle & Far East			
Turkey	Small minority	Majority of Izmir and Anatolia communities, part of Istanbul community	Part of provincial communities; majority of Istanbul; Ankara community
Syria and Lebanon	,,	Most of Syrian, part of Lebanon communities	Chiefly Beirut community
Egypt	,,	Communities in provincial cities; part of communities of Cairo, Alexandria, etc.	Majority of Cairo, Alexandria and other urban communities
Yemen	Entire community	—	—
Kurdistan**	,,	—	—
Persia	Small minority	Villages, provincial cities (e.g. Shiraz, Isfahan), part of Teheran community	Chiefly part of Teheran community
Iraq	,,	Villages, provincial cities (e.g. Basra, Mosul), part of Baghdad community	Part of provincial cities and of Baghdad
Cochin	Large majority	Small minority	—

* The "Cave Dwellers" were the inhabitants of Ghirian Mountain (the so-called Mountain of Caves) in the District of Tripoli. On the slopes of this mountain there were fields, trees and wells but no human dwellings. The Jews of the area lived in caves (dug in the earth or natural); these caves contained living quarters, cattle and shops in conglomeration, the individual households or "yards" being connected by subterranean passage. There is no competent historical study on the background and development of this particular way of life; most probably, however, it originated in fear of bandits. Before immigration to Israel there were in the Mountain two Jewish villages, engaged chiefly in trade and crafts, with agriculture (mostly sheep) as an auxiliary branch. The two villages constituted distinct communities with separate synagogues, ritual butchers, etc.; at the same time they had a common Rabbi, who was also the official representative of the population before the authorities.

** Including Jews from Turkish, Persian and Iraqi Kurdistan—constituting a special cultural group.

status of the Jewish community (including the extent of social autonomy, the attitude towards Judaism, and identification with the community); b) the stability of various primary—and particularly kinship—groups; and c) the nature of local leadership.

This formulation is indeed an indispensable tool for research in this area and we have made extensive and grateful use of it; but also we have found it necessary to modify, extend and operationally elaborate on it, coming up with the following conceptualization:[16]

1. BASIC ABILITY TO ACT IN A NEW REALITY

It was assumed that this ability depended on the wholeness and the security of status in the settler's country of origin, namely, on the extent to which he had undergone successful socialization and been able to fit himself into, and accept, existing institutional norms and openings. This factor, we presumed, was the function of two specific elements:

a. *The stability of the primary group,* that is to say, the extent of solidarity and integration of this group, and its ability to fulfil its functions both in terms of society and of the individual. It seemed to us that, on the general level, this variable is definitely connected with, or embedded in the basic structural types mentioned, in two ways: On the one hand, these structures should determine the very *nature* of the primary group relevant to the actor (whether nuclear, extended, or lineage-based); on the other, they should define the *functions* of this group in the social division of labour, and its actual ability to carry out these functions. We assumed that a congruence of this kind would exist at both extremes; and that both the traditional and modern immigrant groups would be fundamentally characterized by stable primary groups. Or, in other words, that any instability would derive from secondary rather than general factors. This is not so as regards the transitionals, who would be sensitive, in this respect, due to the very ambivalence of the processes of change. Here, then, the situation should be taken to depend on the extent to which a lag developed between the prevalence of familistic orientations and the actual process of social differentiation and diminution of familial functions.

b. *Wholeness of the social person* (beyond the family), i.e., the actor's own integration in the roles expected of and by him, and his consequent assumption of a social status suitable to subjective and objective norms. This factor was again taken to be related to the previous set of variables, and to vary chiefly in the transitional pattern, because, on both extremes, the status of the Jewish community could be interpreted as fitting mutual expectations: isolated and self-sufficient on the one hand, and emancipated on the other (except, of course, for "special" cases of persecution). This was not so as regards the "middle", which was especially susceptible to discrepancy between aspired and achieved status. Here, the degree of discrepancy was attributed to the speed, rate, orderliness and timing of the change process.

2. ABILITY TO ADJUST TO NORMATIVE CHANGE

By this, we mean acceptance of specific change, or change in *contents* as opposed to discontinuity *per se*. We did not refer, however, to the level of *legitimation* of change as such, which we discussed in relation to the basic images of different societies. We meant rather the various social mechanisms through which change can be effected. The mechanism assumed to be potentially most relevant here was a *suitable leadership elite*. This elite was defined as having three characteristics: legitimation by the society which it led; ability and readiness to lead; and an orientation (at least potentially) to change. As before, this variable was assumed to be connected with the structural institutional pattern and largely predictable in terms of it. In the "traditional" society, the elite should thus be traditionally legitimated as such, ensuring its status and continuity. It should also be highly integrated with, and dependent upon, the "in-group". On the other hand, it could not be expected to be able to lead in adjustment in the instrumental spheres involved, nor to promote value change. Consequently, the traditional elite might generally be assumed to be very conservative and expected to resist rather than to advance change. In the "oriental" group, therefore, this predisposition was generally accepted as negative, orderly change being dependent primarily on later processes, chiefly on the emergence of new elites, and the creation of conditions for their activity. Moving "westwards" a progressively professional and flexible elite could be expected. True, such an elite would not necessarily be strongly attached to the group, and might even show an orientation outwards from the *moshav*. But in this type of society the incidence of potential leaders would be high, any specific stratum being expendable and replaceable by another. The crucial factor here—particularly in the "transitional" sector—should be the size of the leadership reservoir (which depends, of course, on group variations,[17] and upon the selectivity of migration).[18]

B. *Cultural-Dynamic Predispositions*

By this we meant the ability to think analytically and abstractly and to generalize, which are faculties of primary importance in a situation requiring learning and reorientation. This ability has two aspects: a) learning ability proper; b) "sociological" ability to analyze new social circumstances, i.e., to distinguish the level of goals from that of means, and to grasp the relationship between both of these and the actor's own values and position.

In other words, this quality ought to enable the immigrant to approach the new reality through conscious and autonomous thought, and help him to differentiate between the significant and the trivial requirements of this reality; to sort out aspects which are truly salient, and those which are actually irrelevant to his own aims and characteristics; and, consequently, to narrow the areas of tension, uncertainty and clash.

Obviously predispositions of this type should, by definition, develop in modern institutions; in fact, they are one of their very features. There would, of course, be considerable differences due to differing educational levels and intellectual capacities; but the basic ability required by the *moshav* could be deduced from, and predicted by, the very type of the society of origin.

This being so, the present factor was used as a separate variable mainly to distinguish between different *traditional* societies. More precisely, we hypothesized that a learning-oriented or "learned" traditional society would differ significantly from a "non-learned" one. It would, in fact, be approximate in this respect to the advanced transitional sectors, irrespective of the marked difference between modern and traditional education as regards content and structure.

C. *Intervening and Mediating Factors*

Here reference was made to those factors assumed to mediate between the predispositions described—both static (or structural) and dynamic—and between the actual, situational supply of resources. Our study included three sets of such factors:

1. THE PROCESS OF MIGRATION

a. *Knowledge of conditions obtaining in the country of migration.* We hypothesized that familiarity with conditions obtaining in Israel would be a significant determinant of adjustment, provided it related both to the immediate confrontation and to future changes—and that it could preclude sudden disappointments. It might, of course, lead the individual to reject the idea of migration to Israel altogether, due to perception of incompatibility. On the other hand, it should help in legitimating the temporary moratorium of migration. And though the immigrant's ultimate goals would remain fundamentally unaltered, their realization would be given a subjective breathing space, a sort of absorptive "credit".

Possession of this basic information was taken to depend *a priori* upon the level of the immigrant's general education and sophistication, and upon his interest in and communication with the country. Without these, the nature of the picture described or any explanations provided—especially by Israeli representatives abroad—is of crucial significance.

b. *Structure of the immigrant group.* This denotes the processes of selection—both voluntary and involuntary—which determine the actual structure of the immigrant group. The selection can derive from the group's own planning, or from immigration policy, or from such chance factors as travelling in different ships and being distributed to different reception camps in Israel. In any case, it would certainly have a significant effect in increasing or decreasing the applicability of predispositions in the new situation, chiefly in areas such as the continued existence of organic or solidary social units, the presence and distribution of elite groups, and household structure.

c. *The nature of the process of migration.* By this, we mean the extent of the problems produced by hardships and their duration, in which the immigrant was involved by coming to Israel. The significance of this factor was taken to lie in its probable effect on the settler's patience, ability to endure, initial flexibility, goodwill, and even, possibly, on his basic motivation.

2. SETTLEMENT OF LAND

Reference is made here to the period between the immigrant's arrival in the country and his actual settlement on the land, and, more specially, to the nature of the various concrete frameworks of selection, preparation and living with which he was familiar prior to arrival on the *moshav*. The significance of these frameworks was analyzed in the same terms as that of the preceding variable and need not be gone into again.

3. CONSOLIDATION OF THE MOSHAV

As explained above, the settlement plan provided for a phase of transition and intensive preparation before the settler and the village assumed their respective functions. The extent to which this period, in fact, met the actual requirements of the situation was consequently regarded as very important in three respects: a) vocational training; b) main value communication[19] and c) rate of development.

(a)+(b) Vocational training and main value communication. Basically, the success of the communicative process depended on the differential distance that had to be covered in both respects. By definition, therefore, it could not be expected to effect changes in factors such as negative value orientations or the very meagre supply of abstract reasoning in most traditional groups. Conversely, it should, on the whole, encounter no particular difficulties in teaching the professional aspects of agriculture to Western immigrants. Predispositional extremes apart, however, several factors inherent in the communicative process itself were assumed to account for its differential success.

I. The vocational competence of the instruction and absorptive teams, which needs no further elaboration. It was seen that financial and professional resources had been insufficient to meet all the requirements, and it was inferred also that, at the beginning of mass immigration to Israel, the settlement authorities had not been fully aware of the extent of these requirements. Consequently, a varied level of performance was expected.

II. Team flexibility. Great importance was attached to the extent to which members of these teams themselves had a sufficiently flexible conception of the *moshav*, and of their own duties. Proper flexibility would have allowed the instructors to make, at least temporarily, allowances for the basic characteristics of the settlers, rather than to demand strict adherence to the normative pattern. However, since most of the original instructors came from old established *moshavim*, we expected them to be ideologically involved in the principles of the classical *moshav*, and we assumed that their role-conception would be rigid rather than adaptable, thus generating tension in, and resistance to, the communicative process.

III. The nature of the communicative situation. Social conditions of communicative receptivity among new immigrants had already been adequately analyzed.

(S.N. Eisenstadt: chiefly *Absorption of Immigrants, op.cit.* and "Communicative Processes among Immigrants in Israel" *Public Opinion Quarterly*, Vol. XVI, No. 1, (1952), pp. 42–58.) Applying the general conclusions of this analysis to the *moshav*, three factors seemed to be of primary importance in this respect:

First, utilization of proper channels as regards the mediation of settler groups and elites. This would seem to be especially significant in "oriental" villages. These settlers had not developed specific and neutral communicative frameworks, and in order to reach them properly it would be necessary to proceed in traditionally sanctioned ways, namely, through their traditional leaders and within their lineage structure.

Secondly, manipulation of communicative settings to suit various types of communication. On the technical level, this would mean a correct choice of medium—as for instance lectures, demonstrations, movies, etc.; and of set-up—whether individual or group. There might, however, also be a deeper, symbolic level, again especially important in the traditional society. For example, the proper and improper communicative uses of the synagogue, the prayer group, the religious festival and so forth.

Thirdly, use of appropriate symbols, concepts and techniques. The language used would be of primary importance, since most of the settlers initially spoke little or no Hebrew at all. Use of simple and familiar concepts, drawn as far as possible from their own culture, might also be extremely helpful, especially with non-modern settlers. And finally, again chiefly in the traditional group, the use of suitable auxiliary methods of education designed to fit the recipients, such as various mnemonic and visual aids.

Obviously, practice of these far-reaching requirements would demand considerable professional as well as vocational competence, especially in education, perhaps also in sociology and social psychology. Few, if any, of the original instructors possessed these qualifications, nor had they initially received any supplementary training. Serious communicative impediments could therefore be expected. The best results, by far, should have been obtained by the few people acquainted with the way of life of the settlers under their jurisdiction (for instance: instructors who had worked with the immigrants abroad prior to their immigration, and had even accompanied them to Israel and later perhaps to the *moshav*).

(c) Rate of development. The last factor considered, under the general heading of development, was the relative rate of this process, i.e., the extent to which handing-over of responsibilities to the settlers actually coincided with their desire and ability to assume it. As has been shown, this responsibility was two-fold, i.e., related to the management of individual farms, and to the administration of the cooperative and the village. Obviously, the right way of doing this would be to meet the differential capacities of the settlers, as determined by previously mentioned predispositional and communicative factors. In reality, however, these transfers were effected almost

uniformly and very early on, and were guided by a rigid *a priori* set schedule rather than by *ad hoc* considerations. The crucial factors here were not the actual mistakes that were made, but the fact that the settler had to pay for them without being willing and able to do so. This was especially true as regards the farm. Although each farmer continued to receive intensive instruction for a long time, very early in the game he had become an autonomous producer (though not on all of the land ultimately destined to be handed over to him).

This, we assumed, might have a double effect. On the one hand, mistakes were clearly inevitable, resulting in production and income even below transitional norms. On the other hand, these mistakes would occur at a time when the settler was most insecure and easily discouraged, and thus possibly they would undermine his motivation. Mistakes are clearly an essential part of any learning process, but here the "adult" role had to be assumed before the educational process had been completed or even advanced much. Consequently, the villager was, in effect, denied the basic right of a pupil, i.e., the right to err. To sum up: the negative impact of an early handing-over of ownership and responsibility would be directly correlated with vocational inadequacy, occupational (i.e., agricultural) insecurity, and motivational ambiguity.

NOTES

[1] In the present context, our interest in this concept is chiefly instrumental, as a research tool, and we offer only relatively brief remarks on this topic. For fuller exposition of our use of the concept of role see:

S.N. Eisenstadt, D. Weintraub and N. Toren, *Analysis of Processes of Role-Change,* (Jerusalem, Israel Universities Press, 1967). In short we assume that the normative definition of role behaviour is not a given and a fixed pattern within the institutional structure of society, to which an individual has only to adjust himself. On the contrary, the very formation of a specific role should be seen as a complex process of crystallization of various components into a system which possesses properties of its own. The complex nature of roles has been recognized and studied before, and the various extensive role definitions such as those of:

R. Merton and A.S. Kitt, "Contributions to the Theory of Reference Group Behaviour", in *Continuities in Social Research,* R.K. Merton and P.F. Lazarsfeld, (eds.), (Glencoe, Illinois, The Free Press, 1950);

T. Parsons, *The Social System,* Ch. X, (Glencoe, Illinois, The Free Press, 1951);

F.J. Davis, "Conception of Official Leaders' Roles in the Air-Force", *Social Forces,* XXXII, (1954), pp. 253–288.

S.F. Nadel, *The Theory of Social Structure,* (Glencoe, Illinois, The Free Press, 1957).

N. Gross, W. Mason and A.W. Eachern, *Explorations in Role Analysis: Studies of the School Superintendency Role,* (New York, J. Wiley, 1958);

All refer to one or more of the following aspects or components:

a. The "positional" one—i.e., the specification of some position in the social structure, the incumbents of which are expected to perform the given role;
b. The "situational" one, i.e., the specification of the setting in which this performance is expected to be carried out;
c. The "contents", i.e., the goals or output of the role:

d. The "exchange" aspect, or the specification of the outputs of different activities specified in the normative definition of a role. Special sub-categories of this exchange are:
e. The personal and interpersonal component—i.e., the specification of the personal relations, the relations with other people or other roles which are involved in the performance of the given role;
f. The normative or institutional, i.e., the definition of patterns of behaviour, which are demanded from the bearers of any given position in terms of norms, values and normative injunctions and sanctions.

Few studies, however, treat all the components together in a systematic way. Moreover, the role has been dealt with mostly as a unified concept which represents a functionally indivisible whole. This study, on the other hand, assumes that, although certain role-components do, in fact, tend to go together, they may also vary independently, and should, therefore, be studied from this point of view. These variations are, of course, limited by the social system within which the role is set; but each of them is often subject to independent influences, and may thus constitute a focus of change which affects the entire role in different ways and to different degrees. A basically similar approach to role analysis—theoretical and empirical—can be found, among others, in:

G. Homans, "Social Behaviour As Exchange", *American Journal of Sociology,* Vol. LXIII, No. 6, pp. 597–606, (May, 1958).

J. Ben-David, "The Professional Role of the Physician in Bureaucratised Medicine: a Study in Role-Conflict", *Human Relations,* Vol. XI, No. 2, pp. 255–275, (May, 1958).

R. Dahrendorf, "Homo Sociologicus", *Kolner Zeitschrift fur Soziologie und Sozialpsychologie,* 10, pp. 178–208, (1958).

A. Southall, "An Operational Theory of Role", *Human Relations,* Vol. XII, No. 1, pp. 17–34, (February, 1959).

D.J. Levinson, "Role, Personality and Social Structure", *Journal of Abnormal and Social Psychology,* Vol. 53, No. 2, pp. 170–180, (March, 1959).

[2] Of course, the role of the settler is a *multiple role,* combining social, cultural and political functions; and the actual input-output analysis relates thus chiefly the various capacities of the individual settler (and the settler group) himself.

[3] In modern economic theory, all material resources can be expressed in terms of capital. In the *moshav* reality, however, this is not so, both because of differential scarcity of the various means, and because of normative restrictions on their interchangeability.

[4] This is the resource, or the mechanism, through which agricultural output is realized in terms of personal income. In the *moshav,* its supply depends primarily on the market (partly free, partly subject to planning and price control), and on farm subsidies.

[5] It seems, in fact, that this "basket" or profile of resources is a generalizing one, applicable to other roles. That is to say, different normative and performance patterns can be expressed, among others, in terms of different structures and configurations of the basic types of resource mentioned. But two qualifications are essential in respect to this proposition:

a. In certain roles, requirements for one or another resource may be nil;
b. Certain roles call for an additional type of resource which can be termed psychological, namely, it relates to traits or qualities of personality, as distinct from skill and motivation (one example: courage in the military role). In the settler's situation this factor, though, is not usually very significant.

[6] These qualities obviously do not exhaust the structure of the family pattern. But in the context of this study, we have referred only to those selected facets directly relevant to the demographic problem. This qualification applies, of course, to the other variables as well.

[7] It is obvious that reference is made here to a special case of the modern economy, one characterized by at least a modicum of free enterprise and autonomy from political intervention. This does not mean, of course, that we ignore the existence of other types. We have concentrated on *this* economic form, however, because of its special relevance to the problems at hand: on the one hand, it obtains in Israel and in the *moshav;* and on the other, it is characteristic of the background of most of the "modern" settlers.

[8] Factors of this type analysed in the project were chiefly the structure of the status of origin; educational level; and occupational category.

[9] See chiefly: S.N. Eisenstadt, *Absorption of Immigrants, op. cit.* This book analyses the way in which different types of discrepancy between general and Jewish aspirations, and between the actual status and situation of the Jews, produced various types of migrational "push" and "pull".

[10] Pioneering immigration in the post-war period has chiefly characterized Jews from so-called Anglo-Saxon—or English-speaking countries—and South America, and has been primarily *kibbutz*-oriented. The few such groups in the new immigrant *moshav* came mostly from the transitional society of North Africa.

[11] At least as ultimate goals. *Temporary* lowering of aspirations to meet the migration requirements as such is discussed later.

[12] See chiefly:

R. Redfield, *The Primitive World and its Transformation,* (Ithaca, New York, Cornell University Press, 1953).

T. Parsons, *The Social System, op. cit.*

M.J. Levy, *The Structure of Society,* (Princeton, New Jersey, Princeton University Press, 1952).

D. Lerner, *The Passing of Traditional Society: Modernizing the Middle East,* (Glencoe, Illinois, The Free Press, 1958).

[13] The table does not attempt to present the entire Jewish Diaspora over the past few decades. The areas we included are those chiefly represented in the immigrant *moshavim.*

[14] There is, of course, a wealth of demographic and other data. These are not susceptible, however, to a breakdown in the analytical terms we have used. The situation is better in regard to communities which belong *entirely* to one identifiable extreme. Yemenite Jewry, for example, can quite safely be classified as wholly traditional. For the interested reader, the following are some selected (non-Hebrew) sources on the background of the main ethnic groups we have analysed.

A. *Yemenite Jewry*

E. Brauer, "Die Frau bei den suedarabischen Juden", *Zeitschrift fuer Sexualwissenschaft und Sexualpolitik,* XVIII, Berlin, (1931).

E. Brauer, *Ethnologie der Jemenitischen Juden,* (Heidelberg, C. Winter, 1934).

E. Glaser, *Reise nach Marib,* (Wien, D.H. Mueller und N. Rhondonakis, 1919).

S.D. Goitein, *Jemenitische Geschichten,* Zfs VIII, (1935).

Hayim, Habshush, *Travels in Yemen,* S.D. Goitein, (ed.), (Jerusalem, University Press, 1941).

S.D. Goitein, *From the Land of Sheba—Tales of the Jews of Yemen,* (New York, Schocken Books, 1947).

S.D. Goitein, *Portrait of a Yemenite Weavers' Village,* (New York, Conference on Jewish Relations, 1955).

K. Rathjens, Sanaa, Eine Suedarabische Stadtlandschaft, (Berlin, *ZGBB,* 1919).

H. Scott, *In the High Yemen,* (London, J. Murray, 1942).

B. *North African Jewry*

J. Berque, *Structures Sociales du Haut-Atlas,* (Paris, Presses Universitaires de France, 1955).

E. Blum, *Les Juifs Algeriens,* (Paris, Librairie C., 1902).

A. Chouraqui, *The Social and Legal Status of the Jews of French Morocco*, (New York, American Jewish Committee, 1950).

A. Chouraqui, *Marche vers l'Occident: Les Juifs d'Afrique du Nord*, (Paris, Presses des Livres Francais, 1952).

A. Chouraqui, "North African Jewry Today", *The Jewish Journal of Sociology*, Vol. I, No. 1, (1959).

Institute of Jewish Affairs, *The Jews of French Morocco and Tunisia*, (New York, World Jewish Congress, 1952).

P. Marty, *Les Institutions Israelites au Maroc*, (Paris, P. Geuthner, 1930).

N. Slouschz, *L'Ethnographie Juive de l'Afrique du Nord*, (Cairo, Imprimerie de l'Institut Francais d'Archeologie Orientale, 1921).

C. *Others and General*

E.N. Adler, *Jews in Many Lands*, (London, Macmillan, 1905).

S.D. Goitein, *Jews and Arabs: Their Contacts through the Ages*, (New York, Schocken Books, 1955).

E.H. Hadad, and P. Fischman, *History round the Clock: The Jews of Iraq*, (Tel Aviv, Wizo, 1952).

Jewish Agency for Palestine, *Memorandum on the Position of the Jewish Communities in the Oriental Countries*, (Jerusalem, 1947).

Jewish Agency for Palestine, *The Jews of Iraq*, (New York, 1949).

C.Z. Kloetzel, *"Auguranam"—Bericht uber eine Reise zu den schwarzen und weissen Juden in Cochin (Indien)*, (Mukacevo, Nekudah Verlag, 1938).

S. Landshut, *Jewish Communities in the Muslim Countries of the Middle East*, (London, The Jewish Chronicle, 1950).

R. Patai, "The Middle East as a Culture Area", *The Middle East Journal*, Vol. 6, No. 1, (1952).

L. Resner, *Eternal Stranger—The Flight of the Modern Jew from Baghdad to Casablanca*, (London, Doubleday, 1951).

N. Robinson, *The Arab Countries of the Near East and their Jewish Communities*, (New York, Jewish Congress, 1951).

A.B. Salem, *Eternal Light: Jew—Town Synagogue in Cochin*, (Ernakulam, S.D. Printing Works Ltd., 1929).

D.S. Sassoon, *A History of the Jews in Baghdad*, (Letchworth, S.D. Sassoon, 1949).

I.I. Schwarzbard, *The Rise and Decline of Jewish Communities in the Far East and South East Asia*, (New York, World Jewish Congress, 1957).

J. Wolff, *Travels and Adventures*, 2 Vols., (London, Saunders, Otley and Co., 1860–61).

15 The approach, and the major findings of this project, can be found in:

S.N. Eisenstadt, "The Place of Elites and Primary Groups in the Processes of Absorption of New Immigrants in Israel", *American Journal of Sociology*, Vol. LVII, No. 3, pp. 222–231, (November, 1951).

— *The Absorption of Immigrants, op. cit.*

— "Sociological Aspects of the Economic Adaptation of Oriental Immigrants in Israel: a Case Study in the Process of Modernization", *Economic Development and Cultural Change*, Vol. IV, No. 3, pp. 269–270, (April, 1956).

16 Formally, the ability to change is a dimension which cuts across the specific-structural types we have already mentioned. If, for simplicity's sake, we imagine this as a dichotomy, we might expect a sixfold table made up of a rigid and a flexible "traditional" type, a rigid and a flexible "modern" type, and a rigid and a flexible "transitional" "middle". But in fact this is not so, or at least not entirely so, because in some aspects flexibility is either delimited, or else rendered irrelevant by static-structural properties. Within the present context, we cannot analyze the theoretical implications of this relationship. We shall only hint, therefore, at their expected incidence among the various groups.

[17] Differences in size and extent of urbanization of communities of origin, in their population and occupational structure, etc.

[18] In fact, migration to Israel from many transitional communities was negatively selective. In contrast to previous waves, in which there has been a relatively high proportion of the young, the dedicated, the fit, and the skillful, these newcomers were often underprivileged. This was especially so in countries where immigration was not actually a compulsory exodus; where the higher Jewish status groups considered themselves safe and better off; and in respect to which there was an institutionalized alternative avenue (chiefly formerly French North Africa contrasted, for example, with Iraq).

[19] Because of the essentially similar implications of these aspects—both communicative mechanisms—(a) and (b) are analyzed together.

INDEX